Courtly Culture and Political Life in Early Medieval India

Scholars have long studied classical Sanskrit culture in almost total isolation from its courtly context. As the first study to focus exclusively on the royal court as a social and cultural institution, this book fills a gap in the literature. Using both literary and inscriptional sources, it begins with the rise and spread of royal households and political hierarchies from the Gupta period (*c.* 350–750), and traces the emergence of a coherent courtly worldview, which would remain stable for almost a millennium to 1200. Later chapters examine key features of courtly life which have been all but ignored by the previous literature on ancient Indian society: manners, ethics, concepts of personal beauty and theories of disposition. The book ends with a sustained examination of the theory and practice of erotic love, in the context of the wider social dynamics and anxieties which faced the people of the court.

DAUD ALI is Senior Lecturer in the Department of History at the School of Oriental and African Studies, University of London.

Cambridge Studies in Indian History and Society 10

Cambridge Studies in Indian History and Society publishes monographs on the history and anthropology of modern India. In addition to its primary scholarly focus, the series also includes work of an interdisciplinary nature which contributes to contemporary social and cultural debates about Indian history and society. In this way, the series furthers the general development of historical and anthropological knowledge to attract a wider readership than that concerned with India alone.

A list of titles which have been published in the series can be found at the end of the book.

Courtly Culture and Political Life in Early Medieval India

Daud Ali

University of London

CAMBRIDGE
UNIVERSITY PRESS

PUBLISHED BY THE PRESS SYNDICATE OF THE UNIVERSITY OF CAMBRIDGE
The Pitt Building, Trumpington Street, Cambridge, United Kingdom

CAMBRIDGE UNIVERSITY PRESS
The Edinburgh Building, Cambridge, CB2 2RU, UK
40 West 20th Street, New York, NY 10011–4211, USA
477 Williamstown Road, Port Melbourne, VIC 3207, Australia
Ruiz de Alarcón 13, 28014 Madrid, Spain
Dock House, The Waterfront, Cape Town 8001, South Africa

http://www.cambridge.org

First published 2004

Printed in the United Kingdom at the University Press, Cambridge

Typeface Plantin 10/12 pt. *System* LaTeX 2ε [TB]

A catalogue record for this book is available from the British Library

Library of Congress Cataloguing in Publication data
Courtly culture and political life in early medieval India / Daud Ali.
p. cm. – (Cambridge studies in Indian history and society; 10)
University of Chicago.
Includes bibliographical references and index.
ISBN 0 521 81627 0
1. India – Court and courtiers – History. 2. India – Civilisation – to 1200.
I. Title. II. Series.

DS425.A645 2004
954.02′1 – dc22 2003055901

ISBN 0 521 81627 0 hardback

For my mother and father,
who must surely be amused that their son has finally taken an interest in manners!

Contents

II. Aesthetics and the Courtly Sensibility

III. Courtly Love and Aristocratic Society

Figures

Cover, crystal intaglio seal of the king Avarighsa. Photo courtesy of Department of Oriental Antiquities, British Museum

Acknowledgements

The seeds of this book were sown in the intellectual environment nurtured by teachers and friends at the University of Chicago. Martha Selby first pointed out to me, in the basement of the Regenstein Library, the fact that while nearly all of Sanskrit poetry was courtly in nature, courtly life itself had remained largely untreated in both historical and literary scholarship. My dissertation supervisor, Professor Ronald Inden, first opened my mind to the important problems of studying culture and practice in medieval India. Through both his teaching and published work, he conveyed to me one of the most important principles for historical research: that a close attention to one's sources was not superflous to or inconsistent with thinking about theory and method, but in fact demanded it. To him I owe an immense debt. Through courses with Sheldon Pollock I gained an exposure to Sanskrit literary culture, both textual and epigraphical. What little I know about this culture is very much indebted to him. His interest in the social world of Sanskrit literature, though only nascent during my studentship at Chicago, has been nothing short of inspirational. The contributions of other teachers at Chicago, notably the Tamil scholars Norman Cutler and A. K. Ramanujan, both of whom are no longer with the scholarly community, as well as Dipesh Chakrabarty, were important in different ways for the conception of this book. The intellectual stimulus that these teachers provided, both individually and collectively, has been sorely missed.

More recently, numerous colleagues, friends and students have provided encouragement and support in bringing this book to completion. Many of the ideas in this book have benefited in some way from discussions with a number of people, including Kunal Chakrabarti, Rachel Dwyer, Bhairabi Sahu, V. N. Jha, Vena Ramphal, Romila Thapar, Bhaskar Mukhopadhyay, Subho Basu, Sudipta Kaviraj, Shruti Kapila, Sarah Hodges, Carol Miles, Letchimi Veeron, Mattia Salvini, Oliver Winrow, Akira Shimada, Sergio Targa and, particularly, Nilanjan Sarkar, Indira Peterson, Sascha Ebeling, Martha Selby and Whitney Cox, some of whom took time to read drafts of various chapters. Francesca Orsini at

Cambridge kindly invited me to participate in her workshops on ‘love’ in South Asia where I had the chance to put forth a number of ideas in this book. Rosalind O’Hanlon, Peter Robb, Chris Bayly, Stuart Blackburn and John Parker all gave important and crucial advice about the revision of the manuscript. My dear friend and teacher K. Srinivasan, lecturer in Sanskrit at Vivekananda College in Chennai, spent long hours discussing the finer points of many difficult Sanskrit terms. Michael Willis, my colleague at the British Museum, offered precious time, thought and resources to help me develop visual correlatives for some of my findings and think about the larger problems of Gupta India. Joe Cribb, from the Department of Coins and Medals at the British Museum, provided advice on (and images of) Kūṣāṇa and Gupta coins, and Tapash Ray and Madhuvanti Ghose helped me locate slide images from Deogarh. Unfortunately, I cannot name the closest and most critical reader of the first draft of this book, to whom its present form is immensely indebted. The anonymous referee at Cambridge University Press, known to me only as ‘reader b’, provided what any author dreams of – a clear apprehension of the nature and significance of the arguments I was trying to make, with detailed and sustained criticism in light of those aims. I owe to this person and the many others who have contributed to my thinking on matters medieval, a deep gratitude, though they bear no responsiblity for the flaws in this book.

The faith and patience which my own colleagues and staff in the History Department at SOAS have shown me through the course of writing and publishing this manuscript provided confidence and stability in the increasingly vexed environment of UK academics. I also owe thanks to the staff at the SOAS library (particularly Jane Phillipson, Romesh Dogra and Mohini Nair) who helped me locate missing volumes, extended borrowing privileges and obliged my incessant photocopying. These small kindnesses allowed me to conduct the research for this book during the busy time of the teaching year. And finally, my greatest thanks goes to my parents, who have offered unqualified support and love to me throughout my long education, and who continue to be a source of great strength, my mother for her humanity and my father for his dreams, to my life in ways they will never know. They, not to mention Sugra and Maryam, will certainly be happy to see this thing put to rest.

Transliteration of Indic words follows the accepted style for South Asian languages. The citation of primary sources, barring inscriptions, in footnotes will not include publication information as in some cases multiple editions and translations, where available, were consulted. For readers who wish to check the original sources, the edition cited will usually be the first entry, unless otherwise noted, under the text’s title in the bibliography. Citation of Sanskrit texts is usually by book, chapter and verse (of the first Sanskrit edition cited in the Bibliography) as necessary. Prose works have been cited similarly, but with reference to chapter and page. In mixed prose and verse works, particularly dramas, note of the act/chapter is followed by a verse number, with '+' referring to following prose sections. For the sake of brevity, I have shortened citations to published inscriptions in important epigraphical journals like *Indian Antiquary (IA), Epigraphia Indica (EI), South Indian Inscriptions (SII), Corpus Inscriptionum Indicarum (CII)*, and *Journal of the Epigraphical Society of India (JESI)* by omitting the details of particular inscriptions and including only the volume, date, inscription number (where relevant) and page number.

Abbreviations

AK	Amarakośa
AS	Arthaśāstra
AV	Atharvaveda
BS	Bṛhatsaṁhitā
BC	Buddhacarita
BSOAS	Bulletin of the School of Oriental and African Studies
CHI	Comprehensive History of India
CII	Corpus Inscriptionum Indicarum
CkS	Carakasaṁhitā
DhVS	Dhūrtaviṭasaṁvāda
DK	Daśakumāracarita
EC	Epigraphia Carnatica (new series)
EI	Epigraphia Indica
GkS	Gaṇikāvṛttasaṁgraha
HC	Harṣacarita
IA	Indian Antiquary
IHR	Indian Historical Review
IHQ	Indian Historical Quarterly
IIJ	Indo-Iranian Journal
ISPS	Inscriptions of the Śarabhapurīyas, Pāṇḍuvaṁśins and Somavaṁśins
JAOS	Journal of the American Oriental Society
JAS	Journal of Asian Studies
JESHO	Journal of the Economic and Social History of the Orient
JESI	Journal of the Epigraphical Society of India
JIH	Journal of Indian History
JRAS	Journal of the Royal Asiatic Society
Kd	Kādambarī
KS	Kāmasūtra
MDh	Mānavadhāramaśāstra
MhB	Mahābhārata
MK	Mṛcchakaṭika

MkA	Mālavikāgnimitra
MR	Mudrārakṣasa
MSS	Mahāsubhāṣitasaṁgraha
NiS	Nītisāra
NiV	Nītivākyāmṛta
NS	Nāṭyaśāstra
Pd	Prīyadarśikā
PIHC	Proceedings of the Indian History Congress
PT	Pañcatantra
PY	Pratijñāyaugandharāyaṇa
RghV	Raghuvaṁśa
Rv	Ratnāvalī
SG	Sigiriya (Sigiri) Graffiti
SII	South Indian Inscriptions
Sk	Abhijñānaśākuntala
STr	Subhāṣitatriśatī
SV	Svapnavāsavadatta
VkU	Vikramorvaśīya

Glossary

ākāra	facial expression or gesture
alaṁkāra	ornamentation, literally 'making sufficient'
amātya	minister
añjali	gesture of greeting involving the putting together of the palms
antaḥpura	a term originally denoting royal palace as a whole but which eventually came to designate women's quarters therein bhāva – state, disposition, emotion
anugraha	favour or kindness
anurāga	attachment, affection
artha	wealth
ārya	'noble', elevated
bhakti	participatory devotion
bhāṇa	genre of monologue play narrated by the viṭa
dākṣiṇya	consideration, courtesy
daṇḍanāyaka	military retainer
digvijaya	a conquest of the four directions necessary to claim imperial overlordship
dūtaka	envoy, messenger
goṣṭhī	salon-like gathering of men for entertainment and conversation
indriya*s*	the senses
iṅgita	physical movement, gesture
kalā	'art' or skill
kāma	pleasure or desire, particularly sexual desire
kañcukin	doorkeeper, chamberlain
kīrti	fame, notoriety
kumāra	prince
kumārāmātya	prince among ministers
lalita	grace or charm
līlā	playful grace or charm

mahāmātra	'one of great estimation', high ranking courtier or official
mahārāja	subordinate king
mahāsandhivigrahaka	minister of peace and war
māna	respect, estimation
manas	mind, locus of feelings, volition, thought
maṇdaleśvara	a lord of a province
mantrin	counsellor
nāgaraka	man of the town, urbane sophisticate
nāyaka	hero of drama
nāyikā	heroine of drama
nīti	political and worldly policy
parīkṣā	test or examination
paṭṭabandha	turban-like fillet or headband
prasāda	favour, particularly as physically manifested by a lord
praśasti	eulogy
pūjā	reverence, honouring
puruṣārtha	four goals of man, referring to kāma, artha, dharma and mokṣa
rājamaṇḍala	'circle of kings', term used to designate a hierarchically ordered array of kings in the *Arthaśāstra*
rājādhirāja	title referring to higher ranking king or emperor
rājayakṣman	'royal disease' of physical attenuation
rasa	essence, flavour, second-order aesthetic experience
rasika	connoisseur, or aesthete
sabhā	assembly or assembly hall
sabhya	fit for an assembly, courtly; courtier, person of good society
sajjana	'good people'
sāmanta	'lord of the marches', a term which came to refer to subordinate vassal-kings
sṛṅgāra	second order aesthetic experience of sexual love
sevā	service
subhāṣita	sententious, gnomic, or pardigmatic verse, literally 'well spoken'
trivarga	'threefold path', worldly life, constituted by the pursuit of kāma, artha and dharma

upacāra	an act of service or courtesy
vaśa	influence or will
vijigīṣu	king desiring paramount overlordship of the rājamaṇḍala
vinaya	discipline, humility
viṭa	a well-regarded man, a former nāgaraka reduced to the role of dependency through poverty
yuvarāja	heir apparent

Introduction

In 1888, R. H. Farmer, the Government of India's political agent to the princely state of Pudukkottai in south India, declared that the palace of the newly installed king Martanda Tondaiman was to be extensively reformed. This task was assigned to the British-appointed *diwān* to the Pudukkotai court, A. Seshaia Sastri.[1] The *diwān*'s most important task was to monitor palace expenditures and guard against the misappropriation of 'public funds' for domestic use by the young prince. Interestingly, Tondaiman's body, deemed obese, was a point of special concern and in 1890 he was removed from the palace to receive 'physical education' near the British military cantonment outside Trichinopoly. Along with this reform of the king's body and sumptuary, various members of the palace retinue, mostly brahmins but also a number of dancing girls who contributed to palace 'vice', were summarily dismissed for fiscal considerations. In the Inam Settlement of 1888 the remaining palace attendants' rights to enjoy the revenue of lands given by the king was substituted by a system of fixed wages, with the old *iṉām* holdings apportioned and deeded to the palace staff as private property subject to taxation.

Some twenty-three years later, Ganganatha Jha of Muir Central College in Allahabad edited an abridged version of the fifteenth-century manual for princes, the *Puruṣaparīkṣā*, for use in schools to replace the 'animal fables' (of the *Hitopadeṣa* and *Pañcatantra*) which were currently in use.[2] The *Puruṣaparīkṣā*, like the texts before it, was to provide young boys at school with an introduction to morals, but without the air of 'unreality' that pervaded the fables. According to one of the several study guides to the text published in subsequent years, the stories of the *Puruṣaparīkṣā*, or 'The Test of Man', were to 'serve as a good social and moral guide

[1] Joanne Punzo Waghorne, *The Raja's Magic Clothes: Re-Visioning Kingship and Divinity in England's India* (University Park: Pennsylvania State University Press, 1994), pp. 55–81.

[2] See the preface of Ganganatha Jha, ed., *Puruṣaparīkṣā* (Allahabad: Belvedere Steam Press, 1911).

for the training of the young and go a great way in forming their moral character and making them live a life worth living'.[3]

These two events, I would like to suggest, represent the contradictory relationship that modernity in India, as elsewhere, has shared with some of its own political antecedents – a relationship which has acted as a perennial irritant in the understanding of pre-colonial India. On the one hand, there has been widespread condemnation. Accounts of the corpulent and decadent bodies of the *ancien régime* characterise the European critique of dynastic absolutism and feudalism as much as the British, and later nationalist, diatribe against the oriental prince. Liberal writers and statesmen of the nineteenth century looked forward to the transformation of the aggressive 'passions' of human life – lust, avarice and the desire for domination – into enlightened 'self-interest' to be pursued through the rational accumulation of wealth. Men would peacefully accrue wealth rather than appropriate war-trophies and women. In Europe, this vision entailed a systematic attack and destruction of the old order, the ideology and practices of the feudal and absolutist classes. In India, it entailed the subjugation of the social order in the name of liberating it from itself. The British political agent's concern over the king's 'home life' in Pudukkottai – his body and manners – was a concern over what might be termed 'the habits of despotism'. The king's body, corrupted by the old order, was to be reshaped to reflect new-found principles of government based on fiscal thrift and public welfare. He was to lose the excess of the past and discipline his appetites. In India, such transformations, part of what one scholar has aptly called the 'colonisation of the political order',[4] relied heavily on particular representations of past Hindu and Muslim kingdoms. Indeed, the various theories of traditional Indian government served the ends of the emerging colonial state in its dismantlement and reconstitution of the political.[5] Throughout the nineteenth century, the bourgeois concepts of 'state' and 'civil society' were repeatedly counterposed to the pomp and despotism of Indian potentates and the choking hold of the caste system. The 'state' in ancient India was a particularly debased form of monarchy, one steeped in sensuality and imagination. But because of its isolation from 'society', rigidly enthralled by the religious sanction of caste, it was at the same time powerless and irrelevant.

[3] *A Complete Guide Key to Purush-Pareeksha, Part II Full Sanskrit Notes* (n.d., n.p.). See also V. B. Dawoo, *A Guide to the Purush-Pareeksha Matric Sanskrit Course for 1915 and Onwards Containing Full Notes in Translation* (Nagpoor: Desh Sewak Press, 1914).

[4] Nicholas Dirks, *The Hollow Crown: Ethnohistory of an Indian Kingdom* (Cambridge University Press, 1987), pp. 324–57.

[5] See Bernard Cohn, 'African Models and Indian Histories', in Bernard S. Cohn, ed., *An Anthropologist among the Historians and Other Essays* (Delhi: Oxford University Press, 1987), pp. 200–23.

Yet the fate of the practices which sustained the *ancien régimes* of late pre-colonial India, both provincial and imperial, were hardly sealed, for they were subject to both wide scale relocation and ideological recuperation. Even as the colonial state sought to reform and re-educate India's 'princes', it also integrated them into its own imperial durbars and splendorous pageantry. These incorporations continued with the rise of nationalism (though India's loyalist princes were consigned to all that was corrupt in the past!). History once again played an important role in ideological transformation, with nationalists defending the critique of Indian despotism and attempting to find the lineages of their own modernity in ancient village republics, benign welfare states and glorious Hindu kingdoms. These visions are perhaps best captured in the Indian state's later adoption of the Aśokan lion-capital as its national emblem, a 'symbol' that was properly ideological, having no organic relationship with the practices of governance and language of state which it so nicely crowned, as symbol of secular unity. At one level, India is hardly unique in this matter, for most modern states have deployed symbols of the past in similarly anachronistic ways.

Yet there is a vast, complex and problematic history here which remains largely unwritten. For perhaps more important than these ideological postures was the gradual 'relocation' of numerous forms (manners, modes of dress, literary cultures, etc.) grounded in practices of polity, both imperial and provincial (and only partly embodied in the princely states the British chose to patronise), to the newly emerging realm of 'civil society' – that is, beyond the borders of the newly christened colonial and post-colonial state apparatus. This process entailed not so much a wholesale movement of practices as their increasing recontextualisation in a world where the political was ostensibly located elsewhere – within the Indo-Saracenic sandstone of the Indian parliament.

This is in fact the process of modernity everywhere, where elements of pre-modern political life survive as apparently depoliticised aspects of 'civil society' and 'national culture', where manuals for princes like the *Puruṣaparīkṣā* become character-building exercises for the nation's youth. Yet what of everyday forms of life beyond the designs of the state's civil authority, forms of practice whose political connotations were now silent? If in some cases these constituted 'social problems' in need of eradication, in others they have formed the ostensible basis of 'social ethics' among various classes and communities in everyday life. The recent and rather misplaced claims for an indigenous Indian 'modernity' notwithstanding, the problem which faces historians in charting the history and evolution of these practices is complex, for while it may be argued that in Europe the evolution of the bourgeois world occurred in open (often antagonistic) dialogue (i.e. dialogic process) with the aristocratic cultures it displaced, and thus were in some sense 'organic', the colonial context prevents any simple application of such a model to India. To put it crudely, while it may be argued that in Europe 'civil society' and 'public life' were complex (and often antagonistic) reworkings of the practices and concepts of *civilité*, *courtoise* and *le monde*, in India, political modernity everywhere has had a more fitful and divided existence. It is an implicit presumption of this book that in order to comprehend this history in more complex and convincing paradigms than either the 'imposition' of Western modernity onto India or the rediscovery of an 'indigenous modernity', it is first necessary to explore critically the evolution of these practices outside the paradigms which have been made for them by those who seek to escape or return to some putative past. This work hopes to make a modest contribution to such a larger project.

The court in early India: approaches

This book is about early Indian courts and the activities that transpired at them. It approaches the court from a broadly conceived 'social history' perspective. That is, it seeks to understand early Indian courts first and foremost as *societies*, coherent social formations composed of individuals whose relationships were governed by particular codes of behaviour and modes of thought. Its primary concern will be with courtly culture – and in particular the emphasis in courtly sources on beauty, refinement and love. It will place these themes, however, within the context of the court as a social institution, focusing on its organisation and structure, protocol and the relational dynamics of its members. Ultimately, this approach hopes to add something to our knowledge of both the sociology of early Indian courts as well as their impressive cultural achievements.

The dynamics of courtly life in India have held remarkably little interest for scholars of Indian history and literature and, barring a handful of important articles on early medieval and Mughal courts, there is very little secondary literature on the subject.[6] This is not, however, because

[6] Krishna Kanti Gopal, 'The Assembly of Samantas in Early Medieval India', *JIH*, vol. 42, pts. 1–3 (1964), pp. 241–50; Ronald Inden, 'Hierarchies of Kings in Early Medieval India,' *Contributions to Indian Sociology*, n. s., vol. 15, nos. 1–2 (1981), pp. 99–125; B. D. Chattopadhyaya, 'Religion in a Royal Household: A Study of Some Aspects of Rājaśekhara's Karpūramañjarī', in B. D. Chattopadhyaya, *The Making of Early Medieval India* (Delhi: Oxford Univeristy Press, 1994), pp. 223–31; John Richards, 'Norms of Comportment among Imperial Mughal Officers', in Barbara Metcalf, ed., *Moral Conduct and Authority: The Place of Adab in South Asian Islam* (Berkeley: University of California Press, 1984), pp. 255–89; Rosalind O'Hanlon, 'Manliness and Imperial Service in Mughal North India', *JESHO*, vol. 42, pt. 1 (1999), pp. 47–93.

of any dearth of source materials. In fact, the source materials on which this book will be based is for the most part well known, having been the ballast of historical, literary and religious scholarship on early India for the last one hundred years. The contribution this study hopes to make, then, is at some level perspectival. In traversing familiar territory through new paths of analysis, this book will parse the evidentiary terrain in different ways and, hopefully, reveal new vistas. It will juxtapose materials which have often been read disparately in order to present a courtly 'world' which is coherent in its own terms.

One region of the current landscape which must be remapped is what we know as 'kingship'. Ancient Indian kingship has been a perennial topic in Indological study. The dominant approaches in recent times have seen the Indian king as a problematically sacred or 'dharmic' figure, locked in eternal struggle with and ideological dependence on, his priestly companion, the brahmin. Such theories of ritual or religious kingship have no doubt advanced our knowledge, particularly with regard to the cosmological and religious dimensions of royal ideology. Yet they have, even from these perspectives, rarely if ever treated the immediate world of either the king or those around him (other than priests) as a topic worthy of study, despite the fact that these are precisely the concerns of the manuals on polity which formed the most important knowledge the king was to acquire.

This book will to a large extent, then, de-emphasise the figure of the king as an embodiment of 'kingship'. It will suggest that greater attention to the court itself as an arena of activity and knowledge will shed fresh light on the ruling classes as a whole in early India. In a sense, such a turn should be obvious, as kings in early India were manifestly complex agents; their coronations, routines, edicts, counsel and pleasures being regularly attended by large numbers of ministrants and companions, whose own agendas and commitments were only partly lived through those of the king. Of course it is not possible to ignore the king altogether, for as the central 'organ' of the kingdom, he remains an unavoidable figure in the study of monarchical political forms in early India. The focus in this book, however, will mainly be on the royal household, the culture and dynamics of which were relevant not only to the king, but to a whole class of élites of which the king was only a part, and from whose ranks he often rose.

A more formidable realm of scholarship which will remain largely unaddressed in this study is the historiography of 'state formation' in early India. This may seem peculiar to those who would assume that a book about early Indian courts should be concerned first and foremost with the procedures and functions of the state. To some extent such a sentiment is justified, but the existing historiography of state formation in early India, as elsewhere, has tended to approach the evidence with an overly substantialist notion of the state as an abstract thing. These models generally view the state as a sort of administrative or bureaucratic polity suspended above a 'society' composed of castes. The major debates in this historiography until very recently have revolved around the relative centralisation or decentralisation and administrative structure of the state. These debates have been useful and important. But they often presume a sort of almost self-evident bureaucratic rationality as the framework of the medieval state. The actual 'activities' of the court, beyond revenue collection and warfare, have, when treated at all, been comfortably glossed, using theories of dharmic kingship, as the 'legitimation' of authority. While this approach has some merits, for the sort of study undertaken here, its overweening faith in a putative bureaucratic or administrative rationality as the 'glue' holding together the organisation of the state itself has been, to my mind, detrimental to coming to terms with the sources themselves. To use the words of Pierre Bourdieu, in trying to 'think the state' this historiography has been 'taken over by the thought of the state'.[7] Since the administrative apparatus of states have a sort of self-evident logic which holds them together, the preoccupations of the court can do little more than sprinkle coloured powder on otherwise 'functional' furniture.

The approach here, drawing on the work of Ronald Inden and others, will conceive of the 'state' as existing more relevantly in the specific activities and ideas of the individual men who composed it rather than any self-evident functional structure. It was the activities of the king's court, composed of dependents and retainers, and attended by underlords and vassals, which constituted 'government' rather than a putative 'administration'.[8] This means relinquishing the idea of the king's court as a sort of

[7] Pierre Bourdieu, 'Rethinking the State: Genesis and Structure of the Bureaucratic Field', *Sociological Theory*, vol. 12, no. 1 (1994), pp. 1–18.

[8] Drawing on the work of A. M. Hocart (*Caste: A Comparative Study* (London: Metheun, 1950)), Inden in a number of important articles has argued for the overall commensurability of caste and kingship, culminating in a theory of polity (rather than a state) as a 'scale of lordships'. Within this framework we may understand the court as standing at the apex of a hierarchy of lordly assemblages and encompassing masteries (different from one another in degree and sometimes in kind, but not in 'species') which stretched from the king's household to the labourer in the field whose mastery barely and tenuously extended over his own person. See R. Inden, 'Lordship and Caste in Hindu Discourse', in Audrey Cantile and Richard Burghart, eds., *Indian Religion* (London: Curzon Press, 1985), pp. 159–79; R. Inden, *Imagining India*, (Oxford: Blackwell, 1990), pp. 213–62. James Heitzman has recently combined a similar theory of lordship with Marxist political economy. See James Heitzman, *Gifts of Power: Lordship in an Early Indian State* (Delhi: Oxford University Press, 1997).

'symbol of authority' representing the actuality of the 'state'. The activities of the court in an important sense *were* the activities of the state. The men and the activities which constituted the state, to be sure, extended far beyond the royal household to the revenue collectors and local lords who may have rarely appeared at the king's assembly. The relevant point, however, is that the royal court stood at the apex of this circle not as a symbol but a superordinate set of human relationships. The approach here thus views the court as a complex agency of rule which continually re-articulated itself in response to diverse relations both within and beyond it. Its focus will be on mental and practical concerns of people of the court within the dynamics of the imperial household as a set of relationships.

Judging from the sources, these concerns were strikingly procedural, aesthetic and even ethical in nature. The people of the court were preoccupied with questions of style and protocol. The largely indifferent attitude toward such concerns in the historiography of early India is at variance with other historiographical traditions (on Europe and elsewhere), which have produced rich and diverse interpretations of courtly societies and cultures.[9] While important evidentiary differences preclude any wholesale application to Indian materials, such scholarship on the whole suggests two broad points relevant to this study.[10] First, and perhaps most obviously, the cultural achievements of courtly societies may be most effectively understood with specific reference to the functioning

[9] The exception to this indifference is the work of a few scholars of post-Gupta India who have treated the court in passing, *inter alia*, with striking and perceptive detail. Particularly notable are V. S. Agrawala, *The Deeds of Harsha: Being a Cultural Study of Bāṇa's Harshacarita* (Varanasi: Prithvi Prakashan, 1969); R. S. Sharma, *Indian Feudalism C. 300–1300* (Delhi: Macmillan, 2nd edn, 1980); R. S. Sharma, 'The Feudal Mind', in R. S. Sharma, *Early Medieval Indian Society: A Study in Feudalisation* (London: Sangam Books, 2001), pp. 266–84; and B. N. S. Yadava, *Society and Culture in Northern India in the Twelfth Century* (Allahabad: Central Book Depot, 1973).

[10] This literature, particularly in European history, is vast, and the more important works reviewed for this research include Stephen Jaeger, *The Origins of Courtliness: Civilizing Trends and the Formation of Courtly Ideals, 923–1120* (Philadelphia: University of Pennsylvania Press, 1985); Joachim Bumke, *Courtly Culture: Literature and Society in the High Middle Ages*, trans. Thomas Dunlap (New York: Overlook Press, 2000); David Burnley, *Courtliness and Literature in Medieval England* (London: Longman, 1998); and relevant sections in Georges Duby and Philip Aries, eds., *A History of Private Life: vol. 2, Revelations of the Medieval World* (London: Harvard University Press, 1988). Important studies of chivalric ideals, a topic which has a much older scholarly tradition, include Georges Duby, *The Chivalrous Society* (Berkeley: University of California Press, 1977); Georges Duby, *William Marshall: The Flower of Chivalry* (New York: Pantheon, 1985); and Maurice Keen, *Chivalry* (New Haven: Yale University Press, 1984). For a study of Ghaznavid and Seljuk courtly culture, see Julie Scott Meisami, *Medieval Persian Court Poetry* (Princeton University Press, 1987); and for Heian period Japan, see Ivan Morris, *The World of the Shining Prince: Court Life in Ancient Japan* (New York: Kodansha, repr. 1994).

and dynamics of these societies themselves. As we shall see, barring a few recent studies, the overwhelming approach to courtly culture in India has been rampantly formalist or blandly reductive in approach, so much so that the courtly basis of much of the literature that has come down to us from early India is almost entirely obfuscated by the secondary scholarship. Second, courtly societies developed peculiar and pronounced, yet coherent, forms of 'sociability' which, as much as they attracted comment and even censure from both contemporary critics and later reformers, are worthy of study for social historians. These norms of behaviour formed important 'socialising' or 'integrating' mechanisms for the ruling classes of medieval society. They also, viewed from a macro-historical perspective, were key and indeed formative 'moments' in the evolution of wider conceptions of individual and social being. In Europe, later notions of civility and morality often grew up in explicit dialogue with courtly precedents.

Concerns around courtly sociability have recently been raised by historians writing on the 'history of manners', inspired at least in part by the eminent scholars Norbert Elias and Michel Foucault.[11] Elias emphasised that the behaviours of men and women at court had to be understood with reference to the *specific conditions* of life there – chiefly, the fact that the court was nothing other than the extended household of the king. Here the courtier's most intimate life and his 'career' were confined to a single field of operation. Appearance, outward bearing and manners, considered mere 'externals' in bourgeois society, were the means through which the people of the court secured their livelihoods. From this perspective, the courtier's preoccupation with appearance and good form was not an intrinsic superficiality, as its bourgeois critics assumed it to be, but was rational behaviour suited to a particular social environment.[12] It is only when these practices were delinked from their social moorings, when professional opportunities were freed from the yoke of feudal and courtly hierarchies, that such social accoutrements took on a potentially 'superficial', or 'hollow', aspect.[13]

[11] Anna Bryson, *From Courtesy to Civility: Changing Codes of Conduct in Early Modern England* (New York: Oxford University Press, 1998); Jorge Arditi, *A Geneaology of Manners: Transformations of Social Relations in France and England from the Fourteenth to Eighteenth Century* (University of Chicago Press, 1998); Jan Bremmer and Herman Roodenburg, eds., *A Cultural History of Gesture: From Antiquity to the Present Day* (Cambridge: Polity/Blackwell, 1991).

[12] Norbert Elias, *The Court Society* (Oxford: Blackwell, 1983), pp. 53–4.

[13] Other sociologists have described this transformation with somewhat different emphasis. For Jürgen Habermas, the shift was from one of 'representative publicness' typical of the medieval nobleman, who was what he *represented*, to a 'bourgeois' or 'authentic publicness' in which the entrepreneur was what he *produced*, J. Habermas, *The Structural Transformation of the Public Sphere* (Cambridge: Polity Press, 1999), pp. 5–13.

Elias connected the behaviours of the courtly elite to wider processes of social transformation. He placed the habits of feudal, absolutist and bourgeois societies in Europe on a continuum which saw an increasingly internalised restraint of human drives, social detachment and individuation – key elements of what the West had defined as 'civilisation'.[14] Methodologically, Elias' key formulation was that each type of society, or 'social figuration' as a network of interdependent individuals, generated a particular set of manners, psychic structures and intersubjective relations which were appropriate to it. This approach allowed historians to see many aspects of courtly life (and other societies), from attitudes to bodily functions to the nature of intersubjective relations, within an historical frame – rather than through vague and psychologising explanations which treated such features as consubstantial with human nature itself.[15] Whatever disagreements scholars have had with Elias' method, this contribution alone, as simple as it sounds, has made his work a landmark in the study of courtly life and manners.

Michel Foucault's contribution to the study of manners has been less direct, partly because he never took up the topic directly, and partly because his approach is less assimilable to normative historical and sociological inquiry.[16] In his uncompleted *History of Sexuality*, Foucault began to develop his ideas about pre-bourgeois forms of discipline in the West.[17] In the first volume of this history Foucault posed the question of how modern individuals came to recognise themselves as the possessors of 'sexuality'. His answer, now famous, was that medical, legal and juridical institutions and knowledges did not so much 'discover' or 'bear down' upon human sexuality, but instead 'implanted' it as a natural and legitimate domain of being human. In retracing the antecedents of this dispensation, Foucault concluded that it would not suffice to follow the threads of pre-bourgeois notions of 'flesh' and 'desire' which sexuality itself had tried to lay claim to. Instead, it was necessary to begin with the larger ethical frameworks in which sex had always been placed – not merely around interdictions regarding sex itself, but its place in a larger sense of how individuals should constitute relations with themselves and others.

[14] Norbert Elias, *The Civilising Process: The History of Manners and State Formation and Civilisation*, trans. Norman Jephcott (Oxford: Blackwell, 1994).

[15] See Roger Chartier, 'Social Figuration and Habitus: Reading Elias', in Roger Chartier, *Cultural History: Between Practice and Representation*, trans. Lydia Cochrane (Ithaca, NY: Cornell University Press, 1988), p. 79.

[16] For discussions of Foucault's work in relation to the history of manners, see Bryson, *From Courtesy to Civility*, pp. 14–16, and Arditi, *Geneaology of Manners*, p. 6 ff.

[17] Michel Foucault, *The History of Sexuality: An Introduction*, vol. I of *The History of Sexuality* (New York: Vintage, 1980); Michel Foucault, *The Use of Pleasure*, vol. II of *The History of Sexuality* (New York: Vintage, 1985).

Foucault argued that the male citizen in antiquity considered his ability to subject himself to techniques of self-discipline (not only with regard to sex but a host of other aspects of his life) as a mark of personal beauty and freedom which set him above his social inferiors. Courtly manners in this sense would probably have gained their significance as specific forms of ethical practice – and their capacity to produce a certain type of ethical 'subject'.[18]

Whatever their differences (and they are considerable), both Elias and Foucault have played influential roles in resisting the common liberal and humanist trivialisations of pre-bourgeois manners in the name of producing a rational 'enlightened' ethics.[19] According to perhaps the chief spokesman of this ethics, Immanuel Kant, the superficiality of manners hinged on their lack of inward self-determination and control: 'affability, politeness, refinement, propriety, courtesy and ingratiating and captivating behaviour . . . call of no large measure of moral determination and cannot, therefore, be reckoned as virtues'.[20] Kant's outline of a rationally determined and universal moral imperative was a defining moment in a general trend which has viewed ethical activity as an essentially 'inner mental' and almost monologic form of ratiocination. This relocation of 'authentic' ethics from the more 'public' and socially mediated contexts it had occupied in pre-Enlightenment society to the 'inner world' of modern man, occurred at the same time as the rise of the new ideas of the public good based on the wholly different principles of utilitarianism. The interiorisation of ethics, in other words, was complemented by the rise of the modern notion of society where men would rationally pursue their enlightened 'self interest'.[21] And it is this dual movement which has made it so difficult to sensitively reconstruct practices like courtly manners in both India and Europe. In India, the reform of the oriental despot entailed the re-education of the prince in the new values of modern society, in ideas of 'public good' and fiscal thrift. It also entailed the trivialisation (through the discourse on oriental pomp and decadence) and

[18] Drawing on Foucault, Arditi has highlighted the ethical foundations of 'courtesy' (and their denudation in 'etiquette'). See Arditi, *Geneaology of Manners*; cf. Michael Curtain, 'A Question of Manners: Status and Gender in Eitquette and Courtesy', *Journal of Modern History*, vol. 57 (1985), pp. 395–423.

[19] See the very useful discussion in Jeffrey Minson, *Questions of Conduct: Sexual Harassment, Citizenship, Government* (London: Macmillan, 1993), pp. 16–40.

[20] I. Kant, *Lectures on Ethics*, trans. L. Infield (New York: Harper Torchbooks, 1963), pp. 236–7.

[21] It is perhaps as significant as it is ironical that modern ethics, to the extent that it has followed Kant, has for the large part regarded altruism as its most authentic ethical posture, while modern society, to the extent it has followed utilitarians like John Stuart Mill and Jeremy Bentham, has for the large part regarded self-interest as its cornerstone.

partial relocation and diminishment of a wide variety of socially mediated ethical practices.

The inspiration that this study has drawn from the history of courts and manners in Europe is largely orientational rather than programmatic. This book will not search for Indian counterparts to ideas like *courtoisie*, *civilité* or *sprezzaturra*. The research for this book began as and remains, an engagement with Indian materials and Indian materials alone. Yet where comparison is illustrative, I will not shy away from it, for it is my belief that the 'spectre' of European categories is not so great as to render critical comparison undesirable. The specificity of Indian materials in fact can often best be illustrated with reference to other traditions. The magisterial projects of Elias and Foucault are difficult to imagine (and not necessarily desirable) in the Indian context, not only because the relationship of pre-colonial cultural figurations and modernity in India was mediated by the complex imposition of European colonialism, but also because so little attention has been paid in the first instance to ethics, manners and rhetoric in any sort of sociological or historical-discursive framework, much less as part of macro-historical processes. Following the generally structural thrust of these scholars, this study will, on the one hand, try to ground courtly behaviours within the logic of social relationships which they were integral to maintaining, and on the other, demonstrate how these behaviours helped to form courtly individuals. It will, in other words, place courtly practices within their social context, and also show how they generated a certain sort of subjectivity.

Interpreting poetry and aesthetics

Parts of this book will focus very centrally on the courtly preoccupation with beauty and aesthetic pleasure, and make copious use of literary and, to a lesser extent, visual sources. It will not do so, however, from an exclusively 'art historical', 'literary critical' or aestheticist perspective. Rather, it will place literature and art against wider practices of self-refinement and beautification which extended beyond the formal boundaries of these 'genres'.

Though scholars of Indian literature have noted in passing the courtly provenance of the great bulk of Sanskrit literature known as *kāvya*, and art historians have noted the courtly influence on much visual art, very few, if any, studies until very recently have taken this context seriously. Not surprisingly, the roots of this critical lacunae stretch back to colonial estimations of Indian art and literature as despotic or debased in nature.

n Ruskin, for example, vilified Indian sculpture as grotesquely ornamental and non-naturalistic. For critics like Ruskin, moral and civilised art, even in its ornamental mode, followed a strict fidelity to the truth of nature, and therefore had an ennobling moral value. Savage art, by contrast, was preoccupied with pleasure rather than truth. It was intricate to a fault and distorted and unbalanced. This, of course, was seen as a symptom of civilisational dissipation, rampant superstition and political tyranny.[22]

Similar estimations of Indian literature were common and given a fillip by the fact 'that the Indians designate what in Europe is called poetics as "the science of embellishment"'.[23] Many European scholars concluded that Sanskrit court literature was characteristically preoccupied with form over content, exhibiting a prurient fascination for long-winded, stereotyped and florid description. Indian poetry had a relish for indirection, and a tendency towards obfuscation, achieved through the accumulation of ever greater numbers of verbal conceits and figures of speech. The inclination towards ornamentation, floridity, and indirection in courtly and religious aesthetic forms reflected the tyranny and superstition of their origins. These traits were thought to reflect the deeper political and philosophical deficiencies.

Later scholars of Indian art and literature reacted to this criticism diversely. There were those who implicitly accepted it, not as a critique of despotism, but as a comment on the 'unreliability' of literary sources. Humanistic scholars tended to either retreat into formalist criticism or Romantic apologetics. One of the chief protagonists of this latter tendency was the art critic A. K. Coomaraswamy, whose work has been inspirational for a generation of humanistic scholars in India today. Coomaraswamy began by distinguishing between modern and traditional art forms (rather than occidental and oriental) and argued that because the rise of modern society had led to an alienation between life and aesthetic production – a divorce between utility and meaning, enjoyment and understanding – it was necessary to break with modern critiques of traditional art to understand its place in both Indian and European

[22] See the excellent discussion in Partha Mitter, *Much Maligned Monsters: A History of European Reactions to Indian Art* (University of Chicago Press, 1977), pp. 198–202; 239–48. Whatever his patrician sympathies and criticism of modern 'materialism' at home, Ruskin's view of oriental art put him squarely on the side of the utilitarians when it came to India. On the relation between utilitarianism and aestheticism in the nineteenth century, see Terry Eagleton, *The Ideology of the Aesthetic* (Oxford: Blackwell, 1990), pp. 31–69.

[23] A fact deemed 'significant' by Maurice Winternitz in *A History of Indian Literature*, vol. III (Delhi: Motilal Banarsidass, 1963 repr.), p. 4.

civilisation.[24] What Coomaraswamy offered in its place was a highly idealist, holistic and even metaphysical interpretation of Indian art which found favour in the nationalist celebration of ancient Indian culture.

In literature, scholars celebrated the already dominant subjectivist *rasa* aesthetics associated with the eleventh-century Kashmiri scholar Abhinavagupta as an answer to the charge of floridity and ornamental extravagance. As much as these interpretations, generally highly theoretical or formalist, have formed the bedrock of scholarship on Indian aesthetics, they have also shied away from exploring the courtly and urbane contexts of this literature. So the problem, as it stands, is that those who have treated the social contexts of literary and aesthetic texts have by and large paid scant attention to the content of these sources, while those preoccupied with their content have done so with very little regard for context.

It is only recently that a number of scholars have attempted to revise earlier assessments and turned seriously to the sociology of Indian courtly art. As the approach here will both build on and depart from this work in different ways, it will be of some value to review briefly the more important of these contributions. David Smith, in his study of Ratnākara's ninth-century *Haravijaya*, composed at the Karkoṭa court, has contested the widespread dismissal by most modern literary critics, sanctioned by their interpretation of Abhinavagupta's corpus, of ornamentalist court poetry. Smith argues that in order to understand ornamentalist literature, we need to move beyond this ideological polemic. In his own analysis, Smith argues that the rise of ornamentalist and eulogistic *kāvya* in the first centuries of the Common Era gradually came to replace older religious (Vedic) ritualism which had the function of shoring up or strengthening royal authority.[25] Smith here is exemplary of scholarship which has rooted the social existence of *kāvya* in the relationship between the poet and the king. This has been the approach of several scholars who have contributed to a volume on patronage and Indian art. These scholars have sought to

[24] For a general discussion of Coomaraswamy, see Mitter, *Much Maligned Monsters*, pp. 277–86; his ideas on ornament will be treated below. Coomaraswamy shared Ruskin's critique of modern materialism and valorised 'traditional' art forms, though his remarkable ecumenism and breadth as a scholar prevented him from the excesses of Ruskin's Eurocentric philistinism. Coomaraswamy was an idealist and Neoplatonist; he argued that good art need not imitate external natural reality but rather translated the idealised and superior reality within the mind of the artist into visible form. The post-Independence celebrants of this approach have largely opposed themselves to Marxist understandings of ancient India, and have recently used debates on orientalism to claim an 'indigenous' perspective.

[25] David Smith, *Ratnākara's Haravijaya: An Introduction to the Sanskrit Court Epic* (Delhi: Oxford University Press, 1985), pp. 55–102.

over the imprint of political power on specific works of art, and how power thus gains 'legitimacy' through art.[26]

At one level patronage is such an obvious and undeniable fact in the production of art and literature in pre-colonial South Asia, and its absence as a problem in the secondary literature so glaring, that any sustained attention to it is to be welcomed. To this extent, the focus on patronage has been a positive development. Yet, when we examine what such scholarship has actually made of patronage relations, there is perhaps less reason for enthusiasm. For it would seem that most of this scholarship has merely returned to theories of sacred kingship which argued that political power in the form of the king, required 'authority' which was to be gained from religion in the form of the brahmin.[27] The political 'imprint' on art thus amounted centrally to legitimating royal authority.

The difficulties with this approach are twofold. First, it has tended to assume that political power is constituted outside the realm of ideation, to which it then desperately repairs in order to gain post facto 'legitimacy'. Yet when we actually enquire about the nature of this non-ideational realm of power, it appears that scholars have relied rather uncritically on supposedly self-evident notions of either kingly power or administrative 'rationality' which I reviewed briefly above. The problem, as we shall see through the course of this book, is that the ideas enshrined in art and literature are in fact identical to the key concepts found in the texts which urge the king and his men to constitute their political actions, which is to say that the supposedly non-ideational realm of power and politics is in fact already ideational. Given this, legitimation theory seems to suggest the rather unlikely and even anachronistic scenario of the court acting collectively on the basis of certain principles, and then representing them back to itself in order to legitimate them. In some particular cases such a model may be appropriate, but for the large part, it is inadequate. I am

[26] Barbara Stoler Miller, 'Introduction', in Miller, ed., *The Powers of Art: Patronage in Indian Culture* (Delhi: Oxford University Press, 1992), p. 4.

[27] The key work here has been that of J. C. Heesterman on Vedic ritualism, who argued that the peculiarities of Indian kingship could be explained by the unresolved tension between transcendentalising ritualism (in the form of the brahmin) and immanent political power (in the form of the king). David Shulman's important work on south Indian kingship extended Heesterman's theory of brahmin and king to the entire ideological fabric of later Hindu kingship, and in doing so seamlessly inserted courtly literature into this problematic. For Shulman all of this literature, from the Vedas to later medieval court literature, revealed the unresolved tension between transcendence and worldly power which characterised Indian kingship, and which helped explain the apparent absence or weakness of 'centralised administrative authority' in the medieval state. See J. C. Heesterman, *The Inner Conflict of Tradition: Essays in Indian Ritual, Kingship, and Society* (University of Chicago Press, 1985); and David Shulman, *The King and the Clown in South Indian Myth and Poetry* (Princeton University Press, 1985).

not for a moment suggesting here that we accept either the claims of political manuals or poetic representations at face value, but only that in the absence of any de-personalised and de-ethicised practice of government, legitimation is a particularly impoverished model for understanding the nature and function of this language or the genres in which it is embodied. Very minimally, theories of 'ideology' would be a great improvement, if for no other reason than that they often tend to ask the question of how representations actually function in constituting social relationships.

This brings me to the second point of criticism, that the patronage/legitimation model typically assumes a very impoverished court sociology, one dominated by the single figure of the king/patron. The dynamics of the court as an institution of complex agencies is completely missing from these approaches. Yet courtly literature, by its themes and currency, had a far more diverse audience of spectators (we need only think of a text as basic as the *Pañcatantra* – ostensibly written for princes but narrated from the perspective of courtiers). If, as this study will argue, the court was a complex agency, then it is possible to read courtly literature, even in its most individually eulogistic mode, as addressing a variety of composite agencies necessary for its operation. The court poem, in other words, addressed a variety of courtly agendas rather than the individual needs of the patron.

Sheldon Pollock has recently provided a more sophisticated approach to the relationship between aesthetics and power which distances itself from theories of legitimation and ideology. In a number of important articles Pollock has attempted to theorise the relationship of Sanskrit *kāvya* and political power in South Asia. He begins with the important premise that the massive and sophisticated corpus of Sanskrit literary culture which suddenly appeared in the second to fourth centuries of the Common Era in India and quickly and volubly spread over a vast geographical space – usually treated as a self-evident expression of classical 'culture' – is actually a historically produced phenomenon in dire need of some account, explanation and analysis. Pollock places special attention on dynastic inscriptions, tracing the rise, spread and eventual decline of Sanskrit as a 'public political language' in South and Southeast Asian polities from the fourth to the thirteenth centuries. Pollock argues that Sanskrit, through the medium of *kāvya*, came to define a global cultural formation or 'cosmopolis' that at once transcended political boundaries and religious affiliations, uniting intellectuals and their masters in a common aesthetic culture which stretched across a wide geographical expanse. He points out that by the fourth century CE a linguistic division of labour emerged in Indian epigraphy in which Sanskrit expressed transcendent political claims linking polities to a pan-regional political culture while regional languages recorded the quotidian material power upon which these claims were inevitably based. Real political power was thus hierarchised by transcendent 'aesthetic power'.[28]

Pollock's approach in a sense is a major breakthrough, for he usefully shifts our focus away from kingship, patronage and legitimisation theory to a more widely defined notion of political power which leaves ample scope for taking more serious account of courtly literature. He has placed Sanskrit *kāvya* at the centre of medieval political life. Moreover, he makes the important observation, a direly needed warning to cultural historians, that the Sanskrit cosmopolis as a cultural formation cannot be readily apprehended through the pat theories of indigeneity which animate the discussions of the modern bourgeois national state. For to participate in the cosmopolitan order meant precisely to supersede and therefore occlude localised forms of belonging. To date, there probably remains no more sophisticated formulation of Sanskrit *kāvya* to the political culture of early medieval India.

Yet Pollock's theories pose certain problems. His main argument, that *kāvya* 'aestheticised' politics by bracketing out the question of material practice, or at least delegating it to regional languages, seems to rely on an *a priori* division between aesthetics and materiality. Pollock's assumption that the eulogies (*praśasti*s) of inscriptions deal only with idealising, non-material claims, I would argue, precludes from its start seeing *kāvya* as connected with political practice in any *formative* way. I think that the problem here lies in the somewhat exaggerated and aestheticist profile which Pollock attributes to the category of 'the Literary', which we are told is immensely 'important', 'influential' and 'significant', on the basis of its formal prevalence and its function as a vehicle for the transfer of 'symbolic goods'. In many respects this is a valuable way to put the problem, showing how Sanskrit itself becomes a 'cultural commodity', but when we enquire into the actual 'goods' being 'transferred' in Pollock's account, they turn out to be not only somewhat undertheorised, but to resemble those objects so familiar from legitimation theory – generic symbols, mythic origins and perduring claims. Pollock's reticence towards combining his important insights into literary Sanskrit as a discursive form with any serious engagement with its content leads him to pose the literary as a sort of empty and hypostasised place-holder,

[28] Argued chiefly in Sheldon Pollock, 'The Sanskrit Cosmopolis, 300–1300 CE: Transculturation, Vernacularization, and the Question of Ideology', in Jan E. M. Houben, ed., *Ideology and Status of Sanskrit: Contributions to the History of the Sanskrit Language* (New York: E. J. Brill, 1996), pp. 197–8; and reiterated in Sheldon Pollock, 'The Cosmopolitan Vernacular', *JAS*, vol. 57, no. 1 (1998): 6–37; and 'India in the Vernacular Millennium: Literary Culture and Polity, 1000–1500', *Daedalus*, vol. 127, no. 3 (1998): 41–74.

functioning, somewhat tautologically, to 'aestheticise' politics.[29] It also, unfortunately, makes Pollock's formulation in some ways vulnerable to some of the same criticisms which he so ably levels at legitimation theorists.

To understand how Sanskrit literature 'aestheticised' life at court, it is necessary to appreciate its content. One of the more serious works in recent times to take up the content of *kāvya* is Robert Goodwin's monograph on Sanskrit drama.[30] Goodwin uses the fact that the audience of drama was ideally to identify with the hero to eschew any formalist approach to his material and open the thematic world of the drama to sustained scrutiny. This point, perhaps an obvious one, has hardly been in evidence in the rarefied world of Sanskrit criticism, where hermetic, formalist interpretation has been the preferred modus operandi. At the heart of the classical Sanskrit plays, and indeed courtly and urbane society as a whole, Goodwin argues, is a dynamic tension between the demands of emotional and erotic life and the ascetical wisdom of Vedantic metaphysics, which Goodwin links to Freud's life and death drives (*eros/thanatos*). The conflict between these tendencies is not so much resolved as symbolically mediated in the aesthetic texts through a Barthesian 'myth' which posits the ideal of detached 'play' (*līlā*) as a transcendental response to the renunciative power on the part of the sentimentalist. Goodwin's approach has much to recommend it. While on the one hand he engages with the categories of the tradition itself, and provides close textual analyses of the plays, on the other he retains enough distance from his sources to ask questions which they themselves do not formulate. But to understand his plays, Goodwin relies, perhaps too heavily, on the subjectivist traditions of Sanskrit aesthetics and metaphysical philosophy rather than enquiring into the sociology of the court itself. The theoretical texts may inflect dramas with important philosophical themes (although immanence/worldliness versus transcendence/renunciation may not be the most significant of these), but there is much more going on in the dramas which is explicable through the everyday concerns of courtly life.

While relying on many of the crucial insights of these scholars, particularly those of Pollock, this book will also depart from their approaches to literature in two ways. First, it will place literature, and the aesthetic

[29] This leads Pollock to suggest that since Sanskrit was 'restricted to the expressive and divorced from the documentary, its relation to power seems to have been far more aesthetic than instrumental, a poetry of power in an aesthetic state' ('India in the Vernacular Millennium', p. 49). In this sense, Pollock tends to wed a very modernist notion of aesthetics with an equally modern notion of 'state'. For a critique of the former, see Terry Eagleton, *The Ideology of the Aesthetic* (Oxford: Blackwell, 1990).

[30] Robert Goodwin, *The Playworld of Sanskrit Drama* (Delhi: Motilal Banarsidass, 1998).

theories on the basis of which it was putatively produced and enjoyed, within the wider context of material life, interpersonal protocols, and ethical practices as they obtained at court. In doing so, this book will use literary sources in two ways. First, they will be used empirically (and hopefully not naively!) to assist in reconstructing the context into which they must then be placed to a much greater degree than Goodwin has done. This may seem like a tautologically self-referential method, but it is justified by the fact that literary texts corroborate many practices known from prescriptive literature, and thus, if read critically, can serve as useful evidence in reconstructing the world of the court. As Goodwin himself notes, it is perhaps striking that literary criticism in Indian studies has only rarely produced scholars with more than a passing interest in the actual themes and content of courtly literature.[31] It is an implicit methodological contention of this book that if a more contextually informed literary criticism is to develop in the study of Sanskrit poetry, then the themes of Sanskrit *kāvya* must be returned to with greater scrutiny.

But this is not all, for I hope to treat literary texts analytically as modes through which individuals were 'educated' and 'interpolated' into the structure of courtly life in a highly reflexive manner. And, rather than exalting the 'literary', I hope instead to place literature within a wider set of aesthetic practices and ethical cultivations which were concerned with the body, the mind and the world. If Sanskrit *kāvya*, as Pollock maintains, constituted a sort of 'aesthetic power' then the question must be asked as to what the nature of this power really was. What were its contours and modes of deployment? Over what domains was its power exercised and to what end? In probing these questions I think that we will see that *kāvya* formed merely one dimension of a much larger field of courtly cultivation which hardly eschewed an engagement with materiality.

George Bühler pointed out long ago that inscriptional encomiums, what he considered to be mediocre specimens of *kāvya*, indicated not simply the existence of writers adhering to conventions, but audiences who understood them. The poet, whose training was ideally to include the study of poetry in conjunction with grammar, music, logic, the sciences of erotics and politics, as well as various martial skills, wrote for an audience more or less familiar with the conventions embodied in his writing.[32] Inscriptional *kāvya* points to the existence, in other words, of an 'interpretive community' or 'literary public', both for itself and the more exalted compositions attributed to the classical corpus. So returning to

[31] The work of V. S. Agrawala (see above) here remains exemplary and unsurpassed to my knowledge.

[32] *EI* 8 (1905–6), no. 6, p. 44. Vāmana, *Kāvyālaṁkāra* 1.3.8–9, 11.

the insights of Pollock I would suggest that one of the first operations of aesthetics as power was the reproduction of the court as an 'interpretive community', a task effected not merely by poetry, but a host of other aesthetic and sumptuary practices. One of the more important concerns of this book, then, will be how the 'interpretive community' of the court was produced and sustained through its culture.

The history and sources of early medieval courts

By and large, this study will not be concerned with the detailed history of any particular court, nor the evolution of a single practice or idea. It is instead concerned with a courtly culture which developed over a period of more than a millennium, and will draw on sources widely dispersed in both chronological and regional ascription. This wide net of inquiry is justified in part because extensive information on any single court in early India remains elusive, but more positively, because the sources themselves reflect a common set of themes and concerns.

The origins of courtly culture in India no doubt extend back to the great imperial court of Magadha under the Mauryas (320–185 BCE), but the scope and number of sources from this period is relatively small. The bulk of sources which we may properly call 'courtly' date from later periods, gaining their first expressions under the early 'post Aśokan' dynasties of northern and central India – the Śakas, Kuṣāṇas and Sātavāhanas (*c.* first century BCE to third century CE) – but fully crystallising under the Guptas and other dynasties between the fourth and seventh centuries CE. The pattern of practices which emerged during this period underwent continual elaboration and development for another half a millennium until they were re-articulated within the context of the new political order established by the Turkish Muslim rulers of the Delhi Sultanate. Thus, the broad chronological limits of the cultural dispensation which this book seeks to illuminate extend from *c.* 300 to *c.* 1200 CE.

These dates are not meant to be water-tight boundaries but approximate limits. A number of the sources cited in the chapters below fall outside this 900-year span at both its upper and lower limits. With some key texts relevant to the study of courtly life varying in ascription up to 800 years, precise chronological limits for a study like this are out of the question. More significantly, if it can be conceded that courtly culture in medieval India arose gradually from post-Aśokan times, then it must be admitted that it was also re-articulated gradually, with some of its elements remaining more or less intact in certain regions well into later centuries. Such qualifications should not diminish, however, the basic cultural unity of the period under question. This unity in part justifies the method of this book. In an important way, this study is a synchronic one, which attempts to analyse certain themes and practices which characterised royal courts as a whole during this period.

This does not mean, however, that this book remains without any historical scope. In laying out the basic sociology and culture of the court in the first section of this book, I hope to highlight the historical shifts which gave rise, both politically and ideologically, to the cultural figuration under question. The Vākāṭaka-Gupta imperial formation (*c*. 350–550 CE) together with the empires which arose immediately after it (the Puṣyabhūtis, Cālukyas and Pallavas, *c*. 550–750 CE), sometimes dubbed collectively as part of a larger 'Gupta ecumene', remain a watershed period from the vantage point of courtly life. It is this 400-year period (*c*. 350–750 CE) which saw the development, crystallisation and proliferation of a common political culture throughout all major regions of the subcontinent. Lineages and courts appearing between the fourth and eighth centuries adopted a series of cultural and political conventions which included not only Sanskrit as a lingua franca but a host of gestural, ethical, aesthetic and sumptuary practices which were distinctly courtly in nature. For purposes of manageability, this book, to the extent that it is possible, will limit its examples from this more restricted span within its overall period of concern. Yet it should be clear from the outset that the currency of these courtly practices would remain stable for another half a millennium, through two successive imperial formations of major courts like the Rāṣṭrakūṭas, Gurjara-Pratīhāras, Pālas, Cōḻas, Western Cālukyas, Paramāras and Candellas. From the establishment of the Delhi Sultanate in the early thirteenth century, this culture was partially and gradually re-articulated in 'vernacular' languages which transformed and extended them, often now in open or implicit dialogue with the practices of Islamic polity.

The sources for this study are diverse. As many texts and genres will be discussed at greater length in subsequent chapters, I provide only a brief account at the outset to make the scope and nature of this study clear. First, and perhaps most importantly, are the treatises known as *śāstra*, prescriptive literatures which sought to advise men of the upper classes on how best to pursue worldly life. These treatises covered a vast range of topics, but those of greatest importance for this study will be those on politics, notably the *Arthaśāstra* and its successors; those on erotic love, primarily the *Kāmasūtra*; and finally, the treatises on aesthetics, most centrally the *Nāṭyaśāstra* but also a number of later texts. A second type of material which this book will draw heavily from are the dramatic, narrative and illustrative works which may be classified under the general title of *kāvya*, or 'ornate poetry', the interpretation of which I have discussed above. This study has consulted a variety of genres and sub-genres of the Sanskrit literary corpus, some of which can be assigned to particular poets whose dates and in some cases patrons are known, while many others remain uncertain. To this may be added some art historical evidence – visual representations in various media which somehow illustrate the themes and conventions of courtly life.

A third type of evidence which will be used extensively in this book is inscriptions. Early India has provided historians with one of the world's richest archives of stone and copperplate inscriptions, with one scholar recently estimating some 90,000 extant epigraphs surviving in India alone. From the Gupta period royal inscriptions, which typically authorise the gift of land or land revenues to religious institutions, came to have an increasingly standard form of a royal order preceded by a eulogistic introduction in *kāvya* style. For this study these inscriptions will be used to glean specific information about the personnel of the court, and more generally, as palpable evidence of the spread and adoption of courtly convention.

Finally, this book will draw on the vast body of didactic and gnomic sayings, aphorisms and single stanza poems which circulated individually at the courts of early India. These verses or clusters of verses took the form of pithy descriptions, sayings or counsels which have come down to us embedded in longer prose or *sūtra* works where they were adduced as authorities, or anthologised in collections or 'treasuries' (*kośas*) from the seventh century. Generically referred to as *subhāṣita*, or 'well spoken', these verses, like inscriptional eulogies, were composed in *kāvya* style.[33] Their subjects ranged across the breadth of the preoccupations of the upper classes – from shrewd counsel on political policy to the sublimnities of erotic dalliance. As specifically reflective, they provide us with a fascinating insight into the mental world of the ruling élite in medieval India.

The upper and lower limits of this study invoke the dates of the once hotly debated period of 'Indian feudalism' forwarded by R. S. Sharma and others.[34] These scholars argued that this period witnessed a contraction of long-distance trade, money circulation and urban development, and a concomitant rise of a 'land-grant economy' where state servants were remunerated in land, thereby fragmenting centralised state

[33] Ludwik Sternbach, *Subhāṣita, Gnomic and Didactic Literature*, vol. IV, of Jan Gonda, ed., *A History of Indian Literature* (Wiesbaden: Otto Harrassowitz, 1974).

[34] The most important works have been the classics, Sharma, *Indian Feudalism C. 300–1300* and Yadava, *Society and Culture in Northern India in the Twelfth Century*. Collections of important articles can be found in R. S. Sharma, *Early Medieval Indian Society* and D. N. Jha, ed., *Feudal Social Formation in Early India* (Delhi: Chanakya Publications, 1987).

authority and leading to the growth of a class of landed intermediaries. The debate which this model of feudalism generated was fierce and protracted. Critics challenged the evidentiary bases for what was deemed the 'closure' of the Indian economy and queried the utility of a specifically European model of 'feudalism' for understanding the Indian evidence. These debates, which once dominated the pages of history journals, seem to have lost the interest of the scholarly community. While it is not the intention of this book to take any definitive position on the applicability of feudalism to Indian history, its writing has implicitly suggested, at least to its author, that some of the perceptive observations made about political relationships by the scholars of Indian feudalism which have subsequently been jettisoned for other themes, still merit serious consideration and exploration from the vantage point of the history of cultural practices. This is because 'feudalist' historians have paid closer attention to the language of political relationships than more recent historiography, which has been concerned with either typologies of the state or theories of state formation.

One positive outcome of post-feudalist scholarship, however, has been a move towards more processual models of political, economic and cultural change in medieval India. B. D. Chattopadhyaya has argued that the rise of the post-Gupta, or 'early medieval' political order in India should be seen not simply as a 'cessation', 'fragmentation' or 'decline' of existing economic and political structures, but, just as importantly, as the growth of new ones.[35] From the macro-historical perspective, Chattopadhyaya has described these developments as tending towards the spread of 'state society' throughout the subcontinent. To my mind, this gradualist approach has not so much rejected as refined and qualified some of the changes described more negatively in the feudalist model. It has stressed the expansion of agriculture and the growth of the agrarian economy, the peasantisation of diverse non-agrarian and non-sedentary populations, the rise of landed lords and intermediaries, the restructuring of urban–rural networks and the growth of ever more complex chains of lordship and political affiliation.

The culture of the court had a special role to play in many of these processes. For though the parameters of courtly life in India, as elsewhere, acted as a great barrier between the lives of 'good people' and the vast labouring populations which supported them, it is also possible to see that over the long durée, the ways of the court formed an acculturative mechanism through which aspiring men and local élites entered into the pale of 'good society'. At the same time, as this process evolved and as

[35] See the numerous articles in Chattopadhyaya, *The Making of Early Medieval India*.

the culture of the court inevitably seeped into the city, the temple, the bazaar and, even its anathema, the village, it was transformed and inflected anew, leading to hybrid forms of culture. A more textured history of courtly practices taking these processes into account is not, unfortunately, to be found between the covers of this book, the remit of which remains largely preliminary.

This book is divided into three parts. The first, comprising three chapters, deals with the rise and spread of royal households and the culture associated with them from Gupta times. In the first chapter, I treat the 'people of the court', focusing on the evolution of the structure and personnel of the royal household, and the relationship between courtly and urban life. The second chapter traces the emergence and basic parameters of a coherent courtly worldview as it took form in the prescriptive treatises on polity and erotic pleasure and the development of courtly poetry from the Gupta period. Here I will also treat the problem of how men acquired this knowledge and the association of notions, lordship and courtly culture with irenic values and enjoyment. Chapter 3 treats the key affiliational dynamics of people at court and then turns, in some detail, to how these relations were embodied in the formal procedures of palace routine, particularly within the court assembly. It examines the exchange of honours and courtesies as well as verbal and gestural protocols. Implicit in this chapter is the argument that court procedure and ethical concepts like humility and courtesy formed not only mechanisms for maintaining courtly hierarchies but also instruments through which people negotiated their relationships at court.

The book's second section is composed of two chapters dealing with the cultivation of aesthetic sensibilities at court. Chapter 4 takes up the courtly concept of beauty, not as a static ideal but rather as a domain of bodily, gestural, verbal and ethical *refinement*. Important here will be the suggestion that the practice of *alaṁkāra*, or adornment, functioned both as a 'technology' of self-transformation and an idiom of communication. In chapter 5, I explore the affective world of the court as embodied in literature and manuals on polity. My research suggests that courtly literature assisted the 'education' of élites in a 'mannered' system of emotions and dispositions central for the maintenance of formal relationships at court. More than this, the emphasis on *rasa*, or aesthetic savour, fostered not only a reposeful 'delectation' of sentiment, but also a mobile or itinerant subjectivity with regard to the affective relations which constituted courtly life.

The third part of the book, comprising two chapters, raises the problem of erotic love in courtly life. I say 'problem' because erotic love, as the preferred theme of courtly poetry and the subject of extended reflection in courtly gnomic literature, seems to have had a hypertrophied ideological life among the people of the court, a fact which I would suggest is in need of explanation. Chapter 6 explores the actual contexts and practice of sexual relationships and courtship among the aristocratic and urban élite and focuses specifically on its representation in the palace dramas composed between the fourth and seventh centuries. Chapter 7 looks more closely at the inner language of erotic love in relation to self and the world, placing the whole discourse against the courtly social dynamics of dependence and autonomy. Finally, a postscript reviews the major themes of this book and briefly explores future directions and possibilities for the study of courtly life in India.

This book does not have a single, overall argument, save the general proposition, which it hopes to demonstrate, that courtly culture should not be seen as a bland form of legitimatory discourse but rather a complex set of practices which were formative and constitutive of political life in early medieval India. By closer attention to actual practices and claims of political élites in early India, we can begin to think about writing a more complex history of manners, ethics and aesthetics in India, a history in which courtly life plays a crucial role. This in turn will provide the tools with which to develop a more nuanced account of political modernity in India. The 'obesity' of monarchs like the Tondaiman king of Pudukottai, from the vantage point of the history of practice, is in desperate need of reassessment.

I shall conclude with a few disclaimers. The scope of this study is both broad and narrow in different ways. The advantages gained in treating materials of diverse genre spanning nearly a thousand years have been achieved at a cost. First, there are major empirical lacunae in this study. For one, the early Tamil Caṅkam texts of south India are not dealt with at all below, though some engagement with them would no doubt have added richness and complexity to the study. Moreover, a large body of literary and epigraphical sources in Sanskrit and Prakrit have generally been treated sporadically, perhaps all too much in the manner which historians have traditionally done – as 'sources'. Specialists in these fields will no doubt be unhappy with some of the interpretations and methods in the pages that follow. Others may find the sometimes empiricist reading of sources highly naive. On the other hand, this study will bring a variety of textual genres together around problems that have been largely ignored by existing scholarship.

Finally, it should be remembered that this book is preliminary and restricted in its scope. It is not intended as a comprehensive survey of courtly life. While it will raise certain questions about protocol, manners and aesthetics in court society, it will touch only briefly on many other topics integral to courtly life, like jewellery, dress and cosmetics, modes of address, palace architecture, gardens, foods, which merit fuller and more extended consideration. Indeed, the research for this volume has suggested just how much work remains to be done in many fascinating areas of medieval Indian social history. This book will altogether neglect other important topics relevant to understanding courtly life, like religious festivals, coronation ceremonies and magical rites, some of which have been treated by other scholars. If one of the major assertions of this study is correct, that the ancient Indian court formed a key context for the production of knowledges that have more commonly been attributed to a generalised 'society' in ancient India – knowledge as diverse as aesthetics, medicine, erotics, prognostication and astrology – then a single monograph can hardly hope to do justice to courtly life in its entirety. The implicit argument of this book is that understanding the court as an important sociological locale for early Indian sources will provide new vistas into the world of medieval India. A fuller picture of this world is yet to be drawn.

Part I

The Rise of Court Society in Medieval India

1 The people of the court

The practices which form the subject of this book may be conceived of as a loosely connected web of bodily gestures, inner dispositions, and ethical preoccupations which developed at royal courts throughout the subcontinent gradually and unevenly from early historic times. These practices, which together formed a coherent courtly 'ethos', evolved as part of a much wider transformation of ways of life in early India, which saw the rise of new political and economic relationships, the proliferation of social structures and changes in religious ritual and theology. This chapter will take up the social composition and basic foundations of courtly life, and the following chapter the ethical and aesthetic elements of courtly culture.

Most fundamentally, courtly life arose in the context of new political institutions and a culture that grew up around these relationships. The historical record reveals a growing complexity of what might be termed the 'apparatus of rule' in early Indian polities from the Mauryan period. It is during the reign of the Mauryan emperor Aśoka (*c.* 268–232 BCE) that we hear for the first time, thanks to the inscriptions of this monarch, of a generic class of men who served the imperial household by continuously reporting events to the emperor.[1] It is also during Mauryan times that priests and intellectuals posed the question of polity – how a king could organise and appoint his household, order his realm and constitute his relations with other princes and kings – as a set of considerations *separate* from the discourses of the Vedic *soma* rituals which until then had been the organising discourse of kingship in north India.

Reliable knowledge of these institutions and theories, however, remains somewhat fragmentary and uncertain, and it is not until the rise of the Sātavāhana kings in the western Deccan and Śaka and Kuṣāṇa kings in north-western India during the first centuries of the Common Era that the historical record again affords us with enough clarity to speculate on the nature of polity and courtly life. There are a few very important

[1] N. R. Rastogi, *Inscriptions of Aśoka* (Varanasi: Chowkhamba Sanskrit Academy, 1990), pp. 65–80.

imperial inscriptions and literary texts composed during this period which form benchmarks in the history of our knowledge of the culture and practices at Indian courts. The real watershed comes, however, in the fourth century, when the inscriptional record grows more certain and more complex nearly every decade. The break up of the Sātavāhana and Kuṣāṇa empires in the first half of the third century CE, which coincided with the rise of the Sasanians in Persia under the emperor Ardashir (*c.* 224–41 CE), saw the assertion of numerous smaller royal households across the subcontinent: the Yaudheyas, Madrakas, Mālavas and Nāgas in the north and the Ābhīras, Ikṣvākus, Cuṭu-Śatakarṇis and Pallavas in the south.[2] Some of these households were undoubtedly families once linked in fealty or marriage to the Kuṣāṇnas and Sātavāhanas, while others were asserting authority for the first time. Their appearance on the historical record, as fragmentary as it may be, is significant. They heralded the great proliferation of royal houses throughout the subcontinent, which from the first decades of the next century would be a steady feature of early medieval polity.

By the middle of the fourth century, a number of families – the Pallavas of Kanchi, the Vākāṭakas of Bundelkhand and the Guptas of Patalipūtra, to name the most prominent – appear to have extended their patrimonial lands and drawn local lords to their courts. The most powerful of these were the Guptas, who under the king Samudragupta (*c.* 340–75 CE) conducted a military expedition known as a *digvijaya*, or 'Conquest of the Directions', which took him as far south as Kanchi. Along with their sometime allies in the Deccan, the Vākāṭakas, the Guptas articulated an imperial polity composed of important subordinate rulers and minor kings, who, unlike the subordinates under the Mauryas, retained a good measure of their own power. The Gupta imperial structure survived, often tenuously, until the middle of the sixth century. Its gradual collapse, under both internal and external pressures, saw an even larger wave of royal families appear on the historical record, each issuing grants of land and naming their ancestors.

The earliest records of some of these families, like the Aulikāras of Mandasor,[3] the Maitrakas of Valabhi,[4] the Paṇḍuvaṁśins in Mekalā,

2 The northern dynasties are known almost entirely through coin issues and those of the south by inscriptions. For the latter, see D. C. Sircar, *The Successors of the Sātavāhanas in the Lower Deccan* (University of Calcutta, 1939).

3 See the Rīsthal inscription of Prakāśadharman, *JESI* 10 (1983), pp. 96–103; R. Salomon, 'New Inscriptional Evidence for the History of the Aulikaras of Mandasor' *IIJ* 32 (1989), pp. 1–36; and the inscriptions of Yaśodharman, see *CII* 3 (1888), nos. 33–35, pp. 142–57.

4 For the earliest record of the dynasty see the Bhamodra Mahota plate of Droṇasiṁha, dated 502 CE, *EI* 16 (1921–2), no. 4, pp. 17–19. The installation of Droṇasiṁha is recorded in Maitraka grants from Dhruvasena I (*c.* 520–50 CE), who himself is described as meditating on the feet of the *paramabhaṭṭāraka*. See, for example, the Palitāna plates

the kings of Sarabhapura,[5] and the Maukharis of Kanauj,[6] suggest that they had once been subordinate to the Guptas, and asserted independence after their collapse. Other families, like the Kalacuris in Malwa,[7] the Gurjara kings of western India,[8] the Vardhanas or Puṣyabhūtis of Sthāṇvīśvara,[9] the kings of Gauḍa and Vaṅga,[10] the eastern Gaṅgas in central Orissa at Kaliṅganagara, the Śailodbhavas in Koṅgoda, and the Māṇas in Oḍra,[11] appeared for the first time. In south India, the largely independent houses of the fifth century – the powerful Pallavas of

of Dhruvasena I, *EI* 11 (1911–12), no. 9.1, pp. 106–109. His successor Guhasena, however, does not acknowledge the *paramabhaṭṭāraka* in his earliest grant (557 CE), a fact which correlates with the final collapse of the Gupta empire sometime shortly after 542 CE, *IA* 7 (1878), no. 9, pp. 66–7.

5 An early grant of the Śarabhapurīya king Narendra, which is explicit about it, renews a land grant originally made by the *paramabhaṭṭāraka* for the 'benefit of his feet': *ISPS*, vol. 2, 1.2, pp. 7–11. H. Bakker (*The Vākāṭakas: An Essay in Hindu Iconology* (Groningen: Egbert Forsten, 1997), p. 29) has argued that the *bhaṭṭāraka* referred to in this grant is the Vākāṭaka king.

6 Compare the recently discovered Shankarpur inscription of the king Harivarman, the first king of the family according to later Maukhari insciptions, dated in the reign of the 'Paramount Lord' (*paramadeva*) Buddhagupta, *JESI* 4 (1977), pp. 62–6 and the later record in *EI* 14 (1917–18), no. 5, pp. 110–20.

7 The Abhoṇa plates of Śaṅkaragaṇa are issued from Ujjain in 595 CE, and Buddharāja's Vadner plates from Vidīśā in 609 CE. See *CII* 4 (1955), nos. 12, 14, pp. 38–43; 47–50. The Kalacuris, who perhaps originated in Mahiśmati after the fall of the Traikūṭakas at the end of the fifth century, apparently gained the loyalty of a family of 'Mauryan' kings in the Konkan and the king Saṅgamasiṁha in Gujarat. The Sunao Kala plates of Saṅgamasiṁha, issued in 541 CE from Broach, clearly indicate subordinate status, but no overlord is mentioned, *CII* 4 (1955), no. 11, pp. 35–7. See the discussion of V. V. Mirashi in *CII* 4 (1955), no. 11, pp. xliii–xlvii.

8 These kings are known from inscriptions in the early seventh century, and were presumably connected to the legendary family of Haricandra, the progenitor of the Gurjara Pratīhāras, detailed in the ninth-century Jodhpur inscription of Bauka, *EI* 18 (1925–6), no. 12, pp. 87–99. See the entries for Lāṭa, Gurjara and Gurjarātra in Irfan and Faiz Habib, 'India in the Seventh Century – A Survey of Political Geography', *PIHC*, 60th Session (1999), s.v.

9 The early kings of the Vardhana family have been reconstructed from the copperplate charters of the king Harṣa in the seventh century and his famous chronicler, Bāṇa. For a review of this evidence, see D. Devahuti, *Harsha: A Political Study* (Delhi: Oxford University Press, 3rd edn, 1998), pp. 67–75.

10 This dynasty has been reconstructed from a handful of separate undated inscriptions of the kings Gopacandra, Dharmāditya and Samācāradeva which though not mentioning their forebears, bear striking resemblance in style. See *IA* 39 (1910), pp. 193–205 and *EI* 18 (1925–6), no. 11, pp. 74–86. Their relationship with the Guptas is unclear, though a king named Vijayasena, who issued the Mallasarul plates as a subordinate to Gopacandra, is also known as the *dūtaka* of the Gunaighar copperplate inscription of Vainyagupta, *EI* 23 (1935–6), no. 24, pp. 155–61. See the discussion in *CHI*, vol. 3, pt. 1, pp. 200–3.

11 The epigraphic record of Orissa in the fifth and early sixth centuries is complex and problematic. The dozen or so Māṭhara/Pitṛbhakta inscriptions do not present any clear dynastic picture. For a review of the evidence, see the discussion in *CHI*, vol. 3, pt. 1, pp. 169–72. Also the brief remarks of David Henige, 'Some Phantom Dynasties of Early and Medieval India: Epigraphic Evidence and the Abhorrence of a Vacuum' *BSOAS* vol. 38, no. 3 (1975), pp. 533–4. The Śailodbhavas, whose first known record is not issued until 619 CE, were probably in the region from the end of the sixth century.

Kanchi, Śālāṅkāyanas of Veṅgi and Kadambas of Vānavāsi, were joined by new families like the Rāṣṭrakūṭas in southern Mahārāṣṭra, the western Gaṅgas around Mysore, the Śendrakas in the Nāgarakhaṇḍa division of the Vānavāsi province and the Cālukyas at the hill-fort of Bādāmi (Vātāpi). By the beginning of the seventh century the most powerful of these houses were the Puṣyabhūtis under king Harṣa (*c.* 606–47 CE), who occupied the Maukhari throne at Kanauj, and the Cālukyas of Bādāmi under Pulakeśin II (*c.* 609–42 CE), both of whom sent emissaries to imperial courts outside India.[12] These two monarchs, accompanied by other kings as their subordinates, met in battle somewhere near the Narmadā river between 630 and 634 CE. Pulakeśin seems to have gained the victory. His success was short-lived, however, as he lost his capital and his life in an attack soon after by the Pallava king Narasiṁhavarman (*c.* 630–68 CE).[13]

This dynastic configuration, entailing multiple power centres in subcontinental regions, marked the consolidation of a pattern which had begun during Gupta times, and which would remain stable for the next half a millennium under dynasties like the Gurjara-Pratihāras, Pālas and Rāṣṭrakūṭas, Cālukyas, Cōḻas and Paramāras. The battles fought between these imperial houses rarely resulted in or even had as their goal the direct annexation of substantial territory any great distance from the core regions of these kingdoms. They resulted rather in the giving of gifts, the offering of tributes and the profession of loyalty within an explicitly acknowledged scale or hierarchy of kingships. This hierarchy of lordships formed the context for the development of an extensive courtly culture.

Paramount overlordship and the rise of lordly houses

Inscriptions containing dynastic information, relatively sparse down to the beginning of the fourth century, literally explode in number from Gupta times. By the end of the Gupta period, royal donative inscriptions are found in all major regions of the subcontinent. The implications of this expanded epigraphic record are manifold. Inscriptions point to the growth and advance of agrarian economy, the spread and consolidation of varṇa ideology, the proliferation of castes and the development and spread of religious ideas. They also have a special significance for court and polity. Inscriptions suggest a transformation of the political order. The appearance of new royal houses in the epigraphic record indicates the passage of pre-state forms of social organisation into monarchical

[12] For Harṣa's emissaries to the T'ang emperor T'ai-tsung see Devahuti, *Harsha*, pp. 238–63 and Pulakeśin II's to the Sasanian emperor Khusru II see B. K. Singh, *The Early Cālukyas of Vātāpi (Circa 500–757)* (Delhi: Eastern Book Linkers, 1991), pp. 91–8.

[13] Devahuti, *Harsha*, p. 109.

states as well as the integration of local political structures into wider regional and pan-regional political networks.[14] This expanding political order took the form neither of a single centralised imperial state nor a plethora of fragmented regional kingdoms, but instead a series of diverse and uneven political orders which, while regionally based, sought to relate themselves, in diverse ways, to ever more integrated political hierarchies which had as their ideal the notion of an imperial polity ruled over by a single supreme overlord, a king over kings.

This political order is described in the *Arthaśāstra*, the final composition of which may be placed in the Gupta period, as a 'circle of kings', or *rājamaṇḍala*, a concentrically conceived structure of contiguous and overlapping relationships of allies and enemies.[15] At the centre of this structure stood the ambitious king, or *vijigīṣu*, who formed the 'ego' of the policy recommended by the treatises. This king was to direct his diplomatic policy towards other political agents within the circle, by warring with bordering kings and allying with other kings spatially contiguous with his enemies. As other kings could operate with the same policy, the *rājamaṇḍala* was not so much the blueprint of an imperial state as a theory of dynastic relationships. It formed the basis of political strategy and diplomatic thinking at the courts of Gupta and post-Gupta India. At the beginning of the seventh century, for example, the Gauḍa king Śaśāṅka declared war against the contiguous kingdom of the Maukharis (who were once his overlords) while at the same time securing an alliance with the king of Mālwā, thereby flanking the Maukhari king from two sides. The Maukharis in turn protected their western reaches by allying with the Puṣyabhūtis of Sthāṇvīśvara, making the Mālwā king vulnerable from two directions.[16]

The theory of the *rājamaṇḍala* took shape within the context of increasingly calibrated hierarchy of kings, at the apex (or centre) of which stood an imperial overlord, or paramount sovereign. The idea of an imperial king over other kings had been a feature of royalty since Mauryan times, when Aśoka styled himself a *cakravartin*, or 'wheel-turning' imperial king. The Kuṣāṇas and Sātavāhanas took various exalted and sometimes cosmopolitan titles, borrowing from Persian and Bactrian usage, which portrayed them as 'kings over other kings' (*rājātirāja*, *rājarāja*).[17] The Guptas continued this tradition, inflating the titles even more to

[14] See the useful discussion in B. D. Chattopadhyaya, 'Political Processes and Structure of Polity in Early Medieval India', in Chattopahdyaya, *The Making of Early Medieval India* (Delhi: Oxford University Press, 1994), pp. 202–11.

[15] The dating of this text will be discussed in the following chapter. For the discussion of the *rājamaṇḍala*, see *AS* 6.1.1 ff.

[16] See Devahuti, *Harsha*, pp. 23, 156–62.

[17] The Kuṣāṇas, for example, represented themselves as ruling an empire along the four rivers of the world (Ganges, Indus, Yarkand-Tarim and Oxus) and took appropriately

'Great King over Kings' (*mahārājādhirāja*), 'Supreme Honourable One' (*paramabhaṭṭāraka*), and 'Paramount Lord' (*parameśvara*). These titles remained stable protocol for would-be imperial kings for nearly a millennium, though they were occasionally supplemented by titles taken by a particular house, like the Cālukyas of Badami, who called themselves 'Beloved of Fortune and the Earth' (*śrīpṛthivīvallabha*).[18]

These exalted titles were complemented by rankings of kings at lower levels. By the Gupta period, it was standard for lesser monarchs and subordinate rulers to call themselves *mahārāja* or 'Great King'. This title often implied acknowledgement of some superior power or the paramount sovereign, either directly, as in the case of the *mahārāja*s of Vālkhā who dated their inscriptions in the Gupta era, or indirectly, as in the case of the Vākāṭaka dowager queen Prabhāvatiguptā, who referred to herself as the daughter of the Gupta *mahārājādhirāja*, while naming her Vākāṭaka relatives as merely 'Great Kings' (*mahārāja*s).[19] Although the evidence is fragmentary, the historical record from the fourth to the beginning of the sixth century suggests a substantial number of individual kings and royal families who in some way acknowledged the overlordship of the Guptas. These included not only the kings of Vālkhā and the Vākāṭakas of Vidarbha just mentioned, but the Maitrakas of western India, the Parivrājakas and Uccakalpikas in Bundhelkand, the Maukharis of Gaya and Kanauj, the Aulikāras of Mandasor, the Śanakānikas of Vidīśa, the Śarabhapurīyas of Dakṣina Kosala as well as a number of other individual kings.[20] The title could also be taken by independent

cosmopolitan titles – 'Great King' (*mahārāja*), 'King over Kings' in Persian (*shahenshahi*), Greek (*basileōs basileōn*) and Prakrit (*rājātirāja*), as well as the Chinese title 'Son of Heaven' (*devaputra*, Chinese – T'ien-tzu) and the Roman 'Caeser' (*kaisara*). The titles 'Great King' and 'King over Kings' were Parthian and Bactrian continuations of the Achaemenid imperial titles *kshāyathiya vazkra* and *kshāyathiyānām kshāyathiya*. See remarks in D. C. Sircar, *Indian Epigraphy* (Delhi: Motilal Banarsidass, 1965), p. 331 and *CHI*, vol. 2, pp. 192–3, 241, 245. The Sātavāhanas took the titles 'Lord' (*svāmin*), 'Great King' (*mahārāja*) and 'King among Kings' (*rājarāja*). *CHI*, vol. 2, p. 313.

18 This title was inherited by later houses of the Deccan like the Rāṣṭrakūṭas of Mānyakheṭa and Cālukyas of Kalyāṇī.

19 See her Poona and Riddhapur Plates, *CII* 4 (1963), nos. 2, 8, pp. 5–9, 33–7.

20 Acknowledgement of Gupta overlordship is usually indicated through the dating of records in the reign of a Gupta king, in the Gupta Era, or by mentioning submission to the emperor, usually as *paramabhaṭṭāraka*. For the Vākāṭakas of Vidarbha, see *CII* 5 (1963), no. 2, pp. 5–10. For the Parivrājaka and Uccakalpa kings in Bundhelkhand, the latter of whom may have also recognised the overlordship of the Vākāṭakas at the end of the fifth century, see *CII* 3 (1888), no. 21, pp. 93–9, *CII* 5 (1963), nos. 20–1, pp. 89–91, *CII* 3 (1888), no. 26, pp. 117–20. For the kings of Vālkhā, see K. V. Ramesh and S. P. Tewari, *A Copper Plate Hoard of the Gupta Period from Bagh, Madhya Pradesh* (Delhi: Archaeological Survey of India, 1990). For the early Aulikāras of Mandasor, see *CII* 3 (1981), nos. 14, 35, pp. 261–6, 322–32. For the Maitrakas of Valabhi, see *EI* 16 (1921–2), no. 4, pp. 17–19, *EI* 11 (1911–12), no. 9.1, pp. 106–9. For the

kings who simply sought to avoid confrontation with imperial monarchs, as in the case of the Māṭharas and Pitṛbhaktas of fifth-century Orissa or the early Pallava kings of the south, both of whom remained beyond Gupta influence after the end of the fourth century.

By the early sixth century subordinate kings began to take new titles like *sāmanta* (lord of the marches, or tributary prince) and *maṇḍaleśvara*, (lord of a province), and these were soon joined by finer gradations in rank.[21] Contemporary inscriptions mention kings with titles like 'jewel' (*ratna*) or 'crest jewel' (*cuḍāmaṇi*) among *sāmanta*s, indicating a titular hierarchy among subordinate kings.[22] And it is from this time that the texts on architecture begin to set out varying sizes of palaces for different ranks of kings and vassals. The early sixth-century *Bṛhatsaṁhitā* speaks of five kinds of palace, of 108, 100, 92, 84 and 76 cubits in width respectively.[23] By the beginning of the seventh century both inscriptions and literary texts abound in references to various grades of *sāmanta*s and *maṇḍaleśvara*s.[24]

Paramount overlordship was typically established by a great military and diplomatic expedition called a 'Conquest of the Directions' or *digvijaya*, in which the ambitious king sought to defeat and/or gain the submission of neighbouring rulers, or to re-establish fallen or collateral lines, rather than to expand the boundaries of his own territory. The Allahabad pillar inscription, praising the emperor Samudragupta's *digvijaya*, states that he defeated and reinstated a number of kings

Śarabhapurīyas of Dakṣiṇa Kośala, see *ISPS* vol. 2, 1.2, pp. 7–11. For the Maukharis of Gāya, see *CII* 3 (1888), no. 48, pp. 221–2. For the Maukharis of Kanauj, see *JESI* 4 (1977), pp. 62–6. For the Śanakānikas, see *CII* 3 (1981), no. 7, pp. 242–4. For the individual kings Suraśmicandra in Arikaṇa, Iśvarāta in Kathiawar and Śatrudamana in central Kalinga, see respectively, *CII* 3 (1981), no. 39, pp. 339–41; *EI* 33 (1959–60), no. 56.1, pp. 303–6; and *EI* 31 (1955–6), no. 15, pp. 89–93.

21 The early use of the term *sāmanta*, seems, as in the second rock edict of Aśoka (*samaṁtā rājāno*, cf. *pratyanta nṛpati*, of the Allahabad pillar inscription) to denote merely a neighbouring king. It is only toward the end of the fifth century that the term clearly comes to mean subordinate king, what Inden has called 'Lord of the Marches'. See Lallanji Gopal, 'Sāmanta – Its Varying Significance in Ancient India', *JRAS* (1963), pp. 21–37; R. Inden, 'Hierarchies of Kings in Early Medieval India', *Contributions to Indian Sociology*, n.s., vol. 15, nos. 1 and 2 (1981), p. 112. For other studies of the term, see K. K. Gopal, 'The Assembly of Sāmantas in Early Medieval India', *JIH* 42 (1964), pp. 231–50. For a discussion of *sāmanta*, along with *maṇḍaleśvara* and related terms see Sircar, *Indian Epigraphy*, pp. 342–4.

22 For the former see the late fifth-century inscription of the Kadamba heir apparent (*yuvarāja*) Devavarman in Kuntala describing his father *mahārāja* Kṛṣṇavarman as *sāmantarājaviśeṣaratna*, *IA* 7 (1878), no. 35, p. 33. For the latter see the early sixth-century, inscription of the Maukhari king Anantavarman of the Gāya region, also referring to his father Śārdula as *sāmantacūḍāmaṇi*, *CII* 3 (1888), no. 48, p. 223.

23 *Bṛhatsaṁhitā* 53.4.

24 See the discussion of Agrawala, *Deeds of Harsha*, pp. 256–60.

(*grahaṇa-mokṣānugraha*, literally, 'capturing and releasing through favour') and re-established (*pratisthāpana*) fallen families.[25] Imperial rule was constituted through the incorporation and re-articulation of separate and distinct lordships rather than the extension of boundaries of land ruled directly by the emperor. The sources represent the paramount sovereign, not as the ruler of a realm, but as an 'enjoyer of the earth', for in this diplomatic language rulers of bounded realms were always lesser kings. The paramount sovereign gained the submission of such rulers, who were incorporated into his empire in the manner of fief-holding vassals.

It would seem that in accepting the overlordship of the paramount sovereign, subordinate kings were allowed to retain a large measure of power in their own realms. In the language of the sources the idea was that subordinate kings gained their own agency to rule through recognising the sovereignty of the overlord. As the Allahabad pillar inscription puts it, many kings 'requested the decrees [of the emperor] so that they might enjoy ruling their own provinces through the seal of his sovereignty'.[26] On the one hand, such lords were expected to offer tribute (*kara*) to the emperor, attend court to pay obeisance (*praṇāmagamana*), offer daughters in marriage (*kanyopāyanadāna*), carry out orders (*ājñākaraṇa*), and 'dedicate themselves' [to military assistance] (*ātmanivedana*).[27] On the other, they tended to issue their own land-grants, raise their own armies, and appoint their own courts, though there seems to have been no consistent or standard set of rights and obligations.

Judging from the sources, the appearance of subordinate *mahārāja*s and *sāmanta*s at the household of the emperor was a matter of considerable importance. It is here that they presented gifts and tribute and displayed the verbal and gestural deference required of their status. Their presence was a constant theme in courtly literature from the Gupta period. Bāṇa portrays hundreds of *sāmanta*s in the outer courts of Harṣa's camp waiting for audience with the king. These kings not only supplied their wives as attendants for the imperial queen, and their sons as companion-servants for imperial princes, they also attended the life-cycle rites of the imperial family – birth celebrations, marriages and even deaths.[28] Clearly the idea was to establish the most intimate of bonds between families, and to reproduce these affiliations from one generation to the next.

[25] *CII* 3 (1981), no. 1, pp. 213–14.

[26] *CII* 3 (1981), no. 1, pp. 213–14.

[27] The duties of subordinate kings as detailed in the Allahabad pillar inscription (*CII* 3 (1981), no. 1, pp. 213–14) correspond well with the accounts of literary texts like Bāṇa's *Harṣacarita* (*HC*, ch. 2, p. 60, *passim*).

[28] Harṣa's father, the emperor Prabhākaravardhana, is carried to his funeral pyre on the shoulders of his mourning *sāmanta*s, *HC*, ch. 5, p. 170.

While the institution of kingship at all levels was hereditary, the inscriptions beginning in the sixth century start to include detailed genealogical introductions, often tracing a king's ancestors back several generations. The importance of these genealogies, which were often invented, lies as much in their ability to facilitate the absorption of new families of diverse social origins into the ruling class as in their stated commitment to birth as a marker of social rank. The diversity of *varṇa* affiliations of the kings mentioned in inscriptions is instructive. Major imperial dynasties like the Mauryas, Sātavāhanas and Guptas, to name the most prominent, came from non-*kṣatriya* origin, not to mention the many minor houses known from the fourth century. Overall, the royal court was a place of exceptionally fluid social identity with respect to *varṇa*. Either direct or indirect acknowledgement of the supremacy of imperial kings seems to have been a major mechanism for men of diverse *varṇa* origins to translate local power into royal status. We have, for example, the case of the *mahārāja*s of Vālkha, who ruled as Gupta underlords in central India. The earliest ruler of this family had the name 'Bhuluṇḍa', probably indicating non-caste or 'tribal' origin, while later kings of the family took Sanskritised names.[29] It is likely that Bhuluṇḍa was a local chief or clan leader who gained the status of *mahārāja* as a result of the Gupta conquests in central India. At the other end of the spectrum are examples like the Kadamba family, originally brahmins of the Mānavya *gotra*. This family, according to its inscriptions, took up arms after one of its men, Mayūraśarman, was insulted by a Pallava noble, but following a display of military strength and valour entered the Pallava king's service with a sign of royalty, a fillet-crown (*paṭṭabandha*).[30]

Whatever is made of such statements, the appearance of so many royal houses between the fifth and seventh centuries throughout the subcontinent from diverse or unstated backgrounds, taking the title of *mahārāja* and acknowledging imperial authority, does suggest the integration of local or nascent power brokers into a composite but increasingly homogenous ruling class. The major source of wealth for these kings was certainly land revenues, although tolls and other forms of tax are known from inscriptions. As a class they were united by their freedom from the physical labour of cultivation, their skill in arms, and their putative birth. Some of these men and their families became powerful agents in the vast political hierarchies which typified subcontinental politics from the early centuries of the Common Era, while others passed into obscurity.

[29] See the discussions and evidence cited in Ramesh and Tewari, *A Copper Plate Hoard of the Gupta Period*.

[30] *EI* 8 (1905–6), no. 5, pp. 24–35.

The palace and its personnel

As early as Mauryan times there had been a standard cadre of royal retainers, called *mahāmātras*, or men of 'great esteem', which in the early centuries of the Common Era became increasingly differentiated.[31] By the time of the *Arthaśāstra*, however, the situation was even more complex, a point which can be seen quite clearly in the expansion of the royal household. While from early historic times, terms like *bhavana, antaḥpura, niveśa, prāsāda, harmya,* were known to refer to large and complex dwellings, earlier literature conceived of royal households in a rudimentary fashion.[32] *Āpastamba Dharmasūtra*, for example, says that in his city the king should build a palace (*veśman*) in front of which there was to be a hall (*āvastha*) of invitation (*āmantraṇa*) and within view of which an assembly hall (figure 1.1).[33] The royal household depicted in later texts like the *Arthaśāstra* and *Harṣacarita*, however, reveals considerable development (figures 1.2 and 1.3). These texts portray the royal residence (*rājaniveśa, antaḥpura*)[34] as an extensive complex of buildings situated either within a fortified town (*durgāniveśa*) or a moveable military camp (*skandhāvāra*).[35] In the later palace plans it is possible to see

[31] For Sātavāhana/Śaka period titles, see U. N. Ghoshal's remarks in *CHI*, vol. 2, pp. 349–51; also Sircar, *Indian Epigraphy*, p. 354.

[32] For a survey of the terminology for dwellings in ancient India, see Amita Ray, *Villages, Towns and Secular Buildings in Ancient India c. 150 BC–350 AD* (Calcutta: Firma K. L. Mukhopadhyay, 1964), pp. 36–45; 79–90.

[33] *Āpastamba Dharmasūtra*, 2.10.25.2–5. Manu mentions only the king's residence (*gṛha*) and audience hall (*sabhā*), *MDh* 7.76, 145.

[34] The term *antaḥpura* here refers not to the women's quarters but to the palace complex as a whole.

[35] The *Arthaśāstra* discusses the layout of the royal palace in two passages, one more general (*AS* 2.4.1–15), which situates it in the residential part (*vāstuvibhāga*) of the fortified city (*durgāniveśa*), and the other, detailing the regulation and orientation of the central buildings at the heart of the palace complex (*AS* 1.20.1–11). For a discussion of the latter, see Hartmut Scharfe, *Investigations in Kauṭalya's Manual of Political Science* (Weisbaden: Harrassowitz, 1993), pp. 142–9. In understanding the former of these passages, I have followed B. D. Chattopadhyaya, 'The City in Early India: Perspectives from Texts', *Studies in History*, vol. 13, no. 2, (1997), pp. 185–90. Chattopadhyaya states that it is unclear whether the regional parts (*bhāga*) of the complex occupy the whole of the *vāstuvibhāga*. His diagram, which I follow, suggests that they do not. I interpret these as part of the palace complex (*antaḥpura/rājaniveśa*) itself, which is said to be walled (1.20.1), and the regions designated as *tataḥ param*, 'beyond there', outside the palace but within the larger *vāstuvibhāga*, which was also walled. Beyond this was the non-residential region (*vāstucchidra*) of the city, which probably contained cultivated land. The *durgā* was surrounded by a fortified wall. The picture seems to be of a three-walled city: an outer wall dividing the fort from the regions beyond it, an inner wall dividing the residential and non-residential parts of the city and a final wall separating the palace complex from the rest of the city. Incidental accounts of the *skandhāvāra* occur in several passages of Bāṇa's *Harṣacarita*. See Agrawala, *Deeds of Harsha*, Appendix 1, pp. 240–55.

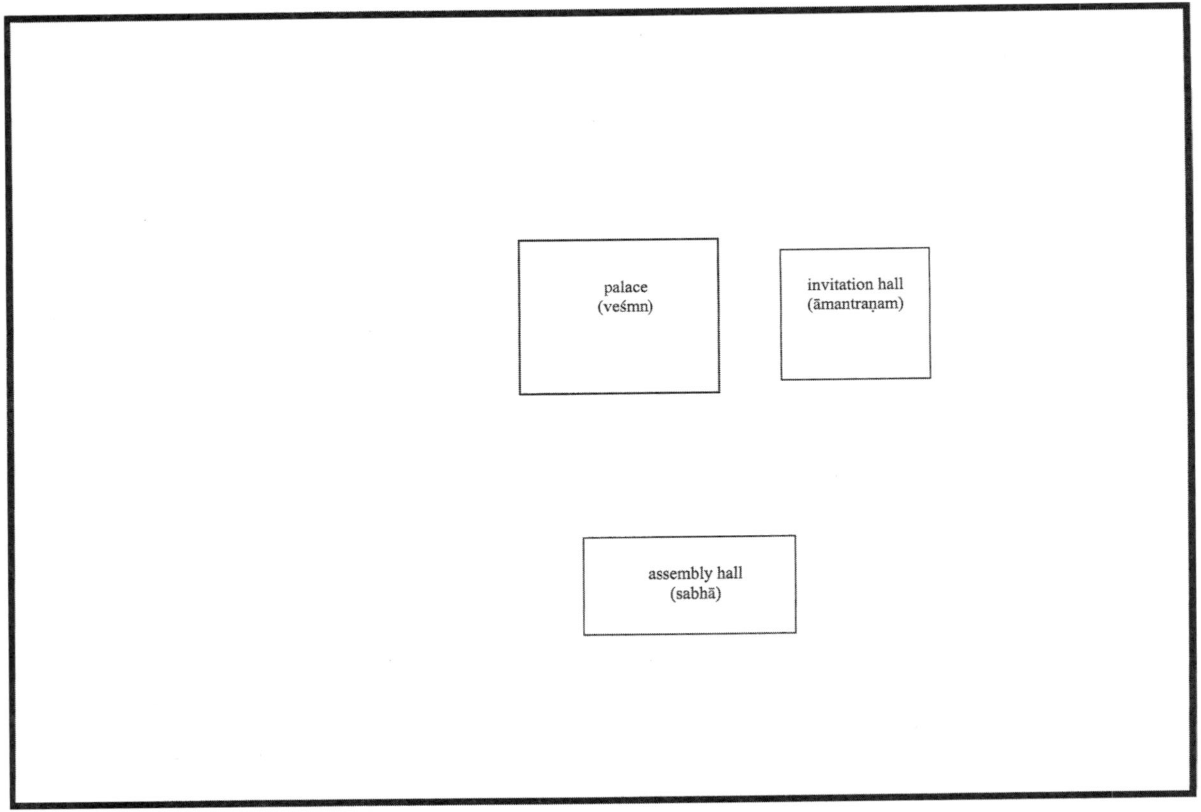

Figure 1.1 Plan of royal city and palace according to *Āpastambha Dharmasūtra* 2.10.25.2–5, *c.* 300 BCE.

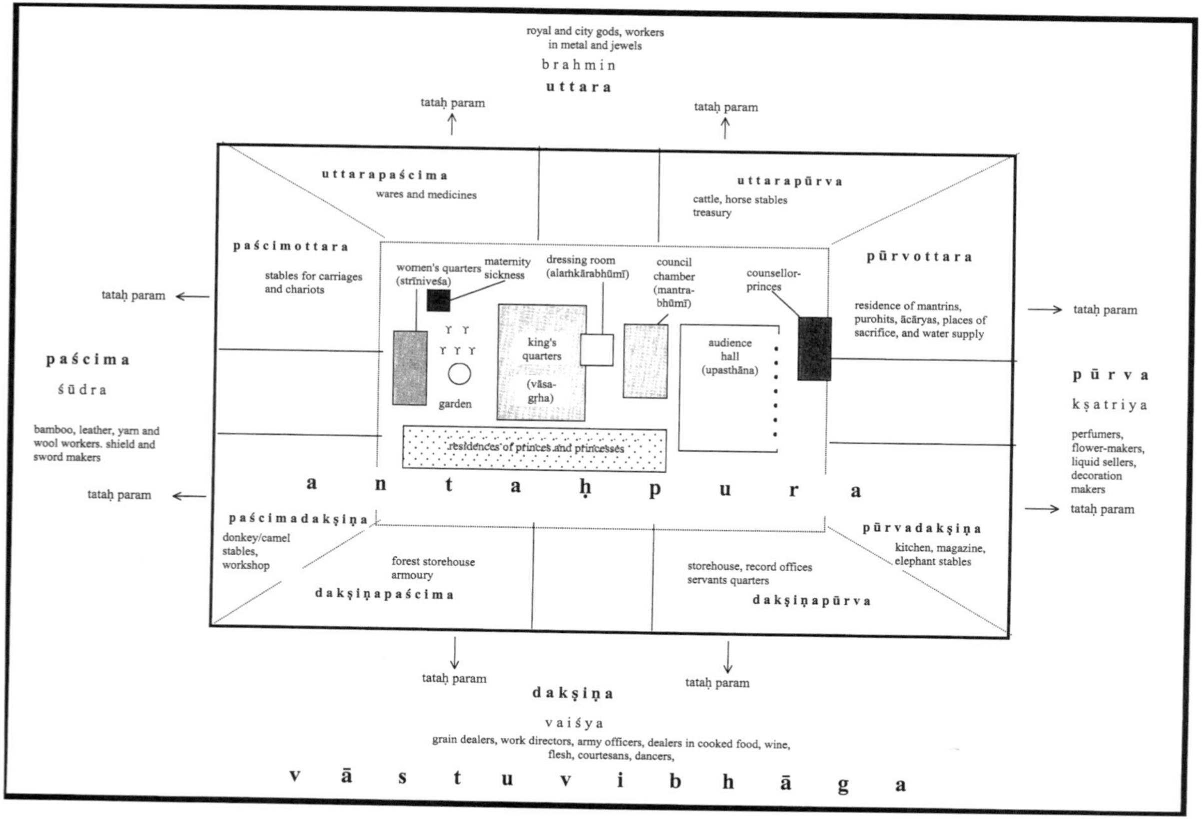

Figure 1.2 Plan of royal palace as situated in residential area (*vāstuvibhāga*) of the fortress-city (*dūrganiveśa*) according to Kauṭilya's *Arthaśāstra* 1.20.1–11; 2.4.1–15.

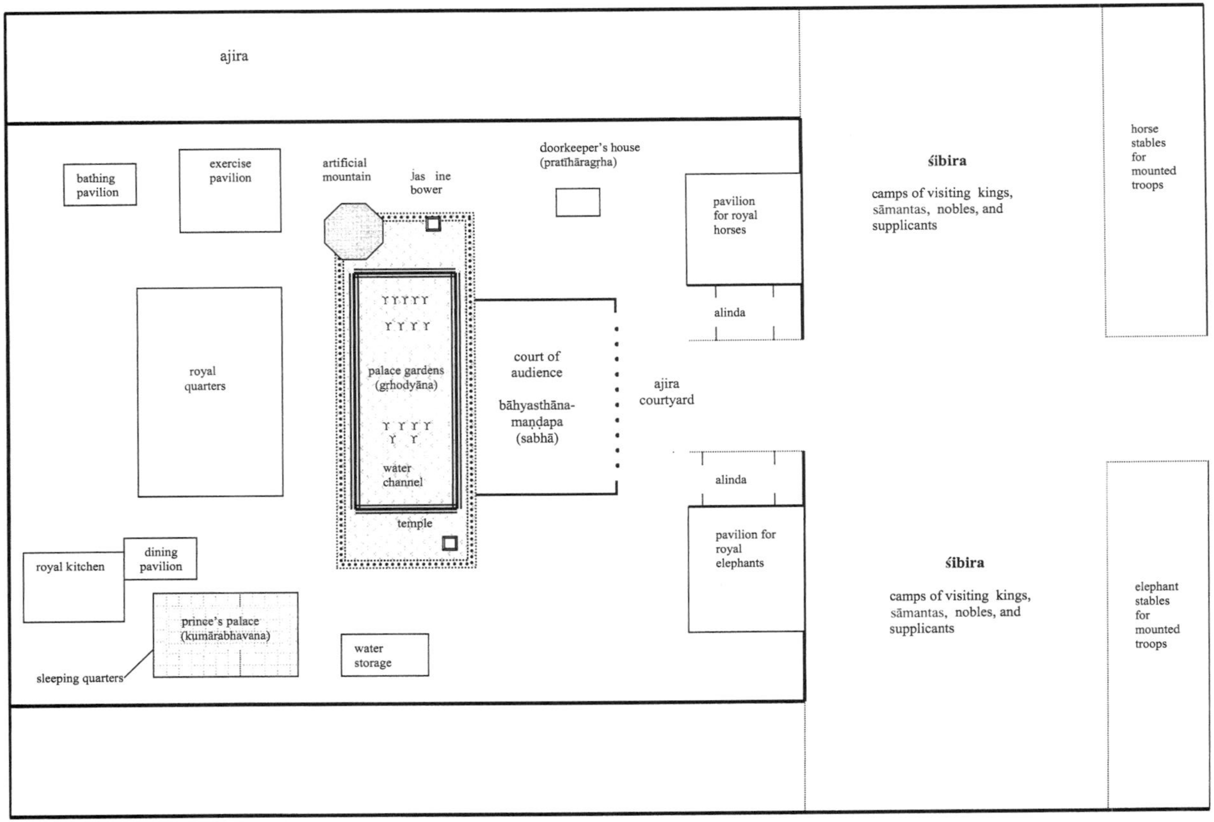

Figure 1.3 Plan of royal encampment (*skandhāvāra*) as reconstructed from the works of the poet Bāṇa, *c.* seventh century CE.

a division of space into a series of structures separated by function, situated in open courtyards (*kakṣya*) and surrounded by a series of walls. The king himself resided in a multi-storeyed building with many rooms and balconies, and there were separate residences or quarters maintained for queens, princes and princesses, heir-apparents, most immediately, but also counsellors, priests, chamberlains and servants.

Space in the palace was divided, on the one hand, by the demands of an increasingly elaborate royal routine, with separate buildings or places for dressing, eating, bathing, exercise, counsel and courtship; and, on the other, by the need to accommodate the growing numbers of people who resided, either permanently or temporarily, within the royal household. The growth of the palace complex thus reflected the elaboration and concentration of the apparatus of rule within the king's household. It is clear that the bulk of the king's affairs were conducted from within the royal household, where he took counsel, heard supplicants, met subordinates, received tax and tribute, stored wealth and issued decrees. It is perhaps no wonder that Bāṇa describes the royal palace of Prince Candrāpīḍa as a place where 'thousands of royal orders were being written down by court scribes who knew the names of all the villages and cities, and who looked upon the whole world as if it were a single house'.[36] Even when he travelled to tour his kingdom or undertook military expeditions, the king was accompanied by large contingents of palace personnel, making his retinue not much more than a moveable household. Numerous inscriptions from Gupta times record orders issued by kings from their touring military encampments.[37]

The expansion of the royal household allowed for the spatial articulation of political hierarchy. This is in part reflected in the elaborate system of courtyards and walls within the palace, which effectively organised the palace complex into successively enclosed spaces of increasingly difficult access. Entry to the inner courtyards was guarded by ascending ranks of doorkeepers. The concentric walled courtyards which surrounded the king's living quarters, and which were to become an important element of the treatises on palace and temple architecture – with the world-ruling king typically said to possess a 'seven walled palace' – functioned both to protect and rank access to the king and his companions. The destination

[36] *Kd*, p. 88.

[37] For a sixth-century example from the Māṇa dynasty of Orissa, see *EI* 23 (1935–6), no. 32a, pp. 201–2; for a seventh-century example from the victory camp of Harṣa, see A. Agarwal, 'A New Copper Plate Grant of Harshavardhana from the Punjab, Year 8', *BSOAS* vol. 66, no. 2 (2003), pp. 220–8. For an early eighth-century example from central India, see *CII* 3 (1888), no. 46, pp. 213–18.

of visitors was the central audience hall or court (*sabhā*, *upasthāna*) where the king sat on a couch or throne attended by other kings, princes and subordinate lords.

The idea which we encountered above, of palaces reflecting rank and power among kings also obtained within the king's household. Contemporary and later 'architectural manuals' mention different residences for ranks of courtiers, generals, ministers and princes.[38] These treatises were concerned not only (or even chiefly) with architecture, but also with the entire material world which centred around the court and kingdom.[39] They sought to develop a precise knowledge of the material world in relation to celestial and atmospheric powers or a divinely ordained cosmos – but in all cases this knowledge conceived of the physical and material world of the court as one calibrated along lines of political hierarchy. Everything about the lives of men of rank – their residences, their clothing, insignia, ornaments, modes of travel and, as we shall see, their bearing, speech and gestures – indicated their status.

Life in the royal household had a markedly 'public' character. This is not to say that the political identities was somehow 'open' or accessible to all; the palace was a hierarchised and differentiated space, organised under diverse logics such as inner and outer, open and restricted, and high and low. Rather, the publicness of the royal household derived from the fact that the political identities of kings and lords who attended court could not be clearly set apart from some inner realm of 'private' identities or associations. All aspects of their 'private' lives signified their 'public' status as men and women of rank and title. The entirety of the king's residence bore this public quality, though certain places remain 'closed' to those of inferior rank. Publicness in this sense was, as Jurgen Habermas has pointed out in the case context of feudal Europe, a sort of 'status attribute', what he called 'representative publicity'.[40]

According to the *Arthaśāstra*, because of the manifoldness, simultaneity and varied location of the king's affairs, he was to appoint ministers to perform his work for him.[41] This justification, which the emperor Aśoka had turned into a boast in his sixth rock edict, reveals an important aspect of royal service – that the king's ministers carried out what was considered to be the personal work of the king, and were thus bound directly and

38 *BS* 43.5 ff.

39 For the *BS* on types of umbrellas, see 73.1ff; conches and seats, see 79.1ff. This text foreshadowed later medieval manuals like the *Aparājitapṛcchā*, *Sāmārangasūtradhāra*, *Mānasollāsa*, *Mayamata* and *Mānasāra*.

40 Habermas, *The Structural Transformation of the Public Sphere*, p. 7.

41 *AS* 1.9.8.

personally to him. Here the text calls the minister *amātya*, a term meaning literally one who resided within the royal household (from *amā*, house), but which denoted a generic rank of 'official', 'courtier' or 'companion', who secured his position by attending the king's household and gaining his favour. The number of these *amātya*s was high; Scharfe estimates that they may have sometimes numbered into the hundreds.[42] The *amātya* was a vital constituent of the kingdom, according to the *Arthaśāstra*, superseded in importance only by the king himself.[43]

The *Arthaśāstra* provides a set of 'tests' to be conducted by secret agents of the king in order to appoint ministers to particular tasks. The most successful were appointed 'counsellors', or *mantrin*s, while others took various positions of service both within and outside the palace complex. Counsellors in turn formed part of a more restricted category called *mahāmātra*, or 'one most excellent in rank', which also included sacrificial priests (*ṛtvij*) the royal preceptor (*ācārya*), chaplain (*purohit*), general (*senāpati*), crowned prince (*yuvarāja*), mother (*rājamātṛ*) and chief queen (*rājamahiṣī* or *mahādevī*), among others.[44] This expanded list of personnel in the textual sources, all of whom had to be accommodated within the royal household, is also attested in the epigraphic record from the first centuries of the Common Era. By Gupta times, inscriptions speak not only of ministers (*amātya*s) and the higher grade of 'ministers of princely rank' (*kumārāmātya*s), but also of counsellors (*mantrin*s), envoys (*dūtaka*s), ministers of peace and war (*mahāsandhivigrahaka*s), generals (*mahābālādhikṛta*s, *senāpati*s) and military retainers (*daṇḍanāyaka*s).[45] Inscriptions also provide a number of positions which relate to the functioning of the royal household like the gatekeeper or chamberlain (*pratīhāra*), the overseer of the royal elephant stables (*mahāpilupati*) and the royal kitchens (*khādyakūṭapākika*).[46] Contemporary and later sources

[42] Scharfe, *Investigations*, p. 126, n. 9. [43] *AS* 6.1.1.

[44] These are drawn from the list of stipends for royal officials and the list of palace officials who the king had to watch over with spies. See *AS* 1.12.6; 5.3.3 ff.

[45] For the Gupta meaning of *daṇḍanāyaka*, see D. R. Bhandarkar, *CII* 3 (1981), pp. 95–7. For the meaning of *kumārāmātya* see, K. K. Thaplyal 'Kumārāmātya – A Reappraisal' in Chhabra, *et al.*, eds., *Reappraising Gupta History (for S. R. Goyal)* (New Delhi: Aditya Prakashan, 1992), pp. 224–31.

[46] The term *mahāpratīhāra* is found on a seal from Basāḍh referring to one Vinayasura and, along with *mahāpilupati*, in the Gunaighar plates of Vainyagupta. See *CII* 3 (1981), pp. 99–100, and *IHQ* (March, 1930), pp. 45–60. A fragmentary inscription from Vidīśa datable to the fifth century mentions a family of men with the title *pratīhāra* attached to their names for three generations, presumably servants of the Nāgas, who were in turn underlords of Guptas. *EI* 41 (1975–6), no. 19, pp. 186–8. The term *khādyakūṭapākika* has been suggested as the proper reading of the obscure *khadyaṭapākika* of the Allahabad pillar inscription of Samudragupta. See D. C. Sircar, *Indian Epigraphy*, pp. 357–8.

mention titles connected with carrying royal paraphernalia – particularly the umbrella, fly-whisk and betel bag.[47] These titled positions were also accompanied by personal servants who attended the king, queen and, no doubt, others of eminent rank, and who were generically referred to as *paricārakas* (literally, those who surrounded the lord) or *upacārakas* (those who performed personal services).

Particularly important among the men of the royal retinue, judging from literary texts and inscriptions, were the envoy and the chamberlain. The envoy, or *dūtaka*, was the temporary executor of the king's will in regard to tasks outside the palace. He acted as messenger to friendly and hostile courts as well as subordinate officials within a king's realm. He appears prominently in historical records because inscriptions, being essentially the orders of kings, were always executed under the direction of a man deputed by the king from the royal court. Land grants from the Gupta period onwards regularly mention the *dūtaka*, who is often (but not always) a prince or retainer of rank at the king's court. In some cases a subordinate king could act as the executor of his overlord's will, conforming to the Allahabad pillar inscription's remark that underlords were required to 'carry out the orders' (*ājñākaraṇa*) of the emperor.

With the growing complexity of the royal household, the doorkeeper and/or chamberlain (*pratīhāra*, *dvārapālaka*, *kañcukin*), were positions of immense importance. Larger royal households, with their many buildings and surrounding walls, typically had numerous entrances and gates which had to be guarded. The overseer of these men, or *chamberlain* (referred to variously as *pratīhāra*, *mahāpratīhāra* or *kañcukin*), though generally subordinate to the highest counsellors, priests and members of the royal family, was trusted with the management of the royal household, acting

[47] All three posts are mentioned by Bāṇa in the seventh century, see *HC*, ch. 5, p. 155 for a *chauri*-bearer (*cāmaragrāhin*); ch. 7, p. 206 and ch. 1, p. 33 for a betel-nut bearer (*tāmbūlika; tāmbūlakaraṅkavāhinī*); ch. 6, p. 176 for an umbrella-bearer (*chatradhāra*). Kauṭilya mentions the umbrella-bearer (*chatragrāhin*) as a possible spy, *AS* 1.12.7. A twelfth-century Kannada inscription dated in the reign of the western Cālukya king Someśvara IV (1180–1200 CE) refers to the chief minister (*mahāpradhāna*) of the *mahāmaṇḍaleśvara* Rāchamalla II, named Becharāja, with the title 'carrier of the king's betel bag' (*haḍapavaḷam*), see *EI* 14 (1917–18), no. 19a, p. 272. For other references, see P. K. Gode, 'References to Tāmbūla in Indian Inscriptions between A.D. 473 and 1800', in P. K. Gode, *Studies in Indian Cultural History*, vol. I (Hoshiarpur: Vishveshvaranand Vedic Research Institute, 1961), pp. 113–20. The *Mānasollāsa*, a compendium composed in the twelfth century at the Cālukya court, says that the officer in charge of the betel-nut (*tāmbūlādhikārī*), the finest of royal enjoyments, was to sit next to the king at all times. See *Mānasollāsa* 3.959–60. A roughly contemporaneous inscription of the Nāgavaṁśī king Jayasiṁhadeva, in Bastar state, describes one of the king's high ministers as the 'prince in charge of the fly whisk' (*cāvarikumāra*), see *EI* 10 (1909–10), no. 6, p. 36.

as mediator between the king and those of lesser rank who had no direct access to the him, as well as the many supplicants and visitors who came to the court. He oversaw the protocol of the royal assembly hall and regulated procedure at royal audiences, managed the flow of movement within the household and ensured that visitors behaved according to rank and title. As Bāṇa arrives at Harṣa's encampment he is met by a tall man named Pariyātra, who his royal escort Mekhalaka introduces as the chief of all the king's doorkeepers (*pratīhārāṇām dvaurika*), adding that anyone pursuing success should treat him with fitting respect.[48] The chamberlain wore special vestments, and is called *kañcukin* or 'one who wears a waistcoat', in court dramas.[49]

From Gupta times inscriptional records show the combination of palace and ministerial titles with those indicating minor royalty, vassal, or military status. Hariṣeṇa, author of the Allahabad pillar inscription, for example, calls himself a military retainer (*mahadaṇḍanāyaka*), a minister of princely rank (*kumārāmātya*) and a minister of peace and war (*mahāsandhivigrahaka*).[50] Similarly, the *dūtaka* of the Gunaighar grant of Vainygupta was one *mahāsāmanta*, *mahārāja* Vijayasena who is also titled a chamberlain (*mahāpratīhāra*) and master of the king's elephant stables (*mahāpilupati*).[51] This accumulation of titles, which became ever grander toward the end of the Gupta empire, signals an important dimension of courtly life, reflected in two processes. First, subjugated kings and princes who attended court were sometimes required to or willingly took up service functions within their overlord's household. In some cases these titles were probably considered ceremonial honours, and did not require permanent residence in the overlord's household. Nevertheless, major imperial houses seem to have kept a large body of retainers who hailed from subordinate royal families. They are frequently mentioned as attending the royal family in courtly texts. Second, it seems that high palace servants, functionaries and ministers tended to be recognised with privileges similar to those of military retainers and vassals. This could mean that they gained titles of royalty, as is implied when Bāṇa describes

[48] *HC*, ch. 2, p. 62. The full account is significant. Bāṇa arrives accompanied by Mekhalaka, who is immediately recognised by the doorkeepers. Mekhalaka enters alone leaving Bāṇa outside and after some time returns with the chamberlain, who then courteously offers Bāṇa entrance for audience with the king. The transpiring events, unmentioned by Bāṇa, probably were that Mekhalaka announced the arrival of the visitor to the chamberlain, who in turn approached the king to enquire whether he was ready to meet with Bāṇa. What is significant here is that the chamberlain acts as the official 'interlocutor' between the visitor and the king over and above the royal escort sent to bring Bāṇa to court, suggesting a strict protocol in access to the king which only the chamberlain oversaw.

[49] In *HC*, ch. 2, p. 61, Pariyātra is described as wearing a waistcoat, or *kañcuka*.

[50] Hariṣeṇa may have resided in the palace, *CII* 3 (1981), no. 1, p. 215.

[51] *IHQ* (1930), pp. 45–60.

'ministers anointed to royal rank' (*mūrdhābhiṣiktāḥ cāmātyā rājāno*) surrounding the grieving prince Harṣa.[52] It could also mean that they took titles like 'enjoyer' (*bhogika*).[53] In both cases, such titles indicated that these men gained the economic privileges of lordship, namely a regular supply of land revenues from territorial fiefdoms.[54]

The more powerful men at court, then, tended to be effectively greater or lesser landed lords, and inscriptions from the sixth century present ever more complex gradations of titles indicating this status.[55] They increasingly formed a class with a homogenous economic base and a similar world of social aspiration. In some cases it is difficult to determine whether these men were first retainers who attended the royal court and as a consequence were assigned lands, or were first defeated kings or landed lords who gained titles by appearance at court. In either case, service titles tended to move towards a ceremonial status, which is to say that such men, though their titles may have signified some position in the house of an overlord, tended to have households of their own set up along similar lines.

The Maitraka house of Valabhi in Gujarat is an interesting case. The early inscriptions trace the family back to the general (*senāpati*) Bhaṭārka, who is said to have 'gained the glory of royalty' by the strength of his many loyal hereditary servants and friends.[56] His sons, therefore, took the title *mahārāja*, though they clearly expressed submission to the paramount sovereign. One of them, Droṇasiṁha (*c.* 500–25 CE), was even anointed into kingship by the paramount sovereign and another, Dhruvasena I (*c.* 525–50 CE), gained the titles *mahāsāmanta* and 'great chamberlain' (*mahāpratīhāra*).[57] After the fall of the Guptas, at the end of the first half of the sixth century, they began to drop all reference to any overlord. It would seem, then, that this family saw its fortune rise as generals of the Guptas. At this stage they also seem to have commanded a powerful household with extensive dependants of their own, and presumably enjoyed some form of land revenue, perhaps at the appointment of their overlords, who

52 *HC*, ch. 5, p. 173.

53 See the authors of the ten Parivrājaka and Uccakalpa land grants in *CII* 3 (1888), nos. 21–31, pp. 93–139, who claim to be the descendants of ministers who held the title of *bhogika*.

54 The evidence for secular land grants from this period has been less well preserved than grants of land to religious beneficiaries. What evidence does exist, however, points overwhelmingly towards the remuneration of royal functionaries in land revenues. See the discussion in Sharma, *Indian Feudalism*, pp. 8–12.

55 For a summary of such terms, see Sharma, *Indian Feudalism*, p. 216.

56 *EI* 16 (1921–2), no. 4, p. 17.

57 The distinction between his own title 'great chamberlain' (*mahāpratīhāra*) and that of Mammaka, 'chamberlain' (*pratīhāra*) is thus explicable. See *IA* 4 (1875), pp. 104–7; *EI* 11 (1911–12), nos. 9.1, 9.2. pp. 106–12; *IA* 5 (1876), pp. 204–6.

must have either bestowed or acknowledged the title of *mahārāja* taken by the sons of Bhaṭārka. Dhruvasena I was further honoured by his overlord with the post of 'great chamberlain', a title which did not prevent him from having his own chamberlain (*pratīhāra*), one Mammaka, who acted as the envoy for his own orders. The trajectory here seems to be from the status of a powerful royal military retainer enjoying revenues and supporting a retinued household to that of subordinate king, taking ceremonial status in the overlord's household. The transition to royalty was crucial for this family, though not all men of the court were able or even wished to do so.

The majority of men who resided at court, even when possessing titles and offices, were generally referred to either as 'retainers' (*parijana, paricara, anucara*), literally those 'surrounding' or 'following' the king, or as 'servants' (*sevaka, bhṛtya, dāsa*), or 'dependants' (*anujīvin, upajīvin*). Most broadly, these terms referred to any man who depended on some lord (*svāmin*) for his livelihood.[58] This category was important enough to form the subject of a special set of recommendations and protocols in the manuals on polity, which contain chapters on how would-be courtiers were to gain entry, audience and favour at court, how they were to perform and report their work to the king, and how to understand his intentions.[59] According to the same treatises on polity, these men were to be recruited from the upper castes, preferably from the priestly class, but as Kāmandakī puts it, 'a man with a treasury and an army is resorted to by all men'.[60] Judging from the sources, there seems to be no way to generalise on the *varṇa* backgrounds of those who entered royal service. The lines of ministers mentioned in the inscriptions of the Aulikāras, Parivrājakas, and the kings of Uccakalpa, suggest *vaiśya* origin. Kāmandaka seems to presuppose diverse backgrounds for royal servants when he recommends the king keep a careful balance in his treatment of dependants, honouring those that were high born, while promoting those of middling and lower rank without offending their superiors.[61] The hundreds of verses throughout Sanskrit literature which lament the difficulties of the 'servant's life' and the evils of 'servitude' refer less to the plight of low-caste menials than to upper-caste men who sought livelihoods at royal courts.

58 The term *sevaka* in the *AK* (2.8.9) together with *anujīvin* and *arthin*, refer to those who repair to a king's household for their livelihood. Other terms refer more generally to servants like *bhṛtya, dāsa, cēṭaka* and *paricāraka* (*AK* 2.10.17).

59 See *AS* 5.4 and 5.5. Also *NiS* 5.1–59. This knowledge is no doubt what the jackal minister Damanaka of the *Pañcatantra* refers to when explaining to his companion that he is familiar with the 'rules for retainers' (*anujīvidharma*). See *PT* 1.18+.

60 *NiS* 5.61. 61 *Ibid.*

It is clear that a substantial cadre of men who participated in courtly life came from monasteries, hermitages or brahmin householder communities which were supported by the kings and men of high rank, usually through grants of land, as we know from the many copper plate inscriptions from Gupta times. Links between royal courts and these eleemosynary communities were varied. At one level, brahmin householder communities provided a steady stream of 'secular' functionaries like ministers, counsellors, poets, physicians and generals, as well as religious ministrants like temple priests and astrologers. Indeed, the presence at court of men trained in religious rites had a profound influence on the development of the courtly ethos in early India.[62] Moreover, mendicants along with other types of men unattached to property formed ideal messengers between lovers, spies and agents of royal intrigue. On the other hand, it would seem that many prominent men of the court took refuge in religious communities and hermitages at the end of their lives or when their masters died, renouncing, as it were, the worldly ways of the court.[63] In addition to the men who actually appeared at court and reported to the king, various poets and śāstric authors who may not have lived at court nevertheless mention royal patrons in their works. Numerous Jain and Buddhist monks like Amarasiṁha, Aśvaghoṣa and Somadevasuri wrote texts which had a predominantly courtly provenance. Kings also sent princes to be educated by individual teachers living in hermitages or householder communities supported by royal largesse.

The reasons why these men might come to court is perhaps best revealed by Bāṇa's long list of reasons why he *isn't* obliged to travel to king Harṣa's court:

> my ancestors never had any love for it, there is no hereditary connection with it for me, nor must I consider past benefits, nor affection from service as a child, nor family dignity, nor the courteousness of old acquaintance, nor the allurement of exchanging information. Nor would I go from the desire for more knowledge, from respect paid to fine appearance, or to practise turns of speech fit for inferiors. Nor does the cleverness needed in the circles of the learned, the skill to win friends by the expenditure of wealth, nor association with royal favourites [interest me].[64]

62 This may be compared to the influence of the courtier-bishop at royal households in Europe from the time of Charlemagne. See Stephen Jaeger, *The Origins of Courtliness: Civilizing Trends and the Formation of Courtly Ideals, 939–1210* (Philadelphia: University of Pennsylvania Press, 1985).

63 See the description of Prabhākaravardhana's court in *HC*, ch. 5, p. 172 ff. See also the remarkable account of the life of Caturnāna Paṇḍita recounted in an inscription at Tirvorriyur which speaks of his service at the court of the Cōḻa king Rājāditya and his decision to enter a Śaiva monastery because he could not join his lord in death on the battlefield. *EI* 27 (1947–8), no. 47, pp. 301–02.

64 *HC*, ch. 2, p. 53. The passage, in continuous prose, has been punctuated for readability.

A number of these abstentions are revealing enough. It is certain that many brahmin families had hereditary connections with royal courts, and that many must have had various reasons to feel indebted in some way to courtly patrons. The quest for literary success, fame, dignity and influence were perhaps equally important. In all, the reasons differed little from those that any man would have for going to court. Yet Bāṇa's speech is revealing at another level, for the subtext of this passage is critical of court careers and seeks to exonerate him from any accusation of vanity, servility or ambition. It thus points to a certain antagonism towards royal service which was a persistent sentiment in didactic and gnomic literature from Gupta times. Yet the criticism of courtly life, which we shall have occasion to touch upon later, was very easily incorporated into courtly discourses themselves.

Certainly by the beginning of the seventh century, when Bāṇa composed his court chronicle, *Harṣacarita*, there had long been a tendency for offices of service at royal courts to become hereditary. Numerous inscriptions from Gupta times record the existence of hereditary (*maula*) counsellors, ministers and military retainers. In an Udayagiri inscription, Candragupta II's minister of peace and war, the brahmin Vīrasena, mentions that he attained the position of minister through hereditary descent (*anvayaprāptasācivya*).[65] It is not uncommon for inscriptions to mention the relatives of a minister. Hariṣeṇa, for example, whom we met above as the author of the famous Allahabad pillar inscription, and who carries several important court titles, mentions that he was the son of another man of rank, the *mahādaṇḍanāyaka* Dhruvabhūti.[66] The land grants of the Parivrājaka and Uccakalpa kings – all subject to the Guptas at the end of the fifth and beginning of the sixth centuries – trace back ministerial families to four generations, with titles like minister (*amātya*) and 'fief-holder' (*bhogika*).[67] Sometimes inscriptions, in recording acts of charity by ministerial families, set out more elaborate genealogies, as in the case of the Naigamas who served at the court of the Aulikāras of Mandasor. In an important inscription praising at length the accomplishments of these

65 *CII* 3 (1981), no. 11, p. 256.

66 *CII* 3 (1981), no. 1, p. 215. The Karamdanda inscription dated in the reign of Kumāragupta records three generations of ancestors for a brahmin counsellor and general named Pṛthivīsena, one of whom held titles, *CII* 3 (1981), no. 21, p. 281. At Sanchi there is an inscription recorded by one Āmrakārdava, a dependant (*anujīvin*) of Candragupta, which includes his father's name, though he is not attributed with a title. See *CII* 3 (1981), no. 9, p. 250.

67 For the Parivrājaka grants, which mention relatives of the ministers Vibhudatta and Śūryadatta for three generations, see *CII* 3 (1888), nos. 21–3, pp. 93–109. For the Uccakalpa grants which trace back the ancestors of the ministers Gallu and Manoratha for four generations, see *CII* 3 (1888), nos. 27–31, pp. 121–39. Also *EI* 19 (1927–8), no. 21, pp. 127–31.

men over several generations, it is boasted that the standing of the family was 'secure and unbroken' through the generations.[68]

Men like these, together with their royal patrons, formed part of a ruling class united by their links with land, their association with royal households, and a common set of norms and values which placed a high premium on both military valour, worldly wisdom and personal refinement. This class was segmented and highly porous. It included not only kings of various rank, and armed retainers, but men of counsel, the upper echelons of palace servants and royal retainers, who tended to share titles and rank with arms-bearing men.

Women and princes

As early as our sources indicate, the royal family was a large and complex institution. This was caused in the first instance by a tendency of royal houses to establish political alliances through the accumulation of marital ties, polygamy being sanctioned by the *dharmaśāstra*s and widely practised among the ruling classes. In the early manuals on polity, marriage was considered an auspicious and solemn 'seal' on various types of political agreement, particularly those which the families wished to be 'continuous' (*santāna*), or lasting over generations.[69] Relations of friendship, fealty and even favour could be established through the 'gift of a virgin' (*kanyādāna*). In some cases, the gift of a king's daughters to an overlord's household was expected as a sign of loyalty, as in the case of the Allahabad pillar inscription's boast that the princesses of subordinate kings were sent to the Gupta house for marriage. In such cases, *kanyādāna* may have overlapped with more coercive situations where the women of conquered households were 'acquired' by victorious kings with the nominal consent of their natal families. Samudragupta's conquest of the Nāga kings, for example, seems to have ended with the accession of a Nāga princess to the Gupta household and her marriage to Samudragupta's son Candragupta. Yet the gift of daughters to other houses could also be a mark of eminence. In the sixth century, a king of the nascent and rising Kadamba family is praised in an elaborate conceit 'as being like a sun who by the means of his light rays, or daughters, caused the lotus groups of other royal families like the Guptas, surrounded by their bee-like attendant kings, to expand and bloom showing their filaments of love, respect and affection'.[70] In other cases, the gift of a daughter simply

[68] *CII* 3 (1888), no. 35, p. 153. [69] *AS* 7.22–29, and *NiS* 9.6.

[70] *EI* 8 (1905–6), no. 5, p. 33. This is probably not a claim of superiority over these families, but one of honourable subordination.

sealed an alliance between equals or even the friendship of a lesser lord, as in the case of the marriage of Candragupta's daughter Prabhāvatīgupta (through his Nāga queen) to the Vākāṭaka house at the end of the fourth century, or Harṣa's marriage of his daughter to a Maitraka Prince in the seventh century.

More important royal households, therefore, had numerous wives, all of whom lived in quarters separate from the king, generally known as the *antaḥpura* or *strīniveśa*. The ranking and etiquette between these women, the introduction of new and junior brides to the household, and the king's attentions to particular wives, not to mention the other women and attendants of these women, were all serious matters, which formed themes not only of numerous courtly dramas, but also of the prescriptive literature. The *Kāmasūtra*, for example, gives a detailed account of how the senior (*jyeṣṭā*) and junior (*kaniṣṭā*) wives were to behave towards one another, and how they might best achieve their interests, depending on how many other wives were present in the household.[71] In residences where this number exceeded two – as was undoubtedly the case in most royal households – the strategies recommended to them to gain the favour of the king over and above their co-wives resembled the policies of building alliances and sowing discord which kings themselves were to pursue in the *rājamaṇḍala*.[72] The chief queen was an appointed rank and was not enjoyed simply by dint of seniority. According to Bāṇa, it was acknowledged by a crown or headband (*paṭṭabandha*) bestowed by the king.[73] The king, for his part, was each day to visit the women of the *antaḥpura* assembled together with courtesans and dancers who resided in the palace, and give them place and honour befitting their status.[74] He was enjoined to treat his wives, like his other dependants, in such a way that they remained happy and satisfied.[75]

Princes and princesses also dwelled in separate residences within the palace complex. They had their own attendants and companions, often drawn from the ranks of the extended family of the king and his ministers and vassals. We know that the two chief Puṣyabhūti princes, Harṣa and Rājyavardhana, at the end of the sixth century, for example, were attended from their childhood by the son of their mother's brother, a prince named Bhāṇḍi, as well as two princes of the subordinate king Mahāsenagupta of the later Gupta dynasty, Mādhavagupta and Kumāragupta, whose house had already given a princess in marriage to the Puṣyabhūtis

[71] *KS* 4.2.1 ff. [72] See the remarks in *KS* 4.2.16–22; 38.
[73] See Yaśovatī's lament in *HC*, ch. 5, p. 167. Headbands will be discussed below.
[74] Compare *KS* 4.2.76 with *NiS* 5.64–70. [75] See *KS* 4.2.85 ff.

(Mahāsenagupta's sister) a generation earlier.[76] The sons of the king, ranked by precedence of birth, were educated as a cadre and closely observed by the most trusted officials of the king. They were expected to take up positions among the underlords and *sāmanta*s who appeared at court and we occasionally find them acting in the capacity of envoys and generals. The Gupta prince Candragupta II, for example, acted as the *dūtaka* for a grant of his father.[77] One amongst the sons of the king was selected by his father at a suitable moment to be consecrated as 'heir apparent' (*yuvarāja*). This prince was ideally the eldest son of the senior queen, but both history and literature suggest that this was often enough not the case. The Allahabad pillar inscription's account of the bestowal of kingship on Samudragupta implies a formal ceremony of selection in which the king chose a single prince from 'among those of equal birth' (*tulyakulaja*).[78] The treatises on policy are clear on this point: the ablest son was to be chosen as successor. Both birth *and* accomplishment were the necessary criteria of the *yuvarāja*.[79]

The relationships between members of the royal family were highly regulated and ritualised. They lived in separate residences within the royal palace, and were attended at most times by their personal servants and companions. They were thus rarely alone in their dealings with one another, and quotidian communications and emotional expressions alike were typically channelled through intermediaries and formalised routines. Filial affection, for example, took visible form in greeting one's mother and father, the 'greatest of deities for princes', with bowing and prostration.[80] These gestures were to be practised from the earliest of ages, indeed, as soon as the child could speak and walk.[81] They were the same gestures that were required of servants and feudatories at court, and were observed among members of the royal family even in the most intimate of circumstances.[82] Conjugal love was equally routinised. The

[76] For remarks on Bhāṇḍi, whose service to the Puṣyabhūti house is corroborated by Hsuan-Tsang, see *HC*, ch. 4, p. 135. The gift of a later Gupta princess to the Vardhana court is suggested by the name Mahāsenaguptā, queen of Ādityavardhana, with that of the later Gupta king Mahāsenagupta, who was probably her brother. Mahāsenagupta was certainly the father of the princes Mādhavagupta and Kumāragupta, whom he sent to the Vardhana court as a token of his loyalty, and whom Prabhākaravardhana assigned to his own sons as loyal companions. This is mentioned in *HC*, ch. 4, pp. 137–40 and is corroborated by the Aphsad stone inscription, *CII* 3 (1888), no. 43, p. 204. For a discussion of the history of the later Guptas, see Devahuti, *Harsha*, pp. 17–28; 73–4.

[77] *CII* 3 (1981), no. 3, pp. 224–7. [78] *CII* 3 (1981), no. 1, p. 212.

[79] See *NiV* 5.32, 36. [80] See *NiV* 24.76.

[81] See the depiction of prince Raghu in *RghV* 3.25.

[82] Arriving at his father's deathbed, the prince Harṣa bows in humility (*vinayāvanamra*) and must be raised (*unnamayya*) before he is embraced by his father, *HC*, ch. 5, p. 158.

king's daily meeting with the palace women was preceded by a formal exchange of gifts, in which the female chamberlain (*kañcukīyā*) or bodyguard (*mahattarikā*) of the *antaḥpura* brought garlands, unguents and clothes to the king from the queens, the king returning them as forms of grace to the queens.[83] Though many women of the court may have spent most of their time within the *antaḥpura*, the politics there were directly continuous with those of the assembly hall (*sabhā*).

The most pressing issue for the king with respect to the royal household, was the transmission of power and authority from one generation to the next – a process which was by no means straightforward, and often involved competing claims among co-wives and their sons, with their allies and agents placed within the household, the kingdom and beyond.[84] In contradistinction to the idealised representations of literary texts and inscriptions, it is safe to assume that succession was usually a complex affair. Though the ideal in the law treatises was primogeniture, in reality it often took a far more irregular form. Not only were eldest sons often passed over or displaced through dispute by uterine or half-brothers, but succession often went to brothers rather than sons. In both of the preeminent royal houses in India at the beginning of the seventh century powerful kings came to power in the context of irregular or contested successions. In the Puṣyabhūti family, Harṣa was chosen over his elder brother Rājyavardhana for succession by his father Prabhākaravardhana before the wars which led to his brother's death at the hands of the Gauḍa king Śaśāṅka.[85] In the Cālukya house Kīrttivarman's younger brother Maṅgaleśa inherited the throne in 597 instead of his son Pulakeśin II, who later left his uncle's court, gathered a contingent of men and killed his uncle to claim his own patrimony in 609.[86] Indeed, a careful examination

83 *KS* 4.2.73–4.

84 See Kumkum Roy, 'The King's Household: Structure/Space in the Sastric Tradition', in Uma Chakravarti and Kumkum Sangari, eds., *From Myths to Markets: Essays on Gender* (Delhi: Manohar, IIAS, 1999), pp. 18–38.

85 After Prabhākaravardhana's death, the king of Mālwā entered Kanauj, killed the Maukhari king Grahavarman, and took his wife Rājyaśrī, sister of the fatherless Puṣyabhūti princes. Rājyavardhana set out to avenge the death of Grahavarman and retrieve his sister, but lost his life through treachery in the household of the Malwa ally, Śaśāṇka of Gauḍa. When his younger brother, Harṣa, arrived in the city with his sister, the widowed Maukhari queen, the courtiers of Kanauj invited him to take the throne. These fast-moving, complex and almost fortuitously timed events which propelled Harṣa to power not only over his own less-prestigious patrimony in Sthāṇvīśvara, but the more powerful Maukhari kingdom, suggests an element of design which the accounts of the court-chronicler Bāṇa and the Buddhist monk Hsuan-Tsang, may have taken pains to overlook. See the careful and suggestive account of Devahuti in *Harsha*, pp. 92–4. For another interpretation of the sources, see R. S. Tripathi, *History of Kanauj to the Moslem Conquest* (Delhi: Motilal Banarsidass, 1989), pp. 61–77.

86 As detailed in Pulakeśin's Aihole inscription, *EI* 6 (1900–1), no. 1, p. 5.

of the evidence of inscriptions suggests that non-primogentural, or 'collateral succession' (non father/son) was far more common than traditional dynastic histories have allowed for.[87]

So while the accumulation of interdynastic marriages secured the king vital political alliances with other royal houses, it also swelled his own household with potential heirs. While the host of greater and lesser princes in the royal household might form a loyal cadre of retainers, they were also a potentially divisive and fissiparous element, particularly as the court attempted to transfer authority from one generation to the next. Unfortunately, far too little is known about the lives of rank and file princes in early medieval India. It may have been the case that they were sent away from the household to serve at the courts of superior kings or to acquire new territories and fortunes for themselves. Larger imperial houses must have retained very large numbers of princes indeed, a point of which court poems often boast. The frequent appearance of collateral branches of the major imperial houses like the Guptas, Maukharis, Aulikāras, Rāṣṭrakūṭas, Cālukyas and Cōḻas, sometimes long after the collapse of the main house, suggests the importance of minor princes as a political factor in the subcontinent.

The great emphasis on the discipline of the young prince and the cultivation of filial loyalty in courtly life thus had a necessary function – to secure stable relations in the transfer of power from one generation to the next. Princes 'unrestrained', according to Kāmandaka, could bring about the ruin of any royal family.[88] The display of self-control and love for one's father was as necessary for any ambitious prince as it was for the stability of the household. It is for this reason that such qualities were to be continually tested by the king's trusted servants and spies according to the manuals on polity. The motives and dispositions of princes were to be ascertained by the king's spies right from their childhood, and authorities recommended different ways of dealing with lapses in discipline and loyalty.[89] Even after his selection before the court, the heir apparent was to be spied upon by agents of the king.[90]

Conflict between fathers and princes, between uterine or half-brothers, often involved other members of the royal household, most notably queens, whose loyalty to their sons was potentially greater than to their

87 See the remarks of Henige, 'Some Phantom Dynasties', pp. 539–44.

88 *NiS* 7.5.

89 Here Kauṭilya disagrees with other thinkers on the subject, who view the princes' temptations as an opportunity to expose disloyalty rather than cultivate propriety. See *AS* 1.17.28–39. Kāmandaka follows Kauṭilya on this point, suggesting that erring princes should never be disowned but instead turned back to the ways of their fathers, lest they seek refuge with one's enemies, *NiS* 7.7–8.

90 *AS* 1.12.6.

husband, whose attentions were necessarily split among the hierarchy of other co-wives.[91] It is perhaps significant that the prescriptions on policies towards wives and sons in the political treatises are invariably juxtaposed to guidelines for the protection of the king's person. As the *Arthaśāstra* puts it, a king could only protect his kingdom when he himself was protected from those close to him, beginning with his wives and sons.[92] Princes were to be guarded from their birth, according to one authority, because they followed 'the law of the crabs' (*karkaṭaka*), mercilessly devouring their fathers (*janakabhakṣa*).[93] It is in this context, which the *Arthaśāstra* presumes to be the norm, that Kauṭilya provides advice for both the prince in disfavour and his father.[94] Queens were particularly dangerous because the king was often vulnerable when he met them. According to Kāmandaka he was to move through the inner apartments of the palace accompanied by guards deemed deformed of body or unattractive to palace women (dwarves, hunchbacks and mountain men) who were unlikely to be seduced into disloyalty.[95] His liaisons were to be pre-arranged by a trusted minister who oversaw the *antaḥpura*, restricting its access and protecting its members from contact with sorcerers, monks and female servants from other households.[96] The king was never to meet the chief queen within her own residence. 'However dear, women were not to be trusted', according to Kāmandaka, and the treatises provide copious examples of kings murdered by queens and their sons.[97]

The counsellor

According to the *Arthaśāstra*, all the undertakings of the king were to be preceded by deliberation (*mantra*), and proper deliberation could never be achieved by a single person.[98] It required the advice of counsellors, or *mantrins*, whose number was to range between three and twenty.[99] These men, appointed by the king and led by the chief counsellor or royal preceptor (*ācārya*, *rājaguru*, *pradhānamantrin*, etc.), were to be experts on the principles of polity as embodied in treatises like the *Arthaśāstra* and were to advise the king on a vast range of matters. They furnished the king with one of the three acknowledged sources of his power, that of counsel (*mantraśakti*), the other two being might (*prabhu*) and energy

[91] Significantly, Kauṭilya tends to wed the interests of son and mother, in citing that princes may become disaffected when a king shows favour to another son or wife (other than his mother), *AS* 1.18.5.
[92] *AS* 1.17.1. [93] *AS* 1.17.4–5. [94] *AS* 1.18.1 ff.
[95] *NiS* 7.41. These types of men were also considered to be useful spies, see *AS* 1.12.9, 21.
[96] See the remarks in *NiS* 7.42–8. It is interesting to juxtapose such with recommendations in the *Kāmasūtra* on how most effectively to infiltrate the *antaḥpura*, see *KS* 5.6.6 ff.
[97] *NiS* 7.50–4. [98] *AS* 1.15.1, 18. [99] See the discussion in *AS* 1.15.34–41, 47–50.

(*utsāha*),[100] and were typically called the 'eyes' or even the 'mind' of the king.[101] Ministers were expected to direct the king away from any faulty action which could arise from weaknesses like pride, anger and conceit.

More than this, the counsellor was thought to conduct the affairs of the kingdom, as many of the inscriptions praising able and competent ministers tirelessly point out. The Mandasor stone inscription of Yaśodharman and Viṣṇuvardhana (532 CE), for example, lauds one of the Naigama ministers as 'bearing, for the sake of his lord . . . the very heavy burden (of rule), not shared by any one else', a role which seems to have entitled him to wear royal vestments (*nṛpativeśa*).[102] The mention of such powerful counsellors in inscriptions was not meant merely to celebrate the minister's abilities, but also to underscore the power of the king whom he served, as the delegation of one's affairs was a mark of power rather than weakness.[103] At court, the capacity to act through agents differentiated men of rank from those that served them, and within men of standing the more powerful from the less powerful. Kauṭilya concludes that by deputing (*āropita*) the burden of the work of the kingdom (*rājyatantrabhāra*) upon his 'chief minister' (*pradhānaprakṛti*, literally, chief constituent), the king was able to remain entirely disengaged (*satatam udyāste*). A common metaphor for the relationship between a counsellor and the king was that of a mahout and an elephant. Kauṭilya muses that kings, like elephants, become wearied and collapse (*sīdanti duḥkhitāḥ*), despite their natural strength, when they must procure food for themselves, and that a kingdom can only cause joy to a king when he is spared the difficulties of its maintenance (*abhiyogaduḥkha*).[104]

According to the *Arthaśāstra*, when the king was infirm or dying, the counsellors were to take control of the royal household to ensure a smooth and uninterrupted passage of sovereignty between the dying king and his successor.[105] In the famous case of Harṣa's 'succession' to the Maukhari imperium at Kanauj, the Chinese traveller Hsuan-Tsang makes it clear

[100] For the threefold power (*trayaśakti*) of the king, see *AS* 6.3.33.

[101] For the counsellor as eyes of the king, see *BC* 9.62; *NiS* 18.28. In a related metaphor, a ninth-century Rāṣṭrakūṭa inscription of Amoghavarṣa compares the king (*rāja*) to the soul, the minister (*saciva*) to the mind, his circle of feudatories (*sāmantacakram*) to the senses, and his servants (*sevaka*) to his speech and other sense-faculties: *EI* 18 (1925–6), no. 26, p. 247.

[102] He claims to wear these 'only as a measure of his distinction' (*kevalaṁ lakṣmamāttram*), *CII* 3 (1888), no. 35, p. 154. For a later example, see the Mau inscription of the twelfth-century Candella king Madanavarman, *EI* 1 (1892), no. 25i, pp. 199–200.

[103] For the delegation of the burden of government to the companions of the king as an act of his grace (*tatprasādāvāptasamastamaṇḍala-cintābhāram*, with some variation) see the numerous twelfth and thirteenth-century inscriptions of the Śilāhāras of the Northern Koṅkan: *CII* 6, nos. 20 (p. 124), 21 (p. 129), 22 (p. 131), 23 (p. 137), 25 (pp. 145–6), 28 (p. 152), 32 (p. 162), 33 (p. 164), 36 (p. 170), 38 (p. 174), 39 (p. 176).

[104] *MR*, 1.14+, 15.

[105] See *AS* 5.6.1 ff.

that the family servant, who acted as minister, one Bhāṇḍi, prevailed upon the disarrayed Maukhari court to accept Harṣa's overlordship.[106] Indeed, it would seem that when it came to the finer points of diplomatic relations, counsellors played a far greater role than the king himself, and in this sense the powerful minister was certainly a king-maker.

The faultless stratagem of the chief counsellor in winning success and advantage for his lord was an important theme in a number of story cycles which circulated at courts from late Sātavāhana/Kuṣāna and early Gupta times. These cycles were enacted in courtly dramas and widely referred to in manuals on polity and didactic literature. They reached their most heightened effect in the court drama, where the tension of the unfolding plot conforms to the minister's strategy. Notable are the figures of Yaugandharāyaṇa, counsellor of the prince Udayana Vatsarāja as he appears in the plays of Harṣa and the Trivandrum author, and Kauṭilya, or Cāṇakya, counsellor of the Mauryan prince Candragupta, the chief character in Viśākhadatta's famous play *Mudrārākṣasa* written at either the Gupta or Maukhari court.

The *Mudrārākṣasa* begins with the counsellor Cāṇakya explaining how, having been removed from the seat of honour (*agrāsana*, literally, first seat) at the Nanda court, he took vengeance by deposing the Nanda family and establishing Candragupta on the throne.[107] The subject of the play is Cāṇakya's conquest and acquisition of the dangerous and fiercely loyal minister of the deposed Nanda king, Rākṣasa, for his own master Candragupta. Cāṇakya achieves this through a series of complicated strategies which, importantly, play on the virtues of his adversary, making him an unblemished trophy, as it were, for Candragupta at the play's denouement. In the Udayana play cycles, the minister Yaugandharāyaṇa masterminds his lord Udayana's escape after an accidental capture by his enemy Pradyota Mahāsena, the acquisition of Pradyota's daughter Vāsavadattā in marriage (the subject of *Pratijñāyaugandharāyaṇa*), as well as two further marriage alliances which are forged through strategies unknown to the king – with Padmāvatī, daughter of the king of Magadha (featured in *Svapnavāsavadatta*) and Ratnāvalī, daughter of the king of Sri Lanka (the plot of Harṣa's *Ratnāvalī*). In the case of both cycles, the king is directed by the minister, often unaware of his overall designs. In Harṣa's *Ratnāvalī*, for example, the king is entirely ignorant of his minister's plans to bring him success by introducing the daughter of the Sinhala king into the royal household as a servant. In Act 3 of *Mudrārākṣasa*, the king is

106 *Si-Yu-Ki*, vol. I, p. 211 ff.

107 This is what Kauṭilya as an historical figure is most famous for. So, he is mentioned by Kāmandaka, author of the *Nītisāra*, as having singlehandedly (*ekākī*) gained the Earth for Candragupta through the power of his counsel (*mantraśakti*), *NiS* 1.4–5.

instructed by Kauṭilya to dismiss him after feigning a quarrel and rule independently, which the king, unaware of his counsellor's strategy to suggest an apparent rift between the two to Rākṣasa's spies, is reluctant to do.

The subject of the counsellor and his intrigue was eminently suited for the stage. The court dramas were able to portray more effectively than either prose narrative or poetry the time sequences and scenic separations necessary for portraying life at court – what we might describe, using the *Arthaśāstra*'s language, as the simultaneity, manifoldness and spatial dispersal of royal affairs.[108] So it is that Rākṣasa compares himself to a playwright:

> sowing a tiny seed of enterprise, planning its expansion, and when the seeds have germinated, unfolding their hidden fruits, pausing skilfully and finally gathering up the results though spread far and wide, such is the burden which the maker of a play and someone like me bears.[109]

In a sense every courtier strove to gain mastery of their own and others' affairs in the manner of the minister. The whole of the science on polity was oriented to this end, and though it often purported to be directed to the king, it was typically the men around him who interpreted and implemented this knowledge for him. It is telling that though the frame story of the *Pañcatantra* begins by saying that the tales were narrated by a famous scholar to the ignorant princes of King Mahiprola, the first and most important story concerns the attempts of two young jackal-courtiers to get ever closer to the king through strategies entirely unknown (and not entirely unharmful!) to him.

The role of the counsellor in both the political treatises as well as in the plots of court dramas makes it very clear that the agency of the court was both composite and complex. On the one hand, the treatises understand the king as the foundation of the kingdom – its primary constituent and metaphorical head. On the other, sovereignty and power required the delegation of powers and functions, and tended to valorise such delegations as signs of a superior and quiescent lordship. This meant that effective power was often wielded by the king's most powerful courtiers. Yet if ministers effectively governed the kingdom, they did so not directly but through the figure of the king, often making him seem to be the sole agent of royal policy to outsiders and, in some cases, even to the king himself. While such shared agency was recommended in the political treatises, it also clearly left ample scope for tension on the ground. The exchange which ensues in the course of Candragupta's and Cāṇakya's

[108] See *AS* 1.9.4–8. [109] *MR* 4.3.

feigned alienation in *Mudrārākṣasa* is revealing enough of the strains that must have existed between powerful ministers and the men they served. Cāṇakya contravenes the king's direct orders, and boasts of his ministerial prowess; the king for his part questions Cāṇakya's wisdom and attributes his successes to fate. Unfortunately, it is not possible to corroborate such concerns in the events of any known historical courts. Yet the theme of the powerful minister in didactic and literary representation attests to a very real concern at courts over the issue of sharing power.[110]

The court and the city

It will be useful, in concluding this chapter, to enquire into the relationship between the people of the court and town life during our period. Unfortunately, any attempt to do so is hampered not only, to a certain extent, by a lack of detailed information about the lives of people at court, but also by a still-incomplete understanding of the scope and nature of early medieval urbanism in India. We can surmise, for example, that the households of more important kings were typically located in cities and fortified towns, while the residences of minor families were undoubtedly located in more rural environments. Yet palace remains from our period have not been excavated, in either urban or rural settings, in any systematic or useful way. Research indicates, however, that it is probably not helpful here to follow European models too closely. It is certain that between Kuṣāṇa and Gupta times, many larger cities slowly declined in size and population. Political élites seem to have continued to live in these diminished cities, or resided in more modest towns.[111] The recession of the larger cities, however, did not reflect a total collapse of urban development. Evidence suggests that hundreds of towns and cities of more modest proportions appeared on the Indian landscape throughout the early medieval period. And in contradistinction to the European case, these towns were inhabited by a local élite composed of both landed and commercial interests, who shared a common ethos and culture. In other words, India did not witness the strong distinction between town and countryside which was to become the hallmark of economic and cultural development in medieval Europe.[112] In towns, revenue collectors and landed men shared a broadly common culture with the urbane and commercial élites. There was, therefore, no strong distinction between

[110] For a comparative perspective see the discussion on the role of ministers in Heian period Japan in Morris, *World of the Shining Prince*, pp. 41–52.

[111] Sharma, *Urban Decay*, p. 151.

[112] B. D. Chattopadhyaya, 'Urban Centres in Medieval India: An Overview', in his *Making of Early Medieval India*, pp. 181–2.

the culture of the court and the city as in some medieval and early modern European contexts.[113] Rather, the ways of the town mirrored those of the court.

Important in this regard is the lifestyle of the 'man about town', called the *nāgaraka* in Vātsyāyana's *Kāmasūtra*. While he formed the chief 'ego' of Vātsyāyana's treatise, the *nāgaraka* was not a city man *as opposed* to a courtier. The term, like the culture of the *Kāmasūtra* itself, was far more porous. According to Vātsyāyana, the *nāgaraka* was to be a man of means, who, having finished his education, established himself as a householder. He had a steady source of wealth (*artha*), drawn either from an inheritance (*anvayāgata*) or from some other source – gifts, conquest, trade or wages – or both, and was to settle down in a city, royal capital, town, or some other place where 'good people' were numerous.[114] The category of the *nāgaraka*, therefore, was chiefly defined by living among the 'good people' of cities, capitals and large towns, and not by occupation. Vātsyāyana's definition left as much scope for landed classes of priestly householders, warrior nobles and prominent dependants at the royal court as it did for wealthy merchants and city men. In fact, the king is treated by Vātsyāyana as the most pre-eminent of *nāgaraka*s and much of the text presupposes the royal household as its context. Nor was it unusual for kings to consider themselves to be 'urbane men'. We have, for example, the seventh-century eulogies of the Gurjara vassal-king (*sāmanta*) Dadda II which describe him as having the 'natural disposition of a clever *nāgaraka*'.[115]

Similarly, the men of the city came to express their prominence in a language they shared with the court. In at least one case, we may glimpse how new urban residents took on the trappings of this culture. An unusual stone inscription documents the emigration of a guild (*śreṇi*) of silk-weavers (*paṭṭavāya*) from the country of Lāṭā to the town of Daśapura (Mandasor) ruled by the Aulikāras, Gupta feudatories, sometime early in the fifth century. The inscription does not explain the reasons for their migration to Daśapura (other than their attraction to the eminent qualities of its ruler) but makes very clear their impressive career in the city.

113 Some scholars of ancient India like Siegfried Lienhard, have drawn sharp oppositions between urban and courtly contexts, though there is little historical evidence for such an assertion. Siegfried Lienhard, *A History of Classical Poetry: Sanskrit-Pali-Prakrit*, vol. III, fasc. 1 of *A History of Indian Literature*, ed. Jan Gonda (Wiesbaden: Otto Harrassowitz, 1984), pp. 53–64.

114 *KS* 1.4.1–2. Yaśodhara in his commentary associates each of these latter methods of obtaining wealth with one of the four estates.

115 See the Kaira plates of Dadda II, dated 628 and 634 CE, *CII* 4 (1955), pt. 1, nos. 16 and 17, pp. 61, 70. See also *VkU* 2.11+ where king Purūravas' *vaidūṣika* is called a *nāgarika*.

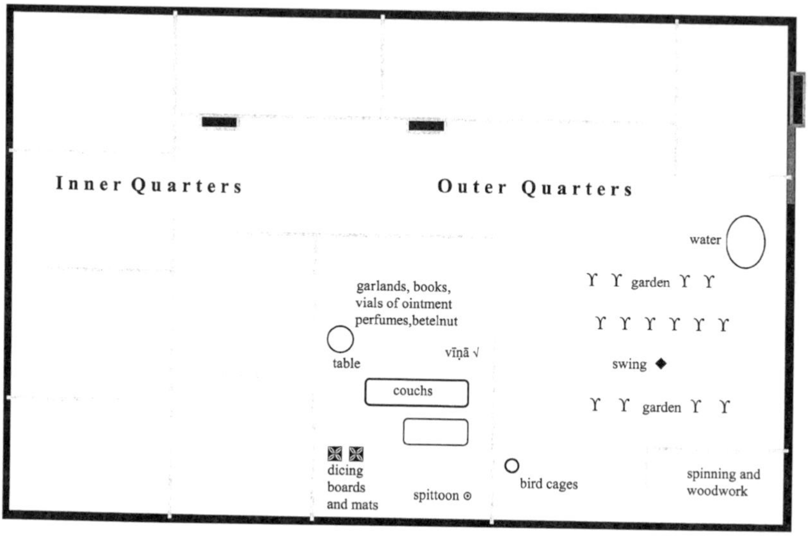

Figure 1.4 Houseplan of an élite urban dweller (*nāgaraka*) as reconstructed from Vātsyāyana's *Kāmasutra* 1.4.4–15.

They themselves sought to complete their good fortune by sponsoring the construction of a temple to the Sun god with their accumulated wealth, and to memorialise themselves by commissioning a local poet, Vatsabhaṭṭi, to compose a standard courtly eulogy introducing the grant. What is significant about this eulogy, whatever its veracity as a record of events, is the worldview which it embodies. After arriving in Daśapura, the weavers are said to be honoured (*pramānita*) by local kings as if they were their own sons, are attributed with a number of qualities typical of the court nobility, including patronising brahmins, mastering various knowledges like astronomy, being fond of music, valorous in battle, enjoying chronicles and colourful stories and, perhaps most tellingly, being clever in bestowing favours to companions.[116] The style of Vatsabhaṭṭi's account is also courtly with its ornate description of Daśapura and the cycle of seasons.[117] The point is that the men who gained their fortune in the city chose to express their own eminence in a style as characteristic of the court as it was of the circles of *nāgarakas*.

Though the architectural prescriptions for the *nāgaraka*'s house set out in the *Kāmasūtra* (see figure 1.4) focus more on the pleasures

[116] See *CII* 3 (1981), no. 35, p. 325.

[117] For a discussion of the poetic qualities of the inscription, see A. L. Basham, 'The Mandasore Inscription of the Silk-Weavers', in Bardwell Smith, ed., *Essays in Gupta Culture* (Delhi: Motilal Banarsidass, 1983), pp. 93–105.

of association than on the calibration of political hierarchy, the preoccupations were as much courtly as they were urbane.[118] Like the descriptions of the royal household contained in courtly literature, the *Kāmasūtra* concentrates on the outer quarters of the house, the chief elements of which seem to be an outdoor garden and a reception room. The garden, which had a well-shaded bower, flowering plants, inlaid floors and a swing, was an important element in both lordly and urbane households. Often called a 'pleasure garden' (*krīḍāvana*) in literary texts, it was the place where men and women retired to 'play' the games which formed such an important theme in courtly literature and it is here that the intrigue of love nearly always took place. The typical reception room contained couches, cushions, tables, gaming boards, mats, spittoons, cosmetics, books, painting materials and a lute.

An element which linked the lifestyle of the *nāgaraka* with the world of the court, judging from this description, was a vast and complex material culture. Men of standing were fastidious about their surroundings, beginning with meticulous care of their own bodies. According to Vātsyāyana, the *nāgaraka* was to bathe every day, have his limbs chaffed and rubbed with oil every second day, have a foam bath every third day, his face shaved every fourth day and his body hair removed every fifth or tenth day.[119] Great use was made of ointments and unguents (*aunlepana*) which had various properties, like sandal paste (*candana*), which was thought to be cooling, or beeswax (*sikthaka*) used as an emollient and adhesive, perfumes (*sugandha*), fragrant oils and incenses (*dhūpam*) for counteracting body odours and the effects of perspiration, betel-nut (*tāmbula*) and citron bark (*mātuluṅgatvaca*) for sweetening the mouth, collyrium (*añjana*) for colouring eyelids and lashes and lac (*alaktaka*) for reddening the lips and feet.[120] Perfumery and cosmetics formed extensive sciences in medieval India which have only been partially understood, their only material remains being the occasional discovery of vials, mirror handles, palettes, combs, hair pins, scrubbers and the like (see figure 1.5).[121]

Fine textiles and jewellery were among the most prized objects among the urban and courtly élite. The most pre-eminent fabric was silk, which during Kuṣāṇa times came *via* overland trade routes from China and

118 The following account is based on *KS* 1.4.4–15.

119 *KS* 1.4.17. Daily bathing, according to Yaśodhara, promoted vitality and purity.

120 Based largely on *KS* 1.4.8, 13 and comm.

121 For accounts of male and female toilette, see Jeannine Auboyer, *Daily Life in Ancient India, from 200 BC to 700 AD* (New York: Macmillan, 1965), pp. 268–72; also *CHI*, vol. 1, p. 497. For illuminating studies of early medieval cosmetics and perfumery, see Gode, *Studies in Indian Cultural History*, vol. I, pp. 3–112.

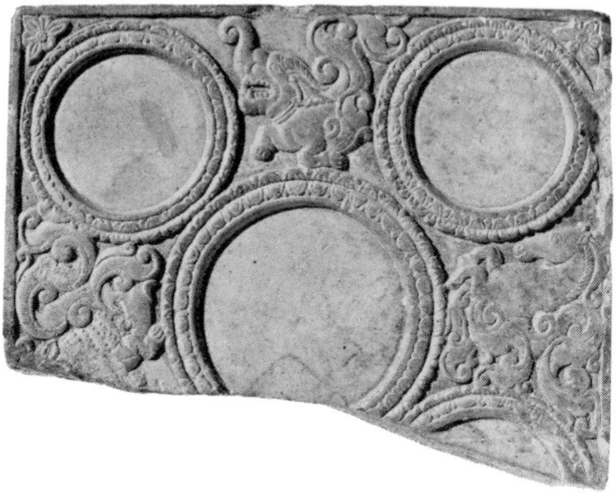

Figures 1.5 and 1.6 Material culture of the court. The fragment of a limestone make-up palette (left), seventh century CE, Deccan, and sealring (right) with identifying royal inscription, western India (Punjab) end of fourth century CE. The seal reads 'the king (*mahārāja*) Maheśvaranāga, son of Nāgabhaṭṭa'.

later from Sasanian Central Asia itself, though local silk was also produced.[122] The fineness and colours of silk clothing are nearly always described in sumptuous detail in sources between the fifth and seventh centuries. As the inscription of the silk-weaving guild at Mandasor puts it, 'a woman, though saturated with youth and beauty and suitably adorned with golden necklaces, betel leaves and flowers, does not attain transcendent beauty until she has put on garments made of silk'.[123] Both men and women wore jewellery on nearly all parts of the body, from the feet to the head, including toe-rings, anklets, waist bands, armlets, bracelets, finger-rings, earrings, tiaras and hair pins. These objects, fashioned from precious metals and stones, were highly personalised. Not only did the king and queen have their own ornaments, sometimes with separate names, residences and servants to attend them, but high-ranking courtiers like ministers and spies were identified by seal or signet rings (see figure 1.6).

[122] Xinru Liu, *Ancient India and Ancient China: Trade and Religious Exchanges, AD 1–600* (Delhi: Oxford University Press, 1988), pp. 6–7; 53–75. See also Xinru Liu, *Silk and Religion: An Exploration of Material Life and the Thought of People AD 600–1200* (Delhi: Oxford University Press, 1996), pp. 20–1.

[123] The poet goes further to say that the guild 'adorned the entire surface of the earth with silk cloth agreeable to touch, variegated with arrangements of different colours so as to please the eye', see *CII* 3 (1981), no. 35, p. 326.

These goods, whether produced locally or imported by merchants, circulated widely among the élite and helped to create common culture among these classes. The royal palace, according to the *Arthaśāstra*, was to be surrounded not only by military and food provisioners, but perfumers, flower-makers, jewellers, smiths and dealers in liquids, decorations and toilet articles. Judging from later sumptuary manuals, these objects were consumed in great quantity by royal households, partly because the giving of such items formed a standard part of the protocols of courtesy between men and women of noble rank. According to the *Kāmasūtra*, the wealthy townsman made similar use of such materials, which were not only enjoyed within his own household but given as favours to friends, servants, paramours and courtesans. Worldly sophistication, according to Vātsyāyana, included a thorough familiarity with these goods, and among the 'auxiliary arts' recommended for the *nāgaraka* are knowledge of garlands and flower arrangements, crowns, jewellery, gems, clothes, perfumes, oils, dyeing, woodwork and food preparation, among other subjects. The point of these 'arts' was not so much technical training or artisanal apprenticeship but sophisticated, connoisseurial knowledge. The provenance of this material culture implied a set of everyday practices, ideational propensities and discursive preoccupations shared between the élite of the court and the city.

A key institution linking these circles was the *goṣṭhī*, which Vātsyāyana defines as a meeting or association of city-men (*nāgaraka*) of equal means, intelligence, disposition and age, who sat together in conversation either in the outer apartments of the townsman's house, the residence of a courtesan, or at the royal court (*sabhā*) itself.[124] The most important activity which transpired at the *goṣṭhī* was conversation, the favourite themes of which were romantic liaisons and poetry. Literature and inscriptions attest to the existence of *goṣṭhī*s both within courtly settings and beyond them. The later Gupta king Ādityasena, for example, is described in his Aphsad stone inscription as 'laughing in a charming manner at the gatherings (*goṣṭhī*) of his beloved servants (*vallabhabhṛtya*)'.[125] The *bhāṇa* monologue plays, on the other hand, depict *goṣṭhī*s as composed chiefly of urbane men. The connections of such circles with royal courts, however, were never far, and the men of courtly rank (usually low-ranking officials or ministers' sons) regularly appear as characters in the *bhāṇa*

[124] This definition, corroborated by widespread use in early medieval poems and plays, is based on *KS* 1.4.34–6. Chattopadhyaya refers to the *goṣṭhī* as a 'salon like gathering': Chattopadhyaya, 'City in Early India', p. 201. In religious contexts the term referred to associations of men looking after the affairs of monasteries and temples.

[125] *CII* 3 (1888), no. 42, p. 204.

literature. The seventh-century court poet Bāṇa mentions time spent at *goṣṭhīs* before arriving at the court of the emperor Harṣa.

It is perhaps worth considering Bāṇa's account of his youthful peregrinations. Partly prodigal and partly educational, they give us a glimpse into the trajectory that might propel a young man to court. Bāṇa recounts how after a depression following his father's death he fell in with a diverse set of companions and friends, left his home and lived an itinerant life without restraint, falling into disrepute in the eyes of the great. He claims to have regained his reputation by observing great lordly houses of elevated conduct, serving at the houses of the teachers of the wise, attending associations (*goṣṭhīs*) of the good which were full of worthy discussions, and entering into the circles (*maṇḍala*) of the clever (*vidagdha*).[126] Bāṇa's youth, both his errors and accomplishments, did not go unnoticed at court, and he was invited for audience by the king's brother Kṛṣṇa, where he eventually obtained favour.

Bāṇa's early career of folly and dissolution remains perhaps as interesting as his later reform. Among the people he claims to have befriended were a Prakrit poet, a panegyrist, a betel-bearer, a goldsmith, a physician, a scribe, a painter, an engraver, a dancing girl, an ascetic, a story-teller, a magician, a juggler, an actor, a shampooer and a dicer.[127] This list of characters, corroborated by their appearance in the treatises on polity as well as court dramas, suggests the existence of an urban and courtly demi-monde, populated by a variety of often itinerant and generally low-ranking men and women who found occasional employment at both the royal court and powerful urban households. The boundaries between court and city, I would suggest were both continuous and porous.

The interstitial proximity of certain classes of low-ranking people to the lives of the élite, their sometimes less-stable relations with family and property (particularly in the case of ascetics, nuns, monks and courtesans) combined, of course, with their particular skills, made them eminently useful as spies, messengers and clandestine agents.[128] The *Kāmasūtra* describes several such 'dependants' (*upajīvin*) who assisted the *nāgaraka* in matters regarding love. These included the *pīṭhamarda*, a man without any wealth but who was nevertheless well-versed in the knowledge of pleasure, the *viṭa*, a well-regarded man who had once possessed the wealth and sophistication to converse among *nāgarakas* as an equal, but had subsequently spent his wealth, and finally, the *vidūṣaka*, who had only partial knowledge of the science of pleasure but was both trustworthy and humorous.[129] The *vidūṣaka* and *viṭa* are well attested from court dramas, the former as the intimate companion and clandestine messenger of the

[126] *HC*, ch. 2, pp. 19–20.
[127] *HC*, ch. 2, p. 19.
[128] See *AS* 1.12.7–9, 21.
[129] *KS* 1.4.44–6.

king in his love intrigues, and the latter as the comic narrator of the *bhāṇa* monologue plays recounting scenes from the prostitutes' quarter of the city. These men were employed by both men and women of rank (including courtesans) as 'counsellors' (*mantrin*s) in the business of love.[130] Well-versed in the arts of pleasure, they acted as teachers, advisers and messengers for the courtesan and *nāgaraka*. Vātsyāyana describes them as being employed to negotiate the 'alliances and wars' (*sandhivigraha*) of these parties.[131] Despite contextual differences, the terminological parallelism between personal and political relationships remains significant, suggesting a set of shared mental categories which linked the court and the wider social world of urban élites.

If the worlds of the city and the court were linked together culturally and materially, they tended to counterpose their own lifestyles not against one another, but against that of the village. Despite their economic links with rural economy, city and courtly élites deemed the village unsuitable for the pursuit of refined activities, particularly courtship and love – in one text which portrays the conversations at a *goṣṭhī*, it is proclaimed that village life was the very death of erotic love (*kāma*).[132] The term *grāmya*, or 'rustic', derived from *grāma* (village), captures this opposition – as it was the antithesis of both urbanity and courtliness. The term had a pejorative meaning in the Sanskrit lexicons, which understood it as coarseness and vulgarity (*aślīla*), particularly in speech, and generally associated it with other terms which denoted slurring, spitting, drooling or incomprehensibility while speaking, as well as with cruelty and severity.[133] In poetics, it referred to an error or blemish in composition, or to words and expressions which would be inappropriate for men of the court (*sabhya*), but extended to any inappropriateness (*anaucitya*) of behaviour, dress, speech, family, class, learning, wealth, age and characters in a dramatic composition.[134] It was a term that could be used to slight or insult men at court, implying an unsophisticated manner or

[130] *KS* 1.4.46.

[131] The comparison is with the *mahasandhivigrahaka*, or great minister of peace and war, frequently mentioned in Gupta period inscriptions. See Hartmut Scharfe, *The State in Indian Tradition* (Leiden: E. J. Brill, 1989), p. 151.

[132] *DhVS* 38. Indeed, the *Kāmasūtra* itself (1.4.49) recommends that the good men who lived in villages should imitate the behaviours of their urban counterparts, by holding discussions (*goṣṭhī*s) and the like.

[133] See *AK* 1.6.18 ff and comm.; also Halāyudha's *Abhidānaratnamālā* 142. Significantly two commentators to the *AK*, Liṅgayasūrin and Mallinātha, gloss *grāmya* as 'uncourtly' or ignoble speech (*asabhyavacana*). In poetic style it had a similar meaning, denoting a coarseness of either sense or language.

[134] See Bhāmaha *Kāvyālaṁkāra* 1.47 ff. and Daṇḍin's *Kāvyādarśa* 1.63 ff. which understands it as the opposite of sweetness (*mādhurya*). For other references, see R. C. Dwivedi, 'Concept of Obscenity (aślīlatā) in Sanskrit', in Pushpendra Kumar, ed., *Aesthetics and Sanskrit Literature* (Delhi: Nag Publishers, 1980), pp. 13–24.

lower social rank. In King Harṣa's *Ratnāvalī*, the minister of the Sinhala king is called 'rustic' (*grāmya*) as he marvels at the splendour of the court of King Vatsarāja of Kauśambi.[135] The whole complex of values and emotions which this book will be exploring was founded on the opposition between high, noble people and low, base people – a dichotomy which was at least partly articulated through the opposition of court and village.

[135] *Rv* 4.12.

2 The culture of the court

The culture of the court can be documented by two great arenas of discourse: treatises advising men (and sometimes women) of rank on conduct and policy, and a voluminous body of verse and prose literature which depicted the lives of these people. Neither of these genres of writing were exclusively limited to the court; they were produced and circulated at a variety of locales in early India. Yet the urbane and courtly milieu outlined in the previous chapter formed a crucial context for a considerable amount of this literature. This chapter will look more carefully at the texts I have already made reference to in order to set out the political context of courtly life. These sources suggest a coherent and relatively stable cultural formation which we may call 'courtly', defined by an aesthetic and ethical emphasis around the 'good' or 'noble' life.

The upper ranks of court society were composed of people who considered themselves, by virtue of both birth and accomplishment, to be 'noble' and 'good', concepts most comprehensively denoted by the term '*ārya*'. Though its early usage had denoted ethnically based Vedic clan-chieftaincies, by the early centuries of the Common Era the term had come to refer to any man (and sometimes woman) born of the upper *varṇas*, and was already acquiring a more generalised meaning of 'virtuous' or 'noble'. In the second century, the Śaka king Rudradāman, in his Junagadh rock inscription, refers to his minister Suviśākha, probably a Persian by birth, as an *ārya*.[1] By the fourth century a poetic lexicon had equated the term with several other words of significant meaning – 'good people' (*sajjana*), 'the worthy' (*sādhu*), 'the high-born' (*kulin*) and, tellingly, 'those fit for the court' (*sabhya*).[2] From Gupta times, similar if not identical lists of qualities can be found in the idealised descriptions of a range of character types associated with the royal court. Indeed, the

[1] *EI* 8 (1905–6), no. 6, p. 44.

[2] *AK* 2.7.3: *mahākulakulīnāryasabhyasajjanasādhavaḥ*. See also *NiS* 18.48 where Kāmandaka defines those of *ārya* standing as having good birth (*kula*), good conduct (*śīla*), kindness (*dayā*), generosity (*dāna*), righteousness (*dharma*), truthfulness (*satya*), gratitude (*kṛtjñatā*) and obedience (*adroha*).

ideal man a king was to attain for his court, according to the texts on polity was to have just these qualities; he was to be well born, noble, fit for the court, learned, honoured, modest and the like.[3] Eventually, these various terms came to denote a class of people who were the bearers of all that was associated with good in the world.

The co-appearance of these terms as descriptors of people we will be treating in this book also suggests common lifestyle. These 'noble' and 'good' people were largely emancipated from the hardship of physical labour for subsistence. Though having various vocations, as a class they tended to regard themselves as 'enjoyers' rather than producers. They counterposed their own lives, deemed 'high' or 'elevated' (*uttama*), in every way superior – in outward appearance, speech, bearing and intellectual and emotional capacities – to those deemed 'low' (*adhama*) – a category which included not only the people of the village, but barbarians and men from the forests who lived far beyond the social order which sustained the élite.[4] The vast cultural edifice erected by the 'noble' people of early Indian society must always be understood with such basic parameters in mind. In this sense, the culture of the court functioned in part as a great barrier between the 'high' and the 'low'. Yet it was never so closed as to function as a system of ascriptive naturalism. Didactic treatises and courtly sayings never cease to emphasise that virtue was never a function of birth and innate qualities alone, but was also a matter of cultivation. The ever increasing number of inscriptional eulogies appearing from the fourth century praising the virtues of kings, *sāmanta*s and courtiers attest to the porosity of the court as an institution and its ability to absorb rising groups and ambitious individuals within its confines.

Worldly knowledge

The men of the court, being of twice-born affiliation, were expected to conduct their lives around three 'goals' or spheres of human effort: rectitude (*dharma*), acquisition (*artha*) and pleasure (*kāma*). These three categories had developed in the post-Vedic Smṛti literature, and together with the pursuit of enlightenment (*mokṣa*), constituted 'goals of human life' (*puruṣārtha*).[5] But unlike *mokṣa*, they were explicitly associated with worldly life. They were together called the 'threefold path' or *trivarga*,

[3] *NiS* 16.30.

[4] Some barbarians (*mleccha*s) and men deemed to be wild (*kirāta*s) were admitted among the dwarves, hunchbacks, eunuchs, shampooers and other menials deemed safe enough to serve in royal households, a point which made them useful as spies. See *AS* 1.12.9, 21. Their utility in this regard, however, did not fundamentally alter their social distance from the 'good people'.

[5] The goals of human life (*puruṣārtha*), though treated as a fundamental 'axiology' of Vedic religion, only appear in later ritual manuals like the *Hiraṇyakeśi Gṛhyasūtra* (2.19.6) where

and their proper pursuit formed the *sine qua non* of good society. Numerous inscriptions from Gupta times praise kings and courtiers for adept pursuit of these three worldly goals.[6]

The pursuit of the *trivarga* was not founded in human nature as much as it was on worldly accomplishment and moral perfection. The realisation of these goals thus required the application of skills or 'means' (*upāya*) which were to be gained through knowledge and instruction as embodied in prescriptive treatises known as *śāstra*.[7] *Śāstra* was a normative literature which sought to prescribe proper action in the world for men of the upper estates.[8] For the courtly élite and in cities, some knowledge of the *śāstras*, together with experience in the world, contributed towards 'familiarty with worldly ways' (*lokayātravid*) – an accomplishment commonly celebrated in inscriptions.[9] Somadevasuri's tenth-century collection of aphorisms on courtly wisdom remarks that 'he who knows the ways of the world (*lokavyavahārajña*), knows everything, while he who does not, though he may be wise, is surely disregarded'.[10]

By the Gupta period, *śāstras* on *dharma*, or rectitude, which had long circulated among the religious élite, were joined by the first separate treatises on acquisition and pleasure, the *Arthaśāstra* and *Kāmasūtra*.[11]

dharma, *artha* and *kāma* are honoured as 'guests' attending rites related to Vedic studies. For relevant citations from śāstric literature, where they appear regularly, see P. V. Kane, *History of Dharmaśāstra*, 5 vols., 2nd edn (Poona: Bhandarkar Research Institute, 1968–75), vol. II, pt. 1, pp. 8–9.

6 See, for example, the descriptions of the Śaka king Rudradāman, *c.* 150 CE, *EI* 8 (1905–6), no. 6, p. 43; of Māyuraśaka, minister of the Gupta feudatory, the Aulikāra king Viśvavarman, *c.* 423 CE, *CII* 3 (1888), no. 17, p. 75; of Cakrapālita, son of the Gupta courtier Parṇadatta, *c.* 457 CE, *CII* 3 (1981), no. 28, p. 301; of the Kadamba king Kakutsthavarman, *c.* sixth century CE, *EI* 8 (1905–06), no. 5, p. 33; of the Kalacuri king Śaṅkaragaṇa, *c.* 609 CE, *EI* 12 (1913–14), no. 7, p. 34; of the Gurjara king Jayabhaṭa I, *c.* 628 CE, *CII* 4 (1955), vol. 1, no. 16, p. 61; of the Cālukya king Pulakeśin I, *c.* 634 CE, *EI* 6 (1900–01), no. 1, p. 4.

7 Vātsyāyana makes this point to justify the need for a *śāstra* on pleasure, which some critics deemed unnecessary on account of its prevalence, *KS* 1.2.18–24.

8 This point is developed extensively in Sheldon Pollock, 'The Theory of Practice and the Practice of Theory in Indian Intellectual History', *JAOS*, vol. 105, no. 3 (1985), pp. 501–12. Pollock discusses Vātsyāyana's arguments justifying the admission of women (usually forbidden access to śāstric knowledge) to the study of his *śāstra* (*KS* 1.3.4. ff.) as an example of this tendency. It is significant that the realm in which śāstric authors recognised a more dialectical relation between theory and practice was that of politics. See *AS* 1.5.8; 1.8.25.

9 See the description of Vīrasena, courtier and companion of the Gupta king Candragupta II, as 'knowledgeable of the world' (*lokajña*) *CII* 3 (1981), no. 11, p. 256; and of the silk weavers' guild in the famous fifth-century Mandasor inscription as 'unparalleled in worldly ways' (*lokayātrāpara*), *CII* 3 (1981), no. 35, p. 325.

10 *NiV* 17.60. According to Kauṭilya, those who possessed such knowledge were most suited to the royal court, *AS* 5.4.1.

11 The dating of these texts has been the subject of detailed investigation and contentious discussion. For many years the *Arthaśāstra* was associated with the Mauryan period on the basis of its ascribed authorship to Kauṭilya, the reputed minister of Candragupta. It

Though these texts certainly represent the culmination and refinement of previously existing traditions of knowledge (which are frequently cited on numerous points), the importance of their compilation in the early Gupta period should not be lost sight of.[12] They together represent a sort of 'enunciative moment' for the concerns they take up. It is very possible that the knowledges which they drew on were dispersed (as Vātsyāyana himself maintains), inchoate or attached to other ideological concerns. The 'rules for the king' (*rājadharma*), for example, formed a standard part of the early *dharma* literature, and the emergence of the *Arthaśāstra* as an autonomous discourse largely displaced and re-oriented this knowledge.[13] The importance of this re-orientation is underscored by the fact that many of the concerns with which these texts were preoccupied seem strangely appropriate to the lifestyles of the political élite which grew up in the first centuries of the Common Era and crystallised during the Gupta period in their full-blown form.

is Thomas Trautmann who showed irrefutably that the text was compiled from a number of sources which reveal considerably later dates by incidental references to places, items of trade, royal orders and coinage types. Hartmut Scharfe has further demonstrated the unreliability of the internal evidence for its attribution to Kauṭilya, suggesting that this ascription is a later accretion to the text, otherwise penned by one Viṣṇugupta. The collective evidence would seem to suggest that the text is datable to the later third or early fourth century CE, just before the rise of the Guptas. For a review of the problem, see Thomas Trautmann, *Kauṭilya and the Arthaśāstra: A Statistical Investigation of the Authorship and Evolution of the Text* (Leiden: E. J. Brill, 1971) and Scharfe, *Investigations*. H. C. Chakladar, on the basis of dynastic references in the text, set a *terminus post quem* for *Kāmasūtra* at 225 CE while Jolly and Schmidt, based on external references, gave a *terminus ante quem* in the fourth century CE. Its similarity in structure and style to the *Arthaśāstra*, and the occasional confusion of their authors in the gnomic literature suggests that the two texts were composed in chronological proximity, priority usually being reserved for the *Arthaśāstra*. See H. C. Chakladar, *Social Life in Ancient India: A Study in Vatsyayana's Kamasutra* (Calcutta: Sushil Gupta, 1954), pp. 11–35; 69–72; J. Jolly and R. Schmidt, 'Introduction', *Arthaśāstra of Kauṭilya*, vol. I (Lahore: Motilal Banarsidass, 1923), pp. 28–9; Maurice Winternitz, *A History of Indian Literature*, vol. III, p. 661 ff.; and R. Shama Sastry, 'A Note on the Supposed Identity of Vātsyāyana and Kauṭilya', *Quarterly Journal of the Mythic Society*, vol. 7 (1917), pp. 210–16.

12 Both texts make reference to pre-existing authorities at the beginning and through the course of their treatises. See *AS* 1.1.1; *KS* 1.15–19. For a discussion of Vātsyāyana's predecessors, see Friedrich Wilhelm, 'The Quotations in the Kāmasūtra of Vātsyāyana', *Indologica Taurinensia*, vol. 7 (1979), pp. 401–12 and S. C. Upadhyay, *Kama Sutra of Vatsyayana* (Bombay: Taraporevala, 1961), p. 47 ff. Vātsyāyana provides a telling explanation for his own project, saying that the origin of knowledge on *kāma* was to be traced to the Vedic deity Prajāpati, who recited 100,000 chapters on the three goals of human life. Passed down by various sages, this knowledge eventually became dispersed, a situation which Vātsyāyana sought to remedy by condensing (*saṃkṣipya*) the treatises on various aspects of *kāma* treated by separate authors. Serious claims to the antiquity of this knowledge must be vitiated by the ubiquitous impulse among *śāstric* writers, who conceived of themselves as expositors rather than innovators, to view their own work as extending what had always already existed.

13 For *rājadharma* sections of the dharma texts, see *Baudhāyandharmasūtra* 1.10.18.1 ff.; *Vasiṣṭhadharmasūtra* 19.1 ff. and *MDh* 7.1 ff.

Most generally, *artha* was considered to be the livelihood of men – specifically agriculture, cattle rearing and trade, all considered beneficial because they yielded products like grain, animals, gold, forest produce and labour.[14] For the king, the realm itself was his livelihood, and thus from his point of view, which is the point of view taken by the śāstric treatises, the science of *artha* consisted of attaining and protecting a realm.[15] The discourse about polity in the *Arthaśāstra*, as in later texts, revolved chiefly around the king and his manifold relations with the elements that composed his realm or kingdom (*rājya*). These elements, or 'limbs' (*prakṛti*, *aṅga*) consisted of the king himself (*svāmi*), as well as the minister (*amātya*), the territory (with inhabitants, *janapada*), the fortified city (*durgā*), the treasury (*kośa*), the army (*daṇḍa*) and the ally (*mitra*).[16] Each 'limb' was more important than the next with the king functioning as the metonymic 'head' and central constituent – though when ordered properly, the limbs of the kingdom were to function in coordination with collective agency, in the manner of a person.[17]

Attaining and protecting a realm was to be achieved by force or coercion (*daṇḍa*), the application of which was effected through 'policy', or *nīti*, a term which came to encompass the entirety of the science of politics. From Gupta times, the *Arthaśāstra* was supplemented by treatises which sought less to comprehensively define a realm of striving around *artha* (as Kauṭilya had done) but instead to assemble, often in the form of anthologies of verse sayings, wisdom on *nīti*, or policy.[18] According to the *Arthaśāstra*, the policy of the king was to consist of the acquisition of things not possessed, the protection of things obtained, the increase of things protected and, finally, the donation to the worthy of things increased.[19] By the use of this wealth, along with force, the king was to bring under his sway both his own 'party' (*pakṣa*), as well as those of others.[20] These rather generic goals – of winning over and deploying wealth and people – both within his household and kingdom, and in the wider *rājamaṇḍala* in which he operated, formed the great obsession and goal of the texts on polity. To achieve these ends they prescribed

[14] *AS* 15.1.1; 1.4.1.

[15] *AS* 15.1.1–2: *manuṣyāṇāṃ vṛttir arthaḥ, manuṣyavatī bhūmir ity arthaḥ; tasyāḥ pṛthvyā lābhapālanopāyaḥ śāstram arthaśāstram iti.*

[16] *AS* 6.1.1; *MDh* 9.294; *MhB* 12.59.51; *NiS* 4.1. All but Kauṭilya use the term *aṅga*, 'member' or 'limb', to describe the elements of polity.

[17] See *MDh* 9.295–7.

[18] Chief among these were Kāmandaka's 'Essence of Policy', or *Nītisāra* (*c.* 450–800 CE), Bhartṛhari's 'Centad on Policy', or *Nītiśataka* (from his *STr*, *c.* 600–50 CE) and Somadevasuri's 'Nectar of Sayings on Policy', or *Nītivākyāmṛta* (*c.* 965 CE).

[19] *AS* 1.4.3–4. For praise of the Gupta courtier Parṇadatta in precisely this formulation, see *CII* 3 (1981), no. 28, p. 300.

[20] *AS* 1.4.2.

various schemes of policy, like the 'six general courses of action' which included alliance (*sandhi*), war (*vigraha*), marching (*yāna*), encamping (*āsana*), seeking refuge (*saṁśrayavṛtti*), and duplicity (*dvaidhībhāva*), or the 'seven means' of dealing with an enemy, which comprised conciliation (*sāma*), gift-giving (*dāna*), sowing dissension (*bheda*), force (*daṇḍa*), waiting (*upekṣa*), deceit (*māyā*) and magic (*indrajāla*).[21]

Such concerns, focused almost entirely around the aspiring king or noble's quest for power, did not rely on ethnic or regional identities, theories of governance or political ideologies. The theory of the kingdom itself, which included the 'ally' (whose territory was not contiguous with that of the aspiring king), was conceived less as a fixed territory than as a set of shifting relationships. The 'boundaries' of the kingdom, so conceived, were always deeply entangled in the wider structure of entities which comprised the multi-nodal and potentially polycentric structure of the *rājamaṇḍala*. The discourses on polity focus on the ambitious king, his acquisition of a territory with subjects, wealth and allies as a generic and universal problem.[22] Beyond general remarks on the king as 'supporter of world' and protector of the social estates of his realm, the manuals on polity were principally concerned with how a lord could protect his realm or office only to the extent that acquiring and retaining possession of it was an end in itself.[23]

Pleasure, or *kāma*, is defined by Vātsyāyana as generally as the consciousness that arises from the contact between the various sense organs (ear, skin, eye, tongue and nose) and their respective sense-objects as directed by the mind along with the soul (*ātmasaṁyuktena*); but particularly when, during the sensation of touch, there is a clear delight in some object, which bears fruit and is permeated by the pleasure of arousal.[24] The specific definition, as the treatise itself bears out, makes it clear that *kāma* referred primarily to sexual pleasure. But the *Kāmasūtra* devotes only one of its seven books to sexual techniques, and thus in contrast to some recent European renditions of the text, the *Kāmasūtra* itself perceived sex as an overwhelmingly 'social' act. The largest part of the

[21] For the six courses of action (*ṣādguṇya*), see *NiS* 11.36–42, for the seven means (*saptopāya*), reduced by some texts to four, see *NiS* 18.1 ff.

[22] Verses *nīti*, for example, often speculate on the relative importance of land, gold and allies for a king in different situations. See *NiV* 29.71–3.

[23] In this sense the texts on *artha* and *nīti* resemble more the genre, known elsewhere, of 'advice to the prince' rather than manuals on government and state administration. For a useful discussion of this distinction, see M. Foucault, 'Governmentality', in Graham Burchell, Colin Gordon and Peter Miller, eds., *The Foucault Effect: Studies in Governmentality* (University of Chicago, 1991) pp. 87–104. Also, Morris, *World of the Shining Prince*, pp. 72–3, for a discussion of similar problems in relation to the basis of politics in Heian period Japan.

[24] *KS* 1.2.11–12.

Kāmasūtra is concerned with how men and women of rank, in the text called 'heroes' (*nāyaka*s) and 'heroines' (*nāyikā*s), were to manage their liaisons.

The knowledge recommended by the *Kāmasūtra* constituted much more than simply knowing how to execute diverse sexual techniques. Sexual pleasure had the character of a carefully cultivated avocation. Its skilful pursuit was a matter of great distinction and pride among the high-ranking men of the court and city, who were routinely compared in their inscriptions to the god of love, Kāmadeva, in beauty and sexual prowess.[25] In the *Kāmasūtra*, the sexual act itself was always accompanied by a vast array of accoutrements, material, verbal and gestural, which were thought to be integral to its enjoyment.[26] These accoutrements were deemed so important that the theatrical traditions considered a number of them (unguents, garlands and ornaments) to be 'determinative' of the very emotion of sexual pleasure (*rati*) on the stage.[27] Vātsyāyana calls these accoutrements 'fine arts' (*kalā*) or 'subsidiary sciences' (*aṅgavidyā*), and lists some sixty-four of them.[28] The skills included in Vātsyāyana's catalogue are so diverse as to almost defy comprehension (see table 2.1).[29] They range from knowledge of gems, precious metals and plants, to swordsmanship, physical exercise and carpentry; from skill in dancing, singing and musical instruments to virtuosity in speech, including knowledge of other languages, riddles, word-games, dictionaries, rhetoric and

[25] A few examples from inscriptions will suffice to convey the character of such claims: the description of the Gupta courtier Cakrapālita as 'having a body lovely as Kāmadeva', *CII* 3 (1981), no. 28, p. 300; of the Gupta feudatory King Bandhuvarman as shining like the 'very embodiment of erotic sentiment' *CII* 3 (1981), no. 35, p. 326; of the Gupta feudatory King Dattabhaṭa as 'the god of love in pleasure', *EI* 27 (1947–8), no. 4, p. 16.; of the Maitraka king Dhruvasena III as 'surpassing Kāmadeva in beauty', *EI* 1 (1894), no. 13, p. 88; of the Gurjara king Dadda II as 'showing his nature as an urbane man by winning with obeisance and sweet words the favour of jealous women', *CII* 4 (1955), vol. 1, no. 16, p. 61; of the Sendraka king Allaśakti as 'delighting the eyes of lovelorn ladies like Kāma', *CII* 4 (1955), no. 26, pp. 119–20; and of the Maukhari king Śardula as 'charming the thoughts of lovely women like the god Smara (Kāma)', *CII* 3 (1888), no. 48, p. 223.

[26] See for example, the description of the start and finish of sex in *KS* 2.10.1ff.

[27] *NS* 7.8+.

[28] *KS* 1.3.1. They are listed in *KS* 1.3.16, and should be distinguished, as Vātsyāyana notes (1.3.17), from a similarly numbered list of sixty-four sexual techniques attributed to Bābhravya of Pañcala. See the useful remarks of Wendy Doniger and Sudhir Kakar, *Kāmasūtra* (Oxford: Oxford University Press, 2002), pp. 186–7.

[29] *KS* 1.3.16. The meanings of a number of the arts remain obscure. For discussion of various arts, see A. B. Ganguly, *Sixty-Four Arts in Ancient India* (Delhi: English Bookstore, 1962); A. Venkatasubbiah and E. Muller, 'The Kalas', *JRAS* (1914), pp. 355–67; Louis Renou and Jean Filliozat, *L'Inde Classique: Manuel des Études Indiennes*, Tome II (Paris: École française d'Êxtreme Orient, 2001), appendix 11; and V. Raghavan, *Bhoja's Śṛṅgāraprakāśa* (Madras: Purnavasu, 1978) pp. 639–43. Similar lists of arts are known from earlier Jain and Buddhist sources like the *Lalitavistara*.

Table 2.1 *The Sixty-four Kalās*

1. singing (*gīta*)
2. playing musical instruments (*vādya*)
3. dancing (*nṛtya*)
4. painting (*ālekhya*)
5. cutting designs on leaf for the head (*viśeṣakacchedya*)
6. making designs on the floor with rice grains and flowers (*taṇḍulakusumavalivikāra*)
7. arranging flowers (*puṣpāstaraṇa*)
8. colouring the teeth, garments and body (*daśanavasanāṅgarāga*)
9. fixing coloured tiles and jewels in the floor (*maṇibhūmikākarman*)
10. arranging beds (*śayanaracana*)
11. making musical sounds with water (*udakavādya*)
12. splashing and squirting with water (*udakāghāta*)
13. various secret formulae and their application (*citrāścayoga*)
14. making various garlands (*mālyagrathanavikalpa*)
15. making head decorations (*śekharakāpīḍayojana*)
16. making costumes (*nepathyaprayoga*)
17. making ear ornaments which look like leaves (*karṇapatrabhaṅga*)
18. preparation of perfumes (*gandhayukti*)
19. making and decorating with ornaments (*bhūṣaṇayojana*)
20. magic and illusions (*aindrajāla*)
21. preparation of sorcery and recipes expounded by Kuchumara (*kaucumāra yoga*)
22. sleight of hand (*hastalāghaba*)
23. cooking vegetables, soups and other things to eat (*vicitraśākayūṣabhakṣyavikārakriya*)
24. preparing sherbets and drinks (*pānakarasarāgāsavayojana*)
25. needlework (*sūcīvānakarman*)
26. creating patterns with yarns and threads (*sūtrakrīḍā*)
27. playing on vīṇā and damaruka drum (*vīṇāḍamarukavādya*)
28. composing and solving riddles and rhymes (*prahelikā*)
29. a game in which one party recites a verse and the opposite party recites another which begins from the same letter which the last verse ended (*pratimālā*)
30. reciting verses difficult to repeat (tongue-twisters) (*durvācakayoga*)
31. recitation from books (*pustakavācana*)
32. staging plays and stories (*nāṭakākhyāyikādarśana*)
33. filling out incomplete verse riddles (*kāvyasamasyāpūraṇa*)
34. caning of wood frames of cots, chairs, etc. (*paṭṭikācetravānavikalpa*)
35. woodworking (*takṣakarman*)
36. carpentry (*takṣaṇa*)
37. knowledge of dwellings and architecture (*vāstuvidyā*)
38. knowledge of precious gems (*rūpyaratnaparīkṣā*)
39. knowledge of metals (*dhātuvāda*)
40. knowledge of the colour and form of jewels (*maṇirāgākarajñāna*)
41. knowledge of gardening (*vṛkṣāyurvedayoga*)
42. art of cock-fighting, ram-fighting, quail-fighting (*meṣakukkuṭalāvakayuddhavidhiḥ*)
43. training parrots and mynah birds to speak (*śukasārikāpralāpana*)
44. proficiency in rubbing, shampooing and hairdressing (*utsādane saṃvāhane keśamardane ca kauśalam*)
45. speaking in sign language (*akṣaramuṣṭikākathana*)

(*cont.*)

Table 2.1 (*cont.*)

46.	talking in a language with deliberate transposition of words (*mlecchitavikalpa*)
47.	knowledge of local or provincial languages (*deśabhāṣāvijñāna*)
48.	making flower carriages (*puṣpaśakāṭaka*)
49.	knowledge of omens (*nimittajñāna*)
50.	constructing mechanical aids (*yantramātṛkā*)
51.	memory training (*dhāraṇamātṛkā*)
52.	game of group recitation (*sampāṭhya*)
53.	improvising poetry (*mānasi kāvyakriyā*)
54.	knowledge of dictionaries and thesauruses (*abhidhānakośa*)
55.	knowledge of prosody (*chandojñāna*)
56.	knowledge of poetics (*kriyākalpa*)
57.	art of impersonation (*chalitakayoga*)
58.	using clothes as disguise (*vastragopana*)
59.	various types of gambling (*dyūtaviśeṣa*)
60.	game of dice called akarsha (*ākarṣakrīḍā*)
61.	children's games (*bālakrīḍaṇakāni*)
62.	knowledge of the rules of modesty (*vainayikīnā*)
63.	knowledge of science of victory (*vaijayikīnā*)
64.	physical exercise (*vyāyāmikīnā*)

prosody; from games of every conceivable sort to preparing drinks and soups and teaching parrots and mynahs to speak. The *Kāmasūtra* recommends these arts to both men and women, and their acquisition was a badge of distinction among people of the court.[30] They were to be enjoyed at the gatherings (*goṣṭhi*s) which met either at court or in the households of prominent men and courtesans.[31] They were an integral aspect of courtship between men and women, and their enjoyment was a sign of general happiness – Bāṇa's *Kādambarī* depicts scores of *sāmanta*s in the outer courtyard of king Candrapīḍa's palace engaged in games and activities connected with the *kalā*s. The point is that sexual relations for the people of the court were part of a wider aestheticised lifestyle. It is perhaps no surprise then that the major discourses which took up and expanded much of the knowledge of the *Kāmasūtra* were increasingly treatises on drama and poetry.[32]

[30] Numerous inscriptions praise kings and courtiers for being 'proficient in the arts' (*kalā*s), often a pun as part of a larger comparison of the hero with the moon, the appearance of which occurred in stages or measurements called *kalā*s. For the Kadambas in the sixth century, see *EI* 8 (1905–6), no. 5, pp. 32–33; the Maukharis in the sixth century, *EI* 14 (1917–18), no. 5, p. 117; the Pāṇḍuvaṁśins in the seventh century, *ISPS*, vol. 2, no. 3.1, p. 97; the early Gurjaras in the seventh century, *CII* 4 (1955), vol. 1, no. 16, p. 60; and the Bhaumanākaras in the seventh century, *EI* 12 (1913–14), no. 13, p. 74.

[31] *KS* 1.4.35.

[32] This may in part explain the seeming attenuation of these wider concerns in the later handbooks on erotics, which focus more on sexual technique.

Courtly literature

The aestheticised lifestyles of the court have been attested most volubly by literary texts, which were produced and heard widely at the households of men of rank. This literature, known as *kāvya* ('ornate poetry' as either verse, prose or dramatic performance), became widespread at Indian courts during the Gupta period, and was to remain a great preoccupation in courtly circles for at least a millennium. Nearly all the early texts of the *kāvya* tradition were composed in courtly environments, including the verse-biography of the Buddha by the Buddhist monk Aśvaghoṣa composed at the Kuṣāṇa court and Hāla's anthology of short Prakrit poems attributed to a Sātavāhana king. They were soon followed by what must have been an explosion of poetic production from about the fourth century. Some of these works may be attributed to poets whose court affiliations are more or less certain, like Bāṇa (*c.* 600–50 CE), Mayūra (*c.* 600–50 CE), and Harṣa (606–47 CE) who flourished at the Puṣyabhūti/Vardhana court, and Kalidāsa (*c.* 400–50 CE?) who probably lived at the Gupta and/or Vākāṭaka courts, as well as others only probable in ascription, like Daṇḍin (*c.* 665–710 CE) and the author of the Trivandrum plays (*c.* 700 CE),[33] both of whom probably flourished at the Pallava court, and Viśākhadatta (*c.* 600 CE?) who may have resided at the Maukhari court. Beyond these are a number of poets whose dynastic ascription and date remain uncertain like Śyāmalika, (400–500 CE?), Viṣṇuśarman (*c.* 400–500 CE), Śūdraka (*c.* 400–600 CE?), Īśvaradatta (*c.* 400–600 CE?), and Bhartṛhari (*c.* 600–50 CE) – to name some of the most important.[34]

The rise of *kāvya* may also be documented effectively by its appearance and spread in inscriptions. While it had been common practice since Aśokan times for kings to record their orders and edicts in stone, in the first centuries of the Common Era these public orders came to be preceded by eulogistic descriptions of the king's attainments in poetic style.[35]

[33] On the authorship of the Trivandrum plays usually ascribed to Bhāsa, see Herman Tieken, 'On the So-called Trivandrum Plays Attributed to Bhāsa', *Wiener Zeitschrift für die Kunde Südasiens*, vol. 37 (1993), pp. 5–44. Tieken has convincingly argued that these plays should be dated to the court of the Pallava king Narasiṁhavarman II (690–720 CE).

[34] For an overview of other poets in this period, see A. K. Warder, *Indian Kāvya Literature*, vols. 3 and 4 (Delhi: Motilal Banarsidass, 1990, 1994).

[35] In the Aśokan inscriptions, the royal proclamation is usually preceded by the simple introduction 'thus speaks king Piyadasī, beloved of the gods' (*devānāṁpiye piyadasī lājā hevam āha*), see Rastogi, *Inscriptions of Aśoka*, p. 24 ff. The early post-Aśokan dynasties – the Ceṭis in Orissa in first century BCE and the Sātavāhanas in the Deccan and Śakas in western India in the second century CE – all introduce eulogistic introductions in their records. For these important inscriptions see the Hathigumpha inscription of the

The eulogistic portions preceding the orders of the Ceṭis (first century BCE), Sātavāhanas (second century CE) and particularly the Śakas (second century CE) are some of the first clearly datable specimens of *kāvya*, corroborated as such by the roughly contemporaneous appearance of the first longer literary texts of the *kāvya* tradition composed at these courts.[36] The co-appearance of inscriptions and literary texts between the second and fourth centuries of the Common Era is again significant, representing not a 'revival' or continuation of a long-standing tradition, but, as Sheldon Pollock has argued, the 'inauguration of a new cultural formation'.[37]

By Gupta times these eulogies had become even more elaborate, and often included descriptions of the donor's ancestors. This has made them invaluable sources for the reconstruction of political history. Their increasingly homogenous style and content reveals an important process from the vantage point of the social history we are tracing here. The stylistic convergence as well as geographical proliferation of inscriptional eulogies from the early centuries of the Common Era form our clearest evidence of the consolidation of the values and lifestyles embodied in 'high' literary texts. They point to the integration of local lords, landed men and urban élites into a common culture of 'worldliness' – a set of commensurable values and codes of meaning shared from one lordly household to the next – which had penetrated all nuclear regions in the subcontinent by the end of the seventh century.

This process of integration can be in part grasped by imagining the public 'performance' of these documents. They took the form of letters, dispatched from the king's camp to various destinations where they were eagerly awaited, received with respect (bowing, processing, etc . . .) by his own agents, local élites, arms-bearing men and learned beneficiaries, read aloud by the king's messengers, who prefaced them with eulogies (*praśasti*s) of the king's family. For those in attendance these announcements not only told the story of the king and his lineage with its particular events and themes, but did so in a luminous language whose form conveyed its own meaning as something sublime and exalted. In this way,

Ceṭi king Kharavela, *EI* 20 (1929–30), no.7, pp. 71–89; the Nasik inscription of the Sātavāhana king Vāsathiputa Pulamavi, *EI* 8 (1905–6), no. 8, p. 61 ff.; and the Junagadh rock inscription of the Śaka king Rudradāman, *EI* 8 (1905–6), no. 6, pp. 36–49.

[36] The close connection between literary texts and inscriptional eulogies was noticed first by George Bühler, who concluded that by the second century 'it was the custom at Indian courts to occupy oneself with *kāvya*', G. Bühler, 'The Indian Inscriptions and the Antiquity of Indian Artificial Poetry', *IA* 42 (1913), pp. 192–3; and D. C. Sircar, 'Kāvya Style in Post-Sātavāhana Epigraphs' in D. C. Sircar, *Studies in the Yuga Purana and Other Texts* (Delhi: Oriental Publishers, 1974), pp. 61–8.

[37] Sheldon Pollock, 'The Cosmopolitan Vernacular, *JAS*, vol. 57, no. 1 (1998), p. 10.

royal *praśasti*s, even if not fully comprehensible to all, still formed a spectacular communicative idiom, dramatically enacted by men of the court, which no doubt contributed greatly to the spread of the courtly ethos among men whose fortunes might someday raise them to prominence.

The viability and coherence of this cultural formation was in part facilitated by the rise of Sanskrit as a lingua franca for royal courts in the first centuries of the Common Era. The first clear incidences seem to have been the Śakas and Kūṣāṇas in north-western and central India who patronised Sanskrit as a language of literary expression and administrative protocol (as opposed to their southern contemporaries, the Sātavāhanas, who continued to use Prakrit). By the fourth century, under the Guptas and other royal houses, this process reached its completion, with Sanskrit becoming the dominant language in both literary expression and public proclamation, a status it would enjoy for nearly a millennium, when it was partially supplanted by Persian and regional languages.[38]

The rise of the highly ornate and regularised language of Sanskrit *kāvya* as the preferred idiom of communication at court presupposed not only the benefits of grammar, but rhetoric and metrics as well. Some of these concerns were addressed by the first handbook or manual on aesthetics, probably assembled in early Gupta times. This sprawling and highly composite treatise, the *Nāṭyaśāstra*, reveals the existence of several discrete fields of knowledge and training required for the composition of literary and dramatic works – including knowledge of metrical patterns, stage and theatre techniques, figures of speech and aesthetic sentiment.[39] By the seventh century, many of these topics had been taken up individually in manuals and treatises. The famous word lexicon of Amarasiṁha,

[38] Sheldon Pollock has demonstrated exhaustively how Sanskrit overtook Prakrit as a courtly language throughout the subcontinent and beyond by the middle of the fourth century CE: Pollock, 'The Sanskrit Cosmopolis', pp. 195–217. For a more gradualist linguistic account, see Richard Salomon, *Indian Epigraphy: A Guide to the Study of Inscriptions in Sanskrit, Prakrit, and the Other Indo-Aryan Languages* (New York: Oxford University Press, 1999), pp. 81–94.

[39] The *Nāṭyaśāstra* has had an extremely problematic chronology, being compiled from a number of different sources. P. V. Kane argues that some work similar in structure to the present text existed by 300 CE. S. K. De assigns the *sūtra* parts of the text to the last few centuries BCE, and the *kārikā* text to as late as the eighth century CE. Particularly convincing is D. C. Sircar's review of geographical and intertextual evidence which would place the current text, in both recensions, no earlier than the Gupta period. Most recently, S. A. Srinivasan has demonstrated definitively that the text represents an unmediated and irreducibly heterogenous compilation. P. V. Kane, *A History of Sanskrit Poetics* (Delhi: Motilal Banarsidass, 1971), p. 47; Edwin Gerow, *Indian Poetics*, vol. V, fasc. 3 of J. Gonda, ed., *A History of Indian Literature* (Wiesbaden: Otto Harrassowitz 1977), p. 225, n. 34; S. K. De, *Studies in the History of Sanskrit Poetics*, vol. I (London: Luzac, 1923), pp. 32–6; Sircar, *Studies in the Yuga Purāṇa*, pp. 17–24, 55–60; S. A. Srinivasan, *On the Composition of the Nāṭyaśāstra* (Reinbek: Verlag für Orientalistische Fachpublikationen, 1980).

the *Nāmaliṅgānuśāsana* (or *Amarakośa*), with its lists of synonyms for use in the new metrical contexts of formal poetry, was compiled in the late Gupta period (*c.* 500–50 CE) and the influential manual on rhetoric and style in poetic composition, the 'Mirror of Poetry' (*Kāvyādarśa*), was written by Daṇḍin (665–710 CE) at the turn of the seventh century.[40] Many of the concerns of these treatises, particularly those on rhetoric and poetic composition, were shared by manuals on politics and governance. The *Arthaśāstra*'s discussion, for example, of the faults and merits in the composition of a royal order, seems to borrow much from the emerging tradition of Sanskrit poetics and rhetoric.[41] Conversely, the early manuals on poetics show a nascent but marked emphasis on the social attributes of both the poet and the spectator as refined persons of noble birth and exalted qualities. Together, then, the sources suggest the existence of a relatively restricted political community with commonly held conventions of speech, in which formalised rhetoric provided the standard of effective communication.

Judging from the texts, Sanskrit was to form an integral part of the education of those of noble rank and high birth, and was a prerequisite for acquiring the worldly knowledge of the *śāstras*. It was typically barred for women, menials and the low-born, who in Sanskrit dramas speak in various 'Prakrit' (unrefined, or natural) languages. Though it is difficult, if not impossible, to ascertain the real extent of literacy among the men of the court, the voluminous epigraphic and literary output from Gupta times suggests that rudimentary knowledge of the language was widespread among the upper echelons of the court. Reading and writing in the language were also distinct and valued skills – reading from books was one of the sixty-four arts (see table 2.1, no. 31) to be mastered by the *nāgaraka* and learning letters (*lipi*), according to the *Arthaśāstra*, was to be mastered by the king as an infant.[42] The king was to surround himself with men capable in the language – counsellors, panegyrists and poets, not to mention priests, astrologers and others familiar with religious rituals.

[40] The *Amarakośa* was followed in the tenth century by the *Abhidānaratnamālā* of Halāyuddha (*c.* 950–1000 CE) who was associated with the Rāṣṭrakūṭa and Paramāra courts. From the eleventh century this literature expands rapidly. See Claus Vogel, *Indian Lexicography*, vol. v, fasc. 4 of J. Gonda, ed., *A History of Indian Literature* (Wiesbaden: Otto Harrassowitz, 1979). In rhetoric and poetic composition, Daṇḍin was followed by Bhāmaha (*c.* 725–50 CE) and Vāmana (*c.* 780–810 CE). For a reliable summary discussion of the chronology of these authors, see D. K. Gupta, *A Critical Study of Daṇḍin and his Works* (Delhi: Meharchand Lachhmandas, 1970).

[41] See *AS* 2.10.1 ff. For a discussion of Kauṭilya's terminology in relation to the works of Bhāmaha and Daṇḍin, see Raghavan, *Bhoja's Śṛṅgāraprakāśa*, pp. 212–14.

[42] *AS* 1.5.7. Kālidāsa says that the prince Raghu 'entered into literature by learning to write correctly the way one enters the ocean through the mouth of a river', *RghV* 3.28. *AS* 1.5.7 says that the prince should learn letters (*lipi*) after his tonsure ceremony.

The inscriptions themselves provide interesting evidence, as they typically involved the work of several men who performed distinctly different tasks, often with varying degrees of literacy – one who composed the eulogy, one who drafted the grant and wrote it on bark or palm leaf and/or the surface onto which it was to be copied, and finally one who engraved the document onto some permanent material like copper or stone.[43] While the last of these tasks was almost entirely manual and was usually performed by an artisan, the others were often performed by titled men and required some degree of literacy. Grants from the fifth century claim to have been written not only by scribes and record keepers, who themselves sometimes held royal titles, but also by princes, and very often 'ministers of peace and war' (*mahāsandhivigrahaka*).[44] The last of these titles is perhaps particularly important, for these men, who were in charge of the diplomatic affairs of kings with other courts, needed to be in a sense both fluent and literate in Sanskrit, for they were responsible for having the eulogies which contained the titles, rituals and military conquests of the king made 'public'; and no doubt were also responsible for being aware of the claims made by rival kings. Somadevasuri, author of the tenth-century 'Nectar of Sayings on Polity' (*Nītivākyāmṛta*), composed at the court of a Rāṣṭrakūṭa vassal, exhorts the king to 'ignore no one's writing, as writing formed the basis of war and alliance and all the affairs of the kingdom'.[45]

This brings us to the authors of the royal eulogies themselves, who were sometimes men of high rank at court, like Hariṣeṇa, composer of the Allahabad eulogy, but were just as often court poets or panegyrists whose sole function was to eulogise the king. In all cases, such men enjoyed royal patronage and favour. Though the genre of the poetic eulogy, or *praśasti* as it is sometimes called in inscriptions, was not taken up extensively in the

43 These tasks were designated in Sanskrit by the roots (*vi-*) √*rac*, to compose, (*vi-* or *ul-*) √*likh*, to write, and *ut-* √*kṝ* or (*ni-*) √*khan*, to engrave. See the remarks of J. F. Fleet in *CII* 3 (1888), p. 99n, and Salomon, *Indian Epigraphy*, pp. 65–6.

44 For typical specimens, see the early fifth-century grant of the Māṭhara king Umavarman, written by a record keeper (*deśākṣapaṭalādhikṛta*), who in a later grant is also called a military retainer (*daṇḍanāyaka*), *EI* 12 (1913–14), no. 2, pp. 4–6 and *EI* 28 (1949–50), no. 31, pp. 175–9; the early sixth-century inscription of Vainyagupta written by a scribe (*kāyastha*), also called a minister of peace and war, *IHQ* (March 1930), pp. 45–60; the sixth-century inscription of the Kadamba king Mṛgeśavarman, written by a general (*senāpati*), *IA* 7 (1878), pp. 37–8; the early seventh-century grants of the Gurjara king Jayabhaṭa III written by numerous military commanders (*bālādhikṛta*), *CII* 4 (1955), vol. 1, nos. 21–4, p. 90 ff; and the early seventh-century inscription of the Paṇḍuvaṁsin king Indrarāja written by a prince (*rājaputra*), *ISPS*, vol. 2, Appendix, pp. 86–92. Records written down by the minister of peace and war, or men who served him, were very common. See the fifth-century grants of the Parivrājakas and kings of Uccakalpa, *CII* 3 (1888), nos. 21–30.

45 *NiV* 32.30.

aesthetic treatises which appear from the Gupta period, there can be no question that these panegyrists participated in the same literary culture as the more famous poets known from longer literary works. They often emulated their style, and occasionally even boasted of similar skill, as when Ravikīrti, author of the famous Aihole inscription of Pulakeśin II, claimed to have attained the fame of Kālidāsa and Bhāravi.[46] It is significant that they constitute by far the largest genre of Sanskrit *kāvya* (in point of numbers of surviving specimen), with thousands being recovered from copperplates, temple walls, pillars and rock faces from Gupta times.

These eulogies were essentially praise poems which recounted the deeds and accomplishments of emperors, subordinate kings and courtiers, as well as their families. Their voluminous number from Gupta times points to one of the most important entities which men of standing sought to attain – 'fame' (*kīrti*, *yaśas*). Reference to the fame of kings is ubiquitous in the eulogies and in courtly poetry as a whole, where it is typically imagined as a sort of substance – a bright, white, spotless light, like the moon, 'covering the world' like a canopy and spreading beyond the oceans. It has been pointed out by scholars that ruling families legitimated their power by employing pliant court poets to invent fabulous genealogies and royal pedigrees. What has been less recognised, however, is the dynamic and dialectical relationship that praise had with power in the courtly context, and the degree to which the quest for fame served to structure the ambitions of men even after having attained power. Indeed, it is difficult to overestimate the importance of fame as a social attribute for the nobility in early medieval India. It was 'reputation' which enabled aspiring lords to draw men to their households, and courtiers to make careers for themselves at court – it seems to have been one of the key mechanisms of social mobility within the world of the court. The nobility saw fame as one of the most desirable attributes a man, or indeed a family, could acquire and possess. This fame was most effectively attained by having one's accomplishments and virtues proclaimed and celebrated by songs and eulogies which circulated in the circles of the good. As the Bhitari pillar inscription of Skandagupta puts it, the celebration of the king's way of living, in songs and panegyrics, raised him to the dignity of an *ārya*.[47] Praise was visibly memorialised by being inscribed on permanent materials, like stones, pillars and plates. A sixth-century pillar

[46] *EI* 6 (1900–1), no. 1, p. 12. On inscriptional emulation of Kalidāsa's *Meghadūta*, see Disalker, 'Indian Epigraphical Literature', *JIH*, vol. 37, no. 3 (1959), p. 330; for Śyāmalika, see G. H. Schokker and P. J. Worsley, *Pādatāḍitaka of Śyāmalika*, vol. I (Dordrecht: D. Reidel, 1966), pp. 13–18; for Bāṇa , see Salomon, *Indian Epigraphy*, p. 235.

[47] *CII* 3 (1981), no. 31, p. 316.

inscription of the Aulikāra king Yaśodharman says that the king had the pillar erected to celebrate his own fame as if it were an arm of the Earth extended to write upon the surface of the moon of his excellent qualities and his birth in a family worthy of praise.[48] Eulogies were often compared to garlands or ornaments offered in devotion to make brilliant the reputations of their patrons.[49]

Yet the poetic dimensions of speech at court far exceeded the demands of praise and eulogy. Literary accomplishment was central to aristocratic and urbane existence as a whole, and among the sixty-four arts to be mastered by the townsman/courtier were prosody, dramaturgy, poetic vocabulary, figures of speech and composition (table 2.1, nos. 32, 53–6) as well as various games (table 2.1, nos. 28–31, 33) which perfected these skills. Numerous inscriptions praise nobles and kings as being accomplished in the composition and enjoyment of *kāvya*.[50] Literary taste formed a topic of discussion and poetic contests were frequently conducted at *kavigoṣṭhīs* in the royal household.[51] Vast numbers of free-floating verses from later medieval times celebrated the poetic renown of key courts, like that of the famous Paramāra king Bhoja, and suggest a vibrant oral context for the literary culture of *kāvya*.

Such verses, however, called *subhāṣita*s (literally 'well-spoken'), first appear in large numbers during early medieval times, when they were incorporated into longer prose works like the *Pañcatantra* or collected in treasuries like Bhartṛhari's famous seventh-century anthology, the *Subhāṣitatriśati*. It is clear from such literary contexts that these verses were to be remembered and recited to provide moral guidance, impart instruction and facilitate discussion. This performative aspect of poetry formed an integral part of the collective life of the court. The composition, exchange and quotation of poems punctuated nearly every aspect of daily life. Not only did kings assert political claims in poetic language, but ministers communicated in verse and supplicants won the attention and favour of kings through the composition and recitation of verses in the assembly.

48 The poet ends by remarking 'these verses were composed by Vāsula, son of Kakka, out of a desire to please this king of good deeds', *CII* 3 (1888), no. 33, p. 147.

49 See the seventh-century Nidhanpur plates of Bhāskaravarman of Assam in which the poet says that the king is adorned by the ornament of fame composed of flowers which were words of praise, *EI* 12 (1913–14), no. 13, p. 75.

50 The Junagadh rock inscription, for example, calls the Śaka king Rudradāman the author of clear, agreeable, sweet, charming and ornamented prose and verse (*gadyapadya*), and the Allahabad pillar inscription of Hariṣeṇa depicts King Samudragupta as a man whose poetry was superlative, *EI* 8 (1905–6), no. 6, p. 44; *CII* 3 (1981), no. 1, p. 212.

51 Rājaśekhara's ninth-century *Kāvyamīmāṃsā* (10.21+) describes a meeting of poets, or *kavigoṣṭhī*, to be held in an assembly hall within the palace and presided over by the king.

Kāvya literature was thus intimately connected to the 'representative publicity' discussed in the previous chapter. The aesthetic dimension of such language, far from being in excess to utilitarian utterance, was its very mark as an exalted and appropriate communicative idiom – and must be seen as an analogue to the rational public discussion which Habermas and others have reserved for the modern public sphere. As the most valued and persuasive form of communication between men at court, poetic speech naturally developed a large supporting literature concerned with rules for the classification of its genres and sub-genres, appraising its virtues and faults, setting its modalities through the enumeration of verbal figures of speech. This literature, known as *alaṁkāraśāstra*, resembled closely what may be more familiar as rhetoric in classical and medieval Europe. The orientation of this entire system was to a simultaneously aestheticised and exalted form of communication at court.

Rather than seeing the authors of the *subhāṣita*s and minor poets (*kavi*s) who composed mostly eulogies as legitimators of royal authority, it makes more sense to see them as forming a class of 'organic intellectuals' for the court, representing and reflecting upon, more or less critically, its values, aspirations and tensions. The worldly training of the poet, according to the texts on poetics which emerged from Gupta times, was to be comprehensive, including not only the study of grammar, prosody and figures of speech, but music, logic, the sciences of *kāma* and *artha*, as well as various martial skills.[52] In short, the poet was to be familiar with and embody the conventions of courtly life. And to the extent that all men at court were to aspire towards accomplishment in public utterance, proficiency in poetry was the *sine qua non* of courtly existence.

Education and the pursuit of virtue

Despite the voluminous prescriptive and didactic literature that has survived from medieval times, we know very little about the education of the people of the court – how and to what extent they acquired the vast worldly knowledge we have reviewed briefly above. Both the *Kāmasūtra* and the *Arthaśāstra* place the acquisition of their own knowledge within the context of the training which a twice-born man was to undertake as a child.[53] This entailed, at least according to the *Arthaśāstra*'s recommendation for the prince, instruction in four spheres of application: reflective

[52] See, for example, Vāmana's *Kāvyālaṁkāra* 1.3.8–9, 11.

[53] See the remarks at *AS* 1.5.7–8 and *KS* 1.2.1–6 and comm. After his tonsure at the age of one or three, the child was taught the alphabet and how to count, and later entered the state of *brahmacārin* with the thread investiture that marked him as a full member of a twice-born estate; he was to remain celibate until his studies were complete at the age of sixteen. The *Kd* mentions that Prince Candrāpīḍa entered his education at six and completed it at sixteen.

examination (*anvīkṣikī*), Vedic knowledge (*trayī*), livelihood (*vārtta*) and politics (*daṇḍanīti*).[54] The most central among these, according to the *Arthaśāstra*, was *anvīkṣikī*, which helped men develop powers of discrimination necessary for learning and application in general, and was therefore known as the 'lamp of all learning'.[55] The most extensive, and probably the most substantively open-ended of the four was the Veda, which in the *Arthaśāstra's* definition meant not only the traditionally accepted sacrificial knowledge known as the triple Veda, the more controversial lore on remedial and injurious rites known as the *Atharvaveda*, and the contested collections of miscellaneous traditions known as the *Itihāsaveda*, but a set of subsidiary disciplines meant to support the Veda, which included phonetics, grammar, rituals, etymology, prosody and astronomy.[56] The knowledge of livelihood included, as we have seen above, those ways by which men gained wealth and *daṇḍanīti* constituted the advice on rule, deemed necessary for all other aspirations. This latter knowledge, to the extent that it was embodied in the *Arthaśāstra*, was deemed important enough to be included, along with *dharmaśāstra*, in the category of the Veda itself.[57] In addition to or within the purview of these larger subjects were discrete fields like familiarity with horses, elephants, chariots and weaponry, and proficiency in the sixty-four *kalā*s or arts.[58]

Though the *Arthaśāstra* and *Kāmasūtra* at one level portray themselves as knowledge for a putative 'protagonist', the *nāgaraka* in the case of the *Kāmasūtra* and the king in the case of the *Arthaśāstra*, they also contain sections directed towards other men and women at court, including wives, princesses, courtesans, ministers, princes and courtiers.[59] This diversity of perspective suggests several things. First, the knowledges themselves were less like set 'textbooks' to be mastered by students, and more like open-ended traditions of knowledge, what one scholar has called 'multicentric' treatises.[60] Their knowledge could be disaggregated as necessary. Second, the knowledge contained within them was probably only rarely mastered in its entirety by any one person. Those with more complete knowledge were no doubt high-ranking counsellors who taught the *śāstra*s

54 *AS* 1.2.1. 55 *AS* 1.2.11–12. 56 *AS* 1.3.1ff.

57 The *dharmaśāstra* and *Arthaśāstra* are included in *AS* 1.5.14 among elements of the *itihāsaveda*. As some manuscripts omit the *Arthaśāstra* from this list, Kangle (vol. II, p. 11 n.) regards the verse as a later interpolation, of unspecified date. On its ideological significance, see below.

58 *AS* 1.5.12. For the king's daily training in the *kalā*s, see *NiS* 1.64.

59 Large parts of book four of the *Kāmasūtra*, for example, seem to be addressed to the wives of the élite household and the whole of the sixth book is addresssed explicitly to courtesans. Likewise the fourth and fifth chapters of book five of the *Arthaśāstra* contain recommendations for courtiers.

60 Thomas Trautmann, *Dravidian Kinship* (Cambridge University Press, 1981), p. 361.

to men during their youth. Indeed, it would not be implausible to suggest that the knowledge of the *śāstra*s was designed more for the advisers of their chief protagonists than for the protagonists themselves. It is these men who, after all, were expected to advise them after their formal education was complete, as *mantrin*s in the political arena and *viṭa*s and *pīṭhamarda*s in matters of love. In the case of the king's counsellors, they were to 'bear the burden' of rule, and to ensure continuous sovereignty in the kingdom from one generation to the next, even if it entailed ruling through weak or immature princes who came to the throne in times of dynastic misfortune.

Formal education was always shaped through the teacher-student (*guruśiṣya*) relationship. Knowledge of the *śāstra* was thought to be best acquired through the instruction of a learned teacher, who was accorded the highest respect and devotion by his pupils.[61] Indeed, submission to one's teacher was the first and most important lesson in the student's education.[62] For the twice-born male, the thread ceremony (*upanayana*) initiated the youth into studenthood within the household of a teacher. Study was rarely solitary. In the case of the court, princes were often trained together with the sons of subordinate kings and ministers, as companionship from youth was seen as an effective way to generate loyalty from one generation to the next.[63] Training typically took place outside of the royal residence, either in the house of a teacher or in a palace or camp especially designed for this purpose. Bāṇa's seventh-century prose romance *Kādambarī* provides an explicit account of the training of King Tārāpīḍa's son, the Prince Candrāpīḍa. When Candrāpīḍa was six years old, Tārāpīḍa had him placed in a strongly fortified and guarded 'palace of learning' built outside the royal city, where teachers in all the sciences were gathered. Candrāpīḍa was joined in study by a retinue composed of the sons of his teachers as well as Vaiśampāyana, his childhood friend and son of the kingdom's chief counsellor, Śukanāsa. He was trained in this palace with his companions for ten years, being frequently visited by his father. He was instructed in a range of knowledges similar to what we find in the *Kāmasūtra* and *Arthaśāstra* – logic, law, royal policy, composition and metrics, the use of books and various types of writing, stories and poetry, *itihāsa* (epics) and the Purāṇas, other languages, the use of various weapons (bow, sword, spear, mace, axe and shield), driving chariots, riding and caring for horses and elephants, musical instruments, dancing,

[61] *NiS* 1.62. [62] See *NiS* 1.61–2, 69–70.

[63] According to Kālidāsa, the Prince Raghu entered his education along with the sons of King Dilīpa's ministers (*amātyaputra*), *RghV* 3.28. For debates on this matter regarding the future role of one's study mates (*sahādhyāyin*) at court, see *AS* 1.8.1 ff.

painting, leaf-cutting, gambling, knowledge of omens and astronomy, architecture, carpentry, gem-testing, etc . . .[64]

Teachers of śāstric learning during the prince's youth were probably drawn either from the court's retainers or the large reserve of literate brahmins supported by the royal household through defrayed tax revenues. In addition, the leading men and women of the court and city could gain instruction from household menials, miscellaneous companions as well as various semi-itinerant and independent teachers.[65] Knowledge of *kāma* could be learned by a maiden, for example, from the daughter of a nurse brought up with her, the daughter of her mother's sister, an older female servant, a companion, a mendicant woman (*bhikṣukī*) who had knowledge of pleasure from her previous life, or her own elder sister.[66] The *nāgaraka* and courtesan could learn of *kāma* and its allied knowledges from one another, from conversation at the *goṣṭhī*, or from men called *pīṭhamarda*s whom they met there, itinerants who made their living by teaching (*upadeśa*) various 'arts'.[67]

There were a number of ways in which education at court extended beyond formal training as a youth. Indeed, śāstric training was never enough for the men of the court. Śukanāsa, in his famous words to Candrāpīḍa in Bāṇa's *Kādambarī*, explains that 'though cleansed by the *śāstra*s, the youthful mind can lose its purity'.[68] Men were exhorted to associate themselves with 'good people', particularly those who were learned (*vidvān*) and older (*vṛddha*). This, according to Kāmandaka, ensured continual success in all one's undertakings.[69] For the prince/king, such association took the form of a personal preceptor (*rājaguru*), whom he continued to honour throughout his adult life, as well as a larger cadre of ministers, who provided instruction in supplementary skills and counsel on various policy matters.[70] The benefits of association were important for all men of rank, and Bāṇa's account of his life as a young man, after he had finished his formal education, is indicative of its role. Having fallen into disreputable company, Bāṇa was able to regain his standing in the world not only by continued service at the houses of teachers,

[64] See the extended description in *Kd*, pp. 126–7.

[65] Bāṇa mentions serving at the houses of teachers (*gurukula*) among the acts which regained him his wisdom and reputation, see *HC*, ch. 1, pp. 19–20.

[66] *KS* 1.3.15.

[67] *KS* 1.2. 13; 1.4.44. Although not strictly teachers, the *viṭa* and *vidūṣaka* (*KS* 1.4.45–46) could also take on didactic functions. The *viṭa*'s advisory role on the ways of courtesans is known from the *bhāṇa* monologue plays. Yaśodhara says that the *vidūṣaka* may on occasion reprimand (*apavadata*) the *nāgaraka* or the courtesan.

[68] *Kd*, p. 167. [69] *NiS* 1.61 ff.

[70] See *NiS* 1.70, *passim*. It is significant that Śukanāsa, who advises Prince Candrāpīḍa on the dangers of courtly life, is his father's chief counsellor.

but by observing royal houses of elevated conduct, attending associations (*goṣṭhīs*) of good men which were full of worthy discussions, and entering into the circles (*maṇḍala*) of the clever.[71]

For young men of the court, such associations were important in part to guide them through the trials they faced as they were integrated into formal service at court. Men of both ministerial and princely rank took part in battle, where they sought to prove themselves before their superiors, and were also subjected to tests (*parīkṣā*) by secret agents of the king to measure their accomplishment, judgement and susceptibility to various temptations, particularly those of concupiscence and disloyalty.[72]

But what such tests sought in part to measure, and what the courtly 'education' to inculcate, was not conceived merely as a set of 'professional competences', but an array of moral perfections. The terms used to designate the men of the court which were noted at the beginning of this chapter all had strong moral connotation, and a very visible ethical thread runs through the whole of courtly discourses – prescriptive, didactic and aesthetic. The tests recommended in the *Arthaśāstra* for courtiers and princes sought to measure the 'virtues' and 'faults' of a man in relation to *artha*, *dharma* and *kāma*. The *Arthaśāstra* sets out lists of virtuous qualities or perfections (*guṇa*, *saṃpad*) to be possessed by ministers, counsellors and kings.[73] Inscriptional eulogies routinely commend the virtuousness of kings, royal families, queens and dependants with phrases like 'abode of royal virtues'[74], 'having virtues extending to the four ends of the Earth'[75], 'having an overflow of a multitude of virtues'[76] and 'possessing

[71] *HC*, ch. 1, pp. 19–20.

[72] See the discussion in *AS* 1.17.28–41. These tests were continuous with open and secret methods of ascertaining the qualities of other royal servants, *AS* 1.9.3 and 1.10.1 ff. Various sources mention princes and courtiers successfully passing all such 'tests'. See, for example, the Junagadh rock inscription of Skandagupta, where after suggesting that the goddess of sovereignty looked into the virtues and faults of Prince Skandagupta before selecting him, also mentions that the qualities of the courtier, Cakrapālita, were tested by his own father, who himself had been found pure in tests of honesty at his master's court. *CII* 3 (1981), no. 28, p. 300. Also, Bāṇa remarks that the later Gupta princes Kumāragupta and Mādhavagupta were found by frequent tests to be free from any faults, *HC*, ch. 4, p. 138.

[73] For qualities of *amātya* and *mantrin*, distinguished by the degree of their possession of virtues, and performance in tests in relation to *dharma*, *kāma* and *artha*, see *AS* 1.8.26; 1.9.1; for the king, *AS* 6.1.2–6; and for qualities of the other constituents of the kingdom, *AS* 6.1.8 ff.

[74] *nṛpatiguṇaniketa*: mid-fifth-century CE inscription of Skandagupta at Junagadh, *CII* 3 (1981), no. 28, p. 300.

[75] *caturaṁtaluṭhitaguṇopahita*: first-century BCE inscription of the Ceḍi king Kharavela of Orissa, *EI* 20 (1929–30), no. 7, p. 79.

[76] *anekaguṇaganotsiktibhiḥ*: late-fourth-century CE inscription of Samudragupta at Allahabad, *CII* 3 (1981), no. 1, p. 213.

ever expanding circles of virtues'.[77] Gupta and post-Gupta inscriptions contain hundreds of variations on this theme – the possession of 'good qualities' by members of the court.

According to the didactic texts, men of the court were to live by their virtues and their presence in a man's character was essential for the development of his career. In the words of a twelfth-century Candella inscription praising a minister who had risen to the post of chief counsellor, 'virtues cause men to prosper'.[78] Damanaka, the jackal-minister of the *Pañcatantra* who wishes to move from the periphery to the inner circles of the royal court, is even more explicit on this point – 'what helps a man to earn a livelihood (*vṛtti*), what prompts good men to praise (*praśasyate*) him at court (*sadasi*) – that virtue (*guṇa*) should be guarded and enhanced (*vivardhanīyas*) by its possessor'.[79] This is why we may conceive of the training of the prince and his courtiers as having a particularly strong 'ethical' dimension.

In order to appreciate what this ethics entailed for men of the court, it is necessary to confront two problems, both of which become apparent from the meaning of the word generally used to denote virtue, *guṇa*. While on the one hand this term had the sense of a 'good quality' or virtue (being opposed to *doṣa*, or fault), it also denoted any innate characteristic, and thus shared the sense of both value and being. In this connection, *guṇa* referred to any one of three innate 'substances' which constituted the cosmos: darkness/inertia (*tamas*), activity (*rajas*), and lucidity/goodness (*sattva*). These categories were at once ontological and moral. Though they were present in each individual, their relative balance differed depending on birth. Activity was preponderant in the *kṣatriya* class, goodness in the brahmin and darkness and inertia in the *vaiśya*.[80] The predominance of a *guṇa* manifested itself through particular symptoms, or 'marks' (*lakṣaṇa*s). The dominance of activity (*rajas*), for example, was marked by pleasure in enterprise, instability, indulgence

[77] *vicaradguṇendvaṃśamaṇḍalam*: early-sixth-century grant of the Kadamba king Kakusthavarman, *EI* 8 (1905–6), no. 5, p. 31.

[78] *EI* 1 (1892), no. 25ii, p. 211.

[79] *PT* 1.26. When Piṅgalaka the lion-king is persuaded by Damanaka to revoke his favours and friendship with Saṁjīvaka the bull, he laments that 'once one has acclaimed a man in court (*saṁsadi*) as possessed of virtue (*guṇavat*), one cannot, while keeping to the promise of his word, declare him devoid of virtue (*nairguṇya*)', *PT* 1.77. This is no doubt because not breaking one's word was a virtue that a king must possess.

[80] *MDh* 12.24 ff. For the prehistory of these ascriptions, see Brian Smith, *Classifying the Universe: The Ancient Indian Varṇa System and the Origins of Caste* (New York: Oxford University Press, 1994), pp. 29–30. Śūdras, along with barbarians, elephants, boars and tigers, together form the middle level of existence to which a life dominated by inertia and lassitude leads, *MDh* 12.43.

in sensual objects and continually straying from one's objective.[81] These were the 'natural' problems, as it were, of aristocratic class. Overall, this thinking sanctioned a hierarchical division of social ranks; each man, based on his birth, was possessed of a certain inner constitution, appropriate to a proper code of behaviours (*svadharma*). The brahmin, being wise, was to teach; the *kṣatriya*, being powerful, was to protect; the *vaiśya*, being ignorant, was to produce; and the *śūdra*, being lowly, was to serve.[82]

It might be tempting to conclude that this conceptual system fostered a behavioural determinism which precluded ethical agency altogether.[83] But it must also be remembered that forms of determinism have often co-existed in close conceptual proximity with notions of ethical free will. People rather easily maintain that *x* is naturally or inherently good, while at the same time maintaining that *x* exercises agency in performing good actions.[84] In ancient India we find discourses about 'innate' qualities juxtaposed quite comfortably with those urging ethical transformation. Such forms of internal agency presupposed the possession of inherent qualities, but they were not wholly reducible to or determined by them.[85] In discussing the training of the prince, Kauṭilya remarks that 'discipline is both acquired (*kṛtaka*) and inborn (*svābhāvika*), for training disciplines suitable stuff (*dravya*), not that which is unsuitable (*adravya*)'.[86] Somadevasuri puts it more elaborately: 'good men do not install on the throne a prince who is not cultivated through preparation (*saṁskāra*), even if born in a noble family, for he is like an unpolished jewel'.[87] So while the prince's natural qualities differentiated him from those of lower birth, their presence could not be presupposed and required cultivation.

Such remarks point to an important aspect of courtly ethics. Moral action was not simply a matter of following rules and ethical norms, but also in developing an ethical *sensibility*. In addition to providing straightforward advice, significant portions of the treatises on *artha* and *kāma*

81 *MDh* 12.32.

82 *MDh* 1.87–91; *Baudhāyanadharmasūtra* 1.10.18.1–6; *AS* 1.3.6–8.

83 For this approach, see McKim Marriot, 'Hindu Transactions: Diversity without Dualism', in Bruce Kapferer, ed., *Transaction and Meaning: Directions in the Anthropology of Exchange and Symbolic Behaviour* (Philadelphia: Institute for the Study of Human Issues, 1976), pp. 108–33.

84 The more frequent attribution is in the negative. Some in our society would maintain, for example, that certain racial groups display lawless characteristics rooted in biological essence, but at the same time would argue that particular acts on the part of such agents should be accountable as moral actions.

85 In one sense, the doctrine of transmigration sutured these two discourses. Being born at a certain rank was a function of one's previous actions. It set parameters and conditions, but it also enjoined a certain ethical agency within those conditions.

86 *AS* 1.5.3–4. See also *NiV* 5.36.

87 *NiV* 5.32. He later remarks that well-imparted education to princes does not vitiate birth and prosperity, *NiV* 24.73.

present a more complex picture, setting out differing viewpoints on a matter, outlining expedients and regional differences. In such cases, they functioned in a 'subjectivising' manner, to borrow a phrase of Michel Foucault, enjoining individuals to constitute themselves as 'subjects' of ethical conduct, to act with reflection and discrimination.[88] It is perhaps this reason why courtly love and political policy became the chief topics of a vast tradition of free-floating didactic verses and story traditions which grew up and circulated at courts from the fifth century. Two of the earliest and most prominent of these collections were Viṣṇuśarman's collection of exemplary tales on the five topics of policy, the *Pañcatantra*, and Bhartṛhari's collection of centads on love, policy and renunciation known as the *Śubhāṣitatriśati*. The stories of the *Pañcatantra* were illustrative narratives for princes and ministers at court in various topics of policy – on securing allies, causing dissension among them, peace and war, losing one's advantage and impetuous action.[89]

The narrative portions of the *Pañcatantra*, like the prose of the *śāstras*, were interspered with pithy verses which captured the spirit of an ethical principle either through apt summation, verbal conceit or exemplary embodiment. Vast numbers of these verses circulated individually or in groups among the people of the court, and were eventually collected into anthologies or treasuries from the seventh century.[90] When occurring in expository or narrative settings, they are usually prefaced with some phrase like 'as it is said' (*ukta*). Such citations, like the anthologies themselves, suggest a second order reflection upon ethical issues. They also suggest that such verses were recalled orally in conversation, discussion and debate among educated men and point to the dialogical aspects of courtly ethics.[91] They also suggest what is explicit from other evidence – that the ethics of the court had a markedly 'public' or 'communal'

[88] See Michel Foucault, *The Use of Pleasure*, vol. II of *The History of Sexuality* (New York: Vintage, 1985), pp. 25–32; also Michel Foucault, 'Technologies of the Self', in Luther Martin, *et al.*, eds., *Technologies of the Self: A Seminar with Michel Foucault* (Amherst: University of Massachusetts Press, 1988).

[89] The full title of the work has been reconstructed as *Nītipañcatantrākhyāyika*, or 'the vignettes relating to the five topics on polity' by George Artola, 'The Title: Pañcatantra', *Wiener Zeitschrift für die Kunde des Morgenlandes* 52 (1955), pp. 380–5. The final word of this title, *ākhyāyika*, referring to a genre of short didactic narrative, appears in the *Arthaśāstra*, as a component of *itihāsa*, which, along with the knowledge of the *Arthaśāstra* itself, was to be studied by the prince. See *AS* 1.5.14.

[90] See Ludwik Sternbach, *Subhāṣita, Gnomic and Didactic Literature*, pp. 4–7 ff.

[91] These verses, which form one species of a larger group of free-floating verses known as *subhāṣitas*, point to a crucial oral element of the 'literary' culture current both at royal courts and *goṣṭhīs*. For an introduction to the oral elements of late medieval literary cultures in south India treating similar independent verses known as *cāṭus*, see the introduction and afterword to Velcheru Narayana Rao and David Shulman, *A Poem at the Right Moment: Remembered Verses from Premodern South India* (Berkeley: University of California Press, 1998) pp. 1–26; 135–200.

character, generally inimical to post-Kantian notions of morality. At one level, the end of virtue was accession to the society of the good, attaining the status of being well-regarded in the world. It is in this context that we can understand the tireless emphasis on the 'fame' of men of the court. The fame and reputation of men, as I argued above, was essential to political success. Conversely, the loss of reputation or public censure could have disastrous effects for one's success and career.

This public aspect of moral cultivation, as embodied in the 'tests' (*parīkṣā*) which men of rank underwent, the conferral of honours on the virtuous, and the celebration of character through public praise, was an integral part of the 'ethicised' worldview, the 'cosmomoral' order, of medieval Indian courts. This of course left the world of the court open to criticism, for its 'virtues' were always potentially poisoned by pride, vanity and ambition. Yet it is perhaps ironic that one of the greatest diatribes against the vanity of kings and courtiers, Śukanāsa's famous advice (*upadeśa*) to the prince Candrapīḍa at the completion of his formal *śāstric* training, ends by warning the prince to avoid being ridiculed, censured and blamed by the wise and the good.[92] Even the criticism of court relied on the putative compulsion of good society as one of its chief bases.

The suggestion that texts like the *Arthaśāstra*, *Kāmasūtra* and *Pañcatantra* were partly concerned with the cultivation of virtue may seem perverse or out of place to some, as many commentators in the past have characterised this literature as 'amoral' or 'Machiavellian'. This is because these treatises do not conform either to the principles of 'religious morality', thought to be embodied in the *dharmaśāstra*, or to notions of 'public good' typical of modern civil society and government. They appear as despotic, as they tend to relate the entire question of pleasure to the interests of the *nāyaka*, and the question of polity to the prince's acquisition and increase of his kingdom. Yet it must be remembered that the acquisition of wealth and the pursuit of pleasure were themselves valorised as ethically proper, and the questions posed by these texts is how to achieve these ends most effectively in conjunction with the pursuit of other virtues and goals. The underlying principle of Vātsyāyana's discussion of pleasures, for example, is not the safeguard and maintenance of the patriarchal family (a prerogative of the *dharmaśāstric* literature) but the self-disciplined enjoyment of pleasures. So when Vātsyāyana recommends the seduction of other men's wives it is not through a laxity in regard to the strictures of the *dharmaśāstra* – he is in fact acutely aware of this morality. It is rather through his concern for loss of self-control on the part of the *nāgaraka*. If a man's attraction to a woman was so great that it could not be controlled but through detriment to his self-composure,

[92] See *Kd*, p. 179.

then Vātsyāyana recommends various means to effect his desires, while still recommending that a man avoid ending up in such a predicament. The type of morality enjoined here by Vātsyāyana is precisely 'subjectivising' – it encouraged the development of a reflective ethical capacity.

An important part of the virtuous life at court was the avoidance of faults (*doṣas*), chief among which were known as the 'six enemies' (*ṣadvarga*): passion (*kāma*), anger (*krodha*), greed (*lobha*), conceit (*māna*), intoxication (*mada*) and excitement (*harṣa*).[93] Yet the discriminating subjectivity which was enjoined by courtly ethics is underscored by the fact that a number of these 'enemies' were not wrong as such, but were unacceptable only under certain conditions and in excessive degree. *Kāma*, the first of the six enemies, was one of the three goals of worldly life; *krodha* could form an important element of lordly demeanour and prerogative in some contexts; and *harṣa* was a largely positive characteristic. It is only when these qualities were uncontrolled or manifested inappropriately that they became the 'enemies' of noble conduct. Conversely, any virtue, if not cultivated properly, could potentially become a fault. It was thus an individual's judicious and careful management of numerous qualities which constituted ethical perfection. This discrimination formed the basis of many of the 'ethical' maxims which have come down to us from medieval courts. The relation between the virtue of sweet (*mādhurya*) speech and the fault of harsh (*paruṣa*) language, for example, could sometimes be reversed. Karaṭaka, Damanaka's jackal-companion in the *Pañcatantra*, cites a verse advising that 'that which is wholesome may be sought in harsh speech, and if found, is nectar indeed while that which is deceptive may be sought in sweet speech, and when found, is poison'.[94] Inscriptional eulogies frequently praise the discriminating ethical accomplishment of kings and courtiers. Two seventh-century inscriptions praising kings capture the spirit quite well: Tīvaradeva of southern Kosala, is described as 'greedy for fame, but not stealing the fame of others' and the Gurjara king Dadda at Ujjain as one who 'though eloquent, was dull-witted in abusing others'.[95] These poetic conceits depend on the appreciation that faults like thirst or ambition (as a vice, greed), if put to the right end, could enhance virtue, and conversely, that virtues like verbal eloquence,

[93] For avoidance of the six enemies in the *śāstras*, see *AS* 1.6.1; *NiS* 1.57; and *KS* 5.5.38 and comm. For mention in inscriptions, see the Mandasore stone inscription of Yaśodharman, *c.* 532 CE, *CII* 3 (1888), no. 35, p. 153. Other authorities give a somewhat different list, replacing *harṣa* and *māna* with delusion (*moha*) and envy (*matsara*).

[94] *PT* 1.143; the phrase *sunṛtavāc* indicated both pleasant *and* true speech. See *EI* 1 (1892), no. 25i, p. 200, for its attribution to a Candella minister.

[95] See the Rājim plates of Tīvaradeva, *CII* 3 (1888), no. 81, pp. 295–6 and the Kaira plates of Dadda II, *CII* 4 (1955), pt. 1, no. 16, p. 61. Also see the sixth-century Haraha stone inscription of the Maukhari king Īśānavarman, *EI* 14 (1917–18), no. 5, p. 116.

if used badly, could actually diminish virtue. This system of ethics sought to develop just such a discriminating appreciation.

One important virtue which will be encountered repeatedly in this study is *vinaya*. This term, which denoted at once the sense of discipline, self-restraint and humility, was tirelessly recommended by courtly treatises particularly in regard to the education of princes. It entailed the restraint of one's senses deemed necessary for submitting not merely to those who commanded respect, but to the rules and norms embodied in the *śāstra*. It was thus both the prerequisite for and the instrument through which one became educated by the learned.[96] It was the 'root (*mūla*) of policy (*naya*)' according to Kāmandakī, because perfect knowledge of the *śāstra* could only be obtained through discipline.[97] The untiring emphasis on *vinaya* in courtly discourses was paralleled in early India only by the religious orders of mendicants, monks and pious brahmin householders, making the hermitage or monastery and the court the two pre-eminent places where men could sometimes spend considerable time, freed from the constraints of subsistence, engaged in tasks of arduous ethical self-cultivation.[98]

Another problem of this ethical system is the relationship between its particularistic and universalist tendencies. The various qualities possessed by different estates, appropriate to their separate codes of conduct (*svadharma*), would seem to preclude any common ethical standards. Virtues, in other words, were partly divided according to social function. The king and the arms-bearing nobility, for example, were associated with valour and generosity while counsellors and ministers with knowledge and wisdom. But once again, the picture is more complex, and it would be a mistake to see in such divisions of virtue the supposedly opposed roles of brahmin and *kṣatriya*, or poet and king held by so many scholars. Particularised codes of behaviour existed alongside more or less universalist injunctions and various moral qualities shared diverse complementary, oppositional and overlapping relations with one another.[99] A stable repertoire of virtues was viewed as appropriate for all men of rank at court, whatever their *varṇa* background and

[96] See *AS* 1.5.3–6. [97] *NiS* 1.21.

[98] Existing scholarship has treated the problem of self-transformation almost exclusively within the confines of religion. What has been less recognised is that worldly practices made similar demands on people to cultivate themselves for the proper pursuit of acquisition, pleasure and righteousness. For a comparison of courtly and monastic disciplines, see Daud Ali, 'Technologies of the Self: Courtly Artifice and Monastic Discipline in Early India', *JESHO*, vol. 41, no. 2 (May 1998), pp. 159–84.

[99] For a discussion of this problem in the Indian context using the work of Stuart Hampshire, see James Laidlaw, *Riches and Renunciation: Religion, Economy and Society among the Jains* (Oxford: Clarendon Press, 1995), pp. 12–14.

office. These included prudence (*naya*), modesty (*vinaya*), generosity (*dāna*), mercy (*dayā*), cleverness (*dakṣa*), politeness (*dākṣiṇya*), tenacity (*sthairya*), resolve (*dhairya*), energy (*utsāha*), valour (*śaurya*), truthfulness (*satya*), intelligence (*matimān, buddhi*), wisdom (*prajña*), charm (*lalita*), beauty (*kānti, saundārya*) and eloquence (*vāgmi*).[100] These virtues, which appear repeatedly in the inscriptional records, were identified with the court, but also formed part of a broader conception of the ethical life which was at once universal in its validity yet confined in provenance. So though such qualities were widely esteemed, they were particularly suitable to people of noble rank. Beauty and courage were not despicable in the low-born man or woman, and could even gain them praise, but lack of training and access to the accoutrements of birth prevented the transformation of such virtues into cultural values of élite status.[101] The qualities of men of the court partially overlapped with and yet were complementary to those who enjoyed 'religious' status – either as brahmin householders or monks. They were, on the other hand, generally opposed or considered antithetical to qualities associated with the low-born, forest people and barbarians.

Warrior values and courtliness

Though military codes are in many ways a crucial topic for the study of the lifestyles of courtly élite in medieval India, they will not be treated in this book. Having said this, I would like to end this chapter with a few remarks regarding martial values and ideas about violence relevant to the themes developed below. To appreciate courtly notions of violence and martial valour, we would do well to keep in mind that warrior cultures were hardly new to India. Since as early as we have any discursive evidence of political life in India, whether it be the internecine conflict of the Vedic chieftaincies or the great wars of India's putative 'heroic' age, some configuration of martial values had found prominence in the culture of the élite. What *is* significant in the courtly sources from the early centuries of the Common Era, however, is a striking combination of martial codes and markedly 'irenic' values.

The irenic emphasis in courtly sources was in fact the culmination of a much longer and more diverse historical development in early India which

[100] The incidence of such lists of virtues in the epigraphic record is so common as to have drawn little or no notice from scholars. For a fifth-century example of such a list describing the Gupta courtiers Parṇadatta and Cakrapālita, see *CII* 3 (1981), no. 28, pp. 301–2.

[101] See king Śūdraka's remarks on the low-born Caṇḍāla maiden who comes to visit his court in Bāṇa's *Kd*, pp. 25–6.

echoed far beyond the court. Yet an integral part of this shift was evolving concepts of rule and lordship which had considerable ramifications for the courtly culture. To present the thrust of these transformations requires that we consider for a moment the later Vedic materials, which form one end of a historical continuum on which I would like to place the texts on polity redacted during the Gupta period. There are of course good reasons for looking at these texts, not the least of which being that the Vedic rites form our earliest extant articulations of political order in the subcontinent, and precede the rise of an autonomous discourse on rule or polity by centuries. Moreover, their rites continue to be occasionally performed by royal courts until as late as the seventh century, when references to them gradually disappear from the epigraphic record.[102]

As is well known, the Vedic texts and the rites they contain largely embody the values of a semi-pastoral and clan-based society in the process of sedentarisation. Vedic rituals do not set out a special realm of political and economic life like the *Arthaśāstra*. They place the question of political order within the larger concerns of public fire sacrifices performed by the king to bring him sons, cattle and wealth. These sacrifices took the form of feasts, where plants and animals were killed and offered to the gods through the fire. Notably, the Vedic sacrificial texts use the idea of sacrifice to characterise the political order itself – viewing society as a 'great feeding chain' where the higher orders fed off the lower.[103] To take a typical example, the *Śatapatha Brāhmaṇa* says that the '*kṣatriya* is the feeder (*attā*) and the people (*viś*) are the food; when there is abundant food for the eater, the realm prospers and thrives'.[104]

The social world of this agonistic order was gradually undermined with the rise of historic India. The spread of agriculture, growth of cities and the possibilities of regularised revenue collection rendered the predatory behaviours of the Vedic clan-chieftaincies and nascent monarchies moribund, and the new religious orders like Buddhism and Jainism were critical of the sacrifice as violent. These religious orders contended that the just king exercised his rule not by 'consuming' the people (*viś*) but by protecting his realm. These orders instead valorised non-violence (*ahiṁsā*), a policy adopted by Aśoka in his pillar edicts and later celebrated by the

102 V. S. Pathak, 'Vedic Rituals in Early Medieval Period: An Epigraphic Study', *Annals of the Bhandarkar Oriental Research Institute*, vol. 40 (1959), pp. 218–30.

103 Observed by Francis Zimmerman, *The Jungle and the Aroma of Meats: An Ecological Theme in Hindu Medicine* (Berkeley: University of California Press, 1987), p. 1, and developed at length by Brian Smith 'Eaters, Food and Social Hierarchy in Ancient India: A Dietary Guide to a Revolution of Values', *Journal of the American Academy of Religion*, vol. 58, no. 22 (Summer, 1990), pp. 177–201.

104 *Śatapaṭha Brāhmaṇa* 6.1.2.25.

Sātavāhana and Śaka kings in the second century CE.[105] Such claims were being made against a rapidly changing ritual context for royal courts. As the reformist literature of the *smṛti*s and *śāstra*s sought to domesticate and recode sacrificial practice within less violent frameworks, they also began to think of polity as a discrete and theorisable domain.[106]

This trend, which culminated in the redaction of the *Arthaśāstra* in the period of early Gupta ascendancy, also reflected an important change in the metaphors of rule and order. If, in the sacrificial texts, the proper relation between rulers and ruled was expressed as one of consumption, the powerful eating the weak, the *Arthaśāstra* viewed this state of affairs rather differently. Kauṭilya refers to it as *mātsyanyāya*, or the 'law of the fishes', where the 'strong swallowed the weak' (*balīyānabalaṃ hi grasate*), and attributes it to an absence or perversion of rule rather than its proper operation.[107] Kāmandaka's manual on polity states that in a realm without rulership (*daṇḍābhāva*), people 'deviated from the proper order and hungered for each other's flesh'.[108] And kings from the Gupta period begin to claim in their inscriptions to have eradicated the 'law of the fishes' in their realms.[109]

The older metaphors of rule as feeding gradually gave way to a wider language of 'enjoyment', expressed by the Sanskrit root √*bhuj* and its derivatives.[110] This idea came to have increasingly wide provenance,

[105] See the Sātavāhana inscription at Nasik of King Vāsithiputa, where he claims that he is 'opposed to hurting life even towards an enemy' (*satujane apāṇahisārucisa*): *EI* 8 (1905–6), no. 8, p. 60, and the Junagadh rock inscription of the Śaka king Rudradāman, who claims that he is 'faithful to his promise made to abstain from killing men until his final breath', but adds 'except in battles' (*ā prāṇocchvāsāt puruṣavadhanivṛtti-kṛta-satyapratijñena anyatra saṃgrāmeṣhu*), *EI* 8 (1905–6), no. 6, p. 43.

[106] See R. Inden, 'Changes in the Vedic Priesthood', in A. W. Van den Hoek, D. H. A. Kolff and M. S. Oort, eds., *Ritual, State and History in South Asia: Essays in Honour of J. C. Heesterman*, (Leiden: E. J. Brill, 1992), pp. 556–77.

[107] Compare *Śatapaṭha Brāhmaṇa* 1.3.2.15, which laments that if the kṣatriya was to be separated from the *viś*, there would be no eater and eaten, with *AS* 1.4.13–14. For similar ideas, see *MDh* 7.20 and *MhB* 12.67.16. There are occasional references to a vaguely similar idea in the Brāhmaṇa literature, but they hardly vitiate their larger vision on this matter.

[108] *NiS* 2.40. See also *NiV* 9.7–8.

[109] See the seventh-century Nidhanpur plates of King Bhāskaravarman, eastern ally of Harṣa, whose ancestor Samudravarman is described as 'devoid of the law of the fishes' (*mātsyanyāyamvirahita*), *EI* 12 (1913–14), no. 13, p. 73; and the ninth-centry Khalimpur plates of the Pāla king Dharmapāla, which declare that his ancestor Gopāla 'took the hand of fortune' to end the law of the fishes (*mātsyanyāyam apohitum*), *EI* 4 (1896–7), no. 34, p. 248.

[110] That rule was no longer signified by metaphors of eating has been noted by Scharfe, *The State in Indian Tradition*, pp. 143, 233. The root √*bhuj* in the Vedic corpus primarily referred to eating, and gained its wider sense only later, see R. S. Sharma, *Material Culture and Social Formations in Ancient India* (Delhi: Macmillan, 1983), p. 42.

denoting variously sensual and mental experience, pleasure and possession of title and/or ownership of property. And given the importance of land to the political order, from Gupta times the political hierarchy was conceived through similar terminology – the king 'enjoying' the entire realm or the earth and his subordinate's smaller domains.[111] The term *bhoga* came to denote the enjoyment of all privileges by way of rank and title. By the twelfth century, nearly all of courtly life could be divided into a vast array of different enjoyments, pleasures and dalliances.[112]

This displacement of sacrificial agonism to the realm of anarchy should not be understood as the complete dissociation of violence from ideas of polity. Such conceptual trends (*mātsyanyāya*, *ahiṁsā*) were founded on the demands of an agricultural society which entailed its own sort of violence. After all, according to the manuals, it was the king's 'rod' (*daṇḍa*), or army, which prevented the elements of his realm from consuming one another.

And warfare between royal houses continued to be a major preoccupation of the ruling élite, as the thousands of courtly panegyrics from Gupta times make very clear. Men spent large portions of their youth not only receiving an arduous training in arms, but in cultivating certain qualities repeatedly mentioned in the inscriptions and in texts like the *Arthaśāstra*. These included strength, dexterity, valour, prowess, energy, steadfastness and even fearsomeness and impetuousness. On the battlefield men demonstrated their skill in arms and their martial virtues before their equals and superiors. Their fame, reputation and indeed their very careers, depended on their performance in these battles. The rise of the Kadamba family recorded in their Talgunda inscription is instructive. After being insulted by a Pallava noble, the Kadamba brahmin Mayūraśārman took up arms, defeated several 'lords of the marches' (*antapālan*) loyal to the Pallavas and retreated northward to the area around Śrīparvata where he levied tribute from other kings. When the Pallavas came to punish him, he demonstrated such strength and valour, according to the inscription, that the Pallavas thought it better to befriend than attack him. Entering their service, he distinguished himself in various battles and was crowned with a headpiece (*paṭṭabandha*) by the Pallava king.[113] Whatever the truth of this panegyrical account,

[111] For the concept of the king as enjoyer of the earth, see J. Duncan M. Derrett '*Bhū-bharaṇa, Bhū-pālana, Bhū-bhojana*: An Indian Conundrum', *BSOAS*, vol. 22, no. 1 (1959), pp. 108–23. For titles of lower officials, like *bhogika*, or 'minor enjoyer', see Sircar, *Indian Epigraphy*, pp. 327–439, esp. pp. 379–83. See Kane, 'Bhukti or Bhoga (possession)', *History of Dharmaśāstra*, vol. III, pp. 317–29.

[112] See *Mānasollāsa*, where twenty royal 'enjoyments' (*upabhogas*), 'pleasures' (*vinodas*), and 'sports' (*krīḍās*) are enumerated.

[113] *EI* 8 (1905–6), no. 5, p. 32.

its underlying message, that the Kadambas gained the recognition and regard of the more powerful family of the Pallavas by 'opposing' them (or their subordinates), suggests that valour formed a sort of collectively recognised code through which men sought to gain recognition from one another.[114] This code placed the noble's military prowess at the centre of his courtly career and self-perception, from the scars and battle wounds on his body from battle, often compared to beautiful decorations in inscriptions, to the personal relations among his own family.[115]

The significant point for this study, however, is that the ritualised and honourable violence which this code encouraged was to be exercised with restraint, to be combined and complemented by the virtues of compassion, kindness and gentility. Both the Śaka and Sātavāhana courts describe their kings not only as valiant and skilled in arms, but as compassionate and kind to their enemies.[116] One context for such 'kindness', by the Gupta period, was the re-establishment of defeated nobles to their title and rank by victorious kings in return for their loyalty and obeisance. Much is made of the restoration of subordinate kings in Hariṣeṇa's description of his lord Samudragupta, who is described as 'blending valour with magnanimity', and as having a 'tender heart won over by loyalty'.[117] By the Gupta period the very nature of nobility was a judicious combination of martial and irenic values. A seventh-century panegyric of the Pāṇḍuvāmśin king Tīvaradeva puts it eloquently when it claims that 'though adorned with power, he is not harsh' and 'though fierce (*pracchaṇḍa*) to his adversaries, he is nevertheless moist (*śaumya*) in countenance'.[118] The latter image here, playing on the contrast between the scorching heat of the sun and the cooling light of the moon, captures

[114] The roughly similar presentation of events between the young prince Malladeva and the more powerful king Jayacandra of Kanauj nearly a millennium later in Vidyāpati's fifteenth-century *Puruṣaparīkṣā*, suggests that such policies were undertaken by lesser kings and nobles to actually gain recognition and distinction on entering the service of more powerful kings.

[115] When the courtier Hariṣeṇa describes his lord Samudragupta as having a body beautified by hundreds of alluring scars from axes, swords, arrows and the like, he expresses a common sentiment among men of noble rank, *CII* 3 (1981), no. 1, p. 212. For other references to wounds as ornaments in inscriptional panegyrics, see the Penukonda plates of the Gaṅga king Mādhava II, *EI* 14 (1917–18), no. 24, p. 335; the Gangdhar stone inscription of the Gupta feudatory Viśvavarman of the Aulikāra family, *CII* 3 (1888), no. 17, p. 75; and later of Yaśodharman himself, *CII* 3 (1888), no. 35 , p. 153. The first known *sati* stone inscription memorialises the ritual suicide of the wife of a Gupta vassal named Goparāja who died in battle at the beginning of the sixth century, *CII* 3 (1981), no. 43, pp. 352–4.

[116] See *EI* 8 (1905–6), nos. 6, 8, pp. 43, 60.

[117] *CII* 3 (1981), no. 1, p. 213–14.

[118] See *CII* 3 (1888), no. 81, pp. 295–6; see also the Kaira plates of Dadda II, who describes his father as 'he whose power was not opposed to forgiveness', *CII* 4 (1955), pt. 1, no. 16, p. 61.

the spirit of the courtly discourses. A king was to possess both an unbearable splendour, which burned away darkness, and a relieving coolness which fructified his realm.

Throughout the Gupta period and beyond, these attributes of gentility and compassion which accompanied martial prowess were thought to distinguish men of nobility and virtue not only from the coarse and vulgar men of the village, but also from the fierce and harsh peoples of the forests and hills. These latter people, who had their own norms of behaviour and religious rituals, were seen as innately wild. They ruled over largely non-agricultural lands, made their subsistence by pillaging and looting, consumed wine and flesh, and made similar offerings to the gods.[119] Their lifestyles were deemed directly opposed to the irenic values of courtly life.

The oppositions between these groups remained a continual theme in courtly literature in part because kings throughout the period under question (and well beyond) regularly established relations with these peoples. The Allahabad pillar inscription claims that Samudragupta 'made all the forest kings (*aṭavika rāja*) into servants (*paricārakṛta*)'.[120] These groups, at the periphery of established agrarian society (and often in predatory relationship with it) could form crucial allies, particularly as they could guarantee safe haven and free movement through inhospitable terrain. Harṣa is said to have sought the assistance of the infamous Śaraba tribes living in the Vindhya forests of central India, in order to be conducted to the hermitage where his sister had been placed in safe keeping. These men were thus viewed with considerable ambivalence by the courtly nobility: they are described as lean and powerful, yet decried as misshapen and prematurely aged from their harsh and violent habits.

Yet the interaction between the people of the hills and forests and the men of 'good society' was far more complex and varied, and may be generally conceived as the diverse integration of the former into the political and economic structures of agrarian society – as peasants, royal servants and even as recognised semi-independent rulers of realms. Though this integration was complex and involved mutual influence and accommodation in specific regional contexts, one element of this process from the sources of the Gupta era would suggest that the opposition between the wild and violent ways of the forest people and the restrained and honourable ways of the nobility formed a behavioural 'continuum' along which men moved to enter the pale of 'good society' and once there exhibited the fact as a mark of their moral superiority over others. When

119 For a survey of these groups as represented in brahmanical sources, see Aloka Parasher, *Mlecchas in Early India: A Study in Attitudes Towards Outsiders up to 600 AD* (Delhi: Munshiram Manoharlal, 1991), pp. 179–221.

120 *CII* 3 (1981), no. 1, p. 213.

Bāṇa in his *Kādambarī* describes the chief of the Śabaras as someone who, though being wealthy, continued to eat roots and fruits, and though being dependent on the king, never understood royal service, he might also have been speaking of those wicked kings predicted by the cosmological histories to overtake the world in the final epoch, constantly fighting among themselves and reducing their subjects to wearing bark and eating fruits and berries.[121]

It might be tempting, then, to see the irenic values of the court, as some have read the chivalric manners of western Europe, as a sort of 'civilising' mechanism by which violent barbarians were transformed and pacified into a 'gentile' nobility. But it should be kept in mind that courtly manners in India, like chivalry in Europe, had a much more complex and ambivalent role with violence.[122] For one, the courtly élite in the agrarian empires of India, like their European counterparts, existed atop a vast hierarchical order safeguarded by ever more complex forms of violence. Among the courtly élite, even as men were encouraged to cultivate gentility and compassion, they were expected to constantly display their skills in warfare, exhibit martial emotions like bravery, impetuosity and revenge on the battlefield, and to brutally chastise any exhibition of 'pride' on the part of equals or inferiors. This forms the unwritten context for the sublime enjoyments and rarefied culture which will be explored in the remainder of this book.

[121] Compare *Kd*, p. 59 and the evil kings of the *kali yuga* mentioned in *Viṣṇu Purāṇa* 4.23.18–20, probably a Gupta period text. Bāṇa describes a Śaraba messenger who meets King Harṣa as 'the embodied fruit of sin and the cause of the *kali yuga*', *HC*, ch. 8, p. 232.

[122] For a useful review of this problem in the context of Europe, see Richard Kaeuper, *Chivalry and Violence in Medieval Europe* (Oxford University Press, 1999), esp. pp. 205–8.

3 The protocol of the court

This chapter concerns courtly protocol and palace routine. Specifically, it will take up the various ways in which men and women conducted themselves before one another at court, what may loosely be called 'manners'. Such conduct included not only the specific behaviours, gestures and speech which regulated social interaction between people at court, but also the more subtle, yet equally studied aspects of physical bearing, verbal style and comportment. Manners so defined were much more than either superfluous triviality or self-aggrandising behaviour, as they have been characterised by modern critics. They inflected people's inner psychological make-up, disciplined their bodily proclivities and structured their relationships with others. They were the 'end product' of socialisation for worldly élites, and formed the implicit 'rules of engagement' which enabled participation in the social world of the court.[1] While the following chapter will take up the emphasis on physical bearing and verbal style within the seemingly incessant aestheticising tendencies of courtly life, this chapter focuses on the procedural aspects of manners at court as interactions between courtly agents. It will set down the basic relationships and most important communicative idioms in courtly interaction to illuminate how manners functioned as both a regulatory protocol and an instrument of social negotiation within the world of the court.

Inevitably, the manners of the court overlapped with conceptions of conduct prevalent in wider society, particularly within religious domains. Because of this, one might be tempted to suggest, as has been done in Europe, that 'courtly' manners were little more than religious values oriented towards everyday sociability rather than salvation.[2] Indeed, key concepts and terms which the reader shall encounter below are well known to scholars of Indian religion, and it is tempting, if not plausible, to see their appearance in the courtly milieu as a sort of borrowing from

[1] See the useful discussion of the term in Bryson, *From Courtesy to Civility*, p. 8 ff.

[2] See Jaeger, *Civilizing Trends and the Formation of Courtly Ideals, 923–1120*. See also the remarks of Bryson, *From Courtesy to Civility*, p. 66.

the religious sphere. Such a conclusion, however, would be over-hasty. The evidence for the origin of early medieval religious ideas points instead to significant interaction with contemporary practices and conceptions of human lordship, and the rise and proliferation of many important ideas in both contexts seems to have been broadly contemporaneous. In fact, religious and political notions of lordship differed more in degree than kind. They formed part of a continuous and homologously structured 'chain of being' which linked the entire cosmos. This, on the one hand, meant that the king's authority and mystique resembled and participated in that of the temple god, giving a theological dimension to relationships at court. On the other hand, however, it meant that the life of gods, housed in their sumptuous palaces, shared striking resemblances to those of princes. This study, concerned with courtly life, has bracketed out the question of religion, partly as a corrective measure to the scholarly preoccupation with sacred kingship, and partly from following the sources themselves which present a set of internally coherent dynamics. Exploring these dynamics will not only help shed light on hitherto ignored aspects of courtly life in early India, but, just as importantly, also recover the important social significance of practices which have been seen as entirely 'spiritual' in content.

The dynamics: service, loyalty, favour

The various hierarchies which converged on the court all tended towards the single conceptual classification of servant (*sevaka*, *bhṛtya*) and master (*svāmin*). The courtier, minister, prince in attendance and chamberlain, regardless of their potentially different privileges, duties and rank – were all ultimately 'servants' of the king. In the manuals on polity these men are described as 'taking refuge' (*āśrayate*) with a king and receiving a livelihood (*vṛtti*, *ājīvya*) from him, but the work they performed for him, the manifold labours of effecting his will, was denoted by the term *sevā*, or 'service'.[3]

It is worth stressing the nature and importance of service for life at court. First, and most important, the vast majority of activities which constituted the 'functioning of the state apparatus' were, in fact, based on relationships of personal service. The 'public' functions of the king's men were grounded not in service to an abstract notion of state or society, but in personal obligation to a lord. The dependant oversaw the business of his superior as a form of service to his person. This idea stretched across the gamut of political relationships, from the duties of palace servants of

[3] *AS* 5.4.1–2; *NiS* 5.1–2. See also *CII* 3 (1981), no. 1, p. 212, for men seeking the refuge (*śaraṇamupagatāḥ*) of Samudragupta.

various ranks, to men of ministerial title, as well as vassals and underlords.[4] Nearly every hierarchical relationship was informed in some way by the language of service and the master/servant dyad. So important was the idea of service that a vast body of sayings grew up around the hardships and disadvantages of service at court (*rājasevā*). In spite of such views, however, service was typically celebrated as an honour or accolade rather than a disability. Counterbalancing the many aphorisms which lament it, an even vaster number of inscriptions praise men of various rank for their skills at royal service. A seal found at Nālandā, probably dating from the early seventh century, is typical: it claims to be the 'token of the illustrious Paśupatasiṁha, whose excellences were his virtues, who completely conquered the armies of his foes, who was just, and who was expert at royal service'.[5]

The manuals on polity set out numerous virtues and accomplishments to be found (and detected by 'tests') in royal servants, including good birth, learning, intelligence, truthfulness and skilfulness, to name only a few.[6] But perhaps the most valuable of these qualities for those in royal service, however, was loyalty, usually denoted by the terms *bhakti*, 'devotion', or *anurāga*, 'affection' or 'attachment'.[7] Though these terms occur among larger lists of qualities to be possessed by men of the court, there are good reasons to pause over their significance. In the first place, service at court, whatever its transactional reciprocity, was ultimately grounded in personal obligation to a lord and his family. Both in terms of ideology and realpolitik, the measure of this obligation was loyalty. While the possession of other accomplishments and virtues secured higher or lower ranks at court, loyalty was crucial as it formed the primary affective basis of the servant/master relationship, at least from the side of the servant. Loyalty or attachment to the lord was the inner disposition which was to inform the actions and labour which constituted service (*sevā*).

Its widespread emphasis in inscriptions, then, is hardly surprising.[8] In the great duel of ministers depicted in Viśākhadatta's play, *Mudrārākṣasa*, loyalty forms the chief virtue of Cāṇakya's opponent, the minister

[4] Numerous ministers and counsellors describe themselves as doing the work of good servants. Giving daughters in marriage, attending court offering themselves (for military support) and requesting the right to rule their own districts through the overlord's sovereignty were all deemed forms of service (*sevā*). See the remarks on these acts in Samudragupta's Allahabad pillar inscription, *CII* 3 (1981), no. 1, pp. 213–14.

[5] *EI* 21 (1931–2), no. 12, p. 76. See also the extensive sixth-century eulogy of the Naigama ministers, who call themselves servants (*bhṛtya*) of the Aulikāra kings, and who claim that their fame spread from refuge or service at the feet of these kings (*pādāśrayād viśrutapuṇyakīrttiḥ*), *CII* 3 (1888), no. 35, p. 153.

[6] *AS* 1.9.1 ff.; *NiS* 4.27–30, 5.13–15.

[7] *AS* 1.8.10–12, 26; *NiS*, 4.25, 37–38; 5.13.

[8] For a typical Gupta example, see Skandagupta's rock inscription at Junagadh which portrays the king asking which of his servants is (among other things) 'devoted' (*bhakto*) and 'attached' (*anurakta*), *CII* 3 (1981), no. 28, p. 299.

Rākṣasa, who continues to avenge his master's house even after its collapse. Cāṇakya praises this virtue at the outset of the play: '[most] men serve their lords when not deprived of lordship, for the sake of worldly gain; they follow him in adversity hoping for his restoration. But rare are the virtuous like you who take up the burden of duty with disinterested devotion, attached to past acts of goodness, even after the complete ruin of your master'.[9] It is this quality which makes defeating and winning over Rākṣasa so important for Cāṇakya. Loyalty which extended not only to the king but also to his family (to the 'house') was valued precisely because in the event of calamity it helped to ensure 'continuous sovereignty' as the *Arthaśāstra* puts it.[10]

The conceit of Viśākhadatta's play and essence of Cāṇakya's strategy is to make loyalty the very downfall of Rākṣasa. Cāṇakya engineers events so as to present Rākṣasa with the choice between either the death of his merchant friend or entering the service of his enemy, Candragupta. Continued enmity to Candragupta, based on his pyrrhic loyalty to a fallen house, will now compromise the loyalty to a friend. Rākṣasa thus agrees to enter Candragupta's court, but with the remark, 'I bow to devotion for a friend'.[11] Cānakya has thus won over his opponent without compromising the very virtue which makes him so desirable a servant, his loyalty.

The 'remuneration' and reward of subordinate kings, ministers and household dependants generally participated in the same affective language that characterised service itself. If service at court was based on personal loyalty, then the obvious goal of such service was to please or satisfy one's lord, and prominent among the recommendations for royal servants in the texts on polity is constant vigilance for the signs of satisfaction (*tuṣṭa*) and dissatisfaction (*atuṣṭa*) of one's lord.[12] Satisfaction created a sort of reciprocal affection which led him to bestow his 'favour' or 'grace', denoted by the terms *prasāda* or *anugraha*.[13] These terms referred to the visible form and external signs of a lord's happiness and compassion towards his servants, which could take the form of gifts, honours and, most importantly for those in the king's retinue, a subsistence (*vṛtti*).

[9] *MR* 1.13. See Cāṇakya's entire speech. [10] *AS* 5.6.1 ff.
[11] *MR* 7.16+. [12] *AS* 5.5.7–8; *NiS* 5. 35–46.
[13] The word *prasāda* derived from √*sad* ('to sit' or 'sink down'), which prefixed meant to be pleased, propitiated, gracious and in good humour. The substantive form denoted grace, favour and good temper. The related term *anugraha*, was formed from √*grah* ('to seize or gain possession of') prefixed with *anu* meaning to lend assistance or support, to promote or uphold, with its substantive form denoting favour, kindness and the conferral of benefits. While both *anugraha* and *prasāda* could refer to royal favour as a specific act of beneficence, *anugraha* could also refer to the general disposition or affective state of conferring favour.

From Gupta times, kings and lords are commonly represented in inscriptions as showing courtesy, affection and largesse to their subordinates through this language of 'favour', which became between the fourth and seventh centuries one of the chief political vocabularies of royal houses in the subcontinent.[14] Samudragupta's Allahabad pillar inscription, for example, describes the Gupta king's favour (*anugraha*) in at least three senses: Samudragupta is said to dispense favour on all of mankind, show favour to subordinate kings by 'capturing and then liberating them' (*rājagrahaṇamokṣa*), and to extend his favour to his courtiers like Hariṣeṇa, author of the eulogy, by allowing them 'to move about in his presence' (*samīpaparisarppaṇa*).[15] Conversely, inscriptions also celebrate the receipt and enjoyment of royal favour and numerous kings, ministers and princes represent themselves enjoying the grace of their superiors. In a typical example, the Gupta courtier Āmrakārdava, in his inscription at Sāñcī dated in 410 CE, describes himself as having his 'livelihood (*jīvita*) increased by the favour (*prasāda*) of the feet of Candragupta (II)'.[16]

Any economic or political transaction between men of rank, including the transfer or sale of lands and the bestowal of individual or corporate privileges, could be cast in the terminology of favour. A number of land-grants from the fifth century include or make references to petitions for royal 'favour' which must have preceded their composition.[17] As these inscriptions were the permanent documents which authorised a subordinate's privileges, they were in some cases described as physical embodiments of the lord's favour. Later texts call these *prasādalikhita*, or 'written favour'.[18] In one case we even have a kingdom being bestowed. Two early Cōḻa copperplates refer to a Gaṅga underlord of the Cōḻa as

[14] Noted by Sharma, 'The Feudal Mind', in Sharma, *Early Medieval Indian Society*, p. 276.

[15] *CII* 3 (1981), no. 1, p. 215.

[16] *CII* 3 (1981) no. 9, p. 250. Other examples from the fifth century include the Eran stone pillar inscription of the subordinate king Mātṛviṣṇu ruling in Gupta domains, who describes his younger brother as 'in receipt of his favours' (*tatprasādaparigṛhīta*), *CII* 3 (1981), no. 39, p. 340; and the Andhavaram grant of the Māṭhara king Ānantaśaktivarman in Orissa, who describes himself as having 'a body, a kingdom, prosperity and prowess obtained through the grace of his father the *bhaṭṭāraka*' (*bappabhaṭṭārakaprasādāvaptaśarīrarājyavibhavapratāpa*), *EI* 28 (1949–50), no. 31, p. 178.

[17] See the various grants from eastern India from Gupta times, particularly the Damodarpur copperplate grant issued during the reign of Buddhagupta at the end of the fifth century, *CII* 3 (1981), no. 38, pp. 335–9, and the sixth-century grants of the time of King Dharmāditya, *IA* 39 (1910), pp. 199–202 and King Samācāradeva, *EI* 18 (1925–6), no. 11, pp. 74–86, all of which include petitions requesting the 'favour' of state officials to buy uncultivated land to settle and support brahmin communities.

[18] According to the later *śāstric* compendium known as the *Vyavahāramayūkha*, Bṛhaspati (*c.* fifth century) defines *prasādalikhita*, as 'a writing of favour, made by the king when, pleased (*tuṣṭa*) with the services (*seva*) valour (*śaurya*), etc. of a person'. See *Vyavahāramayūkha*, pp. 25–7. An inscription from western India at the end of the sixth

'obtaining favour in the form of a (copper) plate which was the means of attaining lordship over the Bāṇa kingdom'.[19]

The quest for and bestowal of grace was one of the most fundamental dynamics of life at court, as it formed the chief mechanism for the redistribution of wealth and power among retainers and subordinates, one which presumed a relation of hierarchy. Sayings on polity recommend that the king maintain an abundant treasury in order that his display of favour or disfavour would not be without substance.[20] The king was to extend his favour judiciously; avoiding gifts to the the unworthy, and excessive favour to any one dependant.[21] On the part of dependants and underlords, the pursuit of the king's favour was the most important means of advancement within the courtly hierarchy, for 'in the favour of kings', as Manu put it, 'lay the lotus-like goddess of prosperity' (*prasāde padmaśrīḥ*).[22]

Together, the concepts of service, devotion and favour came to form the principal elements of what may be called the underlying 'rationality' of courtly life in medieval India. Both conceptually and institutionally, they formed the very sinews of dynastic polity. The gradual proliferation of these terms in the epigraphic record from the fourth century throughout the subcontinent indicates the integration of nascent and local lords into an increasingly standardised set of practices and codes. It is perhaps worth noting here that this terminology is explicitly affective (in contrast to the dynamics of bureaucratic organisation) and sought to orient the inner dispositions of men at court with their external actions. So when an inscription describes a royal chamberlain as having 'a mind attached through favour to his master whom he served completely', it suggests both a formal and institutional arrangement as well as a set of mental and emotional dispositions which obtained between the two men.[23] It is the affective dimension of relationships at court, which we shall return to later, that made their gestural and verbal 'regulation' through protocols of courtesy so important. Nearly every act of the sovereign or master, from sitting, standing, processing and eating, could be considered an act

century records the petition to a *mahārāja* (also called *pratīhāra* and *sāmanta*) named Viṣṇusena on the part of a merchant community for the favour of a document (*anugrahastithipatra*) on regulations (*ācāras*) which they might in turn use to favour their own people, see *EI* 30 (1953–4), no. 30, p. 179, see discussion on p. 169.

[19] *paṭṭamayam prasādam bāṇādhirājapadalambhanasādhanam*, *EI* 4 (1896–7), no. 32, p. 224; see also *SII* 2 (1895–1913), no. 76, p. 384. The word *paṭṭa*, here, however, could also refer to a fillet or headpiece, see below.

[20] *NiV* 11.48; 17.2. [21] *NiS* 5.66–70; see also *NiV* 11.49; 18.36.

[22] *MDh* 7.11; see also *HC*, ch. 2, p. 71, where Bāṇa says that when Harṣa showed favour, he seemed to establish Prosperity, though herself immoveable, in various places (*prasādeṣu niścalāmapi śriyam sthāne sthāne sthāpayantam*).

[23] See the Puri plates of the Śailodbhava king Mādhavavarman Sainyabhīta, dated in 623 CE, *EI* 23 (1935–6), no. 19, p. 129.

of 'grace' or 'favour' by his servants.[24] And concepts of service, devotion and favour structured the speech and acts which constituted proper courtesy between individuals at court.

Palace routine

The manners of the court are best understood in relation to the protocols of the royal household. Our knowledge of the procedures and rules of royal households before the end of the first millennium, however, is fragmentary. It is not until the eleventh and twelfth centuries that we begin to find extensive manuals on architecture and kingship which deal, *inter alia*, with the etiquette and 'sumptuary' codes of noble households.[25] These texts shed important light on the miscellaneous references of earlier times and make it clear that the royal household was conceived as a sort of 'icon' of the kingdom, to use the words of Ronald Inden.[26] The activities which transpired within the household, in other words, had an emblematic character, both in signalling *and* constituting relationships between agents of the political order. We could say that those who congregated at the royal household 'enacted' and affirmed relationships which extended far beyond the royal residence itself. Procedures within the royal household were thus of utmost importance.

Though the protocol of the palace certainly revolved around the king's daily activities, early normative texts and literary accounts present no uniform picture of the king's daily routine. According to the *Arthaśāstra*, after rising and collecting his thoughts about the *śāstra*s and reflecting on tasks to be completed for the day, the king was to dispatch his secret agents, receive the blessings of his preceptor and various religious specialists, and see his physician, cook and astrologer.[27] Afterwards he entered

[24] In inscriptions from the far south the Tamil verbal root √*aruḷ*, appears prefixed to various other verbs indicating the sense of a lord 'deigning' to perform an action. It first appears in inscriptions of the Pallavas, as a translation of the Sanskrit *prasāda*, as in the bilingual Kasakudi plates of the Pallava king Nandivarman, where the *nāṭṭār* are said to have implemented the king's act of grace (*paṇittaruḷi*), clearly a translation of the phrase *prasādāt dattaḥ* 'given with favour' which appears in the Sanskrit portion of the grant, *SII* 2 (1895–1913), no. 73, p. 352. This terminology was greatly expanded by the Cōḻas (*c.* 950–1250 CE) and subsequent dynasties. For a list of varieties of usage, see S. Agesthialingom and S. V. Shanmugam, *The Language of Tamil Inscriptions 1250–1350 AD* (Annamalainagar: Annamalai University Press, 1970), s.v.

[25] These include Bhojadeva's eleventh-century *Sāmarāṅganasūtradhāra*, probably composed in Mālwā, Bhuvanadeva's twelfth-century *Aparājitapṛcchā* composed in Gujarat, Someśvara III's twelfth-century *Mānasollāsa* composed in the Deccan, and *Mayamata* (eleventh century), probably composed in south India.

[26] Inden, 'Hierarchies of Kings in Early Medieval India', pp. 116–17.

[27] The account here is based on *AS* 1.19.6 ff.

the assembly hall (*upasthāna*), where he would hear matters of defense, accounts and the affairs of his subjects. He then bathed, took food and returned to the assembly hall, where he received tributes in gold, and assigned tasks to officials of the realm. Next he consulted with counsellors *in absentia* through correspondence and considered intelligence acquired by secret agents. He then took further counsel or did as he pleased (*svairavihāra*), before reviewing his army and deliberating on military matters with his generals. After seeing his secret agents a final time, he bathed, ate and closed the day with the sounds of musical instruments. It is probably unwise to take this account as definitive or exhaustive, as it does not mention a number of activities we know from other sources, like hunting, meeting with women of the *antaḥpura*, performing religious rituals, etc. Hsuan-Tsang, the Chinese monk who visited Harṣa's court in the early seventh century, mentions that the king divided his day into three parts, and the literary accounts of Bāṇa dwell far more on the attendance of subordinate kings and on royal enjoyments, which also formed the preoccupation of the later texts on courtly life.[28]

Judging from the sources, the king's activities may be divided into at least four tiers or levels – each of which may also be mapped onto the spatial structure of the royal household (see figures 1.2 and 1.3). First, there were the king's most 'private' activities – like sleeping and relieving natural functions – which were generally not detailed in literary or prescriptive accounts, and for which (for reasons of vulnerability) he was probably attended only by his most trustworthy palace guards. These activities must necessarily remain shadowy and obscure, not simply because they rarely, if ever, appear in the sources, but because it is indeed difficult, once we subtract his more 'public' activities, to imagine what is left. Nevertheless, the important point is that the king could, at necessary moments, retire to some secluded place, usually in the most inner chambers of his own quarters within the palace.

Second were a more restricted set of activities which were attended not only by bodyguards, but variously by the royal preceptor, chief counsellors, queens, concubines, intimate servants and the most trusted subordinate princes. These included his bathing, a strikingly ritualised event in which he was showered with scented water from golden pitchers by court women; dressing and adornment; eating, in which he was accompanied by only the most intimate of princes of his own rank; pleasures and diversions with palace women, typically in the palace gardens, where

[28] *Si-Yu-Ki*, vol. I, p. 215. Notable among the various partial accounts in Bāṇa's works is king Śūdraka's daily routine in *Kd*, pp. 30–5. For a comparison with Hsuan-Tsang, see Baijnath Sharma, *Harṣa and his Times* (Varanasi: Susma Prakasan, 1970), pp. 244–5, 256–7.

judging from plays he was attended by his jester; and the receipt and assessment of intelligence, counsel and strategy, which involved the highest men of ministerial rank, trusted princes and secret agents. Significantly, many seemingly 'intimate' activities of the royal routine were, in actuality, experienced in a quite 'public' manner (by modern standards). Separate buildings or pavilions within the palace complex were often separately designated for these activities (along with special retinues and functionaries).

Third, there were the daily activities in the hall of assembly, where the king sat on a throne or couch before a gathering of members of his household, subordinate kings and visiting supplicants. Seated in the centrally located hall of meeting, the king received homage, heard petitions, announced proclamations and distributed favours and honours. This formed the central political event in the daily routine.

Finally, there were those activities which took the king into the outer courtyards of the palace or encampment and sometimes beyond, like military reviews, marches and processions.[29] Hsuan-Tsang noted that the king frequently travelled through his realm on inspection, residing in numerous temporary residences.[30] Such processions were conceived as moveable assemblies; the king or other members of the royal family were attended by a retinue of palace servants, ministers and subordinate princes.

Various moments of the daily routine were emphasised in different sorts of sources. Courtly literature, for example, dwelled especially on palace pleasures – bathing, dressing and romantic diversions in the garden – as well as displays of majesty and grandeur in the assembly hall and on the battlefield. Interestingly, absent from the list of palace pleasures were descriptions of food and feasting, which remained relatively underdeveloped themes in courtly poetry.[31] Eating, in fact, was more

[29] In Bāṇa's account, kings waiting outside the central gate call to the palace servants entering the complex, 'Sir, will the great lord give audience in the hall (*sthāne*) today after he has dined, or will he come out into the outer courtyard (*bāhyām kakṣyām*)?': *HC*, ch. 2, p. 60.

[30] *Si-Yu-Ki*, vol. 1, p. 215.

[31] In the account of king Śūdraka's routine in *Kādambarī*, where after a florid description of the king's bath and anointment with cosmetics and perfumes, Bāṇa says prosaically that 'the king took his meal in the company of princes accustomed to dine with him, delighted by the taste of favourite flavours', *Kd*, p. 33. Bāṇa's later description of the wonders of King Tārāpīḍa's palace includes beautiful horses and elephants, women, ornaments, music, games of various types, cosmetics, perfumes, oils and even wines, but significantly, no reference to food of any kind, *Kd*, pp. 140–52, esp. 148–50. It would seem that the imagery of sounds and light interested courtly audiences far more than taste, a point which may be connected to the critique of eating as violence. See the remarks above on the emergence of irenic values in court.

often used to demonstrate the vulgarity, lowness or foolishness of a character.[32] Though there were no doubt rules for taking of meals, eating was typically understood neither as a sublime enjoyment nor an activity which brought the household or the lords of the realm together. Consequently, the early medieval sources present nothing like the European emphasis on the lordly feast and on manners at table as a defining element of élite sociability.[33]

This importance was reserved for another event, the daily meeting of the household in the pillared assembly hall, known variously in Sanskrit as *sabhā*, *upasthāna* or *asthāna*. Prescriptive texts on polity, predictably more concerned with the technicalities of rule, have much to say about the business (and rather less, until the tenth century, on the protocol) of the assembly hall. It is here that the servants and lords of the realm met before the king to report their work, petition their lord and affirm their offices and functions. Yet it would be untrue to say that the assembly hall evaded the remit of the poets. It formed an important icon of sovereignty and the majesty of the king surrounded by his retinue and supplicating underlords was a favourite theme in courtly *kāvya*. It is perhaps this convergence – of aesthetic and prescriptive discourses – which makes the assembly hall the most significant occasion for any enquiry into the wider sociability of courtly life.

The exchange of honours and courtesies

Though sources from the fourth to seventh centuries provide only partial descriptions of the procedures within the assembly hall, later texts like the Cālukya king Someśvara III's political and sumptuary manual, 'The Delight of the Mind' (*Mānasollāsa*), composed in 1129–30 CE, contains more detailed accounts which were clearly based on earlier precedents (see figure 3.1). The *Mānasollāsa* includes the holding of court among the twenty 'enjoyments' (*upabhoga*s) recommended for a king. According to Someśvara, the king was to sit on a lion-throne in the assembly hall, flanked by his whisk bearers and instruct his chamberlain to issue a

[32] See the portrayal of Saṁsthānaka, the vulgar and comedic villain of Śūdraka's *Mṛcchakaṭika*, who appears in Act 10 recounting his meal of tamarind sauce, meat, rice, sweet cakes, soup, greens and fish and in the opening scenes of the play compares Vasantasenā to a tasty morsel and his heart to a succulent chunk of meat, *MK* 10.29 and 1.18. For a similar, if more generous portrayal, see the treatment of the king's comedic brahmin companion, the *vidūṣaka*, in *VkU* 3.6+, *passim* and other palace dramas.

[33] The only discourses which were regularly concerned with food in the palace, which also formed the avenue of their entry into later sumptuary manuals, were medical and focused around sustaining the king's health.

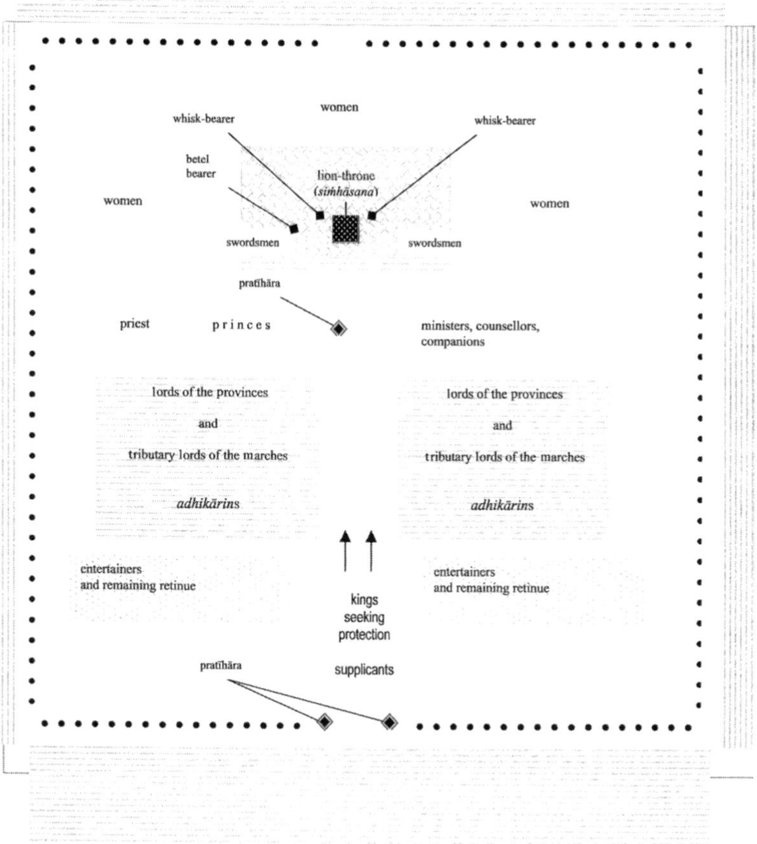

Figure 3.1 Plan of the pillared hall of assembly (*asthānamaṇḍapa*) as reconstructed from Someśvara III's twelfth-century *Mānasollāsa* 3.1161 ff.

general invitation (*sarvāvāhana*) to court.[34] First the doorkeepers were to show in palace women in palanquins (*dola*) covered with curtains, shaded by coloured royal umbrellas and cooled by fly-whisks, while others arrived on horses, mules or on foot. Together, the women were to take seats appropriate to their rank on either side of the throne and behind it (but not in front of it) and to sit in attendance (*paryyupāsate*, literally 'sit around in worship'). They were to gaze at the king and frequently cast glances in his direction to cause him joy.

[34] The following account is based on *Mānasollāsa* 3.1161 ff.

The striking emphasis on the female presence around the king is both ubiquitous and multivalent in courtly sources from at least the Gupta period. On the one hand the king, in his capacity as the embodiment of some deity, typically Viṣṇu, was described in courtly eulogies as the master of various consort goddesses who represented aspects of worldly sovereignty: prosperity and wealth (*śrī*, *lakṣmī*), land (*bhū*), fame (*kīrtī*), learning (*sarasvatī*) and weaponry (*durgā*). These goddesses, and the worldly spheres they embodied, were to be 'enjoyed' (*bhoga*) by sovereigns in varying capacities. And if the king embodied a lordship directly continuous with that which flowed from the divine lord of the cosmos, then the women of the palace, both his wives and the many concubines and female attendants, were analogised respectively to these goddesses and the various types of celestial women who attended the gods in their heavenly abodes.[35] Representing royal authority thus entailed the accumulation of vast retinues of 'palace women', the most important of which were the king's consorts, headed by the chief queen (*mahādevī*).[36] These women functioned generically and symbolically as signs of imperial capacity, and formed, according to Someśvara, 'adornments' to the assembly hall.

After the women assumed their places around the throne, the princes were summoned to sit in front of the king 'at not too great a distance'. The royal priest entered and took his seat close to the princes, and was followed by counsellors, companions and ministers, who were to take assigned places befitting their rank. These men were followed by provincial lords (*maṇḍalādhīśvara*) and tributary lords of the marches (*sāmanta*s or their ministers), who were to sit before the king in rows to his right and left. Next, men appointed to administer and oversee particular tasks and palace functions (*adhikārin*s), like the head treasurer, accountant and master of the wardrobe, entered and were seated as directed by the chamberlains. Trusted swordsman and the all-important betel-nut bearer (*tāmbūladharin*) took places near the king. Then came a host of miscellaneous retainers – brahmins, storytellers, orators, musicians, dancers, bards, chroniclers, magicians and the like. These lower ranks, mostly connected to royal entertainment, were to chant 'victory and long life' to the king.[37] With the household assembled, all were to look at the king

[35] See Bāṇa's remarks on the women (*vilāsinī*s) of Śūdraka's palace in *Kd*, p. 20.

[36] A later (fourteenth- or fifteenth-century) text, the *Mānasāra* (41.10–12), ranks kings by the number of courtesans and queens kept in their palaces. The *Mānasollāsa*, unlike other manuals, makes no mention of the chief queen's presence in the assembly.

[37] The words 'victory and long life', uttered sweetly (*madhurā*) were considered auspicious (*maṅgala*) and were to be chanted by bards and other retainers who walked before the king as he moved about. See the description of King Śūdraka's exit from his court, *Kd*, p. 30, and the expedition of Prince Candrāpīḍa to the royal city, *Kd*, p. 135.

in adoration. At the king's order, the chamberlain was then to lead kings and lords of various regions, who had come seeking protection, into the assembly hall. These kings were assigned places according to their rank.

For the supplicant or subordinate king just arrived at the palace, the first and most important goal was to gain entry into the assembly. Gaining audience, at least judging from the courtly literature, could by no means be assumed. Bāṇa depicts the outer courtyards of Harṣa's camp as filled with kings who waited all day in hope of an audience, many becoming dejected at being turned away.[38] Entry to the court was regulated through those crucial servants we encountered earlier, the doorkeepers and chamberlains (*pratīhāra*). In Bāṇa's case, he is halted at the outer doors of the palace while his companion, the messenger Mekhalaka, brings the chief chamberlain, one Pāriyātra, to escort him to the king.[39] Even then, the king initially rebuffs Bāṇa by declaring, 'I will not see him'.[40]

Upon entering the court, men bowed before the king as a sign of submission. Supplicants and subordinate kings, after bowing, were either raised 'through favour' (*saprasāda*) by the king's own hand (usually placed on the back), or stood themselves and waited to be appointed a seat.[41] They were then assigned a position within the court ensemble by the king and ushered there by the chamberlain. The location of a visitor's place within the assembly hall was a matter of tremendous importance, for it effectively ranked him among the internal hierarchy of the household and among the lords of the realm. The first point of note is that not all people were permitted to sit. Seats were favours and could not be presupposed, as Bāṇa notes on his arrival in Harṣa's court.[42] From Someśvara's account, it would seem that only princes, the royal priest, counsellors, ministers, companions of the king and provincial and tributary lords could sit in the assembly hall. The personal attendants of the king as well as overseers (*adhikārins*), bards and entertainers remained standing.[43] All seats, both in their positioning within the assembly hall and

[38] *HC*, ch. 2, p. 60. Though it was generally considered a royal virtue to be easy of access, courtly poetry often celebrated the power and fame of kings by noting the great crowds who took refuge at their courts. See for example, Bāṇa's account of the multitudes waiting outside the court of Harṣa, which he compares to an entire universe, *HC*, ch. 2, p. 61.

[39] Mekhalaka says to Bāṇa that Pāriyātra was to be 'treated with suitable respect (*anurūpa pratipatti*) by those seeking success', *HC*, ch. 2, p. 62.

[40] See *HC*, ch. 2, pp. 78–9.

[41] *Mānasollāsa* 3.1235. For the king raising a man by placing a hand on his back (*nyastahastaḥ pṛṣṭhe*), see *HC*, ch. 7, p. 214.

[42] He remarks that Harṣa had shown no signs of favour like friendly conversation or the gift of a seat, *HC*, ch. 2, p. 80.

[43] For the position and place of each group mentioned by Someśvara, see *Mānasollāsa* 3.1203–7; 1225; 1231–2.

their quality as objects were graded according to hierarchy.[44] Kāmandaka advises dependants never to occupy places or seats allotted to others.[45] The court assembled spatially from the king's throne outward, so that the sequential entry 'according to rank' (*yathāsthāna*) of various members of the household meant that those arriving first sat closer to the king, while those who came last mostly stood at the rear. Higher-ranking men of the court thus sat on finer seats and near the king, proximity to whom was always a mark of honour.[46] In courtly literature, poets rarely fail to mention the general proximity of a visitor or supplicant's seat to the king.[47]

Men of rank, or royal emissaries arriving at court, typically brought gifts (*prābhṛta*) which were presented to the king. These could include some form of tribute either in money or a vast array of material goods and paraphernalia commonly transacted among kings to express their rank. According to Bāṇa, the Bhaumanākara emissary, Haṁsavega, arrived at court conveying numerous gifts for Harṣa, which included ornaments, crest jewels, pearl necklaces, silken towels, quantities of precious stones, drinking vessels, leather goods, seats, woven silk, sandalwood, camphor, nutmeg, ivory, collyrium and various animals including parrots, yaks and musk deer. The most important gift, however, was a large, magnificent parasol named Ābhoga, heirloom to Bhāskaravarman's family, which signified his house's complete submission and unflinching loyalty to Harṣa.[48]

The gifts of subordinates could also be accompanied by offers to take on specific roles of service within the king's court. As we saw earlier, subordinate kings from Gupta times took on various titles which indicated the performance of duties in the lord's household – like chamberlains, whisk-bearers, and emissaries.[49] The wives of tributary lords of the marches (*sāmanta*s) also served their emperor's queen.[50] These

[44] See *Mayamata* 2.2 for the definition of the seat as one of the four types of dwelling place (*vāstu*) and *Mayamata* 32.1ff. for details on seats. See *Mānasāra*, 3.3, 11–12; 44.1 ff.; *Mānasollāsa* 3.1132–50; 1674–96.

[45] *NiS* 5.18.

[46] The Gupta courtier Hariṣeṇa, author of the Allahabad *praśasti*, says that 'his mind was expanded by the favour (*anugraha*) of walking about in proximity (*samīpa*)' to the king, *CII* 3 (1981), no. 1, p. 214.

[47] Typically with a phrase indicating that the person was 'not too far away' (*nātidurā*; *aviprakṛṣṭa*). See *Mānasollāsa* 3.1203; *HC*, ch. 7, p. 214. Nor were seats to be too near (*asaṁnikṛṣṭa*) the king, according to *AS* 5.4.8.

[48] *HC*, ch. 7, pp. 215–16. For elephants presented as gifts and tribute, see *HC*, ch. 2, p. 58. According to Bāṇa, even a village notary (*grāmākṣapaṭalika*) and his retinue of scribes appear at the emperor's military camp to present him with a golden seal (*mudrā*) embossed with the bull, see *HC*, ch. 7, p. 203.

[49] See *Kd*, p. 191; the evidence from inscriptions has been discussed above.

[50] See the remarks of Yaśōvatī, *HC*, ch. 5, p. 167.

titles did not necessarily require permanent residence within the overlord's household, but were roles which were probably assumed with great fanfare and ritually enacted during the meeting of the assembly. The ultimate submission to another king was signified by fanning him with fly-whisks or marshalling those before him in the capacity of a chamberlain. Such acts were considered ennobling, and even the most powerful of kings, though they may have been served by their underlords, typically took up the role of attending religious images both in temples and when they moved in procession. Hsuan-Tsang mentions that Emperor Harṣa and the king of Assam (Bhāskaravarman) accompanied an image of the Buddha on procession by holding a parasol and fly-whisk above the image, respectively.[51]

These roles, however, were considered honours, and this points to an important reciprocity which the ruling king or emperor was to exhibit towards the entire assembly to varying degrees. The *Mānasollāsa* advises that after having 'respectfully' seated visiting kings within the hall according to their rank, the king was to please them with various gifts – fine garments, many-coloured fillets, golden ornaments, beautiful jewellery, horses, elephants, villages, towns and even countries. In the same way he was to satisfy others in the assembly – princes, counsellors, ministers, companions, lords of provinces, great soldiers, clever servants and even overseers – before retiring to his pleasure house (*keliketana*) accompanied by a retinue of women.[52] The dismissal of the court, not treated by Someśvara, must also have been an elaborate matter. Bāṇa depicts a bewildering scene of men rising after the king and falling over one another in order to bow before him as he exited the hall, preceded by his staff-wielding chamberlains and chanting bards.[53]

Though there were undoubtedly other activities which the king undertook collectively with his underlords and various members of the household (like poetic contests and entertainments), it is the holding of court which was the most important collective event of the king's daily routine. Though it is clear that the adjudication of disputes and the review of revenues and offices took up some time, courtly sources tend to be more concerned with the visible displays of loyalty of subordinates and the distribution of gifts and honours as favours to men of rank. The most important favours entailed either the 're-establishment' of defeated kings to their own territories or the assignment of rule and/or revenues

[51] According to the monk, Harṣa was dressed as Indra and Bhāskaravarman as Brahmā, *Si-Yu-Ki*, vol. I, p. 218.

[52] *Mānasollāsa* 3.1236–44. The court presumably disassembled, and visiting kings retired to residences provided for them.

[53] See Bāṇa's colourful account, *Kd*, pp. 29–30.

of existing or newly conquered territories to loyal generals and servants. Of note here, however, is a repertoire of special objects which were given together with or independent of such privileges to signify favour, respect and authority. These items, which from early historic times had been associated with royalty, were the subjects of extensive and detailed sumptuary regulation by the tenth century. They included war elephants and war horses, as well as emblems (*aṅka*, *cinha*) of political status like parasols, fly-whisks, banners, musical instruments, seats, various types of garments and ornaments. They were either worn on the body (clothes, ornaments, crowns, turbans), held by attendants (parasols, palanquins, fly-whisks), or processed to herald the arrival of a lord (musical instruments and banners).

From the Gupta period, texts begin to set out different types and dimensions of these objects as expressions of political hierarchy. At court, everyone appeared in dress and accoutrements which reflected their rank and function. The concern of texts like the sixth-century *Bṛhatsaṁhitā* over the calibrations of these objects for men of different station highlights the importance of sartorial and sumptuary codes in royal assemblies and processions. The king and his chamberlains ensured not only that everyone was placed in the assembly or procession according to rank, but also that appropriate dress and insignia were maintained.[54] This discipline was most effectively ensured by maintaining a monopoly on the possession *and* distribution of these objects to the lords and servants of the realm. The great emphasis on generosity and on the giving of status objects in the *nīti* literature is surely underwritten by the needs of kings and lords to maintain the delicate hierarchies of their realms and households. The texts on polity always advise that gifts were to be bestowed 'suitably' (*ucita*) and 'according to rank' (*yathāsthāna*). Yet such gifts, by their very nature as acts of favour, often altered the existing hierarchy at court and thus had to be considered carefully so as not to promote discord.[55]

Unfortunately, the sources present no uniform picture, but several practices deserve note. Among the most prized objects during the sixth and seventh centuries was the headpiece known as *paṭṭa* or *paṭṭabandha* – a fillet or band-like piece of silken cloth or gold which was fixed around

[54] Both Kauṭilya and Kāmandaka sternly warn courtiers never to imitate royal dress and attributes, *AS* 5.4.10; *NiS* 5.33. Recall the inscription of Yaśodharman which mentions that a minister was permitted to wear royal clothes (*nṛpativeśa*), though 'only as a mark of distinction' (*kevalaṁ lakṣmamātram*), *CII* 3 (1888), no. 35, p. 154.

[55] This is the implication of Kāmandaka's warning on the subject, *NiS* 5.68–70.

the head and displayed (possibly with a plate) on the forehead.[56] The *Bṛhatsaṁhitā* and *Nāṭyaśāstra* mention varieties of *paṭṭa* or *paṭṭabandha* worn by palace personnel, including the chief queen, chamberlains, ministers, crown princes, generals and the king himself.[57] Inscriptions and literary texts make much of the conferral of these headbands by kings to both palace personnel and subordinate monarchs. According to the famous sixth-century Talgunda pillar inscription it was the tying of the *paṭṭabandha* after entering the service of the Pallavas which formed the crucial moment in the transformation of the Kadamba family from its brahmin origins to royal status.[58] The conferral of a *paṭṭa* formed the central event of some court assemblies, a rite called the *paṭṭabandhamahotsava* or *paṭṭabandhābhiśeka* which was in effect a sort of 'coronation', involving either the gift of land, sovereignty or other powers.[59] Through the conferral of such objects and the powers that went with them,

[56] The *paṭṭa* and *paṭṭabandha*, translated variously as 'head-band', 'turban', 'fillet' or 'badge of honour' in the secondary literature, was wrapped or tied around the head so as to be displayed on the forehead, and could be worn with or without other headgear like crowns. Bāṇa describes subordinate kings of Emperor Tārāpīḍa as having crowns wrapped with white cloth bands, *Kd*, p. 144, though the *Bṛhatsaṁhitā* explains different *paṭṭas* as made of gold. The practice of tying such bands was likely influenced, like other fashions, by Sasanian courts, where tiaras and diadems were common signs of royalty, and was probably more influential in the subcontinent before the thirteenth century than the Central Asian practice of robing. For a discussion of Sasanian practice, see Jenny Rose, 'Sasanian Splendour: The Appurtenances of Royalty', in Gordon, *Robes and Honor: The Medieval World of Investiture* (New York: Palgrave, 2001), p. 38 ff.

[57] *NS* 23.143–4; *BS* 48.1 ff. For examples of *paṭṭabandha* worn by palace servants and chamberlains, see *HC*, ch. 1, p. 24; *Kd*, p. 140; for subordinate kings, see *HC*, ch. 7, p. 207; *Kd*, p. 144; and for chief queens, *HC*, ch. 5, p. 167. The use of *paṭṭas* to mark rank among the queens was important enough that the common term in medieval inscriptions to denote the chief queen was *paṭṭamahādevī* 'the great queen with a headband'. See the Jethwai Plates of the Rāṣṭrakūṭa queen Silamahādevī, *EI* 22 (1933–4), no. 17, p. 101.

[58] The inscription also mentions the Kadamba crown-prince Śāntivarman as having 'a body made radiant by the tying of three *paṭṭas*' (*paṭṭa-tray-ārppaṇa-virājita-cāru-mūrtteḥ*), *EI* 8 (1905–6), no. 5, p. 33.

[59] Ninth- and tenth-century grants from the Deccan refer to such rituals, which, judging from *HC*, ch. 2, p. 58, may have involved the presentation of the fillet on the back of an elephant. For the attendance of Rāṣṭrakūṭa kings at their own and other fillet-tying ceremonies (*paṭṭabandha-mahotsava*), see *EI* 7 (1902–3), no. 6, p. 40 and *EI* 5 (1898–9), no. 16c, p. 129. A tenth-century eastern Cālukya grant mentions sprinkling or bathing (*abhiṣekam*) accompanying the ceremony in the manner of a coronation, *EI* 5 (1898–9), no. 16e, p. 136. This ritual, however, did not necessarily represent elevation to royalty, as an eleventh-century inscription of the eastern Cālukya king Viṣṇuvardhana (himself an underlord of the Cōḻa king Kulōttuṅka I), says that the king anointed with favour into the office of general (*saprasādaṁ senāpatyebhiṣikto*) one Gunaratnabhūṣaṇa by the tying of a fillet (*paṭṭamāropitam*), *IA* 19 (1890), p. 432. R. N. Nandi compares this ceremony (Kannada, *paṭṭam gaṭṭi*) to the European practice of dubbing into knighthood, in *State Formation, Agrarian Growth and Social Change in Feudal South India, c. 600–1200 AD* (Delhi: Manohar, 2000), p. 47.

kings were able to constitute political hierarchies. According to a western Gaṅga inscription, the king Śrī Puruṣa (*c.* 725–75 CE) subjected various kings by the sword (force), on the one hand, and by the *paṭṭa* (conferral of benefits), on the other.[60] From the seventh century inscriptions begin to mention the award of such prized objects as the 'five great sounds' (*pañcamahāśabda*) – musical instruments which heralded the processions of men of royal rank[61] – and later records include the gift of fly-whisks, palanquins, drums, war elephants, umbrellas, thrones and banners.[62]

The particular acts, either individually or collectively, performed in order to please, gratify and convey respect to another person generally of equal or superior rank were denoted by the term *upacāra*. This term included not only gestures and words of respectful greeting, but the presentation of water and food, and gifts to gratify the senses like ornaments, clothes, incense, flowers, unguents and even various entertainments (dance, song and music).[63] By extension, the term came to denote any ministration or attendance of a lord's physical needs, like bathing, adornment, anointment and fanning. It is in this sense that Kauṭilya refers generically to royal attendants as *upacāraka*s and *upacārikā*s.[64] Most generally, *upacāra* could refer to any form of attendance towards a person that was structured by the dynamics of deference typical of the court – what one might call a 'service' or a 'courtesy' in the sense of a specific action or collection of actions.

The idea of *upacāra* probably had its origin in the reciprocal acts of respect performed in a household between a host and his guests – acts of

[60] *EC* 4 (n.s., 1975) no. 354, p. 707.

[61] For early usages of this term, which becomes very widespread from the eighth and ninth centuries, see the Kaira Plates (628 CE) of the Gurjara king Dadda II, *CII* 4 (1955), vol. 1, no. 16, p. 61; the Tiwarkhed plates (*c.* 631 CE) of the Rāṣṭrakūṭa king Nannarāja from Achalapura, *EI* 11 (1911–12), no. 27, p. 279; the seventh-century Baloda Plates of the Pāṇḍuvaṁśin king Tīvaradeva, *ISPS* vol. 2, no. 3.2, p. 102; and the Nidhanpur Plates (*c.* 650 CE) of the Bhaumanāraka king Bhāskaravarman, *EI* 12 (1913–14), no. 13, p. 75. Its meaning has been debated, with some maintaining that the five 'sounds' (*śabda*) referred to titles beginning with *mahat*. More convincing evidence, however, has been accumulated, particularly from the Deccan, to suggest that the sounds in question were types of instruments or music heralding processions. See the discussion in D. C. Sircar, *Indian Epigraphical Glossary* (Delhi: Motilal Banarsidass, 1966), s.v; also *ISPS*, p. 105n.

[62] A ninth-century Cōḻa inscription mentions that one Vikki Aṇṇaṉ received a fly-whisk, palanquin, drum, palace, horn and a troop of war elephants from his Cōḻa overlord, King Āditya, *SII* 3.3 (1929), no. 89, p. 221. For other examples of the conferral of such insignia, see *EI* 4 (1896–7), nos. 10, 25, pp. 89, 189; *EI* 3 (1894–5), no. 15, p. 88.

[63] For *upacāra* used to denote modes of address, see *MkA* 4.1+; bowing and the making of *añjali*, *Sk* 3.17, *RghV* 3.11; and flower offerings, *RghV* 7.11.

[64] *AS* 3.13–9–10.

respect which were required to reflect the varying relations of hierarchy between them. Though the term retained this more generic meaning (the holding of court was, after all, preceded by formal invitation),[65] in the courtly context it could refer not only to acts of propitiation performed by a guest or person of lower or equal rank towards his host or lord, but also to exchanges between men and women within the same household, courtesans and their customers, and various other relationships which obtained at court.[66] The poetic descriptions of the courtesies between people of rank frequently use the metaphor of the flower offering – the folded hands compared to lotus buds, the gestures of the eyes to garlands and words of praise to flower offerings.[67] The collective performance of such courtesies was usually denoted by some form of the more embracing verbal roots √*pūj* or √*arc*, meaning to honour, worship, or revere.[68] Both these terms also developed strong religious connotations, referring to the rites connected with honouring temple deities, which also consisted of set numbers of *upacāra*s.[69]

A number of other terms (*ādara*, *praśraya*, *praṇaya*) referred more generically to deference shown between people of the court, and were frequently used by courtly writers to describe actions performed with requisite and suitable 'respect'. The reciprocation of such courtesies and respect as well as the award or recognition of status on the part of men of superior rank towards subordinates was typically referred to by the verbal and nominal derivatives of the root √*man*, to measure or esteem,

[65] In the Junāgadh rock inscription, Cakrapālita is said to have delighted his subjects by causing reciprocal and free entry into houses (*niryantranānyonyagṛhapraveśa*) and increasing courtesies (*upacāra*) and affection (*prīti*) within them, *CII* 3 (1981), no. 28, p. 300.

[66] For a senior queen to her husband, see *MkA* 4.1+; for a king to a junior queen, *MkA* 3.3. Dealings with courtesans were also renowned for their requirement of courtesies (*upacāra*). See *Gaṇikāvṛttisaṃgraha* 28 and *DhVS* 9.

[67] See *HC*, ch. 2, p. 61; *Kd*, p. 134; *CII* 3 (1888), no. 17, p. 73; *EI* 12 (1913–14), no. 13, p. 78. As the messenger Mālatī (whose betel-bearer is described as composed entirely of flowers) approaches Sarasvatī from a distance, the latter's expressions and sentiments are compared to various courtesies, including meeting, embracing, welcoming, anointing, fanning, adorning and, finally, offering flowers, *HC*, ch. 1, pp. 32–3.

[68] In Daṇḍin's seventh-century *Daśakumāracarita*, the princess Avantisundarī, upon meeting the prince Rājavāhana disguised as a learned brahmin, presents him with a seat, and 'honours him' (*pūjāṃ kārayāmāsa*), as her companion presents perfumes, flowers, barley corns, camphor, betel-nuts, and various other fine substances. *DK*, ch. 5, p. 46. Śukanāsa, the minister of king Tārāpīḍa, honours (*abhyarcya*) the Prince Candrāpīḍa with ornaments, clothes, flowers, and unguents, *Kd*, p. 157. See also *CII* 3 (1888), no. 33, pp. 146–7 and *CII* 6 (1977), no. 43, p. 201.

[69] For the origin of religious *pūjā* and its relation to royal *upacāra*s, see Gudrun Bühnemann, *Pūjā: A Study in Smārta Ritual* (Vienna: De Nobili Research Library, 1988), p. 30.

and, by extension, to honour.[70] The terms *māna* or *bahumāna*, 'honour' and 'much honour', thus had the sense of a specifically demonstrated or conferred respect or recognition at court.[71] Inscriptions and literary texts mention that gifts or acts of favour were conferred with 'honour' (*māna*).[72] According to Someśvara, after the king had allocated gifts to his underlords, he was to dismiss them with a show of 'great honour' (*bahumāna*).[73] This notion of honour, as its etymology suggests, was 'measured', and was extended in varying degrees according to the achievements or rank of the recipient in question.[74]

The immediate context of the courtesies of the assembly hall was often highly charged. Defeated kings were all but coerced to 'seek entry' into the household of a victorious king, as the Allahabad pillar inscription's requirement of court attendance (*praṇāmāgamanam*) for defeated kings and Bāṇa's description of enemy vassals (*śatrumahāsāmanta*) waiting for entry into Harṣa's camp make very clear.[75] The costly and precious objects they presented as gifts and tribute at court, frequently mentioned in inscriptions simply as prizes gained by conquering kings, moved back and forth between families as they rose and fell from fortune. The family of the western Gaṅgas, for example, took part in several campaigns against the Pallavas of Kāñcī as loyal underlords of the Cālukyas, in the course of which they obtained various objects like a royal umbrella and precious necklace containing the gem by the name of *ugrodaya*. Under the retaliatory raids of the Pallava king Nandivarman they were forced to surrender the latter object, which was undoubtedly presented at court as a sign of submission.[76]

One of the most dramatic events which the sources present to us from our period was when Harṣa's elder brother and successor to the throne, Rājyavardhana, visited the court of the ruler of Gauḍa, Śaśāṅka. Rājyavardhana, having just defeated the king of Mālwā, arrived

[70] For the Cālukya king Pulakeśīn II honouring (*saṁmānayati*) officials, *EI* 18 (1925–6), no. 27, p. 259; for the Vaṅga king Viśvavarman treating servants with unparalleled honour (*mānena*), *CII* 3 (1888), no. 17, p. 74. In some cases, $\sqrt{}$*pūj* is used for honouring subordinates, *EI* 8 (1905–6), no. 5, p. 32 and *EI* 28 (1949–50), no. 1, p. 8.

[71] The term *māna* does not seem to be used in the sense of a permanent and substantialised attribute, as in the English sense of the noun 'honour' (which can be lost). Interestingly, its attributional usage tended to be pejorative, meaning 'pride' or 'arrogance', which perhaps arose from being honoured.

[72] For the Gupta courtier and ruler of Saurāṣṭra, Cakrapālita, *CII* 3 (1981), no. 28, p. 300; for the Maitraka king Dhruvasena I, *EI* 11 (1911–12), no. 9.1, p. 106.

[73] *Mānasollāsa* 3.1239. See also Pulakeśin II's Aihole inscription (*c.* 634 CE) which says similarly that Pulakeśin had 'dismissed kings full of honours', *EI* 6 (1900–1), no. 1, p. 6.

[74] After his coronation, Candrāpīḍa receives subordinate kings, honouring each 'appropriately' (*yathocitam saṁmānasya*), *Kd*, p. 182; cf. *Kd*, p. 134.

[75] *CII* 3 (1981), no. 1, p. 213; *HC*, ch. 2, p. 60.

[76] See *SII* 2 (1895–1913), no. 99, p. 520; and for context, *CHI*, vol. III, pt. 1, pp. 356–7.

at Śaśāṅka's court not as a subordinate but as an equal. He was thus due the courtesies appropriate for a guest, which he received and no doubt reciprocated. But something soon went very wrong and according to both the *Harṣacarita* and the inscriptions, he was attacked by Śāśāṅka's men and killed. According to Bāṇa, his confidence (*viśvāsa*) had been increased by 'false courtesies' (*mithyopacāra*) and that 'trusting' (*viśrabdha*), alone and weaponless, he was slain in his quarters.[77] The inscriptions say that he was killed as a result of adhering to the sincerity or trust (*satyānurodha*) required in the exchange of courtesies.[78] According to Bāṇa, when Harṣa was informed of these events, he furiously decried the cowardice of the Gauḍa king and vowed revenge. Though the violation of such codes brought shame on a family, the advice of the texts on polity regarding the king's security would suggest that such violations of courtly protocols were far more common than either the chronicles or inscriptions suggest.[79]

Gestural and verbal protocols

Interactions between men and women at court were accompanied by an elaborate code of bodily movements and verbal protocols. Many of these practices can be documented from early historic times, particularly through sculptural reliefs and the early rulebooks which regulated the lifestyles of the priestly élites. These sources suggest the emergence of a sort of bodily 'grammar' and verbal 'comportment' which were refined and significantly modified by the men of the court from the first centuries of the Christian Era. By the Gupta period, such gestures and protocols formed the necessary accoutrements of daily interaction among men and women of rank. The following section will examine three such occasions for protocol – bowing and prostration; verbal etiquette and modes of address; and the gestures of the eyes. To a certain extent these choices are arbitrary, and much more could be said about other codes of gesture. The *Nāṭyaśāstra* considers nearly every limb of the body capable of some significant gesture (*ceṣṭa*) on the stage, and life at court no doubt followed

77 *HC*, ch. 6, p. 186. While Bāṇa says that he was slain in his 'own quarters' (*svabhavane*), the inscriptional accounts are clear that it was 'in the house of his enemy' (*arātibhavane*), *EI* 1 (1892), no. 11, p. 72. No doubt this means that he was killed in his camp or temporary residence provided while visiting the household of Śaśāṅka.

78 The phrase *satyānurodhena* has been translated as 'adhering to his promise' by most scholars, but the sense of *satya* is more appropriately understood as the good faith or sincerity involved in the exchange of courtesies rather than any particular vow or promise of Rājyavardhana, for which we have no evidence.

79 After Harṣa vows revenge, his minister, Skandagupta, advises caution by citing the demise of numerous kings through treachery.

suit. Gestures even formed part of the new astrological and prognosticatory science which played such an important role at court from the Gupta period.

As we saw above, each man bowed in front of the king before he was assigned a place in the assembly hall. The significance of this act for life at court cannot be overestimated.[80] Such practices had been conspicuous since at least early historic times, as is evident from the railings of Buddhist stūpas which contain many prostrating figures, and the *dharmaśāstra*s which contain details on bowing and saluting.[81] Among kings and their servants bowing was equally important, and Samudragupta's Allahabad inscription mentions 'bowed approaches' (*praṇāmāgamaṇam*) among the requirements for subjugated kings.[82] Inscriptions from Gupta times, and particularly from the sixth century, routinely mention the obeisance and prostration of subordinate kings. The basic gesture was a bending of the head and/or waist, denoted by some form of the Sanskrit root (*pra-* or *ava-*) √*nam*, while sometimes clasping the hands together in a gesture known as *añjali* (-√*kṛ*) (see figures 3.3 and 3.4).[83]

Though our knowledge is once again fragmentary, it would seem that the gestures of bowing and the making of *añjali* in the courtly context were elaborated to express shades of political and palace hierarchy. The *Nāṭyaśāstra* sets out three varieties of *añjali*, made above the head, in front of the face and on the chest, depending on the rank of the person greeted.[84] Bowing was also clearly calibrated to reflect graded political hierarchies, and ranged from simply bending of the head or the waist, with or without making the gesture of *añjali*, to more elaborate forms of bowing as to touch various parts of the body to the ground.[85] In the *Harṣacarita*, when the later Gupta princes Mādhavagupta and Kumāragupta appear before Harṣa and his sons, they bow by touching their four limbs (feet and hands) and head to the ground.[86] Daṇḍin's seventh-century *Daśakumāracarita* describes the same gesture with the

80 Kālidāsa tells us that soon after Prince Raghu learned to utter words and walk as a child, he also learned to bow and prostrate himself, which caused great joy to his father, *RghV* 3.25.

81 *Vasiṣṭhadharmasūtra* 13.41–6; *Gautamadharmasūtra* 6.1–11; *Āpastambadharmasūtra* 1.4.14.7–24, 1.2.5.18.

82 *CII* 3 (1981), no. 1, p. 213.

83 The verb √*vand* tended to be used for bowing and salutation to gods and brahmins, see *Kd*, p. 156 and *VkU* 2.0+.

84 The *añjali* was to be made on the head for the gods (*devatā*), at the face for venerable persons (*guru*) and on the chest for friends (*mitra*). Kings are conspicuously absent from this list. See *NS* 9.127–8.

85 See Agrawala, *The Deeds of Harsha*, p. 155, who distinguishes four types of bowing from a survey of Bāṇa's works: bowing the head, bowing with the hands folded in *añjali*, placing the head at the feet and rubbing the head on the footstool of the emperor.

86 *caturbhiraṅgairuttamāṅgena ca gāṁ spṛśantau namaścakratuḥ*, *HC*, ch. 4, p. 140.

hands folded in *añjali* pressed to (literally 'kissing') the head.[87] This came to be known as the *pañcāṅga* or 'five limbed' prostration, referring to the touching of the two feet, two hands and forehead to the ground. We also hear of the 'eight-limbed' (*aṣṭāṅga* or *saṣṭāṅga*) prostration in other texts, comprising two feet, two knees, two hands, forehead and chest. In these gestures the idea was that the body was to bow (*praṇāma*) or 'fall' (*pāta*) to the ground before one's lord. The most extreme prostration was called the 'staff' (*daṇḍavat* or *daṇḍapraṇāma*), where the entire body was straightened on the ground before one's lord.[88]

Prostration was, in essence, the placement of the highest and purest part of one's own body – the head – towards the lowest part of one's superior's body, namely his feet.[89] It is thus not surprising that the act of prostration came to centre around the feet of one's lord, and no doubt helps to explain the truly remarkable and perhaps unparalleled obsession with feet in the religious and courtly culture of medieval India.[90] Any student of Indian epigraphy will be well-familiar with the copious imagery around imperial feet. According to the poetic descriptions, the king's feet were brushed and scratched by the crowns of prostrating kings, showered and illumined by jewels falling from their crowns.[91] Though the seemingly endless variations on this theme were partly hyperbolic, it is also clear that such descriptions were rooted in actual court ritual. The king sat on an elaborately carved and decorated lion throne, which was not only the grandest seat in the assembly hall, but was also elevated by dias and socle (see figure 3.2).[92] His jewel-sandalled feet, especially washed and smeared with unguents, rested on a jewelled footstool (*pādapīṭha*).[93] Approaching supplicants bowed before the king at some distance, and when signalled, approached the throne to prostrate themselves at his feet. Bāṇa's account of the arrival of Haṁsavega, emissary of

[87] *pañcāṅgaspṛṣṭabhūmirañjalicumbitacūṭa*, *DK*, ch. 8, p. 194.

[88] See *DK*, ch. 2, p. 25; also *Mānasollāsa* 3.1235, where kings seeking protection were to 'bow and fall to the ground like a staff' (*praṇata daṇḍabhuvi*).

[89] In some cases it could entail raising some object infused with the lord's presence to one's head. Later copperplates from the south suggest that royal orders were received by local officials by either prostrating before them or raising them to their heads. See *SII* 3.3 (1920), no. 205, p. 430, l. 143.

[90] Equally remarkable is the almost total neglect of the subject in secondary literature, barring the recent and exceptional study of Jutta Jain-Neubauer, *Feet and Footwear in Indian Culture* (Ahmedabad: Mapin, 2000), esp. pp. 16–79.

[91] Examples are almost too copious to require citation, but see, for a literary example, Bāṇa's description of the emperor Harṣa's feet in *HC*, ch. 2, p. 72. In traditional *kāvya* style, Bāṇa begins his description of the king with his feet and ends with his crown. It should be noted that this 'upward' descriptive movement is also the sequence of vision of one prostrating before a lord.

[92] For the base (*padmabandha*) and socle (*upapīṭha*) of the lion throne, see *Mayamata* 32.14

[93] On the footstool, see *HC*, ch. 2, p. 72. Both anointment of the feet (*pādābhyaṅga*) and the wearing of sandals (*pāduka*) are included by Someśvara among the twenty royal enjoyments treated in his *Mānasollāsa* (3.954–8; 1630–8).

Figure 3.2 Possible dias for a lion-throne at the Pallava complex at Mahabalipuram, *c.* seventh century, CE.

the Bhaumanākara king Bhāskaravarman, at Harṣa's court, is illustrative. The emissary enters, performs a *pañcāṅga* bow with his five limbs touching the ground (literally 'embracing the court') and, when signalled by the king, runs forward to the throne to rub his forehead on the footstool where the king's feet rested.[94]

The focus on feet in courtly circles developed into a rich language of power. From the fourth century, we find common reference in inscriptions to men being 'devoted to' (*bhakta*) or even more commonly 'meditating upon' (*anuddhyāta*) the feet of parents and overlords, and being 'accepted by the feet' (*pādaparigṛhīta*) of these lords. Probably originating at the Gupta court, this terminlogy spread to kingdoms throughout the subcontinent in hundreds of inscriptions within the next two centuries, becoming a common political idiom.[95] It is graphically represented in

[94] *HC*, ch. 7, p. 214.

[95] This terminology, first found in the records of the Guptas and Vākāṭakas, is taken up by numerous courts from the fourth century. For Gupta uses, see *CII* 3 (1981), nos. 1, 9, 21, 22, 24, 31, 38, 40, 41, 44, 45, pp. 215, 250, 281, 285, 289, 315, 336, 344, 348, 355, 358. For the Vākāṭakas, see *CII* 5 (1963), no. 2, p. 7; no. 8, p. 36. For select specimens from dynasties between the fourth and seventh centuries see *CII* 3 (1888), no. 3, p. 25 for the Śanakānikas; *CII* 3 (1888), no. 24, p. 111 for the Parivrājakas of Bundelkhand; *CII* 5 (1963), nos. 21–2, pp. 91–2; *CII* 3 (1888), nos. 26–31, p. 117 ff. for the kings of

Figure 3.3 Relief sculpture depicting Viṣṇu as Varāha rescuing the earth as Bhūdevī from the waters, with a Nāga king performing *añjali* in obeisance. Cave 5, Udayagiri, Madhya Pradesh, *c.* early fifth century, CE.

the Gupta imperial complex at Udayagiri, where a seated figure, perhaps a Śanakānika prince sits meditating on the feet of a Gupta emperor, represented as Viṣṇu's boar incarnation and other Gupta period sculptures (figures 3.3 and 3.4).[96] Often briefly mentioned, these phrases

Uccakalpa; *CII* 4 (1955), nos. 8–9, pp. 24, 27 for the Traikūṭakas; *CII* 5 (1963), no. 19, p. 85; *CII* 3 (1888), no. 81, p. 295; *EI* 7 (1902–3), no. 13, p. 104, for the Somavaṁśis of South Kosala; *CII* 3 (1888), nos. 40–1, pp. 193, 198; *EI* 9 (1907–8) no. 39, p. 283, for the kings of Śarabhapura; *EI* 9 (1907–8), no. 7, p. 58; *EI* 31 (1955–6), no. 1a, p. 4; *EI* 31 (1955–6), no. 1b, p. 9; *EI* 25 (1939–40), no. 7, p. 46, for the Śālāṅkāyanas of Veṅgi; *EI* 17 (1923–4), no. 19, p. 332; *EI* 12 (1913–14), no. 17, p. 134; *EI* 4 (1896–7), no. 25, p. 196, for the Viṣṇukuṇḍins of Śrīpārvata/Veṅgī; *EI* 28 (1949–50), nos. 16, 31, 39, 47, pp. 84, 178, 235, 302; *EI* 3 (1894–5), nos. 3, 20, 21, pp. 18, 128, 131; *EI* 12 (1913–14), no. 2, p. 5; *EI* 23 (1935–6), no. 8, p. 60; *EI* 24 (1937–8), no. 17, p. 135, for dynasties of Kaliṅga; *EI* 15 (1919–20), no. 16i–ii, pp. 289–90; *EI* 2 (1894), no. 4iii, p. 23; *EI* 10 (1909–10), no. 16, p. 74; *CII* 4 (1955), nos. 12–14, pp. 41, 45, 49, for the Kalacuris of western India; *EI* 15 (1919–20), no. 11b, p. 254; *EI* 8 (1905–6), no. 15, p. 162; *EI* 24 (1937–8), no. 18, p. 141 for the Pallavas of Kanchi; *EI* 16 (1921–2), no. 4, p. 18; *CII* 3 (1888), no. 39, pp. 174–8 for the Maitrakas of Valabhi; *CII* 3 (1888), no. 46, pp. 215–16, for the later Guptas of Magadha; *CII* 3 (1888), no. 47, p. 220 for the Maukharis of Kanauj; *CII* 3 (1888), no. 52, p. 232, for Harṣavardhana; *CII* 4 (1955), nos. 28–9, pp. 129, 134, for the early Cālukyas of Gujarat; and *CII* 4 (1955), no. 26, p. 121, for the Sendrakas of Gujarat.

96 For an exhaustive analysis of the Udayagiri panel as a multivalent political signifier, see Michael Willis, 'Archaeology and the Politics of Time' (forthcoming).

Figure 3.4 Detail of a relief depicting a *nāga* and *nāginī* performing obeisance to Viṣṇu and King Gajendra after their defeat. Deogarh, Uttar Pradesh, *c.* early sixth century CE.

indicated relations of allegiance, affiliation and favour between one lord and another. The subordinate repaired to and concentrated on the 'feet' of his lord, who in turn deigned to 'accept him' at his feet. In many cases such gestures indicated the loving devotion of a son to a father, or a vassal to his overlord, usually with the implication of some special relationship which entailed privileges. In other cases the context was clearly coercive and agonistic, as when the Huṇa king Mihirakula is described as being forcefully and painfully compelled to bend his forehead in obeisance, honouring the feet of the Aulikāra king Yaśodharman with the flowers in his hair.[97]

Speech at court was governed by numerous protocols, and speaking effectively within their framework, what we might call 'eloquence', was a highly valued skill among men of rank. Speech could be relatively 'public' as when men spoke before the assembled *sabhā* or *goṣṭhī* to gain favour, assent or support, report business, or maintain their reputations, or it could be relatively more quotidian, as when men greeted and conversed with one another. In either case, verbal interactions were equally structured by protocol. Verbal exchanges were frequently preceded with salutations, gestures, honorific addresses and, when appropriate, words or verses of praise. The act of salutary address, for example, usually denoted by the term *abhivādana*, had entailed a strong gestural component from early times.[98] It generally included rising from one's seat (if seated), touching or embracing the feet of the addressee or making *añjalī*, and finally uttering the appropriate title or name of the addressee, followed by one's own name and the salutation (*abhi* +√ *vad*) itself – 'Noble One (*ārya*), Candragupta salutes (*abhi-vādayate*) [you]'.[99] Greetings to superiors were often prefaced by 'victory' or 'long life'.[100] Forms of address for men of rank typically involved a substantive construed with the third person verb. The most common of these was *bhavant* (male) or *bhavati* (female), probably derived from the title *bhagavant*, or 'lord', but which had wide and generic usage. Other addresses included *āyuṣman*, literally 'long-lived one'; *ārya/ārye*, 'noble' man/lady; *deva/devī*, 'your Highness' (king and queen); *svāmin/svāminī*, 'lord'/'madam'; *bhadra*, 'sir'; as well as a host of other terms related to specific titles from the lowest ranks of

97 *CII* 3 (1888), no. 33, p. 147.

98 See *MDh* 2.119 ff. for greetings between priests.

99 See *MR* 7.8+ where Cāṇakya greets the defeated Rākṣasa in this manner, and later (7.11+) king Candragupta does the same. That this greeting involved touching the feet is indicated by Rākṣasa's response to Cāṇakya after being greeted – 'please do not touch me, I have been defiled by a Cāṇḍāla'.

100 See Vaiśampāyana's greeting of King Śūdraka, *Kd*, p. 26; or the chamberlain Bādarāyaṅa's request for forgiveness for not greeting the king with 'fame' (*prasīdatu*) in *PY* 2.8+.

handmaids to eminent religious men. The *Nāṭyaśāstra* devotes the better part of a chapter to setting out the rules for how men and women of the court were to address one another according to their rank and birth.

Generally speaking, personal names were used only when speaking to one's equals and inferiors, but rarely if ever in addressing those of superior rank. The king, for example, was to be addressed as *deva* or *āyuṣman* by his subjects and retainers.[101] By sages and brahmins, however, he could be addressed by the title 'king' (*rājan*), by his patronym (*apatyapratyaya*), or even directly by his name (*namnā*), a practice 'to be excused' (*kṣāmya*) because brahmins were to be honoured (*pujyā*) by kings.[102] Kings, in turn, were to address brahmins as 'noble one', or *ārya*, though this general honorific could apply to all those of standing and high birth in the courtly environment.[103] Relative rank was important as well, for while all kings could be referred to as *deva*, paramount kings were to be addressed by the special term *bhaṭṭa*.[104] Similarly, chief princes and wives were differentiated from their inferiors by special terms of address.[105] Relations of equality were often expressed through the term *vayasya*, meaning literally 'of the [same] age'.[106] In at least the case of the king and his jester, this title probably meant more than just rank according to 'age', but instead that the men grew up playing with one another.[107] The overall tendency of avoiding 'intimate' or direct second-person forms of address, along with the propensity towards the use of titles reinforced hierarchies of interaction at court by creating verbal distance between speakers across rank.[108]

A smaller set of terms of address (*bhavant*, *ārya* and *bhadra*) had very wide provenance. The term *ārya*, for example, was used not merely to address brahmins, but had a wider and far more generic usage as its meaning, discussed in chapter 2, suggests. Extant sources present cases as diverse as the servants of an eminent courtesan using the term in addressing their mistress, a king combining it with the personal name in addressing his chamberlain, and the Gupta emperor addressing his son by the term.[109] The reality of the situation, therefore, seems to have been somewhat fluid. There was ample scope for individual preference and personal variation, not as 'private expressions' set against the rigidity

[101] *NS* 19.16. [102] *NS* 19.6, 17. [103] *NS* 19.5. [104] *NS* 19.16.
[105] See *NS* 19.12; 19.23–4. [106] *NS* 19.10. [107] *NS* 19.18.
[108] As noted by Sharma, 'The Feudal Mind', p. 278, who observes a tendency toward increasingly variegated registers of address throughout medieval India.
[109] The courtesan Vasantasenā is addressed by her servants as *ārye* (Prakrit: *ajja*), *MK* 2+ *passim*; the king Purūravas addresses his chamberlain as 'noble Lātavya' (*ārya lātavya*), *VkU* 3.4+; king Candragupta II in calling forth his son Samudragupta as heir apparent, *CII* 3 (1981), no. 1, p. 212.

of formal speech, but as pliable instruments with which to articulate subtle shades of favour and disfavour. Protocols of address should thus be conceived less as fixed dictums than as flexible guidelines through which people constituted their shifting relationships. The *Nāṭyaśāstra* recognises as much when it concedes, against its general principles, that superior persons could indeed be addressed by their personal names when inferiors had been granted the specific privilege to do so.[110]

Once granted the opportunity of an audience, retainers had to ensure that their speech was well-timed and effectively used. Indeed, for supplicants and men of low rank seeking promotion, the opportunity to speak before the assembly probably came infrequently, and thus had to be used to the greatest effect.[111] In their discussion of various aspects of court service, the jackal retainers of the *Pañcatantra*, Damanaka and Karaṭaka, eager to ascend the court hierarchy, view the chance to speak as a precarious opportunity. Damanaka remarks that one must 'not speak out of turn (*aprāptakālam*), for doing so, even if one is Bṛhaspati himself, results only in contempt and disdain'.[112] The courtier's speech, according to the *Pañcatantra*, was to be considered and measured, but not verbose.[113] These ends are captured in Damanaka's strategy to achieve his aspirations as a counsellor by seducing the king through conversation, where:

> A reply will generate a reply
> and that reply will lead to further speech
> as one seed is born from another
> well-furnished with the quality of rain.[114]

The idea was to generate dialogue without speaking too much, for verbal exchanges kept open the possibility of speaking, yet again, of effecting one's purpose. If his replies gave his superior the opportunity to conclude the audience, the opportunity might not come again.

Verbal interactions among men of rank, either conducted directly or through intermediaries, were often more elaborate. After initial greetings, people of noble rank enquired after each other's well-being.[115] They then engaged in 'conversation' (denoted variously by terms like *ālāpa*, *ābhāṣana*, *saṁkathā*) which was pleasant and agreeable. Polite conversa-

110 *NS* 19.8. 111 See *AS* 6.1.6; 1.9.1.
112 *PT* 1.23. Bṛhaspati was preceptor of the gods.
113 *PT* 3.38. The courtier was also to speak in a friendly manner (*hitavaktā*) and in refined speech (*saṁskṛtavaktā*), the former of which will be dealt with below and the latter in the following chapter.
114 *PT* 1.22.
115 Usually with the term *kuśalin*, also used in grant portions of copperplate inscriptions, to begin the king's order: 'the king, being in good health (*kuśalin*) informs all servants . . .' See Sircar, *Indian Epigraphical Glossary*, s.v.

tion was considered one of the highest enjoyments of life at court and was the chief activity of the courtly and urbane circles known as *goṣṭhīs*, a term which significantly also meant 'conversation'.[116] It formed the subject of hundreds of sayings which circulated at court throughout post-Gupta India, one of which, attributed to the seventh-century scholar Bhartṛhari, extolled the benefits of amusing conversation (*līlāgoṣṭhī*) with beloved 'good people' (*sajjana*) as more beneficial than camphor, sandal water, betel-nut, moonlight and rare victuals.[117] The enjoyment of courteous and pleasant conversation also had an iconic aspect. The land-grants of the later Cālukyas of Kalyāṇi and some courts influenced by them, for example, are prefaced by the formulaic phrase 'while the king is engaged in the enjoyment of pleasant conversation'.[118]

The exhortations to speak kindly and pleasantly were widespread. The *Arthaśāstra* includes pleasant speech (*śakla*) among the personal excellences of a king, and other sources frequently mention pleasantness in speech as one of the important characteristics of people of high standing.[119] Kāmandaka in his 'Essence of Policy' makes clear that the opposite of pleasant speech was harsh, angry language (described as *krūra*, or 'cruel'), which was to be avoided during all interactions, particularly difficult ones, for cruel words, even in the best of circumstances, caused unnecessary excitement and distress to people.[120] He remarks further that just as the call of the peacock enhances its charm, speech having the quality of sweetness adorns a prudent man.[121] Gesturally, such speech was marked by facial expressions like smiling, and the *Arthaśāstra* recommends not merely pleasant speech but speaking with smiles (*smita*) for the king.[122] Smiling was a sign of favour, and according to the *Arthaśāstra*, when the king deputed tasks with a smile, the courtier was to know that he was satisfied.[123] The Gupta courtier Cakrapālita is praised in the Junagadh rock inscription as delighting the men of his realm by gifts (*dāna*), honours (*māna*), and 'conversation preceded by smiles' (*purvasmitābhāṣaṇa*).[124]

116 Vātsyāyana (*KS* 1.4.34) makes conversation (*ālāpa*) the chief activity of the *goṣṭhī*.

117 Cited in *MSS*, vol. 6, no. 10002. See entries under speech in the subject index of this and other volumes.

118 *sukhāsamkathāvinodadin irutta*: *EI* 14 (1917–18), no. 19a, p. 271. Also used by their underlords, the Śilahāras of Kolhapur, *CII* 6 (1977) no. 43, p. 202, *et al.*, and the Yādavas of Devagiri, *EI* 28 (1949–50), no. 18, p. 97.

119 *AS* 6.1.6; the Somavaṁśi king of South Kosala, Tīvaradeva, is described as 'pleasant in fine speech' (*śaklaḥ subhāṣiteṣu*), *CII* 3 (1888), no. 81, p. 295; and in *HC*, ch. 1, p. 26 the courtier Vikukṣi remarks to Sarasvatī that 'sweet speech (*priyavadatā*) is a hereditary knowledge among the good'.

120 See *NiS* 3.23–34, esp. 3.23–5. 121 *NiS* 3.27.

122 *AS* 6.1.6. 123 *AS* 5.5.7. 124 *CII* 3 (1981), no. 28, p. 300.

'Let alone conversation, even the interchange of glances with the noble raises one to an exalted state.'[125] These words, uttered by the courtier Vikukṣi in Bāṇa's *Harṣacarita*, point to an important aspect of courtly gesture: the movement of the eyes. Seeing was arguably the most developed sense in courtly circles, and the act of looking and viewing was imbued with heavily coded meaning.[126] The normal posture of the eyes for men and women of rank was to be straight, and without furrowing the eyebrows, which indicated malicious intent.[127] A firm gaze indicated virtue; as for men of low birth and menials, their eyes and glances were congenitally unsteady. The *Nāṭyaśāstra* describes menials as having glances which dart from place to place.[128] Just as speech was to be delivered with a smile, so too the eyebrows were to have a pleasant appearance, delivering the gaze as the lips did the voice.

Yet the eyes, like other limbs, were thought capable of gesture, and the *Nāṭyaśāstra* catalogues some forty-four 'glances' or 'looks' (*dṛṣṭi*), in addition to a further twenty-five gestures of the eyeballs, eyelids and eyebrows – together used for conveying various emotional states in drama.[129] These classifications, which in some cases may have been exaggerated for the stage, were clearly drawn from what must have been a complex ocular 'language' at court. The presumption in the courtly manuals was that inner dispositions of people were indicated by the movement of their eyes. The *Arthaśāstra* warns that the contraction (*nirbhoga*) of the eye or eyebrow on the king's face indicated his unhappiness with a courtier or subordinate king.[130] Many inscriptional eulogies boast of the prowess of their patrons by remarking on the ominous consequences of such a gesture for refractory kings.[131] For their part, courtiers were to avoid such gestures in the king's presence lest they be taken amiss. Someśvara recommends that the entire court gathering, having bowed, made *añjali*, and assumed their proper positions, should gaze intently at the king 'as if he were the newly risen moon'.[132] Indeed, in the language of the sources,

[125] *HC*, ch. 1, p. 26.

[126] For visual dimensions of Hindu worship, which are of course related to the courtly material, see Diana Eck, *Darśan: Seeing the Divine Image in India* (Chambersburg: Anima Books, 1985) and Lawrence Babb, 'Glancing: Visual Interaction in Hinduism,' *Journal of Anthropological Research*, vol. 37 (1981), pp. 387–401.

[127] *AS* 6.1.6. [128] *NS* 13.148. [129] *NS* 8.38–125.

[130] Contraction of the lips is also mentioned, *AS* 5.5.9.

[131] For a seventh-century Viṣṇukuṇḍin inscription which describes the king Indrabhaṭṭārakavarman as scattering his rivals by merely contracting his eyebrows (*bhrūbaṅgakara*), *EI* 4 (1896–7), no. 25, p. 196. For similar examples from the sixth century referring to Maukhari and Pallava kings, see *CII* 3 (1888), no. 48, p. 223 and *EI* 8 (1905–6), no. 5, p. 32.

[132] See *Mānasollāsa* 3.1225, 1233. For the courtier's avoidance of displeasing eye movements, see *AS* 5.4.10.

the goal of the supplicant or man of ambition in attending court was not to receive the king's 'audience' but to gain a 'viewing' (*darśana*) of him.[133]

Approval, affection and favour were also typically indicated by glances at court. The first sign of a favourable disposition on the part of the king towards a courtier, according to Kauṭilya, was pleasure or happiness in seeing him (*darśane prasīdati*).[134] Two accounts, one from Samudragupta's fourth-century Allahabad pillar inscription, and the other from Bāṇa's seventh-century *Harṣacarita*, will give a sense of the importance of visual gestures as signs of favour at court. In the first example, the courtier Hariṣeṇa recounts Candragupta's public selection of his son Samudragupta as his successor. After calling him forward and embracing him, the king looked intently (*nirīkṣya*) at the prince with an eye laden with tears (*bāṣpāguruṇā*), unsteady from affection (*snehavyāluḷitena*), yet perceiving his essence (*tattvekṣinā*), and announced to him, 'protect the whole earth', while those of equal birth gazed upon (*udvīkṣita*) him with languishing faces, and courtiers sighed in happiness.[135]

The second example is Bāṇa's account of his arrival at Harṣa's court, which forms the subject of the second chapter of his *Harṣacarita*. Bāṇa is first greeted at the gate by the doorkeeper Pariyātra's distant glance, 'as if it were a flower garland offering', a promising welcome to his summons. Conducted before Harṣa, sitting surrounded by attendants and courtiers, Bāṇa is awestruck at the magnificence of the king, causing his hair to stand on end and his eyes to well up in tears. Yet Harṣa announces that he will not see him, and gives a sidelong glance, his pupils darting to the side, to his favourite companion, declaring Bāṇa to be a dissolute gallant. Bāṇa, who hears this, returns a spirited defence of his youthful follies. The king is silent, offering no sign of favour (*prasāda*) like friendly conversation, a seat or gifts – save, that is, a single affectionate glance (*snehadṛṣṭipāta*), which at once 'revealed his inward satisfaction and bathed Bāṇa in a shower of ambrosia'.[136] At the end of his first audience Bāṇa concludes, on the basis of a glance, that the king is well-disposed towards him.

[133] This terminology has been explored only in the religious context, though the earlier sources are courtly in nature. See *HC*, ch. 2, p. 60, for *sāmanta*s outside of Harṣa's court waiting to have a sight (*darśana*) of the king.

[134] *AS* 5.5.7. Harṣa's chief doorkeeper Pariyātra, is described as *cakṣuṣyah*, or '[pleasant to the] sight [of the king]', *HC*, ch. 2, p. 62. See explanatory notes in Kane's edition, pp. 75, 124.

[135] *CII* 3 (1981), no. 1, p. 212.

[136] Summary of relevant details from *HC*, ch. 2, pp. 61–80. See also *HC*, ch. 7, p. 209, where the emperor Harṣa is said to 'purchase' the lives of subordinate kings in the form of their adoration of him, by distributing among them as tokens of favour partial glances (*netravibhāga*), side glances (*kaṭākṣa*), full glances (*samagrekṣita*), raised eyebrows (*bhrūvañcita*), half-smiles (*ārdhasmita*), laughter (*parihāsa*), conversation with double-meanings (*chekālāpa*), enquiries after health (*kuśalapraśna*), return bows (*pratipraṇāma*), agitated movements of the eyebrows (*unmattabhrūvīkṣita*) and commands (*ājñādāna*).

Both of these accounts portray eye movements as indicative of important inner dispositions accompanying the conferral of favour at court. In the Allahabad inscription, the simultaneous focus and unsteadiness of Candragupta's eyes, their welling with tears, all underscore the king's love for Samudragupta and are carefully contrasted with the envious gazes of his rivals for the king's affection. All the significant moments in Bāṇa's account – his first welcome to the palace, his first sight of Harṣa, his initial rejection and his final acceptance by the king – are all accompanied by gestures of the eyes. Harṣa's final glance, an acquiescence to Bāṇa's appeal, is clearly all the more satisfying for its subtlety – at once revealing the king's refusals to have been little more than paternal scolding, and exonerating Bāṇa's character.

The spirit of courtesy

This chapter began with an outline of the key dynamics of the relationships between men at court: service, devotion and favour. It then explored how these dynamics were enacted through courtly protocol and embodied in speech and gestures. The final section will discuss two key ethical concepts which lay behind courtly interaction.

Perhaps the closest Sanskrit equivalent to the ethical meaning of 'courtesy' or 'civility' in the European context, is the adjective *dakṣina*, and particularly the abstract noun deriving from it, *dākṣiṇya*. While *dākṣiṇya* never gained the wider political and ideological currency of 'courtesy' or 'civility' in the west, its semantic range is so close to the common usage of these terms that it has regularly been translated with them.[137] According to Kāmandaka, *dākṣiṇya* was one of the virtues which made a king or man of rank 'attractive' (*abhigamya*), and its pre-eminence among the political élite – both men and women – is attested by its frequent appearance in inscriptional eulogies and courtly dramas alike.[138] At one level, *dākṣiṇya* meant something like 'kind', 'considerate' or 'respectful', but was differentiated from similar terms by its connotations of accomplishment and sophistication, a sense it carried from its root, *dakṣa*, meaning 'skilful' or 'clever'. It thus entailed an embracing familiarity with the particular elements of courtly protocol. As a quality, it was as important as physical beauty itself, which it was always to accompany. In Aśvaghoṣa's

[137] The only scholar to consider *dākṣiṇya* at any length to my knowledge is Robert Goodwin, who translates it as 'courtly refinement'. His discussion, which relies heavily on Kālidāsa's romances, tends to see it as 'noble pretence' and differs from the approach taken here. See Goodwin, *Playworld*, pp. 72–8.

[138] *NiS* 4.6. It appears very frequently in inscriptional eulogies. For an early usage, see the descriptions of the Gupta courtiers Parṇadatta and Cakrapālita, *CII* 3 (1981), no. 28, pp. 299, 300. For its possession by women, see *VkU* 2.22+; *MK* 4.0.+; *HC*, ch. 1, p. 27.

Buddhacarita, the minister Udāyin instructs the young prince Śākyamuni that 'beauty without courtesy is like a garden without flowers'.[139] In a *bhāṇa* play entitled 'The Conversation between the Libertine and the Rogue' (*Dhūrtaviṭasaṁvāda*), there occurs a debate on the relative importance of beauty and *dākṣiṇya* as virtues in a woman, in which the *viṭa* Devilaka maintains that in *dākṣiṇya* reside all other desirable qualities except beauty: good speech, good dress, modesty, being endowed with emotion, gratefulness, not staying angry too long, not being covetous and compliance. This was because romance, according to the *viṭa*, was founded on a sort of compliance or suitable regard for others, an 'attendance' toward their persons (*anuvṛtti*), which arose from *dākṣiṇya*.[140] Thus the *Nāṭyaśāstra* defines *dākṣiṇya* as the obliging or attendance of another person accompanied with a pleasing and joyful face, words and movements.[141] *Dākṣiṇya* thus was not merely kindness or consideration for others, but skill and accomplishment at doing so, particularly within the delicate context of courtly hierarchies.

This skill is well-illustrated by a passage from the *Harṣacarita* describing King Puṣyabhūti's acceptance of the gift of an inlaid silver lotus from the ascetic Bhairavācārya. Receiving such a gift would have been difficult for the emperor, for the accepted relationship between the secular nobility and religious figures like ascetics was the reverse – kings were to be the givers, and spiritual men the recipients, of worldly wealth. Yet to refuse such a gift would have insulted his friend's act of respect (*praṇaya*). The king's solution to this dilemma, according to Bāṇa, revealed his proficiency at *dākṣiṇya*. When the ascetic's messenger offered him the gift, he hesitated for a moment, his mind visibly wavering, before accepting it, thus 'yielding' in Bāṇa's words, to his own nobility.[142] The king's hesitation subtly conveyed to the messenger and onlookers both his reticence to accept the gift as well as his inability to refuse it.

One of the most typical contexts in which *dākṣiṇya* was required was the ubiquitous problem in courtly circles of balancing affections and favours – how a lord would ensure that he gave respect and courtesies to others when he was showing special favour to one. As we have mentioned above, the favouring of one person necessarily altered the delicate balance of hierarchies at court. In this context *dākṣiṇya* came to have the sense of the skilful placation of multiple subordinate agencies through a balancing of courtesies.[143] A favourite theme in courtly drama was this problem

[139] *BC* 4.70. [140] *DhVS* 55+, 56. [141] *NS* 17.30. [142] *HC*, ch. 3, p. 102.

[143] Hence fate (*daiva*) was seen to be, among other things, highly discourteous (*nirdākṣiṇya*) because it favoured some men excessively while disregarding others who were worthy. See Savitrī's remarks to Sarasvatī regarding the subject, *HC*, ch. 1, p. 16.

as transposed to the royal harem or *antaḥpura*, where the king's new infatuation with a woman implicitly threatened the existing hierarchy of wives in the household.[144] This is particularly the case in the palace romances of Kālidāsa and Harṣa, where the king placates his jealous wives as they discover his new affections. In a famous passage from Kālidāsa's *Mālavikāgnimitra*, King Agnimitra, chided by his beloved Mālavikā about his fear of a junior queen, defends himself by explaining, 'Oh you with Bimba like lips, *dākṣiṇya* is indeed the family vow of the Baimbika clan, so cast your long-eyed glances on me, for my life is dependent upon you'.[145] Though scholars have understood *dākṣiṇya* in such passages to mean 'false courtesy', wider usage makes it clear that *dākṣiṇya* here referred to the *virtue* of consideration for past commitments in the context of new and permitted affections.[146]

Another important virtue mentioned in inscriptional eulogies and manuals on polity which bears directly on the issue of courtly manners was humility or modesty, usually designated by the term *vinaya*.[147] If the political culture of the court tended towards the display of power and eminence, a seemingly countervailing ethical code ran alongside it which recommended constant vigilance against the vice of pride. Pride was understood as the arrogation to oneself of undue respect or honour. It

[144] See *Sk* 6.5, where the chamberlain remarks that due to his grief at seeing the ring of recognition, the king is unable to speak properly to the women of the *antaḥpura* with *dākṣiṇya*, but instead stumbles over their names and retreats in shame. The commentator Rāghavabhaṭṭa (who flourished in the fifteenth century) remarks that *dākṣiṇya* refers to 'great consideration' (*atyantānurodha*) for the women of the *antaḥpura*, citing *MkA* to suggest that this was a matter of paramount obligation.

[145] *MkA* 4.14.

[146] The aesthetic texts divide the hero of the drama into several types, the highest of which is the courteous (*dakṣiṇa*) hero, who pays due consideration to all of his wives. Lower types are the *śaṭha*, who deceives his queens about his new found favourite and the *dhṛṣṭa*, who callously lies and disregards his queen when discovered (see Dhanañjaya's tenth-century *Daśarūpaka* 2.6 and Viṣvanātha's fourteenth-century *Sāhityadarpaṇa* 3.35–8). Most of the heroes of the household dramas, as Goodwin has pointed out (*Playworld*, p. 73), flit between *dakṣiṇa* and *śaṭha*, for they typically attempt to conceal their infatuations, but upon being discovered propitiate their queens, exhibiting *dākṣiṇya*. *Dākṣiṇya* here is an admirable quality, and its translation as noble 'pretence' or false courtesy by modern scholars has more to do with the critique of courtly manners than anything from the poetic tradition itself. The use of the term 'false courtesy', (*alīkadākṣiṇya* or *anṛtadākṣiṇya*) in various contexts (see *MK* 4.0+, *Rv* 3.17+, 18) would also suggest that *dākṣiṇya* as such was not pretence, though like all forms of amelioratory courtesy it remained vulnerable to the charge of being false. So when Udāyin advises the young prince Śākyamuni to show courtesy to the women of the palace even if it was false (*anṛta*), the Buddha responds that he cannot reconcile falsity and courtesy in any way, see *BC* 4.66–71; 92.

[147] This term could also mean variously self-discipline, training and propriety. In some cases, it is difficult to differentiate its sense, as humility was conceptually related to and perhaps even derived from the idea of self-restraint.

was a peculiar vice in that it could arise from virtue and accomplishment, as its etymology suggests – for among the common words for pride were *māna* and *abhimāna*, both of which also had the positive sense of 'honour' and 'respect'. Pride, as the eleventh-century poet Kṣemendra demonstrates in his poem *Darpadalana*, could grow from and undermine all the major virtues like prowess, beauty, learning and generosity. It thus became understood as the chief vice and downfall of the men at court.

Yet if pride could poison all virtues, humility was thought to temper them. *Vinaya* was consequently thought to be the crown of virtues, its presence ensuring the fruition of a properly lived ethical life. The critique of pride and exaltation of humility was less a quietistic or spiritualist condemnation of secular court life and the 'vanity of kings' than a powerful worldly idea, organic to life at court, which functioned to create a specifically courtly ethic. The eulogies present virtuous and world-ruling kings who 'uproot' and 'chastise' the pride of their rivals and enemies. Given the fine line between positive honour and negative pride, it is possible to understand the courtly emphasis on *vinaya* as a sort of internalised self-regulating mechanism which tended towards the maintenance of courtly hierarchy. This is perhaps nowhere more clear than its effect in structuring courtly manners. All men of noble birth were to cultivate within themselves a strong sense of humility before others of rank – both their natural superiors like parents, teachers and lords, as well as their equals. Such exhortations explain the widespread tendency in courtly speech and gesture towards self-effacement, a tendency which spanned the entire palace hierarchy, from king to menial. Prince Raghu's body, according to Kālidāsa, though excelling his father's, appeared low on account of humility (*vinaya*).[148] At the other end of the spectrum, a fifth-century inscription of the Nala king Bhavadatta records two untitled court officials, the composer and engraver of the royal eulogy, referring to themselves, respectively, as having 'little intelligence' (*alpabuddhi*) and 'no virtue' (*nirguṇa*).[149]

Yet humility, being a virtue, had the natural effect of exalting one's character, giving acts of humility a somewhat paradoxical logic. Restraint, deference and even effacement before others actually signified one's eminence, and thus was folded back into the discourse of power they safeguarded. Yet humility could also be used strategically. Humility was such a powerful virtue precisely because it signified the presence of virtues

[148] *RghV* 3.35.

[149] *EI* 21 (1931–2), no. 24, p. 156. See also the self-description of Vikukṣi, hereditary servant of prince Dadhīca's father, as being the 'least of servants', a fact belied by his selection to guard the king's son, *HC*, ch. 1, p. 27.

and capacities not immediately apparent, because, presumably, they were being restrained. As in the many stories of sages and kings, the modest appearance of one man often exposes the pride of another. Yet as has been argued with regard to Elizabethan court life, modesty had the potential to 'arouse inference in excess of the facts'.[150] Humility thus formed the safest demeanour to pursue one's own ambitions at court.

One of course had to be careful, for too self-deprecating a demeanour was thought to be debasing. According to the crow-minister Aḍīvin in the *Pañcatantra*, 'A man's shadow will lengthen when he bows, like that of a stick when bent, but if bent too much (*ati namatām*) will disappear'.[151] Suitable deference increased (*vivṛddhi*) a man's stature; too much brought its diminishment (*kṣaya*). Though Aḍīvin is adamant that a man should never bow to anyone lower in rank (*asama*), the reality of court life was clearly more complex, and many relationships among the upper ranks of men at court involved considerable reciprocity. The king's closest companions, particularly his preceptor and highest counsellors, often enjoyed such status as to demand the deference of the king himself. When, in Viśākhadatta's *Mudrārākṣasa*, the minister Rākṣasa is forced to enter King Candragupta's service, the king pays obeisance to him, a gesture Rākṣasa immediately recognises as a sign of his new position as a 'servant' (*bhṛtya*) of the king, though for a moment he wonders if this is another trick of Cāṇakya's. Significantly, he concludes that the deferential gesture comes from genuine 'humility' (*vinaya*).[152]

Courtly sources are filled with descriptions of how men of virtue deftly and skilfully exhibited humility in their social interactions. In conversation the tendency to place oneself in the position of supplicant or subordinate was deemed a mark of high manners. The relations of service, devotion and favour, which we outlined at the beginning of this chapter, not only structured courteous verbal exchange but were also deployed as conscious rhetorical devices. Gratitude, for example, was typically expressed by phrases like 'I am favoured [by you]' (*anugṛhītāsmi*), and in polite conversation speakers often requested the 'favour' of a response, or assumed an exaggeratedly deferential posture, as when Sarasvatī in the opening

[150] Frank Whigham, *Ambition and Privilege: The Social Tropes of Elizabethan Courtesy Theory* (Berkeley: University of California Press, 1984), p. 99.

[151] *PT* 3.4.

[152] *MR* 7.10 ff. See M. R. Kale's comments on this passage, p. 341 in his edition of the work. I prefer this interpretation of such royal acts rather than understating them as expressions of the obligatory respect given to brahmins as a category by kings. We have numerous examples of kings addressing brahmins without such deference, as in the case of Bāṇa's appearance at Harṣa's court, and the jester (*vidūṣaka*) figures in Sanskrit drama.

scenes of Bāṇa's *Harṣacarita* courteously importunes Mālatī for news of Dadhīca, by calling herself Mālatī's 'servant' (*pratisarā*).[153]

A particularly illustrative example, once again from Bāṇa, is the arrival of the young prince Candrāpīḍa in the Kādambarī, at the residence of his father's chief minister, Śukanāsa. Upon entering Śukanāsa's household, the prince, accompanied by his companion Vaiśampāyana (Śukanāsa's own son) approaches the minister, who is seated among many subordinate kings. Candrāpīḍa bows with his head 'very low' (*durāvatena*). Śukanāsa quickly gets up from his seat and advances several steps forward, 'respectfully' (*sādaram*), to meet the pair. Immediately, the subordinate kings in the court now stand up from their own seats. With tears in his eyes Śukanāsa embraces Candrāpīḍa, and then his own son Vaiśampāyana. The prince is then offered a jewelled seat, which he refuses, instead taking a seat on the bare ground, followed by Vaiśampāyana. This act causes the entire assembly, in turn, to leave their own seats and assume positions on the ground. The prince's behaviour only confirms the pleasure that Śukanāsa feels upon seeing him – his heart is filled with joy and the hair on his body stands on end.[154]

This scene captures the important association of power and humility which was at the heart of courtly manners, and which made them not merely 'expressions' of hierarchy, but powerful instruments for the negotiation of relationships at court. In the example above, Bāṇa is keen to show how Prince Candrāpīḍa's gestures of humility at once underscored his submission and obedience to his father even as it potentially chastised the attendant nobles. Like any ideational theory of relationships tied to power, courtly manners functioned as a system whose rules could be adhered to, as in the examples above, violated, as when Śaśāṅka murdered the Puṣyabhūti prince Rājyavardhana while he was a guest in his own household, or even deployed as subterfuge, as when Cāṇakya advises King Candragupta to address him without the respectful title 'noble' so that this would be noticed immediately by the chamberlain.[155] The practice of manners at court was both polyvalent and complex. If manners conformed to and reinforced the hierarchical structures of courtly life, they were also important instruments through which men might make their careers within them.

[153] *MK* 1.53+; *HC*, ch. 1, p. 34. [154] *Kd*, pp. 156–7.

[155] 'What, no honorific even? No "good sir Cāṇakya", just "Cāṇakya"' (*katham nirupapadameva cāṇākyo nāryacāṇākya iti*) *MR* 3.31+.

Part II

Aesthetics and the Courtly Sensibility

4 Beauty and refinement

To the various skills and accomplishments to be possessed by men and women at court reviewed thus far, a final and important association must be added: an enduring concern with beauty. Taken as a whole, the corpus of evidence left to us from Gupta and post-Gupta India suggests that beauty, elegance and style formed striking preoccupations – even obsessions – in the lifestyles of the 'good people' who attended court. Aesthetic concerns applied not only to the formal arts but also to nearly every aspect of the lives of the élite at court – their bodies, movements, speech, clothes, surroundings and even their souls. Indeed, I will suggest below that the theory of beauty was something like a worldview, an idea through which people conceptualised relationships with both themselves and others. This immediately connects the question of beauty to the realm of social ethics, an association which has made it no easier to understand. For beauty, like so many other virtues, was viewed not merely as a set of attributes (though it was indeed this too), but a capacity, partly bestowed by birth, which was to be realised through individual agency. It was deemed beyond the aspirations of common people, but, within the society of the good, it formed a ceaseless and life-long vocation.

In this chapter I will take up several questions in relation to courtly aesthetics. First, what were the positive attributes which constituted beauty in physiology, bearing, speech, dress and environment for the men and women of the court? Second, what was the relationship between beauty, so conceived, and some of the concerns laid out in previous chapters of this study? How did beauty, in other words, take its place among the 'courtly' virtues? Third, what was the 'organising theory' which stood behind the positive attributes of beauty? And finally, what was the larger significance of the discourse on beauty in the courtly world, both as a practice and as a set of ideas?

The body

At court, much depended on one's appearance. In courtly dramas and stories, characters are often drawn to or repulsed by one another on the basis of first appearances. We need only think of Sarasvatī's first sight of Dadhīca, Bāṇa's first sight of Harṣa, or Agnimitra's first sight of Mālavikā to be reminded of the affective power of first appearances. In all of these cases, the marked emphasis on the physical beauty of the men and women of the court is striking, both for the power it held upon the viewer and in its unerring signification of something beyond itself. Beauty itself was often considered a virtue (*guṇa*), and like the other worldly virtues with which it was associated, it tended to signify the presence of its siblings. As Kālidāsa puts it in describing the prince Raghu, his 'intellect matched (*saddṛśa*) his appearance'.[1] Physical beauty regularly appeared alongside other virtues in the inscriptional eulogies of kings, ministers and courtiers. This did not mean that all beauty was beyond criticism, for there was a strong tradition among intellectuals both at court and beyond which denigrated physical beauty as ephemeral allurement. Yet such criticism rarely, if ever, presented the court with a character whose physical appearance was at variance with their moral character.

The association between physical beauty and moral concepts was not, however, original or specific to the court. Virtue had been thought to inhere in the human body since at least early historic times, when Buddhist monks enumerated lists of auspicious and beautiful characteristics or 'marks' (*lakṣaṇa*) which appeared on the body of a 'great person' (*mahāpuruṣa*) destined to become a Buddha or world-ruling king.[2] Such theories were part of or at least contributed to a vast prognosticatory knowledge gradually taking shape in the early centuries of the Common Era which made great use of the human body as a sign of past actions and future events. By the sixth century, when Varāhamihira composed his 'Great Compendium' or *Bṛhatsaṁhitā*, it was thought that close observation of the properties and proportions of a person's body – its height (*unmāna*), weight (*māna*), motion (*gati*), solidity (*saṁhati*), essences (*sāra*), colour (*varṇa*), oiliness (*sneha*), voice (*svara*), natural elements (*prākṛti*), vitality (*sattva*) and lustre (*mṛjā*) – could reveal a person's

[1] *RghV* 1.15.

[2] See the 'Lakkhaṇa Suttanta', *Dīgha Nikāya* 3.1.145. For Buddhists these marks were at once signs of beauty and the outcomes of moral actions in previous lives which permitted their bearers certain priveleges. For example, by refraining from killing, being gentle and compassionate to all living creatures, the *mahāpuruṣa* was born with projecting heels, long fingers and toes and divinely straight limbs, which, in turn, bestowed upon him longevity and protection from murder in his life as either a monarch or Buddha.

moral worth, as well as his or her past and future.[3] In this spirit the *Bṛhatsaṁhitā* sets out lists of bodily attributes for men (*puruṣalakṣaṇa*), great men (*mahāpuruṣalakṣaṇa*) and unmarried women (*kanyālakṣaṇa*), among others.[4]

The effect of these assumptions, which were widespread at court, was to give physical features and bodily health a multivalent character. Good health and the possession of physical attributes deemed auspicious and beautiful signified moral worth and portended worldly success. It is in this context that we may understand descriptions of kings which emphasise their physical beauty. The second-century inscription of the Śaka king Rudradāman from Junāgadh provides an early, if telling, example. The poet describes the king as having a beautiful body (*kāntamūrti*) possessed of the highest marks and signs (*paramalakṣanavyañjana*) with regard to breadth (*pramāṇa*), weight (*māna*), height (*unmāna*), voice (*svara*), motion (*gati*), colour (*varṇa*), essence (*sāra*) and vitality (*sattva*).[5] In this case, these bodily features indicated the king's fitness to rule. Conversely, physical afflictions and irregularities in bodily function were interpreted as the outcomes of moral actions or as ill omens.[6] Bāṇa's description of the emperor Harṣa is illustrative:

> His vision is not defective and soiled by the deadly poison of selfishness; his speech is not characterised by stuttering and convulsive sentences caused by the disease of the throat due to the heavy poison of presumption; his postures are not stiff due to the loss of consciousness in epilepsy of the heat of astonishment; his changes of feelings are not agitated by the paroxysms of the inflammatory fever of unrestrained self-will; his movement is not stiff or jerky from the derangement of the three humours due to pride; and his speech does not have harsh syllables uttered from distorted lips under the tetanus of intoxication.[7]

The praise of the king's appearance here is advanced negatively as an absence of various vices. Each moral fault is correlated with some physiological manifestation or disease which, in turn, produces symptoms

[3] *BS* 68.1. A related prognosticatory science known as *aṅgavidyā* sought to predict the outcomes of a wide variety of events (like thefts, etc . . .) by observation of the petitioner's bodily gestures. See *BS* 51.1 ff.

[4] *BS*, chs. 68–70. The text also includes enumerations of portending characteristics of animals, plants, gems, umbrellas and other objects.

[5] *EI* 8 (1905–6), no. 6, p. 44. This list is similar to that of *BS* 68.1 ff.

[6] Any throbbing, spasm or contraction of a limb or part of the right side of the body, for example, generally augured fortune, while the same on the left side forbode ominous events. See *MR* 2.11+ where the left eye of the minister Rākṣasa throbs in spasms (*vāmākṣispanda*), auguring misfortune and *Sk* 1.14 where the (right) arm of King Duṣyanta throbs (*sphurati*) portending love.

[7] *HC*, ch. 2, p. 54. The description is conveyed from Harṣa's brother to Bāṇa through the emissary Mekhalaka.

marring various aspects of the body's comportment.[8] Though the passage here is no doubt hyperbolic, it nevertheless underlines the close association between the health and outward appearance of the body, on the one hand, and internal moral states, on the other. It also forms the backdrop against which we may understand the courtly obsession with physical beauty.

The most common accounts of physical beauty in courtly poetry were highly conventional, typically relying on a finite if ever-varying set of stock-metaphors used to describe parts of the body. Longer descriptions typically began with the feet and, moving upward, finished with the tip of the head. Women, tirelessly described by poets, had feet like lotuses, toenails which were brilliant and thighs shapely and smooth like plantains. Their buttocks were heavy, hips wide and waists narrow. Considerable delight is taken in describing the folds of skin visible below the navel. The arms were like the tendrils of lianas and hands like lotuses or lotus sprouts. Breasts were large like golden pitchers; lips red and full; and cheeks smooth. The eyes were large and wide, extending to the ear, with the eyebrows perfectly arched like a bow. The hair was invariably long but often tied up into elaborate coiffure.[9]

Men were both more differentiated and less palpable in description. Yet the accounts of heroes in dramas and arms-bearing men of the court, regardless of their *varṇa* affiliation, tended to be similar, and their physical beauty was often emphasised, the most eminent characteristics being reserved for the king. Like women, such men had 'lotus-like' feet with shining toenails. Their thighs, however, were strong like pillars, and their shanks were lean. The chest was broad and powerful, the shoulders rounded and arms long and pendulous, though the hands were to be graceful and were typically compared to plant tendrils.[10] The forehead was bright like the moon, the eyes were pleasantly clear and wide, extending to the ears, and the eyebrows also perfectly shaped like a bow.[11] The hair was also long and usually curled close to the head.

[8] All of these diseases are attested to in the medical literature except the first. See editorial note in P. V. Kane's edition, *HC*, p. 251.

[9] For useful discussions of feminine beauty, see Sushil Kumar De, *Ancient Indian Erotics and Erotic Literature* (Calcutta: Firma K. L. Mukhopadhyay, 1969), pp. 38–44; and Smith, *Ratnākara's Haravijaya*, pp. 180–8.

[10] See the description of the Paṇḍuvaṁśin king Tīvaradeva's hands as 'sprout-like' (*pallava*), *EI* 7 (1902–3), no. 13, p. 104; a similar metaphor is used through a pun on the family name Pallava (*pallava*, 'sprout') in the sixth-century Talgunda pillar inscription of the Kadamba king Kakutsthavarman, *EI* 8 (1905–6), no. 5, p. 32.

[11] A sixth-century inscription praising the Hūṇa king Mihirakula describes him as having large (*pṛthu*) and pellucid (*vimala*) eyes, *CII* 3 (1888), no. 37, p. 162. A fifth-century inscription of the Aulikāra king Viśvavarman describes a courtier as having eyes stretching to the edge of his ears (*karṇāntapratisarppamāṇanayana*), *CII* 3 (1888), no. 17, p. 75; see also Kalidāsa's description of Raghu in *RghV* 4.13.

A number of points in these descriptions are worth pausing over. It is notable that both men and women shared broadly similar ideals of physical attractiveness. The words used to describe their beauty tended to be the same (*kānta*, *cāru*, *lāvaṇya*, *rūpa*), and several key features united their appearances: large eyes, lotus-like feet and hands, full red lips and shining toenails. By European standards, this parity would seem to give greater effeminacy to men than masculinity to women, though in actuality this was a function of a number of other gendered traits coming into play which tended to flatten the ideals of femininity even as they provided men with more diverse and nuanced forms of masculinity. Descriptions of men at court thus often rather curiously (at least to European standards) combine seemingly feminine attributes with qualities which were clearly masculine. In the fifth-century Gangdhar inscription of the Aulikāra king Viśvavarman, for example, the courtier Mayūraśaka is described in the same breath as having 'eyes stretching to the tips of his ears' and 'skin like that of a tender-aged girl', as well as 'long and round pendulous arms' and a 'body scarred (literally 'decorated') with battle-wounds', from 'destroying haughty enemies on the battlefield'.[12] In this sense the courtly ideal of masculinity was thought to incorporate and include (but was not exhausted by) many of the positively idealised aspects of physical beauty also attributed to women. The delicate and tender beauty of women thus formed a subset of wider attributes possessed by men which included physical strength, bodily prowess and other martial virtues.[13] What was unique to women (delicacy as frailty of body and weakness of will), as we shall see, was typically negative.

The skin and musculature of women and men as depicted in literary and visual sources from Gupta times is also significant. For both men and women, the beautiful body was depicted as rounded rather than angular, and the flesh smooth and slightly 'plumpened' (though not corpulent), rather than lean and muscularly defined.[14] Excessive leanness was variously associated with hard exercise, old age, asceticism, illness and, significantly, various agitated emotional states, the chief of which was lovesickness. The underlying principle in these representations, as F. D. K. Bosch pointed out some time ago, was similar to and continuous with those used in the representation of plants.[15] Like the lotuses and flower buds to which they were constantly compared, human limbs in

[12] *CII* 3 (1888), no. 17, p. 75.

[13] See above for a discussion of combination of tenderness and valour as courtly attributes.

[14] This has somewhat older precedents, as in the description of the *mahāpuruṣa*'s bodily marks in Buddhist sources, which include 'purely round shoulders, pure round shanks, with smooth limbs'. See the 'Lakkhaṇa Suttanta', *Dīgha Nikāya* 3.1.145 ff.

[15] F. D. K. Bosch, *The Golden Germ: An Introduction to Indian Symbolism* (Mouton: Hague, 1960), pp. 222–3.

their ideal state were to be smooth and tautly expanded, or 'blown' like the tender and succulent new growth of plants. Poets used plant analogies to describe courtly lovers, whose limbs 'plumpen', breasts 'expand' and cheeks, eyes and faces 'bloom'.[16] Such language was used not only to denote a certain quality of skin and musculature, commonly evident in sculptural representations of the body, but also to understand the specific physiological processes which accompanied love and affection of various kinds, namely, the 'bristling of body hairs' (horripilation, *romāñcita, lomaharṣaṇa, pulaka*, etc.) and 'reddening' of the complexion (from the root √*rañj*, 'to redden', 'to be attracted').[17]

The images of anatomical perfection which lay behind courtly conceptions of beauty were clearly ideals, endlessly celebrated in ever more elaborate metaphors, and most men and women no doubt rarely saw them in their own appearance. Nevertheless, they formed the 'lenses' through which people of the court viewed both themselves and others and judged them as more or less 'beautiful'. They were connected, however, to deeper attributes, and physical features formed only one dimension of personal beauty in its complete sense. What the men and women of the court lacked in bodily perfection could be, to some extent, compensated by other cultivations.

Bearing

The teachings of the *Nāṭyaśāstra* form an important source for studying the role of physical appearance in courtly life. One of its implicit concerns is with how best to present the actors on the stage – kings, ministers and servants – so as to be immediately recognisable to courtly audiences as the characters they are playing in the drama. This was conveyed not only by sartorial codes, but also by a number of other markers like speech, comportment and bearing. To the extent that it is possible to take these norms as more than simply stage conventions – that is, where dramatic directives are supported by other source material – they present us with two important insights. First, they provide us with important positive data on

[16] For early examples, see Hāla's Prakrit anthology, *Gāthāsaptaśatī* 1.23; 4.9; 4.42; 6.97.

[17] For bristling of the body hair through affection and pleasure, see *HC*, ch. 2, p. 77, where Bāṇa's facial hair stands on end after he sees the emperor Harṣa. See also *Kd*, p. 157; *CII* 3 (1981), no. 1, p. 212. For examples of women, see Vidyākara's eleventh-century *Subhāṣitaratnakośa* 596, 597. These physiological responses might be fruitfully applied to the theory of 'tumescence' developed by S. C. Upadhyaya (borrowing from Havelock Ellis) to describe processes of physical and psychic excitation towards members of the opposite sex. See S. C. Upadhyaya, 'Introduction', *Kama Sutra of Vatsyayana* (Bombay: Taraporevala, 1970), p. 9. Yet it should be kept in mind, as our examples suggest, that such 'excitation' or 'attraction' was hardly limited to sexual response.

courtly conventions – how people moved, spoke and held themselves at court. Second, they suggest just how sensitive people of the court were to physical bearing and verbal style. On the stage, as in life, the movements and postures of people made their birth and social rank almost immediately apparent to onlookers. When King Udayana in Harṣa's *Priyadarśikā* first spies the heroine Āraṇyaka (Priyadarśikā) in the garden with a serving girl, he announces to his jester companion what the audience must have already known: 'her noble birth is clearly revealed by her *gravitas* [in demeanor]'.[18]

The idea of social hierarchy was built into all conceptions of the body and its movement. In sculpture from the Gupta period onwards more important personages were typically represented larger than the attendants who accompanied them (compare the depictions of courtiers in figures 4.1 and 4.2; see also figures 3.3 and 3.4).[19] Their expressions and postures were also different. When we turn to aesthetic treatises like the *Nāṭyaśāstra*, we see a similar concern with hierarchy in the staging of bearing and gesture. The *Nāṭyaśāstra* divides its characters into 'high' (*uttama*), 'middling' (*madhyama*) and 'low' (*adhama*), each of which were to walk, gesticulate and speak differently. Bharata admonishes the playwright not to confuse or misapply the physical bearing of one class with another.[20]

Yet at the same time sources suggest that certain ground rules obtained in respect to the comportment of everyone at court. First, proper physical bearing at court required the control of various bodily functions which drew attention to oneself by sounds or appearances which were deemed unpleasant. The texts on polity demand that courtiers avoid breaking wind (*vāta*), coughing (*kāsa*), yawning (*jṛmbhana*), stretching the limbs (*gātrabhaṅga*), spitting (*ṣṭhīvana*) and finger-cracking (*parvāsphoṭa*) while in the presence of their superiors at court.[21] These prohibitions were so basic as to find little mention in poetic or dramatic descriptions. But beyond this, all men were to walk and hold themselves in a manner reflecting their rank. In dramatic performances, according to the *Nāṭyaśāstra*, as the curtain was drawn away from the stage at the outset of the drama, the characters entered in specific gaits (*gati*) and assumed particular standing postures (*sthāna*),[22] which indicated their position as superior, middling or low characters.[23]

[18] *Pd* 2.6+.
[19] See the remarks of R. S. Sharma, 'The Feudal Mind', in Sharma, *Early Medieval Indian Society*, pp. 267–8.
[20] *NS* 13.34. [21] *AS* 5.4.9; *NiS* 5.23.
[22] It is not clear exactly how this was to be sequenced. Perhaps the character entered the stage in his assigned gait and assumed this posture.
[23] *NS* 13.3 ff.

Figure 4.1 Relief sculpture of a male courtier/attendant, on toraṇa, great Stupa, Sanchi, Madhya Pradesh, first century CE.

Figure 4.2 Female attendant/courtier. Khajuraho, eleventh century CE.

Though during the course of the play characters combined a variety of other movements and gestures to convey different emotional states and sentiments, the 'natural' (*svabhāva*) gait of the characters reflected their innate dispositions.[24] The stride (*kṣepa*) of the step for kings and gods (high characters) was to be four *tāla*s (a measurement of space) in length, for middling characters, two *tāla*s, and for women and inferior characters, one *tāla*.[25] The time for each stride was correspondingly to be measured to four *kalā*s (a division of time) for high characters, two *kalā*s for middling and one for inferior.[26] Finally, the tempo (*laya*) of the gait of high characters was to be firm and calm (*sthita, dhairya*), that of low characters, fast (*druta*) and copious (*pracura*), and of middling characters, in between.[27] The height of the step was also a sign of ranking, as the highest category lifted their knee in striding to the waist.[28]

The idea behind these assignments was the higher the character, the longer the stride, the slower the gait and the firmer and calmer the step. It is in this context that we may understand the common likening in *kāvya* of the walking of men and women to that of the elephant, as this creature, along with the lion, was considered the strongest and most eminent of animals, its natural gait being slow, placid and firm.[29] Steadiness and deliberation of gait were counterpoised to uncontrolled and agitated movement. The movements of lower characters were copious, hurried and excessive. The *Nāṭyaśāstra* advises characters playing ministers and merchants – middling characters – to refrain from moving excessively (*parivāhita*) and stiffly (*stabdha*).[30] The example of the *śakāra*, known from the *Mṛcchakaṭik* of Śūdraka, is instructive. This figure, the brother of a lesser wife of the king, appears as a villainous character, dominated by cruelty and pride. These faults were choreographed into his manner of walking. The *Nāṭyaśāstra* describes him like this: 'his gait will be with presumption (*sagarvita*) and while walking, due to incessantly touching and looking at his clothes and ornaments, and because of the scattered agitation of the movement of his limbs, his garlands and the drapes of his garments move to and fro (*cūrṇapadā*).[31] The *śakāra's* vanity and preoccupation with his appearance caused both excessive and sudden,

[24] Literally, their movement was 'independent' (*svacchandagamanam*) of the constraints of anger and other sentiments, *NS* 13.29–30. For the use of *svabhāva* as 'natural' or innate movement, see *NS* 13.15.

[25] *NS* 13.9–10. [26] *NS* 13.10–11. [27] *NS* 13.12–13. [28] *NS* 13.15.

[29] Having a slow, elephant-like walk was a common epithet for people of rank. For men, see *RghV* 4.4; for women, *Rv* 4.3. For inscriptional references, see *EI* 8 (1905–6), no.8, p. 60; *CII* 3 (1888), no. 49, p. 224; *CII* 4 (1955), no. 26, p. 120.

[30] *NS* 13.78. [31] *NS* 13.148–9.

jerky movement. Excessive movement was a sign of clumsiness or internal agitation, and suddenness and stiffness of gesture suggested intoxication, surprise and lack of control.[32] These states, deemed highly undesirable in one's general carriage, may be directly opposed to the value placed upon ease, economy and dexterity of movement.

Posture, or how one held the body while standing, was generally denoted by the terms *sthāna* or *sthānaka*. The most exalted posture, according to the *Nāṭyaśāstra*, was the stance relating to the god Viṣṇu, the *vaiṣṇava sthāna*. This stance, in which the feet were two-and-a-half *tāla*s apart, with one foot level and the other obliquely placed with its shank bent, was to be assumed in the course of conversation *(saṁlāpa)* and activities that were innate (*svabhāvaja*) to the upper and middling characters.[33] The *Nāṭyaśāstra* advises that the high and middling characters should assume this stance of the feet while the upper limbs were to be in the *caturasra* posture, where the breast was raised (*samunnatam*) and shoulders at rest (*prasanna*) and not raised too much (*nātyukṣipta*), and the arms held at navel and the waist.[34] The limbs in the *vaiṣṇavasthāna* were to have a certain 'excellence' or 'beauty' in carriage (*sauṣṭhava*): they were unwavering (*acañcala*), uncrooked (*akubja*), at ease (*sannagātra*), not too raised (*atyucca*) and not collapsing (*calapāta*).[35] The waist, ears, elbows, shoulders and the head were to be in the normal or even (*sama*) position, and the chest, as in the *caturasra* pose, was to be raised.[36] We may compare these recommendations with the posture of the servants (*ceṭa*) and low (*nīca*) people, who were to walk with one of their sides, their heads, or a hand and foot lowered.[37] The famous Kashmiri satirist Kṣemendra, who wrote a treatise on the relations between servants and masters in the eleventh century, dwells at length on the shrinking postures of servants, whom he describes as having 'drooping faces (*adhomukha*) from their loss of honour' (*māna*).[38]

Taken together, then, beautiful bearing (*sauṣṭhava*) for those of superior movement can be understood through a series of oppositions:

[32] See the mid-fifth-century inscription of Kumāragupta and Bandhuvarman at Mandasor, where the brahmins of Daśapura are described as 'free from surprise' (*asmayita*) and King Bandhuvarman as 'never carried away by intoxication (*mada*), surprise (*smaya*) and other faults', *CII* 3, (1888), no. 18, p. 82.

[33] *NS* 11.51–3; see also *NS* 13.4–7.

[34] For the assignment of the *caturasra* with the *vaiṣṇavasthāna*, see *NS* 13.4. The definition of the *caturasra* is given in *NS* 11.91–2.

[35] Elsewhere, ministers and merchants are urged to avoid drooping (*niṣaṇṇa*) limbs, *NS* 13.78.

[36] *NS* 11.88–91. [37] *NS* 13.147–8. [38] *Sevyasevakopadeśa* 18.

stiffness of motion	ease of movement
agitated, jerky movement	calm, even movement
hurried movement	slow, deliberate movement
lowly carriage	elevated carriage
excessive movement	economic movement
inflated posture	calm, relaxed posture
drooping, broken-limbed	raised, firm-limbed
crooked posture	straight and upright posture

These oppositions present a set of subtle distinctions: the body was to be elevated, yet not puffed up; firm, but not stiff; calm, but not drooping; straight, but not rigid; slow, but not heavy. The combination of these opposing poles into a 'golden mean', often the basis of elaborate poetic conceits, may be usefully understood as forming an ideal of 'graceful' or 'elegant' bearing. One of its obvious principles was moderation. The dictum of 'not overly' or 'not too much' (*nāti*) precedes many of the directives for courtly movement. Too much curvature or a collapsing, drooping posture was a sign of lowness, and too erect a bearing was a sign of arrogance and pride. The ideal was a gentle curvature of the body, captured by words like *añcita*, which meant 'graceful beauty', but derived from the root √*añc*, 'to bend [slightly]'. A gentle curvature and relaxedness in posture was the hallmark of 'elevated' (*audārya*) bearing.[39]

These principles of posture and carriage are also quite apparent in the evolution of figural iconography, both royal and religious, from Kuṣāṇa through post-Gupta times. Not only do the more muscular physiques of Kuṣāṇa-Mathura sculpture give way to increasingly slender bodies with smoother surfaces and rounded angles during the early Gupta period (typical of the 'blown' physiognomy described above), but postures also become more fluid and relaxed.[40] Relaxed and reposing postures, only occasional and sporadic in pre-Gupta art, become increasingly widespread from the fifth century in the depiction of both men and gods – and by the seventh century are clearly the norm of representation. Typically, standing figures show a slight flexion of the torso and gentle thrust of the hip to one side as a result of the body's weight being supported on one leg. This trend is clearly illustrated in the royal portraits in coins and stone from the first to sixth centuries in north India. While images of the Kuṣāṇa kings (figures 4.3 and 4.4) typically present rulers in rigid

39 The cow and bull are typically associated with these relaxed postures. See the *NS* 24.33 which recommends a graceful (*añcita*) walk like that of a bull, for the male hero. Cf. *RghV* 2.18, where the slightly bent gaits (*añcitābhyām gatābhyām*) of Nandini and Dilīpa decorate their path home from the forest.

40 See the remarks of Susan Huntington, *The Art of Ancient India: Buddhist, Hindu, Jain* (New York: Weather Hill, 1985), pp. 190, 201.

Figure 4.3 Portrait sculpture of Kaṇiṣka, Māt shrine, Mathura region, Uttar Pradesh, *c.* second century CE, Mathura Museum.

postures with angular shoulders, those of the Guptas show a fluidity of movement and flexion of the body (figure 4.4). From post-Gupta times, nearly all standing sculpture has this pronounced flexion of the body (compare figures 4.1, 4.3, and 4.4 with figures 4.2, 4.5, and 4.6).

Graceful bearing at one level was an expression of humility (*vinaya*), that moderator of inner virtue. The gentle curvature and fluid postures

Figure 4.4 Gold stater of Kaṇiṣka standing in rigid posture (see Robert Göbl, *System und Chronologie der Münzprägung der Kusanreiches* (Wien: Verlag der österreichischen Akademie der Wissenschaften, 1984), type 71.)

Figure 4.5 Gupta gold coin, depicting king Candragupta standing with bow (see John Allan, *Catalogue of the Coins of the Gupta Dynasties and of Śaśāṅka, King of Gauda* (London: British Museum, 1914), archer type, no. 63).

in this sense were precisely the opposite of the stiff and presumptuous bearing of the *śakāra*. But an equally, if not more important source, however, came from a different direction and introduces an important topic in some ways at the heart of courtly aesthetics. This is the idea of 'playfulness' or 'sportiveness' – an important and polyvalent concept denoted by a large lexical set, including various derivatives from the verbal roots √*krīḍ*, to play; √*lal*, to play; √*ram* to rejoice or play; (*vi* +) √*las*, to shine, glitter or frolic; (*vi* +) √*nud*, to pierce, play (a musical instrument), or entertain; and perhaps most importantly, the noun *līlā*, sport or play, from which the denominative verb *līlāyati* was derived.[41] In the courtly context, these terms could refer to specific games, contests and entertainments enjoyed by men and women at court (the chief of which, as we shall see, was the game of romance), but also, partly by extension from this, a sort of physical inclination and even behavioural disposition.[42]

[41] For a discussion of the origin of these terms with an alternative understanding of their significance, see Johan Huizinga, *Homo Ludens: A Study of the Play Element in Culture* (Boston: Beacon Press, 1955), pp. 31–2, *passim*.

[42] Many of the sixty-four 'arts' (*kalā*) detailed in the *Kāmasūtra* were later called 'entertainments' (*vinoda*, *krīḍā*) in the sumptuary manuals like the *Mānasollāsa*.

Figure 4.6 Ivory sculpture of woman with lotus, *c.* ninth or tenth century, Brahminabad, Sindh.

In either case these amounted to a style of comportment or bearing, and words like *vilāsa*, *ramaṇa*, *lalita* and *līlā*, could refer variously to a playful nonchalance, mirthful spontaneity or a charming insouciance.

These words, frequently used to describe the highest men and women of rank at court, did not suggest any sense of undisciplined wildness, reckless abandon or transgressive carnival; to the contrary, they both presumed and embodied the highest forms of self-control and discipline valued by the people of the court. They are thus better conceived, somewhat akin to the Renaissance concept of *sprezzaturra*, as denoting a sort of cultivated spontaneity or playfulness which operated well within the protocols of respectability and received expectations of bodily carriage.[43] These terms evoked the ideological emphasis on enjoyment and pleasure which formed the court's chief image of itself, and also suggested the ease with which lords mastered difficult tasks. This sort of playfulness in bearing was thus nearly always a mark of high eminence and was typically applied to kings and lords rather than aspiring courtiers, though they were no doubt encouraged to do the same in regard to their inferiors and in the contexts of romantic liaison.[44]

Bāṇa's elaborate description of the emperor Harṣa is, once again, apposite. When he first glimpses the emperor, seated on a finely wrought couch of stone cooled with sandalwood water, he notes that Harṣa is not seated rigidly, but rather rests his weight on one arm placed at the edge of the seat with his foot dangling gently onto a brilliant sapphire and ruby footstool. This relaxed posture, which differentiated the king from his companions, immediately evokes an image of graceful dalliance for Bāṇa, who says that he seemed to be 'playing' (*ramamāṇa*) with his subject kings in a vast canopied lake composed of the light emitted from his body, with his foot, 'sporting' (*salīla*) on the jewelled footstool as if he was Kṛṣṇa dancing on the head of the demon Kālīya.[45] These conceits proceed from a subtle yet unmistakable nonchalance and ease which Bāṇa perceives in the emperor's bearing, which when combined with his imposing majesty,

[43] The term *sprezzaturra*, coined by the Italian noble Baldesar Castiglione (1478–1529) in his *Book of the Courtier*, referred to the ability to conceal or move attention away from the effort and labour put into one's self-cultivation by a sort of studied disregard and spontaneity of manner. See Baldesar Castiglione, *The Book of the Courtier*, trans. George Bull (Harmondsworth: Penguin, 1984), p. 67.

[44] Consequently, these terms cannot easily be read as part of a culture of anxiety and suspicion as some have understood the Renaissance *sprezzaturra*. See Harry Berger, *The Absence of Grace: Sprezzaturra and Suspicion in Two Renaissance Courtesy Books* (Stanford University Press, 2000), pp. 9–25.

[45] *HC*, ch. 2, pp. 70, 72. In this conceit the footstool is compared to the dark-jewelled hood of the demon Kāliya and the darkness of the Kali age. The touch of the left foot was humiliating.

form a perfect embodiment of eminent yet graceful carriage. Bāṇa concludes his description with the contradictory qualities which such bearing naturally evoked: 'though foreboding, unfathomable, and full of *gravitas*, the emperor was at the same time open, gracious, sportive and delightful'.[46]

Harṣa's graceful sitting posture evokes perfectly the 'irenic' notion of lordship discussed at the opening of this book. Lordship, according to this complex of ideas, was compassionate and articulated as a form of 'enjoyment'. The sitting posture here, shared by both courtly modes of representation as well as religious sources like the Bodhisattva ideology emerging sculpturally in the first centuries of the Common Era, clearly points to a new and profoundly mannered conception of lordship.[47] On the one hand, it was powerful and benefactive, indicated by the hand-gestures of assurance and favour (particularly on religious images). On the other, it was 'reposeful', signified by a relaxed or reclining torso with legs in different positions, one extended playfully onto a footstool. Several Gupta emperors are depicted seated in this or similar postures on their coins (see figures 4.7, 4.8), including the famous depiction of Samudragupta playing the lyre.[48] A particularly exemplary and beautiful depiction of this posture can be found in the fifth-century sculpture of a Nāga prince flanked by two female attendants and/or consorts at the Ajanta cave complex, patronised heavily by the Vākāṭakas of Vatsagulma (figure 4.9). As commentators have sensed, the brilliant execution here captures both confidence and elegance, and no better depiction of courtly bearing can be adduced.

The presence of a seated female companion beside the Nāga prince points to another arena where playful grace was particularly prominent – in the comportment that men and women were to take towards one another in courtship and romance. The *Nāṭyaśāstra* uses the terms *lalita*, *vilāsa* and *līlā* (among others) to differentiate various 'graceful' qualities that were to apply to heroes and heroines in courtship as represented on stage. For a woman, *līlā* was the delightful and affectionate imitation (*anukṛti*) of her beloved's speech, gestures and qualities; *vilāsa*, the appearance of relevant particularities with regard to standing, sitting and walking postures and particularly the actions of the hands, eyebrows and

[46] *HC*, ch. 2, p. 77. Bāṇa uses the figure of speech known as *virodha*, where seemingly antithetical descriptions are revealed to be compatible.

[47] The first known depiction of the Buddha in this posture, later known as the 'sportive repose' (*lalitāsana*), is at Amarāvatī (first or second century CE). I thank Akira Shimada for this information.

[48] For an epigraphic corroboration from Gupta sources, see the Bhitarī pillar inscription which describes the emperor Skandagupta with 'his left foot placed on the royal footstool' (*kṣitipacaraṇapīṭhe sthāpito vāmapādaḥ*), *CII* 3 1981), no. 31, p. 315, 316n.

Figure 4.7 Gupta gold coin, depicting king Candragupta seated on couch with foot dangling on footstool (see John Allan, *Catalogue of the Coins of the Gupta Dynasties and of Sasanka, King of Gauda* (London: British Museum, 1914), couch type, no. 102).

Figure 4.8 Gupta gold coin, depicting king Samudragupta seated on couch, playing lyre (see John Allan, *Catalogue of the Coins of the Gupta Dynasties and of Sasanka, King of Gauda* (London: British Museum, 1914), archer type, no. 51).

eyes (when seeing or meeting the lover); *lalita* was the position of the hands, feet and body, along with the eyebrows, eyes and lips produced by tender and beautiful gestures; and *vichitti*, the beauty that arose from a slight (*svalpa*) disregard in the arrangement (*anādaranyāsa*) of garlands, clothes, ornaments and unguents.[49] For men, relevant concepts were *vilāsa*, marked by the straightforward movement of the eyes, smiling when speaking and a graceful (*añcita*) walk like a bull; and *lalita*, romantic gestures and expressions which were undeliberate and grew out of a tender nature (*sukumārasvabhāvaja*).[50]

One theme that emerges from these usages is that grace was in part conceived as an insouciance or disregard for the fastidious discipline of physical bearing required for courtly protocol, akin to the concept of *disinvoltura*. The principle behind such comportment was a sort of controlled spontaneity; gestures and sartorial demeanor were to be 'undeliberate' (*abuddhipūrvaka*, literally 'not conceived before'). The irony of such recommendations on spontaneity is only partly attributable to

[49] *NS* 24.14–16, 22. [50] *NS* 24.33, 37.

Figure 4.9 Nāga prince with female attendants, Ajanta, Cave 19, Maharashtra, late fifth century CE.

their obvious function as dictums for actors on stage, for the 'play' concept which lay behind them implied not only a commitment to grace and spontaneity, but an acknowledgement of its boundaries and limits as well. This is underscored by the contrast between the playful disregard of protocols which was deemed 'graceful' and the violation or ignorance of them due to moral failing or low birth. The character of the *śakāra*'s stiff demeanour and constantly maladjusted clothes may be contrasted here with the physical grace and sartorial disregard of high characters. The *śakāra* is constantly readjusts and touches his clothes and ornaments from presumption, and so the dishevelment of his appearance takes on a totally different meaning. So too with men and women of the 'village' who were seen as incapable of understanding the playful graces of people of the court and city.[51]

Despite these common themes, male and female lovers tended to inhabit graceful modes of comportment somewhat differently. Female grace often emphasised delicacy, weakness or unsteadiness, which at its best was deemed charming, but also had a negative side. It was often taken as a sign of frivolity and inconstancy. For men, by contrast, tenderness and sportive grace were usually combined with *gravitas* and fortitude in bearing which reflected their stronger inner constitution. The common image used to denote this contrast was that of the tree and the creeper, both tender in different ways, but one stable, firm and supportive, the other delicate and unsteady. In *kāvya* the common characterisation of women was that they more easily 'lost control' in love-play, becoming vulnerable to indiscretion, intoxication and even wildness, thereby breaking codes of grace. Yet even this weakness, as we shall see, was deemed the particular charm of women in love-play, and signals an important anxiety which underwrote the courtly obsession with romance.

Decoration

Though the accounts of anatomical perfection and bodily grace outlined above suggest the extent to which courtly notions of beauty were mannered and stylised, neither formed the first and foremost *principle* of beauty prevalent among men and women of the court. This place was occupied by the idea of 'ornamentation' – a cultural figuration of practices and ideas so vast and significant as to subsume within it both anatomical

[51] See the fifteenth-century verse lamenting the condition of a sophisticated woman, whose lover cannot appreciate her urbane habits, including her slow (and graceful) gait, her indirection in speech and playful side glances. He is termed a man who only appreciates 'vulgar village' (*kugrāma*) girls, *MSS* vol. 7, no. 11673.

and gestural beauty (both of which were ornaments of the self), as well as various other concerns I shall take up below.

Early words for ornament were connected to ancient Vedic ritual. The term *ābharaṇa*, derived from the verb *ā* + √*bhṛ*, originally meant 'the bringing near, the attracting (of a magical power . . .)' and the term *alaṁkāra*, from *alam* + √*kṛ*, 'to make sufficient', denoted that which 'makes *alam* [sufficient], which gives strength required for something'.[52] Sometime during the early historic period these terms shed their earlier associations and were refocused, along with other terms, around a more restricted, if widely applicable, meaning – namely the 'decoration' of anything, particularly the human body.[53] By the inception of the aesthetic traditions in the first centuries of the Common Era, decoration had become a key idea among the courtly élite. As Heinrich Zimmer noted, 'the model' for what was deemed beautiful 'the ornamentation of the human body with jewellery'.[54]

The semantic origin of these terms as 'strengthening' remains significant at a number of levels which together suggest the importance that ornamentation came to have for life at court. Jewels, according to legends codified in the Gupta period, originated from the different body parts of the celestial being Bala. While rare specimens of different gems were thought to possess special powers (a belief which connected their use to the world of alchemy and magic commonly invoked at court), all gems had a 'luminosity' which derived from Bala's celestial origins and the purity of his actions.[55] It is the 'shining' quality of gems and jewellery which is emphasised in courtly descriptions and which linked ornaments with a vast imagery of splendour and illumination in early Indian society.

52 Jan Gonda, 'The Meaning of the Word Alaṃkāra', in Jan Gonda, *Selected Studies*, vol. II *Sanskrit Word Studies* (Leiden: E. J. Brill, repr. 1975), p. 271; Jan Gonda, 'Ābharaṇa', in Jan Gonda, *Selected Studies*, p. 176.

53 Among the other terms which come to denote some dimension of the process of adornment are *bhūṣaṇa*, *prasādhita*, *pralambita*, *pratimaṇḍita*, *śobhita*, *rājita*, *vicitrita* from roots like √*maṇḍ*, √*prasādh*, √*pralamb* and √*śubh*.

54 Heinrich Zimmer, *The Art of Indian Asia*, vol. I (Princeton University Press, 1960), p. 269.

55 The earliest treatments of gems include Buddhabhaṭṭa's *Ratnaparīkṣā*, sections of the *Garuḍapurāṇa* (1.68.1 ff.) which both probably date from the Gupta period, and the sixth-century *Bṛhatsaṁhitā* of Varāhamihira, which almost certainly draws on these earlier sources. Ascribing their origin to the seeds arising from the scattered remains of the celestial being Bala, the treatises set out general properties of gems and the prophylactic powers of rare specimens. See Louis Finot, *Les Lapidaires Indiens* (Paris: Librairie Emile Bouillon, 1896). Courtly dramas and didactic texts attest to these powers. See *NiV* 27.51, which claims that gems and gold could purify water; and King Udayana's remark in Harṣa's *Rv* 2.4.+ that 'the power of plants, incantations and jewels is inconceivable'. For gems in later alchemical and 'tantric' literature, see David Gordon White, *The Alchemical Body: Siddha Traditions in Medieval India* (University of Chicago Press, 1998), pp. 188–91.

As Daniel Ingalls pointed out, a number of words for beauty in Sanskrit *kāvya* have originary or concurrent meanings of 'shining' and 'illumining'.[56] Light was associated not only with beauty, but also with other virtues like strength, goodness and wisdom.[57] People of rank at court are often described as shining with a light which indicated their eminent virtue. Kauṭilya includes brilliance (*sūcī*) as an important quality of a minister, and the imagery of 'fame' is most often associated with spotlessness and brilliance.[58] The majesty of kings was thought to derive from a luminous energy (*tejas*) which infused the king's person, and royalty was variously associated with the two most luminous bodies of the heavens, from which the most important royal families from the Gupta period were thought to descend: the enlivening (or furious) splendour (*pratāpa*) of the sun and the cooling and beneficent rays of the moon.

Gems enhanced these attributes, less as a part of any coherent causality than a sort of associational symptomology. The association of jewels with light, beauty and virtue was older, and had been a theme in several post-Vedic religious practices in early historic India, particularly in Buddhism, where it amounted to nothing short of an obsession. Buddhist culture, particularly among the Mahāyāna sects which grew up and flourished in late-Kuṣāṇa and early Gupta times and clearly had close relationships with courtly life across northern India, was pervaded with endless lapidary imagery – gem doctrines, jewel bodies and celestial realms composed of every conceivable type of gem.[59] Buddhist texts imagined paradises where wish-fulfilling trees made of different jewels (*ratnavṛkṣa*s) chimed in the breeze and dropped unfading gem-flowers onto the ground.[60] The effulgent brilliance of the jewelled Bodhisattva

[56] Daniel Ingalls, 'Words for Beauty in Classical Sanskrit Poetry', in Ernst Bender, ed., *Indological Studies in Honor of W. Norman Brown* (New Haven, CT: American Oriental Society, 1962), pp. 100–2.

[57] In this connection it is difficult to agree with Ingalls' assertion (in 'Words for Beauty') that Indian traditions (unlike the west) never associated beauty and virtue. While it is true that beauty never becomes a metaphysical concept equated with the good in early India as it was in certain forms of neo-Platonic thinking, it nevertheless always formed an indissociable dimension of both virtue and power.

[58] *AS* 1.9.1. This is widely corroborated in epigraphic accounts.

[59] This topic is far too vast to enter into here. For preliminary discussions of the role of gems in Buddhist doctrine and ritual see Liu, *Ancient India and Ancient China*, pp. 88–102; and Phyllis Granoff, 'Maitreya's Jewelled World: Some Remarks on Gems and Visions in Buddhist Texts', *Journal of Indian Philosophy*, vol. 26 (1998), pp. 347–71.

[60] Notable among Mahāyāna texts are the accounts of the celestial heavens in the *Sukhāvativyūhasūtra* (paras. 16, and esp. 21) and the *Saddharmapuṇḍarikasūtra* (ch. 11, para. 6 ff.), composed in the third or fourth century CE. The *Sukhāvatīvyūha* remarks that if the inhabitants of paradise desire any kind of ornament – whether it be diadems, earrings, armbands, bracelets, chains, seals, gold strings, girdles, gold nets, pearl nets, jewel nets, nets of bells – they will see them shining everywhere, first on ornament trees, and then on themselves.

paradises was meant to signify the spiritual advancement and blissful enjoyment of their inhabitants. As social 'imaginaries' current among the worldly, they certainly reinforced the association of jewels and jewellery with both light and moral perfection.

Though few actual specimens have survived, all evidence suggests that jewellery and ornaments of every conceivable kind were worn by people of the court. Men wore crowns, earrings, necklaces, finger rings, forearm bands, bracelets, armbands, breast ornaments and waist ornaments while women wore various headdresses, *tilaka*s for the forehead and cheeks, earrings, necklaces, breast ornaments, armbands, finger rings, girdles, anklets and toerings.[61] Flowers and leaves were also an important element and supplement to jewellery, particularly for women. Not only were flowers and leaf cuttings themselves used as ornaments on the ears, forehead and face,[62] but plant motifs of various kinds were also used as prototypes for fashioning metal and stone jewellery.

Both men and women were to appear at court fully adorned with ornaments. It is important to stress that the acceptable ideal of personal beauty in the eyes of people at court nearly always included jewellery and ornaments. Physical descriptions of men and women of courtly rank in Sanskrit *kāvya* often focus on bodily ornaments.[63] Such accounts were attentive not only to light, but sound and movement. The swaying and jingling of ornaments, a favourite theme in poetry, immediately evoked dalliance and enjoyment.[64] For people of the court, the unadorned naked body had little aesthetic appeal. In fact, the absence of ornaments was invariably seen as indicating grief, abstinence or calamity. In Kālidāsa's *Abhijñānaśākuntala* King Duṣyanta removes his ornaments (save a single golden bracelet) when separated from Śakuntalā; in Viśākhadatta's *Mudrārākṣasa*, the minister Rākṣasa takes off his ornaments as a sign of defeat, disgrace and determination to avenge the calamities of the Nanda

[61] See *NS* 23.15–37. For a survey of ornaments as represented in early Indian sculpture, see Anne-Marie Loth, *Les Bijoux*, Fascicule IX (Première Partie), *La Vie Publique et Priveé Dans L'Inde Ancienne (IIe Siècle av. J. C. –VIIIe Siècle Environ)* (Paris: Presses Universitaires de France, 1972). Numerous studies take up literary references to ornaments, see Anupa Pande, *The Nāṭyaśāstra Tradition and Ancient Indian Society* (Jodhpur: Kusumanjali, 1993).

[62] See *Sk*, 1.4, and particularly 6.18 for Śakuntalā's flower ornaments. On the skill of constructing ear ornaments from flowers, see Ganguly, *Sixty-four Arts in Ancient India*, p. 87. The art of *viśeṣakachedya*, according to Yaśodhara (*KS* 1.3.16, comm.), referred to the cutting of designs from various substances (including leaves) into the shapes of creepers, leaves and flowers for the forehead and face (corroborated by Kālidāsa's *Ṛtusaṃhāra* 6.7). It seems that aloe-paste (*aguru*) was used as an adhesive for these leaf-designs, see Jean Auboyer, *Daily Life in Ancient India*, p. 271, nn. 66–7.

[63] See Bāṇa's description of Harṣa, *HC*, ch. 2, pp. 70–3.

[64] Typical is Bāṇa, who imitates jingling girdles with '*jhaṅ*' and swaying earrings with '*raṇ*', *Kd*, pp. 29–30.

throne; and in Bāṇa's *Kādambarī*, Queen Vilāsavatī takes off her ornaments from grief at her failure to bear a child for King Tārāpīḍa.[65]

As early as the *Mānavadharmaśāstra*, it is recommended that the king appear 'adorned' (*alaṃkṛta*) to inspect his soldiers, vehicles, weapons and jewellery (*ābharaṇāni*).[66] By the time of the *Arthaśāstra*, palace plans included a separate room or pavilion for the daily adornment of the king (*alaṁkārabhūmi*). Significantly, this room is situated outside the royal sleeping quarters (see figure 1.2). The king must have proceeded there each day before going to the counsel chamber or audience hall. The activities which transpired in this room were of great ritual and symbolic importance, for adornment, like bathing, formed one of the *upacāra*s or daily courtesies integrated into the royal routine. In Kālidāsa's *Raghuvaṃśa*, the prince Atithi, after his coronation-bath (*abhiṣeka*) takes a seat on a stool in the midst of a courtyard in his palace to receive his royal dress, which is brought to him by his dressing attendants (*prasādhaka*). They adorn his hair, apply cosmetics and fasten his garments, garlands and ornaments.[67] Later eleventh-century records of the Cōḻa dynasty show royal decrees issued from bathing and dressing pavilions,[68] and we know from the Cōḻa inscriptions at Tanjavur that there were stipended palace establishments (*vēḷam*s) for both the bathing (*tirumañcaṉa*) and adornment (*abhimānabhūṣaṇa*) of members of the royal family.[69]

From the Gupta period, treatises make very clear that bodily ornaments to a great extent for men, and a lesser extent for women, were governed, like sartorial manner itself, by sumptuary regulation.[70] Ornaments formed the most prized objects of the king's treasury, and the

[65] *Sk* 6.6: *MR* 2.10; and *Kd*, p. 103. In the last of these examples, King Tārāpīḍa asks his queen, 'O thin-waisted one, why have you not decorated yourself? Why haven't you put *alaktaka* dye on your feet . . . why haven't you favoured with the touch of your lotus-like feet your jewelled anklets, why is your waist silent, your girdle being laid aside, why is the ornamental design . . . not painted on your expansive breasts . . . why haven't you decorated your slender neck with a pearl necklace . . . why have the line decorations on your cheek been washed off by your tears . . . why is your forehead without a *tilaka* mark . . . and your hair unbound . . .?'

[66] *MDh* 7.222.

[67] *RghV* 17.21–6. Interestingly, the description of the prince's dressing and adornment exceeds that of the coronation-bath ceremony itself.

[68] For a twelfth-century inscription referring to a grant issued from the royal bathing hall (*tirumamañcaṉacālai*) at the Cōḻa palace at Gaṅgaikoṇḍacōḻapuram, see *SII* 3.1 (1929), no. 20, p. 35; and at the bathing hall (*kuḷikkumiṭattu*) at the Cōḻa palace at Kāñcī, see R. Nagaswamy, 'Archaeological Finds in South India: Esālam Bronzes and Copper-plates', *Bulletin de l'École Française D'Extrême Orient*, vol. 76 (1987), p. 34.

[69] *SII* 2 (1895–1913), no. 94, p. 436 ff.

[70] Loth has observed that while female figures in sculpture tend to show a uniformity of adornment, male figures show a gradation of complexity, number and quality in relation to rank, Loth, *Les Bijoux*, p. 14.

Arthaśāstra names more than twenty different types of stringed ornaments, denominated by the number of jewels and threads they possessed.[71] Treatises like Varāhamihira's *Bṛhatsaṁhitā* and later sumptuary manuals like *Aparājitapṛcchā*, *Mānasollāsa* and *Mānasāra* are more explicit about the relation of ornaments (particularly crowns and headbands or *paṭṭa*s, but other ornaments as well) to political hierarchy, and place them alongside thrones, umbrellas, fans and other royal insignia which were regulated by rank.[72] The presumption, expectedly, is that the higher the rank of king the more numerous, elaborate and costly the ornaments. The *Mānasāra* remarks that no king other than the emperor should wear any necklace chain (*hāra*) above the chest, and neither should lesser kings wear armbands (*keyūra*, *kaṭaka*).[73]

Ornaments were worn by nearly all men of rank at court and were often highly personalised, being acquired either through favour, war booty, or inheritance. They often had names and were the subjects of considerable celebration in courtly eulogies. Personal seals and seal rings (often too large for a single finger but probably worn around the neck), which bore an imprint of the bearer's name and were used to authenticate communications, though less elaborate than jewelled ornaments, seem to have been ubiquitous among men of upper ranks (see fig. 1.6). The plots of several court dramas turn on the recognition or use of seal rings and other ornaments. In *Mudrārākṣasa*, the minister Rākṣasa's whereabouts are revealed and his demise carefully planned through the clandestine discovery and use of a seal-ring. Cāṇakya's designs against Rākṣasa are further advanced by the strategic placement of two sets of body ornaments belonging to Prince Malayaketu's family, which, when recognised by the prince at a key juncture in Act 5, implicate Rākṣasa in a plot against his lord.

Personal ornamentation in the eyes of people at court entailed not only jewellery and flowers, but an entire gamut of 'body culture', including body oils, pastes, cosmetics, fragrances, dress and hair coiffure. Anything applied to the body – garments (*vastra*), perfumes (*gandha*), ornaments (*alaṁkāra*) or garlands (*mālā*) – was considered to 'adorn' it, and a large number of the skills or 'arts' (*kalā*) to be mastered by the *nāgaraka* entailed expertise at various aspects of this elaborate regimen of self-beautification.[74] Vātsyāyana includes details of the preparation of the courtier's body for his daily routine beginning with the application of ointments, perfumes, beeswax, lac, betel, mouth freshener and garlands,

[71] *AS* 2.11.6–26.
[72] See *Mānasāra* 49.1 ff. for crowns; and 50.3–45 for body ornaments.
[73] *Mānasāra* 50.39–40. [74] See *NS* 13.42; *KS* 1.3.16 (table 2.1).

and finally jewels themselves.[75] The material record has also been revealing, as large numbers of vials, hairpins and other cosmetic implements like make-up palettes (figure 1.5) have been recovered from early Indian sites.

Unfortunately, little by way of clothes has survived, and we are almost entirely dependent on sculptural representations and literary accounts to reconstruct the dressing habits of people at court. Dress styles in the period from the fourth to seventh centuries, it would seem, were particularly cosmopolitan. By the fourth century CE, the traditional attire of (*dhoti*-like) wrapped garments covering the lower body with optional upper garments, known widely from representations on early historic monuments,[76] had long been supplemented by Central Asian dress fashions from the courts of the Parthians, Śakas and Kuṣāṇas.[77] The Gupta court continued many of these fashions and adopted others from Sasanian Iran. While the traditional wrapped lower garments (*adharavāsa*) remained standard, Sasanian headbands, fillets, coats, sashes, girdles and even pants, were popular among people at court in north India until as late as the seventh century.[78] This was particularly true with military and ceremonial court dress, as attested to at sites like Ajanta and on the coins of Gupta monarchs. Bāṇa portrays the kings of Harṣa's court wearing garments which clearly indicated Sasanian and Central Asian influence. These included the *kañcuka*, a long, coat-like garment extending to the ankles worn by either men or women (including the chamberlain or '*kāñcukin*' in Sanskrit dramas); the *vārabāṇa*, derived from a mail-like coat of armour worn by Sasanian nobles, which extended down to the knees; the *kūrpāsaka*, a shorter tunic-like garment with variable sleeve length, also of Central Asian origin; the *cīnacolika*, a coat worn over all outer drapery, perhaps, as its name suggests, of Chinese origin; and the *ācchādanaka*, a scarf or short cape covering both shoulders, knotted in front of the chest, probably from Sasanian Iran.[79]

[75] *KS* 1.4.16, 22.

[76] The basic form of dress, similar for both men and women, was a wrapped garment extending from the waist to below the knees, drawn up between the legs, and secured again at the waist with a sash tied to one side. The upper body in the case of both sexes was for the most part bare, though scarves and coats were also worn. For a review of the evidence, see Moti Chandra, 'Indian Costumes from the Earliest Times to the First Century BC', *Bharatiya Vidya*, vol.1, pt. 1 (1939), pp. 48–50.

[77] These included covered shoes, trousers and hairstyles. See Anne-Marie Loth, *Les Costumes*. Fascicule VII (Premiere Partie) of *La Vie Publique et Priveé dans L'Inde Ancienne: IIe Siècle av. J. C. –VIIIe Siècle Environ* (Paris: Presses Universitaires de France, 1979), pp. 31–5, 50, 62–3, 90–3, 103–4.

[78] For Sasanian influences on Indian court fashions as evidenced in literature and sculpture from Deogarh and Ajanta, see V. S. Agrawala, *Deeds of Harsha*, pp. 42, 104, 105, 181–7 and Loth, *Les Costumes*, pp. 117–18, 121–4.

[79] *HC*, ch. 7, p. 206–7. I have followed the intrepretation of this passage by Agrawala, *Deeds of Harsha*, pp. 181–7.

While court poets like Bāṇa probably exaggerated the prevalence of unusual garments worn by courtiers and kings in order to portray the courts of their patrons as cosmopolitan and exotic, several general features of courtly garments remain significant and worthy of note. Cotton cloth (*bādara*) was common but the preferred fabric was certainly silk, indicated by a large number of terms denoting different qualities and styles – *paṭṭa*, *netra*, *dukūla*, *lālātantuja*, *patrorṇa*, *aṁśuka* and *kauśeya*.[80] Silk was either imported from China or Central Asia or produced locally.[81] Garments for both men and women were typically in bright colours, patterned with floral or animal designs with variegated borders and embroidered or inlaid with jewels. The *vārabāṇa*, for example, was made of a thick brocaded silk known as *stavaraka* imported from Sasanian Persia, which was inlaid with clusters of pearls.[82] Finer silks, however, were far more common. Generally, it would seem that what appealed to the tastes of the court were 'fine' (*sūkṣma*) and 'diaphanous' (*vimala*) fabrics which were typically compared to a snake's slough (*nirmoka*). The diaphanous and semi-transparent features of garments were cleverly used by sculptors to portray the contours of the body while it was fully clothed and adorned.

In conclusion, it should also be noted, if at least in passing, that the principle of beauty as ornament not only applied to the bodies of men and women at court, but to their surroundings as well. The later text *Mānasāra* distinguishes from 'bodily ornaments' (*aṅgabhūṣaṇa*) another category of 'external ornaments' (*bahirbhūṣaṇa*) which included items as diverse as lamp-posts (*dīpadaṇḍa*), fans (*vyajana*), mirrors (*darpaṇa*), swings (*dolā*), balances for kings (*tūla*), leaf-seals (*patra*), pens (*karṇa*) and cages (*nīḍa*) for a host of different animals.[83] These objects were in turn decorated with paintings and engravings of creepers, flowers, jewels and animals. Architecture too was conceived of in 'ornamentalist' terms. Not only did increasingly ornate and elaborate external embellishment characterise stone architecture from the sixth century, but ornament also formed a key concept in later sumptuary and architectural texts. This ornamentalist understanding is clearly prefigured in earlier texts and inscriptions, as the Vākāṭaka record from Ajanta (*c.* 500 CE) that is explicit about it, describes a cave monastery as 'adorned' (*alaṁkṛta*) with windows, doors, beautiful picture galleries, ledges, statues of Indra's nymphs

80 For a discussion of these terms, see Agrawala, *Deeds of Harsha*, pp. 101–3.

81 On the reputation of Sasanian silk in India, and elsewhere, see Liu, *Silk and Religion*, pp. 20–1, 52–3.

82 On the *stavaraka*, cloth, see Agrawala, *Deeds of Harsha*, p. 184; also V. S. Agrawala *Terracotta Figurines of Ahichchhatrā* (Varanasi: Prithvi Prakashan, 1985), pp. 74–5.

83 *Mānasāra* 50.23–8. These external ornaments are also variously 'adorned' with creepers, flowers, jewels, and animal figures. For the ornaments on swings, see *Mānasāra* 50.84; on mirrors, 50.56, 59–60, 65–6; on pens 50.103; on cages 50.134–6, 42, 44.

and the like, and as ornamented (*bhūṣita*) with beautiful pillars and stairs.[84] But by the time of texts like *Mayamata* and *Mānasāra*, not only were the basic architectural elements joined with one another through the language of ornament – buildings being 'decorated' (*alaṃkṛta*) by various types of bases, pillars, stereobates and attics, and gate-towers (*gopura*) 'decorated' (*maṇḍita, alaṃkṛta, prabhūṣyate*) with windows, arches, vestibules and corner towers[85] – but sculptural reliefs of jewels, flowers, creepers and animals of various sorts were also said to 'adorn' (*bhūṣita, maṇḍita, śobhita, vicitrita*, etc.) various architectural elements – doors (*dvāra*), arches (*toraṇa*), pavilions (*maṇḍapa*), pillars (*stambha*), gateways (*gopura*), thrones (*siṃhāsana*), palanquins (*śibikā*) and chariots (*ratha*).[86]

The refinement of speech

Beauty in appearance and bearing was to be complemented by charming and elegant speech. At court, good speech operated at a number of levels. Most basically, it was to be 'refined', and here it is necessary to consider what has recently been called the 'ideology of Sanskrit' as an integral feature of élite society generally, and specifically life at court. Overlapping this notion of good speech as a 'refinement' was the idea that beautiful verbal utterance should be embellished with figures of speech known as 'ornaments'. The treatises which classified these figures, our earliest texts on 'poetics' (called the 'science of embellishment', or *alaṁkāraśāstra*), are significant for any understanding of beauty in early India because they produced arguably the only theoretical discourse on beauty which has survived from this period. When one of its important early theorists, the scholar Vāmana, probably a minister at the court of the Karkoṭa king of Kashmir, Jayāpīḍa (779–813), began his treatise with the assertion that 'beauty is ornament' he enunciated by then what would have been more

[84] Mirashi supplies *bhūṣitam* from missing letters, *CII* 5 (1963), no. 25, pp. 109, 111. See also the fifth-century *BS* 56.1 ff. on temple architecture.

[85] *Mayamata* 21.28; *Mānasāra* 33.154, 213, 242, 258, 271.

[86] See for example, *Mānasāra* 39.39, which in describing the construction of doors says that they should 'be adorned with all ornaments and decorated with leaves and creepers' (*sarvālaṁkārasaṃyuktam patravallayādivibhūṣitam*). For other references to the sculptural adornment with creepers, flowers, jewels, ornaments, lions, *vyāla*s, painting, etc. for doors, see *Mānasāra* 39.32, 34–8, 41, 57, 79; for arches, *Mayamata* 21.72 and *Mānasāra* 46.20–31 where different arches are named after their style of ornament; for pavilions *Mayamata* 25.76–9, 117–19 and *Mānasāra* 33.33, 66; for gateways *Mayamata* 30.114 and *Mānasāra* 33.173; for windows *Mānasāra* 33.287, 292, 295; for pillars *Mayamata* 15.20, 27, 49 and *Mānasāra* 15.18–19, 84–5; for thrones *Mānasāra* 45.62, 92–3; for chariots, *Mayamata* 31.60; for palanquins *Mayamata* 31.14–15. The terminology is so pervasive in architectural texts that more generic terms, such as *anvita* and *saṃyukta* meaning 'furnished with' are used synonymously with the words for 'adorned'.

than common sense, and what, as we have seen above, had resonances with a wide range of activities at court.[87]

It is perhaps significant that though there were certainly antecedents, the first fully enunciated theory of 'Sanskrit' is to be found in an aesthetic rather than grammatical text. That text, the *Nāṭyaśāstra*, remains our first codification of courtly aesthetics, and the theory of Sanskrit (what authors typically call 'classical Sanskrit') was inextricably tied to the culture which we have been setting out in this book. According to the *Nāṭyaśāstra*, stage-recitation could be divided into two varieties of speech – 'refined' (*saṃskṛta*) and 'natural' (*prākṛta*).[88] The central feature of refined speech was its adherence to phonetic and grammatical rules as set down in treatises on grammar. It was described with derivatives of the root *saṁ*+ √*kṛ*, denoting something manipulated, refined or even adorned to achieve a specific result. Natural speech, by contrast, did not have this quality of phonetic and grammatical refinement (*saṃskāraguṇavarjita*) and was deemed, at least by the standards of refinement, as 'inverted' (*viparyasta*).[89] There was another important distinction between natural speech and refined speech. Natural speech was diverse and particular. The *Nāṭyaśāstra* lists a variety of such ways of speaking (*prākṛta*s) each, known by its region of origin – Māgadhī, Āvantī, Śauraseni, etc. . . . In contrast to the varieties of natural or unrefined speech which varied according to region, Sanskrit was deemed universal and implacable.

As might be expected, these forms of speech were associated with different social ranks, and like the postures and gaits in the drama, they reflected the essential qualities of the characters who spoke them. The *Nāṭyaśāstra* says that refined recitation was only to be used in the case of upper-caste males and heroes of different varieties, while natural recitation was to be assigned to women, people in disguise, Jains, ascetics, mendicants, jugglers, children, people possessed of low houses, transvestites and women of low birth.[90] If refined speech was deemed superior to natural speech, natural speech itself was differentiated into higher and lower forms, as Śauraseni, for example, was spoken by heroines and courtly women while Magadhi was suitable for guards of the royal harem.[91] Though each form

[87] *Saundaryamalaṁkāraḥ*, Vāmana, *Kāvyālaṁkāra* 1.2.

[88] See *NS* 15.5. This is generally accepted as the first textual usage of the term Sanskrit to refer to a language or discrete style of speech. For discussion of the importance of this passage in the history of Sanskrit as a language, see M. Srimannarayana Murti, 'On the Nomenclature Saṃskṛta', *Adyar Library Bulletin* 57 (1993), p. 58 and Ashok Aklujkar, 'The Early History of Sanskrit as a Supreme Language', in J. Houben, ed., *Ideology and the Status of Sanskrit: Contributions to the History of the Sanskrit Language* (Leiden: E. J. Brill, 1996), pp. 70–1, n. 18.

[89] *NS* 15.5–6; 18.2. [90] *NS* 18.31–35. The entirety of this list is somewhat unclear.

[91] *NS* 18.49–50.

of natural speech could function as a mode of communication in its own right, as a whole they were considered less intelligible (*gamakatva*) and expressive (*abhihitatva*) than refined speech.[92]

Though the linguistic picture which emerges from this world was probably more ideal than real, its contrast with modern notions of linguistic identity is worth considering. First, 'natural' speech forms were viewed as inferior to speech which was conceived of as modified and transformed, or 'refined'. Second, local and particular forms of speech were once again deemed inferior to that which had a universal or non-locative character. Indeed, as Sheldon Pollock has argued, intellectuals and men of the court sought to participate in a 'cosmopolitan' order which occluded forms of local belonging.[93] While all men possessed familiarity with some form of 'natural' speech, only those of moral and political worth had access to the universal provenance of refined speech known as Sanskrit. The people of the court, like men of religion, moved in a world which valourised the cosmopolitan over the localised, a world where atavistic identities had little place. This is, of course, not to say that the 'languages of the regions' (*deśabhāṣa*), as they were called, had no place. Familiarity with at least one regional language was assumed and knowledge of many was a mark of accomplishment. Mastery of regional speeches is mentioned among the sixty-four arts of the urbane man or courtier, according to the *Kāmasūtra* (see table 2.1). Vātsyāyana advises that in certain contexts the *nāgaraka* should speak with neither too much Sanskrit nor regional language (*deśabhāṣa*), for only then would he be well regarded in the world.[94] The overall picture which emerges is of a great pyramid of linguistic registers at the top of which sat refined speech, or Sanskrit.

The courtly provenance of the 'ideology of Sanskrit' in early India is amply demonstrated not only by the many poems in the language that have come down to us from the courts of kings, but more powerfully, as Sheldon Pollock has shown, by its rise and spread as the dominant epigraphic language from the early Gupta period. Sanskrit came to form the lingua franca of diplomatic transaction – a language which integrated the hundreds of royal houses which emerged between the fourth and thirteenth centuries into a single cultural figuration. Proficiency in Sanskrit was associated not only with virtue and sophistication, but also with correct policy. A rather eloquent testament to this association is made in an eighth-century inscription which praises the Maitraka king Śīlāditya V as

92 Srimannarayana Murti, 'Nomenclature Saṃskṛta', pp. 68–9, citing Patañjali.
93 See Pollock, 'The Cosmopolitan Vernacular', pp. 13–14.
94 *KS* 1.4.50.

> being clever (*nipuṇa*), on the one side at determining combinations (*samāsa*) of treaties (*sandhi*) and wars (*vigraha*) and on the other at analysing euphonic combinations (*sandhi*) into their separate parts (*vigraha*) . . . on the one side at assigning commands (*ādeśa*) appropriate (*anurūpa*) to rank (*sthāna*), and on the other placing substituted forms (*ādeśa*) in suitable (*anurūpa*) places (*sthāna*) . . . and who on the one side was lord among those eminent (*sādhu*) in refinement (*saṁskāra*) arising from the use of (*vidhāna*) increased (*vṛddhi*) virtue (*guṇa*), and on the other, of those who excel (*sādhu*) in the perfection (*saṁskāra*) arising from the use (*vidhāna*) of *guṇa* and *vṛddhi* changes in vowels.[95]

In each case an aspect of grammatical knowledge also denoted an accomplishment in the science of polity. The perfection of speech through knowing its constituent parts, their order, exchangeability and the method of their transformation is analogous to the knowledge of the 'rules' of political relationships – the combination of alliance and war, the assignment of place and, most importantly, the cultivation and refinement of virtue.[96]

The conceit of this passage suggests an even higher level of verbal refinement, and one particularly associated with court. Refined speech and conversation at court drew very heavily on literary registers, and in the debates which must have taken place in the early centuries of the Common Era over the defining characteristics of a poetic composition, consensus came to gravitate around the idea of verbal figure, or 'ornament' (*alaṁkāra*) as the defining feature of poetry. Though the *Nāṭyaśāstra* includes ornament (*vibhūṣaṇa*), with its four sub-varieties, as merely one of some thirty-six *lakṣaṇa*s or 'marks' of a proper *kāvya*, it cannot help but refer to these marks themselves as 'ornaments' (*bhūṣaṇa*s),[97] auguring the importance that this concept would have in subsequent treatises which tended to replace the theoretical centrality of the enumeration of *lakṣaṇa*s with lists of poetic ornaments.[98] These early treatises, as noted above, were akin to the tradition of rhetoric in the West, and defined the literary as an 'embellishment' (*alaṁkāra*) of direct discourse – the classic image being the decoration of the 'body' (*śarīra*) of language through figures of speech, each of which was considered to be an 'ornament'.[99] Proper and beautiful speech for refined men was always presented, like the

[95] *CII* 3 (1888), no. 39, p. 175.

[96] Given that both diplomatic and revenue transactions were recorded in Sanskrit, the basis of this conceit was more than plausible. *PT* 3.38 recommends 'refined speech' (*saṁskṛtavaktā*) as a prerequisite for the successful minister.

[97] *NS* 17.1–5.

[98] On the history of *lakṣaṇa* in subsequent poetic theory, particularly its partial absorption by the idea of *alaṁkāra*, see V. Raghavan, *Studies on Some Concepts of the Alaṁkāra Śāstra* (Madras: Adyar Library, 1973), pp. 1–52.

[99] On this idea, see the well-known passage in Daṇḍin's *Kāvyādarśa* 1.10; also Bhāmaha, *Kāvyālaṁkāra* 1.30; Vāmana, *Kāvyālaṁkāra*, 1.2.

body itself, in ornamented form. The formal science of rhetoric which came to be known as *alaṃkāraśāstra*, or 'the science of [poetic] ornament', conceived of its task, beyond identifying the faults and virtues of aesthetic language, as the enumeration and classification of these ornaments (*alaṁkāras*), *in extenso*.

Though later theories of the literary departed from the idea of ornament as the definitive feature of poetic utterance, replacing it with notions of 'speech-bending' (*vakrokti*) or 'suggestion' (*dhvani*), they still worked with the assumption that connotative meaning was essential for exalted forms of public discourse. The ninth-century aesthetician Ānandavardhana, famous for his theory of 'suggestion' as the essence of poetry, argued in his *Dhvanyāloka*, that the most essential matters were best conveyed through suggestion rather than direct statement, for 'in the assemblies of the clever and learned it is well known that one does not display one's inner wishes through open expression (*sākṣādvācyatvena*) but instead through suggestion (*vyaṅgatvena*)'.[100] The basic idea, however, remained true to the spirit of ornament – that seemly and appropriate speech at court departed in some way from direct discourse.

The oral-literary culture of the court laid tremendous value on speaking beautifully. If the courtier was to cultivate a certain studied 'play' or 'dalliance' in his bearing, his speech was also to be clever and charming. Verbal accomplishments like grammatical refinement (*saṁskṛta*) and eloquence (*vāgbhūṣaṇa*), according to Bhartṛhari, were ornaments superior to jewellery because they lasted forever.[101] And 'cleverness in speech' (*vāgvidagdha*), according to the rhetoricians, required skill in composing poetry.[102] Forms of eloquence like this tended to push courtly speech into ever rarefied domains, a trend which was sanctioned by the idea that sophistication in speech, just as familiarity with Sanskrit, was a preserve of the élite and a badge of distinction.[103] Yet even so, Daṇḍin tells us that poetry thus helped foster 'well-deployed' speech, which brought success in the world.[104] This drive towards a sort of verbal comportment (where formal poetry was joined by verbal games, riddles, secret scripts and the like[105]) underwrote and sustained the incessant aestheticising

[100] *Dhvanyāloka* 4.5. [101] *STr* 1.15.

[102] See Bhāmaha, *Kāvyālaṁkāra* 1.4.

[103] See the exchange between the spy, an aspiring courtier-minister, and the counsellor Cāṇakya in Viśākhadatta's *Mudrārākṣasa* where the spy conveys secret information to his master in the presence of his novices through a cryptic verse suggesting his knowledge of day lotuses, who are enemies to the moon (*candra* = Candragupta), *MR* 1.19, +.

[104] *Kāvyādarśa*, 1.6

[105] It is perhaps signficant that during the period between the fourth and eighth centuries a number of verbal games like *pratimāla*, *kāvyasamasyapūraṇa*, *manasikāvyakriya*, and *prahelikā* are first recommended for courtiers (*KS* 1.3.16, see table 2.1), and discussed

tendencies of courtly speech. To ask of a young man's background, for example, was politely expressed through enquiring what kingdom or family was 'adorned' by his birth, or 'burned by the fire of his absence'.[106] As abhorrent as this prolixity of speech has been to modern commentators, it was utterly integral to communication in the courtly environment, even in the most intimate of situations. As Robert Goodwin has perceptively pointed out, when characters in court dramas attempt to discover the real intentions of those they suspect of disloyalty, they do not do so by 'cutting through' verbal formality, but instead by observing them through spies or concealment.[107] What is significant about such dramatic conventions is the refusal to retreat from formal ornamented registers of speech even at moments of the most intimate emotional truth. The embellishment of direct utterance was not seen as superfluous to basic intentions and emotions – rather it was the preferred expression of them.

Alaṁkāra as a cultural figuration

Yet we must ask whether there exists any 'internal' logic to the incessant aestheticising tendencies and almost pedantic obsession with style among the courtly élite? As suggested in the Introduction, the existing traditions of scholarship have tended to understand courtly aesthetics – and ornament in particular – as either a debased form of aesthetic perception (at best an exotic menagerie of sublime delectation), or alternatively as part of a holistic humanist and/or spiritual 'view of life' typical of Romantic modes of thinking.[108] Neither of these characterisations, however, grasp the full significance of aesthetics for the people of the court. In the final section of this chapter I suggest why we should see courtly aesthetics as something different, a sort of 'root idea' in courtly life.

in poetic manuals (Bhāmaha, *Kāvyālaṁkāra* 2.19; Daṇḍin, *Kāvyādarśa* 3.96–124). Writing during this period also reflects the drive towards aestheticisation, with not only the increasing stylisation of the 'box-headed' and *siddhamātṛkā* scripts of central and northern India, but also the emergence of special ornate or calligraphic scripts like fancy Brahmī and the 'shell script' – both still undeciphered. The latter was very widespread, with over 600 known examples. See Salomon, *Indian Epigraphy*, pp. 69–70.

106 See Śakuntalā's friend Anasūyā's enquiry to King Duṣyanta, *Sk* 1.21+; and Sarasvatī's enquiry to the courtier Vikukṣī about the background of prince Dadhīca, *HC*, ch. 1, p. 26.

107 See Goodwin, *Playworld*, p. 75.

108 For the former of the trend, looking at Japanese courtly culture, see Morris, *World of the Shining Prince*, pp. 170–98; with Indian materials, see Devangana Desai, 'Art under Feudalism in India (*c.* 500–1300)', *IHR*, vol. 1, no. 1 (1979), pp. 10–17. For the latter approach, see E. H. Gombrich, *The Sense of Order: A Study in the Psychology of Decorative Art* (Ithaca, NY: Cornell University Press, 1984) and in the Indian context, A. K. Coomaraswamy, 'Ornament', in *Coomaraswamy: Selected Papers* (Princeton University Press, 1977).

We have so far been reviewing concepts of beauty as they applied to an individual's appearance and speech at court and, to a lesser extent, to his or her surroundings. We have seen that the predominant conceptualisation of this beauty was through the language of ornament, or *alaṁkāra* (and related terms), which, though having old roots in India, came in the first centuries of the Common Era to refer to beautification as such. The purview of this idea, however, was far more wide-reaching than we might first imagine.

Each of the 'attributes' of beauty reviewed above often appears among the lists of 'ornaments' which decorated people at court. Physical marks, anatomical perfections, bodily movement, gestural grace, playful demeanour, brilliant attire, jewellery, verbal style and eloquence – all these attributes 'adorned' their bearers.[109] Just as commonly, abstract qualities, moral attributes and worldly accomplishments are described as 'adorning' their possessors. The inscriptional eulogies present hundreds of examples of virtues decorating men and women of rank. The famous sixth-century Talagunda pillar inscription of the Kadamba king Kakutsthavarman is typical, describing the dynasty's founder, Mayūraśarman, as being 'adorned' (*alaṁkṛta*) by Vedic knowledge, moral conduct, purity and other virtues.[110] Good actions could adorn a person or his virtuous qualities. Mayūraśarman is further described as shining with his actions (*ceṣṭitaiḥ*) as if they were ornaments (*bhūṣanairiva*) and the Gupta emperor Samudragupta is described as 'possessing many virtues adorned by hundreds of good acts' (*sucaritaśatālaṁkṛtānekaguṇa*).[111] This emphasis on moral action suggests that the ideas of physical beauty which we have been reviewing above were not merely linked to ethical presuppositions, but that outward appearance formed part of a larger conception of personal beauty which included ethical and worldly accomplishment. In the end, physical beauty itself was merely one of the many 'virtues' (*guṇa*s) which could adorn and thus beautify an individual.

[109] See for example the Kaira Plates (*c.* 628), where the Gurjara *sāmanta* Dadda II's grandfather is described as having a body 'adorned with a multitude of excellences', *CII* 4 (1955), no. 16, p. 60; or the Rajim plates (*c.* 650–700) of Tīvaradeva which describe the king as being 'adorned with a serious, clear and bright facial countenance', *CII* 3 (1888), no. 81, pp. 294–5. The *Nāṭyaśāstra* understands women's bodily gestures and modes of bearing as 'ornaments', see *NS* 24.4, 12–13. Bhartṛhari remarks that a woman's face, eyes, complexion, hair, breasts, forehead, hips, eye movements, voice, laughs, postures and gait, are all 'ornaments', *STr* 2.3; 2.5.

[110] *EI* 8 (1905–6), no. 5, p. 32. For a literary exhortation, see the *viṭa*'s remark that the best paramour was 'adorned with courtesy' (*dakṣiṇyena vibhūṣitam*) in *DhVS* 29, 30.

[111] *EI* 8 (1905–6), no. 5, p. 32; *CII* 3 (1888), no. 1, p. 8.

The idea of adornment also extended to relations between people. The virtuous, wise and powerful in the king's retinue were considered to be the jewels or ornaments of his court.[112] Kings and ministers were praised as 'ornaments' of their families and lineages, which were in turn considered 'ornaments' of the earth.[113] The famous seventh-century Aihole inscription of Pulakeśin II, for example, opens with a praise of the Cālukya family as the birthplace of jewels of men that were ornaments to the diadem of the earth.[114] The Cālukyas here join mountains, cities and seas as the ornaments of the feminised earth. As one of the goddesses of sovereignty and the potential consort of the world-ruling king, the earth was commonly imagined as being decorated by or for her king. The fifth-century Mandasor temple inscription, describes the city of Daśapura as the forehead-mark (*tilaka*) of the earth, 'adorned' with mountains and 'decorated' with earrings in the form of flower-laden trees.[115] Another fifth-century inscription of the Aulikāra king Viśvavarman describes irrigation wells, tanks, divine residences and audience halls, pleasure gardens and pools as decorations to the city established by the king as if he were decorating his wife.[116]

Ornament was thus used to denote the complete relationship of two elements of any kind which was thought to be proper and good, whether it be ornaments and the body, virtue and self, an attendant and a lord, a prince and his house, or that house and the earth, to name some of the most common usages. The great chain of being which linked all the elements of the universe into a coherent set of relationships was thus typically represented in courtly sources as a vast 'ornamental order'. The king, particularly in his role as the worldly embodiment of a cosmic overlord, often formed the centre of these representations[117], his sovereignty itself conceived of as adhering to his person like a vast array of ornaments. Consider this representation of a Cōḻa king from a twelfth-century Tamil poem:

[112] See *Cāṇakyarājanīti*, 182. Later architectural and sumptuary manuals treat various elements of the king's retinue in this manner, as *Mānasāra* 41.4–5 ff., which implies that the elements of the royal retinue (*rājāṅga*) are 'jewel–like'.

[113] For the claim of the Vākāṭaka king Pravarasena II (420–55 CE) to be the ornament of his family (*vaṃśālaṁkāra, vākāṭakalalāmasya*) in various *praśastis* and on his seals, see *CII* 5 (1963), no. 6, p. 26; no. 7, p. 301, ff.

[114] *EI* 6 (1900–1), no. 1, p. 4.

[115] *CII* 3 (1888), no. 18, p. 81.

[116] *CII* 3 (1888), no. 17, p. 75.

[117] The Kashmiri poet Śambhu (eleventh–twelfth century) praises a king, 'like generosity in a wealthy person, efficient policy in a man of virtue, bashfulness in women of good families, good poetry in the mouth, ichor in an elephant, a male cuckoo in the garden, a bee in a lotus, the imprint of nailmarks on the cheeks of a beloved wife, a charming girl in the bed – oh king, these are ornaments as you are an ornament to the earth!', *MSS*, vol. 4, no. 8249.

On his face, where the goddess of Eloquence resided, glittered *makara* earrings like bees hovering about a bloomed flower. On his shoulders, where the broad-breasted lady of the Earth resided, were epaulets brilliant with jewels. On his hand, the place of the unsteady goddess of Fame, sparkled a bracelet of gems. On his chest, where Prosperity embraced him with desire, shone with increasing splendour a sea-jewel. On his hip, where the beautiful goddess of Victory resided undistressed, was a beautiful sword.[118]

Each goddess, signifying a different element of sovereignty (and personified as a virtue) resides at and is equated with an ornament on the king's body. The picture which emerges is of the kingdom, as embodied by its principle element or 'limb', the king, as a totality both perfectly ordered and radiantly charming.[119] From this perspective, the emphasis then was on the proper deployment of the elements of sovereignty. In the jackal-minister Damanaka's exhortation to his lion-master, Piṇgalaka, he remarks that success for the king depends entirely on recognising distinctions among one's servants and placing them accordingly, like placing ornaments properly on the body. One does not, he explains, fasten a crest-gem to the foot or encase a costly gem in tin.[120]

If the ornamented body formed the great metaphor for the aesthetic-moral order, the act of adornment also formed a key way of conceiving of human capacities in at least two senses. First, it suggested a model of ethical development quite unlike the rationalist and universalist systems of modern ethics. Courtly ethics was not concerned either with outlining a universal moral faculty or in elevating its exercise through the making of moral judgements as the *sine qua non* of ethical life. Instead, it was the acquisition of moral 'qualities' or 'virtues' which formed the great concern of courtly ethical practice and the end of the moral life. This is why much of the didactic literature was in the first place concerned with the enumeration of lists of virtues appropriate for the offices of the court. People of noble rank were to 'acquire' these virtues as badges of their rank, birth and moral eminence. It is this acquisition of virtue which was the most important of ethical activities, and which was deemed a decoration of the 'soul'. There is also great emphasis in the sources on the effective and proper disposition of these virtues in relation to one another. Numerous ethical maxims make this point, as when Somadeva says that 'modesty is the ornament of prowess'.[121] A thirteenth-century Kannada inscription describes a minister as acting in a manner such 'that humility was an ornament to peerless learning, abundance of brilliant

118 *Vikkirimacoḻaṉulā* 45–9.

119 Contemporary theories of the kingdom imagined it as a 'body' composed of seven 'limbs' (*aṅga*). See *NiS* 4.1 ff.

120 See *PT* 1.33–6.

121 *NiV* 15.22. See also *STr* 1.80.

bounty (an ornament) to fortune, stainless conduct (an ornament) to youth, widespread fame (an ornament) to age and truthful speech (an ornament) to eloquence'.[122] The presence of the ornamenting virtue in each case tempers or somehow completes the other.

Ethical agency in the courtly world, then, focused on acquiring the moral accoutrements suitable to one's birth or station in life and *associating* them harmoniously in one's character. Ratiocinative activity and collective moral introspection tended to occur over how best to bring virtues together and order them correctly – what might be considered a 'refinement' of character. The god Brahmā, according to one maxim, took strength from Garuḍa, courage from the mountains, depth from the sea, gentleness from the moon and resplendence from the sun, to create a picture decorated by these invaluable virtues.[123] My contention is that the sources suggest that the most widespread conceptualisation of this sort of ethical 'refinement' (both the acquisition and disposition of virtue) was the idea of *alaṁkāra*, perhaps akin to what Michel Foucault has called, in another context, a 'technology' of selfhood, the capacity to act upon oneself.

Perhaps ironically, one can see the importance of ornament as a principle in ethical ordering in the many maxims which denigrate the utility of body ornaments. Somadeva Suri is typical when he says 'good character (*śīla*) is the ornament of men and not exterior decorations which only bring distress to the body'.[124] Likewise, Bhartṛhari describes the virtuous as having their ears ornamented not by earrings but by the Veda; their hands not by bracelets but by gifts; bodies illuminated not by sandalwood but by doing good for others.[125] The critique of exterior ornament here should not be deemed as invective against courtly life as such, but merely the elevation of some virtues over others.[126] What is significant about such tropes, which were common enough in the *subhāṣita* literature, is not so much the denigration of jewellery, but rather the unwillingness to depart from the language of ornament as the basic concept for self-refinement.

The act of adornment also served as a way of conceptualising and enacting relationships between people at court. Putting on ornaments (*alaṁkāra*) along with bathing (*snāna*), anointing with oils (*anulepana*),

[122] *EI* 13 (1915–16), no. 3b, p. 33.

[123] From the anthology called *Subhāṣitanīvi* of Vedāntācārya (1268–1369 CE), cited in *MSS*, vol. 7, no. 12808.

[124] *NiV* 26.63. [125] *STr* 1.62.

[126] These same thinkers use such tropes to celebrate worldliness. Bhartṛhari, for example, uses the same trope to celebrate the erotic gestures and graces of women as their 'real' ornaments, *STr* 2.3; 2.5.

dressing (*vastra*) and decoration with flowers (*puṣpa*) had early on been integrated into the services or 'courtesies' (*upacāra*) which constituted the proper reverence (*pūjā*) to a superior.[127] And as an integral element of courtesy, adornment came to have the same 'meta-conceptual' character as *prasāda* in polite conversation. The basic idea was that one's moral being was completed and perfected (ornamented) by various forms of association. There is great emphasis in both the manuals on polity and ethical literature on maintaining 'associations with the good' – for, as king Harṣa himself put it, 'as a rule, a thing attains eminence through proximity to something great'.[128] In various contexts, men of the court are praised as being adornments to their superiors, and sometimes to adorn their inferiors through their grace. When in Śūdraka's *Mṛcchakaṭika*, Cārudatta apologises that his touch may have defiled her, Vasantasenā replies that he had in fact 'adorned her by his touch'.[129]

Ultimately, self-refinement and comportment towards others were related. The perfection of the self through the ornamentation of one's soul and body enabled one to take one's place as an 'ornament' in a morally ordered polity, fit to 'decorate' one's family or one's lord. This is the understanding of the numerous inscriptions which praise men as the ornaments of the court. The Kadamba king Kakutsthavarman claims that bravery against superior foes in war, compassion for the unfortunate, relief for the distressed and honouring the twice born were his 'ornaments of discriminating excellence' (*prajñottaram bhūṣaṇam*), and allowed him to be an ornament to his family (*kulabhūṣaṇa*).[130]

Nothing expresses this dual nature of ornament more clearly than aesthetic speech. On the one hand, eloquent speech was to be beautified by ornament. The speaker 'dressed up' the 'body' of speech or direct discourse with various *alaṁkāra*s. On the other hand, aesthetic speech, particularly as verbal praise, also functioned itself as an ornament – a courtesy (*upacāra*) – to its recipient. Praise, whether in formal verse or not, was deemed the source of fame and reputation at court. As the Nidhanpur plates of Bhāskaravarman put it, the king was 'adorned with the wonderful ornament (*aṅka*) of splendid fame made of the flowery words of praise (*nutivacanakusuma*) by defeated kings'.[131] It is for this reason that

127 In religious ritual, the earliest examples mentioning reverence by 'adorning' with flowers, garlands, silk and jewels were Buddhist (*Mahāparinibbānasütta* 5.26, 6.27) but were soon integrated into Śaiva and Vaiṣṇava ritual. See Bühnemann, *Pūjā: A Study in Smārta Ritual*, p. 36; also Joanne P. Waghorne, 'Dressing the Body of God: South Indian Bronze Sculpture in its Temple Setting', *Asian Art*, vol. 5, no. 3 (1992), pp. 9–33.

128 *Pd* 3.1; see also *NiS* 3.14 *passim* and the numerous verses indexed under 'association' in *MSS*. Expectedly, the maxims stress avoiding association with the wicked.

129 *MK* 1.53. 130 *EI* 8 (1905–6), no. 5, p. 33.

131 *EI* 12 (1913–14), no. 13, p. 75. See also *MK* 1.55+: *alaṃkṛtāsmyetaiḥ akṣaraiḥ*.

so many poems are named with ornamental imagery, after jewellery, garlands and flowers. Poems were the verbal counterparts to the physical ornaments (unguents, clothes, flowers, jewellery) which 'dressed' or 'decorated' their addressees. Eulogies (*praśasti*s, *stūti*s) both secular and religious clearly imagine themselves as decorations presented towards their objects. The author of a twelfth-century Kalacuri eulogy, for example, one Kumārapāla, describes his *praśasti* as resembling a necklace of pearls, 'which has the merit of being composed in good metres (as the necklace has that of having well-rounded pearls), which is rich in merits (as the necklace is in threads), which (like a necklace) appears brilliant and is full of deep sentiments (as the necklace is possessed of great charm)'.[132]

Alaṁkāra thus returns to the social world as a communicative idiom, where like western notions of rhetoric, it acted as 'technique' aimed at the refinement of conduct, demeanour and social relationships among the nobility. Some time ago the celebrated art critic A. K. Coomaraswamy wrote an important essay on 'ornament' in Indian art which argued that to understand early Indian concepts of beauty it was necessary to break with the 'modern' conception of ornament as artificial superfluity. Coomaraswamy argued that the Sanskrit words for ornament (*alaṁkāra, bhūṣaṇa, ābharaṇa*) originally referred to endowing an object (or person) not with a fanciful superfluity, but with its 'necessary accidents, with a view to proper operation'.[133] At one level, the material here fully bears out this observation. Yet at another level it allows us to extend it. For though Coomaraswamy grounded his insights in theology, the evidence reviewed here suggests that the importance of *alaṁkāra* can also be understood with reference to courtly life. The approach here has suggested that aestheticised lifestyles and their ethical dimensions were in many ways the closed preserve of the élite classes, and one need only compare the baroquely ornamented world of medieval Indian sculpture to the agrarian world which supported it to dispel Coomaraswamy's Romantic vision of an unbroken and holistic aesthetic world. The meticulous and sublime adornments of people at court – of their bodies, their souls and their surroundings – were in an important sense the *necessary* and distinguishing 'supplements' or 'luxuries' of the ruling classes. As emblems of rank, they assisted, as Habermas would have it, the 'staging' of 'publicness' among the early medieval nobility. Yet the obsession with style was far

[132] *CII* 4 (1955), no. 96. p. 511.

[133] A. K. Coomaraswamy, 'Ornament', p. 242. Here Coomaraswamy drew on the work of the Indologist Jan Gonda (*Selected Studies*), to give ornament a religious grounding. Coomaraswamy noted that medieval Hindu conceptions of god moved from abstraction to sensible forms through a process of 'adornment', or endowment with qualities (*saguṇa*).

more significant than simply marking status through pomp, style and display, as the apologists of the bourgeois world order have suggested. The important point is that aestheticised lifestyles of men and women of rank – the obsession with beautifying themselves and their surroundings – formed the means through which they acted upon themselves as well as negotiated their relations with others in the wider world of the court.

5 The education of disposition

Just as an actor is, so is the king; just as the king is, so is an actor.
Nāṭyaśāstra[1]

It would not be an exaggeration to say that life at court was 'suffused' with a certain sort of emotionality. Crucial moments in the daily lives of the nobility, as depicted in courtly literature, are typically portrayed in highly charged affective terms. Indeed, it would seem that the people of the court viewed their entire lives primarily in terms of shifting affective relationships with their environments. Men and women were expected to indicate openly their inner dispositions towards one another at appropriate moments through the display of collectively recognised gestures and words. An eleventh century eulogy, for example, asks 'which man has not been filled with delight (*āptapramada*), shaken his head (*dolitaśiras*) or felt a thrill in his body hair (*udbhūtaroma*) from attachment towards his conduct (*vṛttānurāga*)?'[2] We encounter here not simply the generic praise of a good man but a specific repertoire of gestures which were to indicate a social disposition – intense affection.

Such dispositions were deemed the fundamental basis of relationships both within and between lordly houses. It has already been asserted that the political or 'public' relationships of the court were, in a sense, nothing more than the personal relationships of its individual members. The ties that held the court together as an institution were essentially personal affiliations; without these, the court would have hardly functioned. In fact, it is ethical inclinations and personal relationships rather than any rationalised discourse of public good, which are repeatedly portrayed in courtly sources to explain political actions. This in part explains the coincidence of the terminology of emotions and political dispositions in courtly texts – a single affective language was used to denote a range of relationships which modern commentators might assume to be distinct. In the language of the court, for example, there is no distinction between

[1] *NS* 35.61. [2] *EI* 8 (1905–6), no. 21, p. 212.

the concepts of 'ally' and 'friend' (*mitra*), which in modern discourses have different valences, one being 'personal/private' and the other being 'political/public'. There remains a single word, *maitra*, to designate what we would perceive as two very different relationships. The proper relations between kings in alliance (*sandhi*), thus, was the affective disposition of friendship (*maitra*).[3]

It is therefore no surprise that even interactions of the most 'formal' kind – the protocols mentioned in chapter 4 – were typically conceived in affective terms. Consider, for example, Bāṇa's account of the meeting between the emperor Harṣa and courtier Haṁsavega, emissary of his subordinate ally, King Bhāskaravarman of Assam. Harṣa receives Haṁsavega with suitable 'honour' (*sabahumāna*), but extends him several privileges or favours which immediately differentiated him from others. After raising him from prostration with his own hand, indicating a place (or seat) for him in the assembly close to the throne 'with an affectionate (*snigdha*) glance', and asking his fly-whisk bearer to step back so that he might address Haṁsavega face to face, Harṣa enquires 'respectfully' (*sapraśraya*) after his master's health. The significance of these subtle gestures are not lost upon Haṁsavega, and his response is just as telling: 'now he is fine since your majesty so respectfully enquires with a voice bathed in affection and moist with the flow of friendliness'.[4] The moisture metaphor here is highly appropriate, as we shall see, but the emissary makes very clear what such courtesies were really all about – the indication of inner dispositions.

Yet for all of the emphasis on affective life in courtly literature, we know precious little about the inner lives of people at court. No diaries or private letters have survived from this period, and indeed, such forms of interiority seem out of place in the world of the court.[5] In fact, the only sources which *do* speak of the inner lives of people at court are indeed the same ones which speak of their 'public' lives, and which are preoccupied with disposition and sentiment. These are the literary compositions known as *kāvya*. Theories of poetry from their very inception were concerned centrally with the portrayal of emotional and dispositional states in poetic

[3] See for example, *Pd* 1.0+ where the condition or emotion of being friends (*mitrabhāva*) is used to describe the nature of the alliance between King Dṛḍhavarman of Aṅga and Vindhyaketu, king of the forest.

[4] Perhaps 'dripping with friendliness' (*sauhārdadravārdrayā girā*), *HC*, ch. 7, p. 215.

[5] Letter-writing was not unknown, and letters formed a common literary device in court dramas. Yet epistolary communication, from the manuals on letter-writing which emerge from the thirteenth century, participated in the same communicative idiom which characterised courteous speech in general. The *Harṣacarita* portrays the reception of a letter by Bāṇa from the king's brother as merely a supplement to the more important oral message delivered by the courier. See *HC*, ch. 1, p. 53.

compositions, particularly works which were to be seen (*dṛśyakāvya*), or 'acted out' on the stage, but later in all forms of literary composition. Judging from these sources, the emotions of people at court were highly formalised and 'mannered' – they appear with predictable regularity, have a standard repertoire of symptoms, and exhibit a self-conscious and almost 'performative' aspect. It is tempting to attribute this mannerism to their treatment in a highly conventionalised literature. This may be true, to be sure. Yet the important and significant point is that this literature provides us with our only discourse on emotions in early India, save those of the religious orders, with which it differed crucially during our period. Consequently, literary portrayals must be explained as such in any inquiry into the affective world of the court.

This chapter will be concerned less with the actual content of emotions at court – which to some extent are taken up in other sections of this book – than with their form, and particularly the role of aesthetic traditions in the delineation, interpretation and reproduction of the 'affective' structures of courtly life. By 'traditions' here I mean not only literary works themselves, but also, and perhaps more crucially, the theories set out in manuals from the Gupta period which constitute the formal tradition of 'aesthetics' in medieval India. These latter traditions have been routinely treated by scholars, in part following strands of high medieval aesthetic theory itself, in overly 'idealist' and 'subjectivist' frameworks.[6] The hope here will be to place aesthetic theory alongside other knowledges we have from early courts to illuminate the work they performed and the effects they had on everyday social interaction at court.

A taxonomy of emotions

An outline of emotions and sentiments was first set out by the author(s) of the *Nāṭyaśāstra*, and eventually taken up by later writers on poetics. The *Nāṭyaśāstra*'s account of the system of emotions, however, is not without contradictions and incoherencies, a fact which renders it problematic as a source for understanding the history and evolution of aesthetic ideas before the tenth century.[7] Yet for our initial purposes, its account is reliable, clear and essentially uncontested by later scholars. The *Nāṭyaśāstra* sets out forty-nine 'emotional states', or *bhāva*s, which it divides into three basic categories.[8] The most important were known as the 'permanent emotions' (*sthāyibhāva*s) – pleasure (*rati*), laughter (*hāsa*), sorrow

[6] See the apposite remarks of Goodwin, *Playworld*, pp. ix–xviii.
[7] See Srinivasan, *On the Composition of the Nāṭyaśāstra*.
[8] The account is based on *NS* 7.6 ff.

(*śoka*), anger (*krodha*), energy (*utsāha*), fear (*bhaya*), disgust (*jugupsā*) and surprise (*vismaya*). These permanent emotions acted as the basis and shelter of some thirty-three 'transient emotions' (*vyabhicāribhāva*s) which flowed in and out of the permanent emotions, and which included a rather large set of heterogenous elements, as well as eight 'involuntary states' (*sāttvikabhāva*s) which were chiefly noted by their physiological symptoms.

In addition, the *Nāṭyaśāstra* sets out a variety of 'causes' (*vibhāva*) and 'effects' (*anubhāva*s) for each primary emotion. The *vibhāvas* were situations which could potentially give rise to one or more experiential states. They were later subdivided into objective (*ālambanavibhāva*) and stimulative (*uddīpanavibhāva*). *Anubhāva*s were the visible and audible evidences of the presence of this emotion. These categories referred to semantically fixed and palpable signs relating to dispositions, rather than dispositions themselves. The *sthāyibhāva* of pleasure, or *rati*, for example, had as its objective causes (*ālambanavibhāva*) the lover and beloved, and as its stimulative causes (*uddīpanavibhāva*) the seasons, flower-garlands, unguents, ornaments, the enjoyments of a house, going into the garden and enjoying oneself there, hearing the beloved's words, playing and sporting, and the absence of rejection.[9] The effects (*anubhāva*s) of *rati* included smiling faces, sweet words, clever motions of the eyebrows, soft and delicate movements of the limbs, glances and similar indicators.[10] In addition, *rati* could also be supported by various of the thirty-three transitory states like joy (*harṣa*), and in the case of separated lovers, anxiety (*cintā*) and longing (*autsukya*), as well as involuntary physical reactions (*sāttvikabhāva*s) like horripilation (*romāñca*) or weeping (*aśru*).[11]

This scheme raises important questions over the nature and semantic domain of the term *bhāva*, usually rendered as 'emotion'. Derived from the root √*bhū*, 'to be', *bhāva* could refer to any more or less changeable state of being, condition or disposition experienced by a person. The general consensus of both philosophical and aesthetic theories was that *bhāvas* arose within the 'mind' or *manas*, an internal 'organ' (*karaṇa*) whose function was discriminatory, constructive or analytic (*saṁkalpa*) in relation to the sense faculties (*indriya*s). The aesthetic traditions maintained that a *bhāva* was experienced when certain feelings arose in the mind as a result of external stimuli such that the person in question was concerned with nothing else.[12] *Bhāva*s hence 'pervaded' the substance or meaning (*artha*) of any literary work to the extent that it portrayed characters interacting with one another on a dispositional level.[13]

[9] Based on *NS* 6.45+, 46–8; 7.8+, 9. [10] *Ibid.*
[11] *Ibid.* [12] Cf. *KS* 1.2.11–12. [13] *NS* 7.0+.

The potentially wide and open purview of the term *bhāva* as portrayed in the *Nāṭyaśāstra* is significant. The transient emotions included some states quite recognisable to modern people as 'emotions' (despondency (*nirveda*) and joy (*harṣa*)). Some, however, appear closer to mental or dispositional states (recollection (*smṛti*), cruelty (*ugratā*) and deliberation (*vitarka*)), while others are apparently physiological in nature (waking up (*vibodha*), disease (*vyādhi*), intoxication (*mada*) and dying (*maraṇa*)!). The *sāttvikabhāva*s complicate matters further, being chiefly states manifested physiologically through activities like sweating, crying and trembling. This rather capacious semantic domain suggests that *bhāva* is not precisely translatable as 'emotion' in its traditionally accepted sense, i.e., a psychological state which by definition excludes physiological response and ratiocinative activity.[14] And here lies one of the most important keys to unlocking the 'affective' world of the court. If the affective states experienced by people of the court included not only what we today recognise as emotions, but also a range of other states like inclinations or dispositions, cognitive appraisals, physiological conditions and even ethical qualities, then it is easy to understand how it is that the affective world of the courtly representation occupied such a prominent role in the conceptualisation of 'public' life in medieval India. It is not, therefore, that the lives of the people at court were 'dominated' by their emotions, but that they viewed what we today consider human emotions as necessarily continuous with a variety of other social and physiological responses and mental dispositions.

These states were conceived of as capacities of social rank, a point which helps to explain the sometimes embarrassingly hierarchical, anti-humanistic elements of courtly aestheticism for modern critics – that, for example, the primary emotion of energy (*utsāha*) was appropriate only for characters of the superior type, while those of fear (*bhaya*) and disgust (*jugupsā*) were suitable only for women and inferior characters.[15] Such differentiations suggest that we are faced not so much with a humanistic psychology as the basis of art but a system of emotions and dispositions as the accoutrements of social class and courtly rank (and continuous

[14] For a brief review of European philosophical approaches to the emotions in the context of understanding India, see Owen Lynch, 'The Social Construction of Emotion in India', in Owen Lynch, ed., *Divine Passions: The Social Construction of Emotion in India* (Berkeley: University of California Press, 1990), pp. 3–36. For the proponents of Sāṁkhya, for example, the *bhāvas* were fundamental conditions or dispositions experienced by the mental faculty of *buddhi* in various circumstances. They included knowledge and ignorance, virtue and vice, attachment and detachment, lordly power and impotence. See Gerald Larson, *The Meaning of Classical Sāṃkhya* (Delhi: Motilal Banarsidass, 1979), pp. 191–4.

[15] See *NS* 7.20+, 21+, 25+.

with the other attributes of rank) – an ideal vision of the world which the people of the court conceived as the basis of both life and art. Taken as a whole, the system of *bhāva*s seems to suggest, on the part of the aesthetic theorists, an attempt to account comprehensively for the specific range of situations and states that were relevant to the lifestyles of the élite in early India.

This sketch of the 'emotions', however, remains incomplete, for the aesthetic traditions also postulated a set of second-order 'sentiments', or *rasa*s (literally 'juice' or 'flavour'), which have long been at the heart of traditional Indian aesthetics. Unlike the concept of *bhāva*, the interpretation of the role and nature of *rasa* was a matter of protracted and lively debate within the aesthetic traditions in post-Gupta India, particularly from the ninth and tenth centuries. All theories more or less agree that each of the eight permanent emotional states, when combined with the various 'transitory feelings', gave rise to a corresponding 'sentiment', or *rasa*: pleasure to the erotic (*śṛṅgāra*), laughter to the comic (*hāsya*), sorrow to the pathetic (*karuṇa*), anger to the furious (*raudra*), energy to the heroic (*vīra*), fear to the terrible (*bhayānaka*), disgust to the horrible (*bībhatsa*) and surprise to the marvellous (*adbhuta*).[16] The metaphor for this process in the *Nāṭyaśāstra*'s well-known formulation was gastronomic: just as the combination of different ingredients produced a flavour or taste in food, so the various *bhāva*s came together in combination (*saṁyoga*) to give rise (*niṣpatti*) to a sentiment.[17] When the permanent states were 'tasted' or enjoyed, they became 'sentiments'.[18] The enjoyer of these sentiments came in the aesthetic traditions to be known as a 'taster' or *rasika*.

The stage and the world

This, such as it is, is the 'system' of emotions and sentiments as laid down by the *Nāṭyaśāstra*. By the end of the first millennium CE a nuanced and complex series of debates had emerged among court intellectuals around key aspects of this system. Assuming that this 'system' represents a valid framework for understanding the ways in which literary works were produced and received, I would like to pose the larger question of the relationship of this aesthetic system in its totality to everyday life at court. It could, of course, be maintained that the elaborate systems of the aestheticians probably had little if anything to do with how literary

[16] *NS* 6.15. [17] In the famous passage of *NS* 6.31+, 32–33.

[18] *NS* 6.32–3. The gustatory metaphor at first glance may seem an exception to the earlier noted indifference of courtly sources to food and eating. Yet Bharata's metaphor here points more to a world of sublime and experiential 'enjoyment' rather than gastronomic relish.

works were actually received by most audiences. In this view such theories were largely scholastic exercises which may have had an intrinsic value as thought, but cannot be relied upon for much else. Such scepticism is tempting, particularly given the abstruse scholastic propensities of Indian intellectualism. Yet there are several reasons to assume that both authors and audiences were generally aware of the theoretical framework of aesthetics as set down in manuals like the *Nāṭyaśāstra* that they together formed part of an 'interpretive community'.

The first, and perhaps most important reason, is that the *Nāṭyaśāstra* spends considerable time thinking about the types of spectators (*prekṣaka*s) fit to appreciate the drama. The ideal spectator possessed not only certain generic courtly qualities like upstanding conduct, noble birth, peaceful demeanour, erudition, appreciation of fame and virtue, impartiality and maturity, but a series of qualities which related directly to aesthetic appreciation, including proficiency in all six limbs of drama (*ṣaḍaṅganāṭyakuśala*), skill in playing the four kinds of musical instruments (*caturātodyakuśala*), acquaintance with costumes and make-up (*nepathyajña*), knowing the rules of local speech (*deśabhāṣavidhānajña*), familiarity with the four kinds of dramatic 'conveyance' or representation (*caturdhābhinayajña*), knowledge of pronunciation and prosody (*śabdachandovidhānajña*), expertise in different arts and crafts (*kalāśilpavicakṣaṇa*) and, perhaps most importantly, a keen understanding of the sentiments and dispositions (*sūkṣmajña rasabhāvayoḥ*).[19] It would seem that one of the explicit concerns of the aesthetic traditions, in other words, was not simply in advising authors, but in producing viable audiences. From another angle, this explains why connoisseurship in literary arts was so valued in urbane and courtly contexts, why for example, the sixty-four arts to be attained by urbane men and courtiers listed in the *Kāmasūtra* (table 2.1) includes proficiency at viewing dramas and court narratives (*nāṭakākhyāyikadarśana*) as well as a number of other skills related to doing so.[20]

Importantly, the *Nāṭyaśāstra* realises that no actual spectator could fulfil its ideal completely, and that inferior members of the assembly (*pariṣad*) could not hope to experience drama in the same capacity as their superiors.[21] The point, however, is not so much that courtly audiences differed in their capacities, but that there was a clear acknowledgement of these capacities on the part of the aesthetic traditions as a precondition for the

19 *NS* 27.50–3.

20 *KS* 1.3.16. Being a spectator (*prekṣaṇaka*) of dramas was also one of the qualities of the noble man as paramour, or *nāyaka*, see *KS* 6.1.12 (Yaśodhara glosses *prekṣaṇaka* with *naṭādidarśaṇa*).

21 *NS* 27.56–7.

success of a production. The *prastāvana*s or dramatic 'prologues' of many plays, where the stage-director (*sūtradhāra*) addressed the audience and introduced the first scene of the drama, often address the sophistication and expertise of their courtly audiences. In King Harṣa's *Ratnāvalī* and *Priyadarśikā* the putative audience of subordinate kings attending the play are addressed as being appreciative of poetic qualities (*guṇagrāhiṇī*).[22] In a later tenth-century play, the *sūtradhāra* tells his assistant that he bears a message from the poet to the courtiers (*sabhāsada*), 'who were proficient in the knowledge of drama (*nāṭyaveda*), conversant with the sciences and arts and familiar with ways of the world (*lokajña*)', asking them to overlook faults and see only the merits of the play.[23] Audiences are often implored by the same courtesies which formed the vehicles of mannered disposition at court. They are asked to show favour, courtesy and bestow honour by giving their attention to the performance.[24] While hardly conclusive, such addresses suggest a general familiarity, or at least the ideal of familiarity, with themes, protocols and conventions of the aesthetic manuals.

How, then, can we characterise the relationship between the theory of emotions and sentiments as embodied in literary works and the everyday lives of people at court? On the face of it, the *Nāṭyaśāstra* says that the relationship between drama and the world was imitative. Brahmā informs the Daityas that the drama portrayed the ways not only of the gods and demons, but the world of men as well. It 'imitated (*anukaraṇa*) the conduct of the world, was rich in various dispositional states, and had as its essence various situations'.[25] Men and women were expected to understand the conventions and themes of drama, even when they were stylised, for the drama presented a picture of their own society with the totality of its situations and aspirations. Emotionally, audiences were to empathise with the characters in the drama. A fit spectator, according to the *Nāṭyaśāstra*, was one who experienced satisfaction when observing satisfaction on the stage, felt sadness when seeing sorrow and misery when seeing misfortune.[26] This theory of empathy eventually led to the emergence in later treatises of the ideal spectator as a *sahṛdaya*, literally 'one who had a heart with it' or *rasika*, one who 'experienced

[22] *Pd* 1.3, *Rv* 1.5. Recall that the aesthetic manuals preoccupied themselves with enumerating the merits (*guṇa*s) and faults (*doṣa*s) of literary compositions.

[23] See Kṣemīśvara's *Caṇḍakauśikam* 1.4+, probably composed before 950 CE at the Gurjara-Pratīhāra court in Kanauj.

[24] See Kālidāsa's *VkU* 1.2 where the *sūtradhāra* requests the audience to listen attentively to the composition through kind consideration (*dākṣiṇyād*) or respect (*bahumānāt*) for a man of a noble house. In *MkA* 1.3 the *sūtradhāra* claims to have taken the command of the audience-assembly (*pariṣad*) to his head, like an attendant skilled in service (*sevādakṣa*).

[25] *NS* 1.106, 111.

[26] *NS* 27.55.

sentiment'. This sympathy allowed one to relate to any character in the drama, but particularly the hero and heroine. In the *Nāṭyaśāstra*, less accomplished or inferior spectators were expected to relate to the characters of their own rank and status, implying conversely that superior spectators were able to relate to the emotions of various characters in the drama.[27]

Yet the authors of the treatises did not see the literature as simply a mirror to life. In the course of explanation of the mimetic character of *nāṭya* in relation to the world, Brahmā informs the Daityas that *nāṭya* also gave birth, in its dispositions, sentiments and actions, to instruction (*upadeśa*).[28] It provides:

> *dharma* for those who go against *dharma*, pleasure for those who pursue pleasure, restraint for those who are poorly disciplined, acts of self control for those already restrained, acts of boldness for those who are cowardly, energy for boasters, intelligence for those of poor intellect, and erudition for fools . . . drama, will give birth to the instruction of the world (*lokopadeśa*) – it is conducive to *dharma*, fame and long life, and promotes intelligence.[29]

According to Brahmā, drama was to uplift the world through its sublime instruction, a claim consistent with the *Nāṭyaśāstra*'s self-nomination as the 'fifth Veda', as well as the remarks of later aestheticians.[30] We have already commented on the role of aesthetics in the ideology of self-refinement at court, but here the claim is very explicit: that art provided a series of exemplars for the people of the court through which they could learn various virtues.

If we translate this didacticism to the affective realm, it becomes possible to speculate how the structure of emotions and dispositions, laid out in the aesthetic manuals and enshrined in literary works, functioned as a sort of 'education of disposition' at court. I shall return to important technical aspects of this 'education' shortly, but here it may suffice to make it clear that this 'education' was not so much about teaching people what to feel, but instead *how* to feel. The objective basis for the affective structures of courtly life lay in the social conditions and relationships which obtained between its members, and not in literary representation. But the role of the aesthetic realm, however, in shaping how emotions were experienced was absolutely crucial. The proper and exalted expression of love for people of rank included an aesthetic element – what was love, after all, without flowers, unguents, ornaments and beauty?

[27] See *NS* 27.58. [28] *NS* 1.113. Ghosh reads this verse as an interpolation.
[29] *NS* 1.108–9; 114.
[30] For Brahmā's creation of drama as the fifth Veda, containing the essence of the four Vedas, see *NS* 1.5–23.

What is more, the constant thematisation of emotions in literary works and on the stage created a sort of mannered emotionalism at court. The great concerns of the aesthetic literature – when and where particular emotions should be experienced, how they should be indicated (physiologically, gesturally, verbally), for whom were they appropriate and with what other dispositions could they be inflected – shaped the affective habits of people at court. This, on the one hand, meant that drama helped interpolate the emotional experience of men and women into a system which prioritised certain dispositions over others. Women learned, for example, how longing and anxiety for one's beloved, should surrender to that experiential state which they, as inferior emotions attended, desire (*rati*).[31] On the other hand, the associational logic of this system also meant that the *bhāva*s could be indicated in a highly precise and systematic fashion. The putting on of an ornament or flower, a darting glance, a trip to the garden, the playing of a water-game, for example, were all imbued with association in life as in drama. Overall, the aesthetic world fostered an affective 'semioticity' in everyday life at court, which in turn gave the expression of emotions a rich and complex, yet mannered, quality.

Understanding the relationship of those second order 'sentiments' or *rasa*s to affective life at court is a far more complex problem, not least because the nature and location of *rasa* was a matter of considerable debate among court intellectuals themselves from the ninth century. The *Nāṭyaśāstra*'s gustatory metaphor succinctly captures the problem: if sentiment was likened to taste produced by savouring food, then it may be asked what aspect of this process was of primary importance – did taste reside most importantly in the food itself, in the taster, or in the interaction between the two? The *Nāṭyaśāstra* is ambiguous on this point, and later scholars differed considerably. Judging from important recent work on the history of Sanskrit poetics, it would seem that the dominant theory until the tenth century was that the primary existence of *rasa* was in the characters depicted in literary works, and came by extension (and analogously) to exist in the spectator through empathetic processes similar to the experience of *bhāva*.[32] Later theorists, particularly those associated

[31] The various *bhāva*s are compared to 'attendants' surrounding the king. *Nāṭyaśāstra* says that just as some people have identical marks on their hands, feet and stomachs, and, due to their family-birth, manners, learning, actions and proficiency in the arts, attain the office of king while others of lesser intelligence become their attendants (*anucāra*), so the *sthāyibhāvas* become masters over the other states, which take refuge (*upāśrita*) in them, *NS* 7.7+, 8.

[32] Briefly noted, *inter alia*, by Daniel Ingalls in differentiating the views of Ānandavardhana and Abhinvagupta. See 'Introduction' to Ingalls *et al.* translation of the *Dhvanyāloka*, pp. 18–19. More recently, it has been definitively demonstrated in an important article by Sheldon Pollock on the Paramāra king Bhoja's *Śṛṅgāraprakāśa*. See Sheldon Pollock,

with Kashmir in the ninth and tenth centuries, decisively moved the arena of concern away from the presence of *rasa* in literary works to how it arose in the minds of readers/spectators. Some modern commentators have used this seemingly 'subjectivist' turn to treat the experience of *rasa* as exclusively aesthetic – implying that the only experience which could appropriately be understood as relating to *rasa* arose in the spectator/reader while experiencing art, and not other contexts.[33] Whatever the fidelity of this claim as truthful representation of the Kashmiri school from the tenth century, it would seem that during the period treated in this book, the assumption in courtly circles was that *rasa* was experienced by men and women of rank not merely in art but in their worldly dealings – that the capacity to experience *rasa* was a way of experiencing the affective world around them. Aestheticians of this tradition were concerned with producing *rasa* within the characters of the drama precisely because drama imitated the world.

Conversely, the *rasika*-spectator was expected to share the same exalting qualities and refined sensibilities as the *rasika*-hero within the literary work. The theorists all assume that only men of moral refinement (and high birth) could be expected to possess the capacity to 'savour' emotions and attain the status of the *rasika*. In short, the *rasika* was at once a moral and aesthetic category. What is absolutely crucial in this conception of *rasa*, as we shall see, is the fact that it was essentially a second-order abstraction which men of culture were to feel towards the world through a self-conscious apprehension of their own emotions. According to King Bhoja, in his literary treatise *Śṛṅgāraprakāśa*, *rasa* was the sense of self which produced the experience of the consciousness of the emotions as agreeable to the mind.[34] *Rasa* was a sort of 'meta-disposition' which aestheticised every aspect of an individual's experience. The remainder of this chapter will attempt to uncover the social implications of such an engagement with the world.

Hermeneutics

One of the more important concerns of the *Nāṭyaśāstra* was the correlation of visible manifestations of inner dispositions. In a sense such a concern was quite natural, for the problem which faced any playwright

'Bhoja's *Śṛṅgāraprakāśa* and the Problem of *Rasa*: A Historical Introduction and Annotated Translation', *Asiatische Studien*, vol. 52, no. 1 (1998): 117–92, esp. 123 ff. I have relied here on Pollock's careful and clear presentation of the problem. For a later work which follows this earlier tradition from Bhoja, see the *Rasakalikā* of Rudrabhaṭṭa, associated with the court of the Hoysala king Vīraballāla II (1172–220 CE).

[33] This has led to a stifling formalism in the interpretation of Indian aesthetics, as noted by Goodwin, *Playworld*, pp. xiii–xv. See also pp. 79–80.

[34] As cited by Pollock, 'Bhoja's *Śṛṅgāraprakāśa*', p. 144.

or author was how actors could most effectively simulate the inner affective states of the characters they played in ways which would be immediately recognisable to audiences. A knowledge of outward signs and their correlation with inner dispositions was thus a necessary requirement for dramatic production. The general term for the presentation of these and other causal states, which 'carried' the dominant emotions of the drama, was *abhinaya*, literally 'vehicle' or 'conveyance', four kinds of which are specified in the *Nāṭyaśāstra*: accoutrements (*āhārya*), physical states (*sāttvika*), words (*vācika*) and bodily gestures (*āṅgika*).[35] Elsewhere these conveyances are said to function both as 'determinants' or *vibhāva*, explained as 'cause' (*kāraṇa*), 'reason' (*hetu*) or 'concomitant' (*nimitta*), as well as 'consequents' (*anubhāva*), which enabled the audience to 'follow' the representation.[36] The conveyances as *vibhāvas* and *anubhāva*s 'determined' (*vibhāvyate*) the inner states of the play and caused the audience to understand (*anubhāvayati*) those states.

One way of understanding this emphasis on affective symptomology in the manuals on aesthetics is as theatric technique: what came 'naturally' for the people of the court had to be rehearsed, catalogued and even turned into a system for those who sought to reproduce these emotions in an artificial environment. Yet I think that it is also possible to attribute a different and deeper significance to the preoccupation with the interpretation of outward signs of inner disposition in this literature, one which will help us understand an important function which drama played in the lifestyles of the court. After all, if we follow the profile of the *Nāṭyaśāstra* itself, it is clear that only a small minority of spectators possessed the subtle capacity needed to understand the display and nature of emotions and sentiments. While some of these correlations may have been self-evident, others clearly had to be learned. In this section I will explore the wider significance and parallels that this system of 'interpretation' or hermeneutics, particularly with reference to appearance and gesture, had with other aspects of life at court.

Among the conveyances outlined by the *Nāṭyaśāstra*, those of bodily gesture (*āṅgika*) received the most detailed attention, and are further divided into those relating to the limbs (*śarīra*), the face (*mukhaja)* and movements (*ceṣṭākṛta*). We have already seen how the outward appearance and attributes of objects were deemed to be reflective of their practical utility and inner moral value. Varāhamihira's 'Great Compendium' contains many lists of auspicious and inauspicious attributes, or *lakṣaṇa*s, of

[35] *NS* 8.9. See the discussion of Pramode Kale, *The Theatric Universe: A Study of the Nāṭyaśāstra* (Bombay: Popular Prakashan, 1974), pp. 117–50; also G. H. Tarlekar, *Studies in the Nāṭyaśāstra* (Delhi: Motilal Banarsidass, 1975), pp. 67–144.

[36] *NS* 7.3+, 4; 7.4+, 5.

every conceivable sort of object relevant to courtly life – including human bodies. Instead of *lakṣaṇa*, which usually referred to an intrinsic, stable or permanent 'mark' or was 'characteristic' of an entity, the courtly texts used a number of other terms to denote temporary appearance or gestures which were thought to indicate the internal states.[37] These include *iṅgita*, referring to any behaviour or movement of the body other than its normal posture, and *ākāra*, denoting the facial expression or appearance.[38]

The literature on political policy laid great emphasis on the importance of paying attention to gestures and facial expressions as the external signs of a person's inner feelings. It formed a common theme in the *subhāṣita* sayings.[39] The advice of the early manuals on polity to the courtier is striking in this regard. According to the *Arthaśāstra*, *Nītisāra* and other texts, the courtier was to observe the king's gestures and facial expressions (*iṅgita*, *ākāra*), for they indicated his internal disposition, or, as Somadeva put it, 'that which abided in his mind' (*manastha*).[40] By observing these signs, a courtier understood the pleasure (*kāma*), aversion (*dveṣa*), joy (*harṣa*), distress (*dainya*), resolve (*vyavasāya*) and fear (*bhaya*) in the king's mind as well as whether the king was 'pleased' (*prasanna*), angry (*kopa*) or indifferent (*mādhyastha*) at the sight of him, or anxious (*śaṅkā*) about his counsel.[41]

Though many of these states were *sthāyibhāva*s and *vyabhicāribhāva*s outlined in the *Nāṭyaśāstra*, for the courtier they formed part of a hierarchy of significations which ultimately ended in the discernment of a lord's satisfaction (*tuṣṭa*) or dissatisfaction (*atuṣṭa*), attachment (*rāga*) or antipathy (*aparāga*) towards him – for this was the basis of the favour (*prasāda*) upon which his livelihood depended. Understanding such dispositions was a strategic preoccupation for men at court.[42] The texts on polity even recommend that the courtier discover the king's inclinations secretly, by finding out his reaction at the mention of his name, whether the king recalled him during meals and in discussion with others.[43] We may sum up with Kāmandakī, that:

> an intelligent dependant capable of reading either the attachment or indifference of his master expressed through physical gestures (*iṅgita*), expressions (*ākāra*) and emblems (*liṅga*) should act accordingly as if he were an expert in interpreting such physical manifestations and appearances.[44]

[37] In some cases the term *lakṣaṇa* is used as well for such conditions, see *NiS* 5.46.

[38] *AS* 1.15.8–9.

[39] See *MSS*, vol. 3, nos. 4269, 4272, 4274, *et al.*

[40] *NiV* 10.27; *AS* 5.5.5; *NiS* 5.34.

[41] *AS* 5.5.6; 5.5.7; *NiS* 5.35–6; 5.39. See also *NiV* 10.37.

[42] For an example of a courtier apprehending the king's disfavour by observation of his gestures and demeanour, see the story of Vasurakṣita and Anantavarman in *DK*, ch. 8, p. 195.

[43] *AS* 5.5.7; *NiS* 5.37.

[44] *NiS* 5.34.

It was not only subordinates who were enjoined to scrutinise men for signs of their inner states, but men of rank and power as well. This could take the form of lords ascertaining the inner dispositions and thoughts of supplicants, as in a verse which praises men so skilled at understanding the inner desires of supplicants from their facial expressions that they never even have to hear verbal supplications.[45] The bodily gestures of those who approached the court as litigants and criminals were also examined as indicators of the moral validity of their claims. Manu advises the person occupying the seat of justice (*dharmāsana*) at the king's court to discover the internal states of men by 'external signs' (*bāhyaliṅga*), including voice, colour, eyes, aspect, gestures and movements. This is because, according to Manu, the interiority of the mind (*manaḥ*) is perceived through changes in the eye and face (*netravaktravikāra*), by gestures (*iṅgita*), facial expression (*ākāra*), movements (*ceṣṭā*) and speech (*bhāṣita*).[46]

This skill was an especially important qualification for courtiers who held posts in which knowing the designs of others helped protect or further the interests of their superiors. They form important attributes of the palace doorkeeper and the royal envoy, men who acted as intermediaries, in the former case within the king's household and in the latter outside it, typically in the households of other lords in his absence.[47] Chamberlains were responsible for ministering to the needs of visitors to the royal household and were thus required to be attentive to their needs. In *Pratijñāyaugandharāyaṇa*, King Mahāsena even asks his chamberlain Bādarāyaṇa, in attending the wounds of his captured rival Vatsarāja, to pay attention to his every gesture and facial expression to meet his needs.[48] The *Arthaśāstra* directs the royal messenger to discover the intentions of rival kings through observing (*lakṣayet*) their facial expressions, speech and glances for signs of satisfaction and dissatisfaction.[49]

The final domain where the scrutiny of external gestures formed a veritable preoccupation at court was romance. The *Kāmasūtra* advises that before a man attracted a woman to himself he should have a proper understanding of the signs of a woman's desire. The *nāgaraka* was to observe the behaviour, gestures and facial expressions (*pravṛtti*, *iṅgita*, *ākāra*) of the woman to discern her inner states (*bhāva*); and likewise, the *nāyikā* was to discover the true intentions and mental inclinations of

[45] See *MSS*, vol. 3, no. 4262. [46] *MDh* 8.25–6.
[47] For the doorkeeper see *MSS*, vol. 3, no. 5748; for the envoy, no. 5746.
[48] *PY* 2.13+.
[49] *AS* 1.16.12. *NiS* 14.46 advises the king to observe carefully the envoys reporting to him.

the man through facial expressions, changes in mood and his actions.[50] Courtesans too, according to Vātsyāyana, were to be perpetually vigilant as to signs indicating the growing and waning of attachment on the part of their lovers.[51] Indeed, all who participated in the elaborate rituals of courtship were to know and understand the outward signs of attraction. Bālacandrikā, female companion of the heroine Avantisundarī in Daṇḍin's *Daśakumāracarita*, notices immediately the mutual attraction when Avantīsundarī and Prince Rājavāhana meet, due to her 'careful discrimination of dispositions (*bhāvaviveka*), which revealed the state of their minds (*antaraṅgavṛtti*)'.[52]

What the sources suggest is that interpreting inner dispositions from outer gestures and expressions was an important skill which required experience and training. That this skill was not considered merely a natural human proclivity or an element of basic communication is partly evident from the very fact that such talents needed to be recommended, and the adjectives which accompany them ('clever', 'intelligent' and 'skilful'). Moreover, numerous verses deride people of the village or countryside for their ignorance of such accomplishments. A verse anthologised by the poet Jalhaṇa in his thirteenth-century *Sūktimuktāvalī* says:

> young men of this village are dull (*jaḍa*) enough, being undone by speaking plainly (*ṛju*); they cannot grasp facial expressions (*ākāra*) nor have the intelligence to understand subtle meanings of puns and innuendos; ladies nobly born do not communicate their intentions directly through words; hence the fever of love must be endured till such time as a traveller, who has a pleasing understanding, comes along.[53]

The comprehension of facial expressions and gestures is here made continuous with the ability to communicate and interpret indirect and suggested meaning in language. The important point is that bodily gestures and facial expressions were regarded, like language, as capable of suggestion. We may recall the emperor Harṣa's subtle glance of approval towards Bāṇa after his self-apology at their first meeting.

Several points are important about the emphasis in courtly sources on interpreting gestures as signs of inner disposition. First and foremost, it must never be lost sight of (and thus bears repeating) that as affective states or inner dispositions were deemed the basis on which people of the court maintained their 'official' relationships, their display and detection

[50] For the hero's attention to the gestures of his beloved, see *KS* 3.3.22; 3.3.24; 3.4.34; 5.3.1 ff. For the reverse, see *KS* 3.3.22; 3.4.42; 5.1.24; 6.3.27.

[51] *KS* 6.3.27. [52] *DK*, ch. 5, p. 46.

[53] Cited in *MSS*, vol. 3, no. 4275. An earlier verse from the *Mahābhārata* praises men from Magadha as understanding gestures (*iṅgitajña*) and derides men from the south as being ignorant of them, cited in *MSS*, vol. 3, no. 5745.

through external signs (gestures and expressions) formed an enduring preoccupation for the people of the court. It, of course, follows that emotions in this world were never viewed as exclusively (or even sufficiently) 'internal states' – all affective states had gestural and behavioural symptoms. It is telling that the vast courtly literature of the time never presents a character so typical of the modern novel, whose inner emotional or mental 'world' is formally separated from his or her social environment, as either narrative technique or literary theme. The characters of courtly epics and dramas thus appear 'flat' and 'exterior' by modern literary standards.

Yet such judgements are certainly premature and inadequate, for courtly literature was quite capable of conveying emotional nuance and shades of meaning. This was not achieved by an interiorisation of character, but through ever more complex or ingenious descriptions which captured subtlety in exterior comportment and mien. We need only recall Bāṇa's extended description of his emperor's hesitation in receiving a gift from the emissary of the Bhairavācārya. Bāṇa portrays perfectly Harṣa's skilful resolution of the predicament he faced. If we may translate such literary descriptions into life, it would seem that if the court was a place where affective relationships were signified through clearly defined and highly choreographed external markers, then shades of meaning were typically expressed through subtleties within this system of gesture.

It should now be clear that the repeated exhortation to discern the inner states of men and women from their outward appearances contributed to what must have been something like a 'science of observing people' at court. Terms used to denote the process of observation were most often derived from the verbal root √*īkṣ*, 'to see', like *pra* + √*īkṣ*, 'to behold or look in front' (as the spectator of a drama, or *prekṣaka*), and *pari* + √*īkṣ*, to move the eye over (as in *parīkṣā*, 'inspection' or 'examination'), or derivatives of the root √*lakṣ*, 'to note, observe or recognise', which in its causative form meant to 'indicate', and by extension, to designate or define (hence *lakṣaṇa*, characteristic).[54] Such observation was not, as Norbert Elias has usefully remarked in his treatment of the European court society, a 'psychology' in the modern sense, but a capacity, springing from the necessities of court life, which enabled men and women to understand the dispositions, designs and mental make-up of other

[54] For uses of the verb *lakṣ*, see *NS* 24.159 where, in advising the director on the proper portrayal of erotic love, Bharata says that the expert should 'note' (*samupalakṣayet*) the signs (*iṅgita*) of men and women who desire one another. In *AS* 5.5.5 Kauṭilya urges the dependant to 'note' (*lakṣayet*) the gestures (*iṅgita*) and appearance (*ākāra*) of the king.

people.[55] It was complemented by a pronounced self-regard or circumspection, for just as a man was to know the dispositions and capacities of others, he was to know his own if he was to deploy them to his advantage. This may be one way in which we can understand the tireless recommendations towards affective self-restraint mentioned in the manuals on *artha* and *kāma*. This was less an expression of any 'ascetical' or renunciative tendency in Indian culture than very worldly advice to worldly men. Utmost care and regard were to be applied to the proper management and display of inner mental states.

The pronounced emphasis on the subtle appreciation of the external signs of people's inner mental states may partly be explained by the widespread compulsion at court towards their concealment. Numerous courtly adages recommend the masking of one's inner dispositions, a point which seems to be assumed by the many verses which praise the ability of detecting them – that despite the attempts of men to conceal their feelings, they could often be discovered.

The famous story of the jackal-ministers Damanaka and Karaṭaka from that didactic text on courtly life, the *Pañcatantra*, illustrates the utility of careful observation of others at court. One day the lion Piṅgalaka, king of the forest, hears a roar on his way to the river for a drink and becomes frightened. He immediately 'hides his [facial] expression (*ākāram ācchadya*', but is noticed by an ambitious retainer, Damanaka, who confides to his friend Karaṭaka that they now have an opportunity to rise to prominence (*pradhāno*) at court. When queried by Karaṭaka as to why, he lectures him on the virtue of being observant. Even a beast, according to Damanaka, grasps the meaning of things expressed directly in words, like horses and elephants responding to orders. It is only the intelligent man who understands what is *not* said, for the fruit of intelligence is understanding the gestures (*iṅgita*) of others.[56] Later, when Damanaka approaches the king and asks him why he has curtailed his journey, Piṅgalaka realises that his minister has discovered his apprehension. Cornered, he confides his fear to Damanaka, who suggests (to the king's relief) that he should investigate the matter. Yet as soon as Damanaka departs, Piṅgalaka begins to worry that he has inadvertently revealed a weakness to his servant and may now be vulnerable, and retreats elsewhere in the forest to safety. When he sees the returning Damanaka, who has meanwhile discovered that the source of the roar was nothing more than a grass-eating bull, Piṅgalaka returns to his former place in order to conceal his countenance (*ākārapracchādana*) lest

[55] See Elias, *The Court Society*, pp. 104–6. [56] *PT* 1.18.

Damanaka think him a coward.[57] His fears are calmed by the jackal who arranges a meeting between the lion and the bull, who become best of friends. Their original fears, however, are exploited by Damanaka, who cleverly sows dissension and eventually arranges through false counsel a confrontation between the two. In the end the lion Piṅgalaka kills his friend the bull and Damanaka is elevated in rank.

One message which could hardly fail to be observed in such a story was not only the importance of observing, but of guarding and managing the external signs of one's own disposition. As Somadeva put it, 'bodily gestures, facial expressions, intoxication, excessive delight, carelessness and sleep are the causes of plans being ruined'.[58] They therefore had to be both carefully guarded and carefully scrutinised. Kāmandaka recommends that the messenger, for example, conceal (*rakṣet*, literally 'protect') his own inner states (*svaṁ bhāvam*), while detecting those of others.[59] This skill found its most perfect embodiment in the king's agents in disguise, his spies, who were to be able to discern the designs and dispositions of others, even when expressed covertly through speech, gestures and expressions.[60] Kauṭilya stresses the necessity of careful attention to gestures and expressions precisely because a knowledgeable man may, 'for the purpose of concealing (*saṁvaraṇa*) his plans, produce through his gestures and expressions (*iṅgitākārābhyaḥ*) a reversal (*viparyāsa*) of the pairs of desire and aversion, joy and distress, resolution and fear'.[61] Such dissemblance was widely sanctioned by the texts on *nīti*, and it should be kept in mind that deception (*chalita*) and related skills are numbered among the accomplishments of the man of sophistication (see table 2.1). As a maxim of Cāṇakya says, 'one should not be overly straightforward. In a forest, the straight trees are cut down and the bent (*kubja*) ones left standing.'[62]

Drama and poetry, I would suggest, played an integral part in the development of this self-styled emotional sophistication among people at court. The hermeneutic relationship necessary for the ideal spectator, or *prekṣaka*, of deducing the inner states of characters from a formulaic and mannered set of external indicators not only united the spectatorship of drama with the social texture of courtly life, thereby reinforcing the nexus between external indicators and inner dispositions, it also cultivated the

[57] *PT* 1.53+.
[58] *NiV* 10.35. See also *MSS*, vol. 2, no. 3642: 'By not keeping careful guard over facial expressions secrets of the king get divulged, and just like a pot with a single hole holds no water, he can hardly hope for a prosperous reign.'
[59] *NiS* 13.15. [60] *NiS* 13.25; 13.27.
[61] *AS* 5.5.6. Kauṭilya's advice here is to the courtier in relation to the king's dissemblance.
[62] *Cāṇakyarājanīti* 130. See also *NiV* 28.30.

skills of its audience in inhabiting this nexus – that is, interpreting and deploying these signs.

Towards a courtly subjectivity

We are now in a position to conclude with a few reflections on the social life of that savouring of emotions, known as *rasa*. As noted above, the concept of the connoisseur (*rasika*, or *sahṛdaya*) was not only a view of literature and drama, but also an orientation towards the world itself. We know this because *rasa* was felt in the first instance by the characters within the drama in regard to one another and their fictive environments, and only then, by extension, by the audiences of the drama. It follows, given the widespread assumption that art imitated the ways of the world, that *rasa* was an experience which the men and women of the court ideally shared with one another and their wider environments. That is, the *rasika* was not merely a literary connoisseur, but a man who cultivated a certain meta-disposition towards his entire affective life. The *nāyaka* or hero on the stage thus becomes the idealised projection of the emotional concerns of the *sahṛdaya* community.[63]

What was the nature of this meta-disposition? At one level, it denoted a certain quality or intensity of emotional feeling. The Allahabad pillar inscription describes subordinates not only 'savouring with their emotions' (*bhāvaiḥ āsvādaya*) the marvellous acts of King Samudragupta, but as 'having minds expanded by clearly manifest affection with an excess of *rasa*' (*sphuṭabahurasasnehaphullaiḥ manobhiḥ*).[64] Here the word *rasa* is used in both its literal meaning of 'juice' and its more abstract sense of 'essence' or 'sentiment'. The idea was that the mind bloomed or expanded like a plant full of sap or juice.[65] The proper intensity of an emotion (like *sneha*, or affection), had to possess an 'essence' or intensity of value which was *rasa*. And just as in the formulation of the *Nāṭyaśāstra*, flavour existed not only on the palate of the taster, but also in the dish itself. So the intensity of feeling which these men felt with regard to the Gupta king was also a mark of the quality of feeling within the king. It is thus that we find many eulogies which praise men of the court as possessing or embodying *rasa*. In a sixth-century Aulikāra inscription the prince Prabhākaravardhana is described as being bestowed sovereignty (*śrī*) by his father because he was 'captivated by the flavour of his good qualities'

[63] See the useful discussion of Goodwin, *Playworld*, pp. x–xiii.
[64] *CII* 3 (1981), no. 1, p. 213.
[65] One may thus perhaps speak of a sort of emotional 'tumescence' which reflected the ideal physiognomy treated above.

(*guṇarasāpahṛtena*).[66] In an early Prakrit poem from Hāla's anthology, a well-born man is compared to sugar cane, as producing juice, or sentiment, through his speech.[67] *Rasa*, in these examples, is deemed at once intrinsic to the subject's being and at the same time capable of being conveyed to those who had the capacity to enjoy it. Ultimately, the distinction between the taste in the food and the taste in the mouth is false, for one could only perceive *rasa* in another if one possessed the capacity to feel/produce it within oneself. *Rasa* thus functioned as a sort of affective or dispositional 'essence' which 'flowed' between people of birth and sophistication.

Affective sympathy lay at the base of the experience of *rasa*. From the first formulations of the perfect spectator (*prekṣaka*) in the *Nāṭyaśāstra* to later elaborations of the ideal *rasika* or *sahṛdaya*, the fundamental emphasis was on the ability to sympathise with the feelings depicted in the drama and also more generally with the affective world which constituted courtly life. As Robert Goodwin has noted, the sympathy which marked the connoisseur of art was the 'same sentimental bond which link[ed] members of the courtly or *nāgaraka* [urbane] community to one another'.[68] When in *Svapnavāsavadatta* the princess Padmāvatī hears the maid Avantikā's response to the plight of King Udayana, she concludes immediately that Avantikā is sympathetic 'tender-hearted' (*sānukrośa*), a characteristic which makes her desirable and fit for the role of heroine, like King Udayana himself.[69]

Yet the experience of *rasa* celebrated in the aesthetic treatises was not simply a sharing of feelings themselves. It was not enough that a man felt sad upon seeing sadness, happy upon seeing joy, etc . . . The *Nāṭyaśāstra* designates this type of audience response as a 'human' (*mānuṣī*) form of dramatic success, but clearly prefers what it calls 'divine' (*daivikī*) success, when the audience was silent, filled with emotion and pure.[70] This undoubtedly refers to what later critics would come to emphasise as the abstractive and contemplative aspect of *rasa* as a form of second-order subjective enjoyment. The idea was that the experience of *rasa* was a higher level of consciousness through which one enjoyed primary emotional intensity. The *rasika*, in this sense, was enjoined to take a detached

66 *JESI* 10 (1983), p. 99. Here I follow the reading of R. Salomon, 'New Inscriptional Evidence for the History of the Aulikaras of Mandasor', *Indo-Iranian Journal*, vol. 32 (1989), p. 4.

67 *Gāthāsaptaśatī* 6. 41.

68 See Goodwin, *Playworld*, p. 143.

69 *SV* 1.12+. Avantikā, of course, is Queen Vāsavadattā in disguise, and so her 'sympathy' is not entirely unmotivated. See the illuminating analysis of this term in relation to the love triangle of Udayana, Padmāvatī and Vāsavadattā in Goodwin, *Playworld*, pp. 143–4.

70 *NS* 27.3–17.

and reposeful posture towards the affective structures of courtly life. He enjoyed a sort of once-removed savouring of emotion.[71]

What were the implications of this peculiar sort of experience? If we refuse to take the claims of this discourse at face value and resist the largely formalist interpretations which modern scholarship has attributed to *rasa*, then we may notice at once some fundamental similarities between the *rasika* concept and other courtly themes touched on in this book. The 'transcendent' posture of the *rasika*, for example, was broadly similar to the notion of lordship as reposeful and detached enjoyment of the world, or ethical perfection as the beautiful array of effulgent virtues which decorated the self as the sublime enjoyments of previous merit. In all of these cases, the claim of removal from the world, the representation of the self as sovereign and 'transcendent', should be seen as claims about agency in the world. This once-removed relationship that the people of the court had with the world around did not reflect so much a transcendence, but a particular sort of engagement with the social world.[72]

If the system of emotions and sentiments as set out in the *Nāṭyaśāstra* and later texts is juxtaposed with the treatises on political policy and courtship, it seems clear that the detached sense of enjoyment encouraged fostered a sort of 'subjective itinerancy' with regard to disposition, something akin to what Stephen Greenblatt has called in the context of Renaissance Europe, a *mobile sensibility*.[73] A cultivated sensitivity towards (and detached enjoyment of) commonly held dispositional states allowed the courtier/spectator to engage and disengage with the mental states of others. The 'mannered' nature of this system of dispositions – wherever simpler signifiers could indicate, through hint and suggestion, deeper mental attitudes and emotions – not only provided courtly sophisticates with a sublime delectation of discerning the unexpressed, but also afforded them with a sort of affective 'playing field', the elements of which could be used by individuals to negotiate the experience and display of

[71] This comes to the heart of the aestheticians' technical concern with *rasa*, and the characterisation here hardly pretends to any complete representation, as the point is to place these ideas within a courtly sociology. It is notable that this sense of detachment as integral to the experience of *rasa* (which distinguished it from mere emotional sympathy) characterised those who placed *rasa* primarily in the characters of the literary text as much as those who located it exclusively in the audience though formulations as to the nature and origin of this experience differed.

[72] As Goodwin has pointed out in regard to *Svapnavāsavadatta*, but applying equally to other palace romances like Harṣa's *Ratnāvalī* and *Priyadarśikā*, the protagonist/*rasika* is portrayed as fundamentally innocent of the power politics which bring him new marital alliances. His sublime erotic dalliance thus remains uncompromised by strategic calculation. See Goodwin, *Playworld*, pp. 154–7.

[73] Stephen Greenblatt, *Renaissance Self-Fashioning from More to Shakespeare* (University of Chicago Press, 1980), pp. 224–5.

their own dispositions. I am not suggesting that emotions and dispositions were not genuinely 'felt', or that they were the mere instruments of some underlying rationality. Yet it remains the case that dispositions were not generally viewed in the manner of humanist psychology as fundamental parts of human interiority. They were instead considered more or less transient states which arose in the mind, and were experienced by internal capacities of the self. This, of course, hardly detracted from their importance as the rationale and basis of all worldly relationships. Yet proper 'discipline' (*vinaya*), as defined by all the manuals on worldly life, emphasised their mastery as a precondition for success in the world. This mastery entailed both their restraint and expression according to guidelines of propriety and strategic considerations which varied in different contexts. The ability, more or less constrained by various exigencies, to fashion and manipulate these dispositions was thus not only a mark of affective sophistication, but also worldly success. The agency of the people at court was exercised precisely through the calculated habitation of these formal structures. Aesthetic sensibility fostered by *kāvya* played no small role in this sophistication and skill. The keen understanding (*sūkṣmajña*) of sentiments and dispositions required of the ideal spectator – an understanding which was itself 'educated' by drama – entailed not merely knowing how to identify the range of dispositions and sentiments of others from their symptoms, but how to recognise and deploy his own dispositions with their concomitant symptoms and affectations.

This dual aspect to the experience of dispositions and emotions explains two contradictory images of the court which have come down to us from medieval sources. First, the court was known as an association of *sahṛdaya*s or *rasika*s – men of taste, who by virtue of their superior and ennobling sympathy, attained to a level of aesthetic-moral refinement. But the court was also known as a place of pretence and deception. Many of the medieval gnomic and didactic sayings (*subhāṣita*) deemed courtly relationships, particularly those between lord and dependant, to be based on deceit. In Daṇḍin's *Daśakumāracarita*, Vihārabhadra, a close servant of the king, in advising his lord against the science of politics, says that whatever is given, esteemed, or spoken dearly of by a prince trained in the science of politics is not to be trusted as it is a deception (*aviśvāsa*).[74] Like the friendship of a snake or the affection of a merchant, one could never trust the respect of a king. Kings and their families were compared with liars, thieves, and courtesans.[75] Importantly, such criticism had from Gupta times formed an occasional but persistent theme in the

[74] *DK*, ch. 8, p. 193.
[75] See verses cited in *Gaṇikavṛttasaṁgrahaḥ* 437, 476, 484, 530–6.

wider circles of the court itself. Yet it is perhaps ironic that it reached its height in the satires and farces written by poets like Kṣemendra in Kashmir, a generation after Abhinavagupta and others there had taken aesthetic subjectivity to its apogee.

The masking and discernment of internal dispositions and the larger calculus of which they formed a part, gave courtly life a markedly 'theatrical' quality. I do not mean to suggest, as others have done, that life at court was infused with any over-ritualised dream or play-like quality as opposed to 'real' action and rational thought as has been suggested by the theorists of the Asian 'theatre state'[76], but rather that the lives of people at court, with their manneristic emotional interactions and mobile subjectivities, quite clearly resembled the calculated expressivity essential to the performance of the theatre and poetry which formed such an important part of their lives. It is thus not surprising that this comparison formed a perennial theme in the aphoristic sayings which circulated at court.[77] It is unwittingly foreshadowed by the *Nāṭyaśāstra* itself, in its discussion of how a mere actor (usually men of low status) could possibly impersonate as great a man as the king.[78] The treatise's answer to the problem, that through various conveyances like ornaments, body paint and the *sauṣṭhava* posture, as guided by the director, the actor could 'become one with the perfections of dignity (*gāmbhīrya*) and exalted bearing (*audārya*) which were the hallmarks of kingship (*rājacinha*) . . . and thus bear the quality of a king'. This may seem logical enough, but Bharata quickly adds the significant reflection with which we began this chapter 'the king too is like an actor (*rājāpi naṭavat bhavet*)' for 'the king is like an actor in the same way that the actor is like a king (*yathā naṭastathā rājā yathā rajā tathā naṭaḥ*). The both of them will express their internal dispositions (*bhāvaniṣpatti*) by similar *sauṣṭhava* of limbs and pretence (*samalīlāṅgasauṣṭhavāḥ*).'[79]

The most general argument of this chapter has been that in order to understand the affective preoccupations of courtly life, we must engage with the copious aestheticisation of human emotions enjoyed by men and women through courtly literature. Yet we have also seen that this relationship was a complex one, for the preoccupation with dispositions and

[76] Clifford Geertz, *Negara: The Theatre State in Nineteenth Century Bali* (Princeton University Press, 1980). In the Indian context the 'dramatic' as opposed to the 'real' nature of Indian kingship has been stressed by Shulman, *The King and the Clown*.

[77] See *MSS*, vol. 3, no. 5580, vol. 7, nos. 12054, 12065, 12935. Notable is Rākṣasa's speech in *MR* 4.4, where he compares the troubles which faced a minister to those of a playwright: that he must first cast the seeds of a plot, and then cultivate and produce the hidden and impenetrable fruits of those impregnated seeds, make them increase and bring together the bundle of actions into the climax (*vimarṣa*).

[78] *NS* 35.57–60. [79] *NS* 35.60–2.

emotions in courtly literature was in turn linked to and supported by a more general affective texture in courtly life, where men and women regularly, as a matter of course, interpreted the outward signs of inner disposition. Aesthetics, in this context, provided its courtly audience not only a sort of 'objective' education in the subtlety of its own affective structures, but also a *subjective* orientation to this system, one which allowed both a reposeful delectation of emotions *and* a strategic itinerancy which enabled men and women to negotiate more effectively the relations of alliance, loyalty and antagonism which structured the affiliations of their lives.

Part III

Courtly Love and Aristocratic Society

6 Courtship and the royal household

Erotic love, if we follow our sources, was one of the most important concerns of the collective life of people at court. It not only formed the subject of a robust prescriptive literature from the Gupta period when the famous *Kāmasūtra* was assembled, but also was indisputably the key theme of the vast literary corpus that has come down to us in Sanskrit from medieval India. It formed the central topic, for example, of every single court drama, save one, that has survived from the fourth to seventh centuries, and continued to be the predominant theme of literary endeavour throughout the larger period with which this book is concerned. Of the eight *rasas* enumerated in the *Nāṭyaśāstra*, the sentiment of erotic love, or *śṛṅgāra*, was the most 'lordly', being attended by more subsidiary emotional states than any of the other sentiments.[1] By the eleventh century, the sentiment of *śṛṅgāra* had become so important that the Paramāra king Bhoja (1011–55 CE) in his *summa poetica*, the *Śṛṅgāraprakāśa* or 'Light on Passion', made it the basis of a superordinate experiential 'sense of self' which encompassed not only erotic love, but all the emotions and sentiments of an exalted life.[2] It is for these reasons that any sensitive apprehension of courtly life must come to terms with the collective preoccupation among the people of the court with erotic love.

Yet whatever its prominence in the sources, trying to undersand its significance as a theme in the mental world of the court and what relation it may have had with actual practice is a far more complex and vexing matter. Barring a few classic text-based studies of erotics and erotic literature which remain useful, and a few very recent essays, most of the scholarship from the 1970s and '80s preferred rather more decontextualising approaches – either humanist formalism, religious structuralism or psychoanalysis.[3] While these latter approaches shed light on some important

[1] See *NS* 7.108–9.

[2] As Pollock has put it, 'the capacity to experience the world richly'. See Pollock's discussion and translation of key passages of the text, 'Bhoja's *Śṛṅgāraprakāśa*, pp. 126, 144–5.

[3] The most exhaustive treatment of the technical and aesthetic literature on the subject still remains Richard Schmidt's *Beiträge zur Indischen Erotik. Das Liebesleben des Sanskrit*

issues, they do little to help us understand the world of the sources with which we are concerned in this book. More useful are a handful of recent essays on the royal household and the *Kāmasūtra* itself.[4] In fact, the topic of courtly love is vast and complex enough to merit an entire study unto itself, and the interpretations presented below may be considered preliminary at best. This chapter seeks, instead, only to begin answering what I think to be important questions, some concrete and others more speculative, pertaining to the sexual lives of people at court. First, what are the sources, who were their 'audiences', and what can they actually tell us about sex and romance at court? Who was involved and what was the nature of sex and courtship in the courtly milieu? What are we to make of the highly idealised and almost fantastic depictions of courtship within the royal household found in the early court dramas? These problems will be taken up in this chapter. In the following chapter I will explore the specific language used to characterise courtship and sex with a view towards understanding the role that sexual pleasure played (as the predominant theme of courtly literature) in the ethical self-perceptions of people of the court.

The very juxtaposition of terms as redolent as 'love' and 'court' may immediately invoke for the reader expectations or connotations related to 'courtly love' as it evolved in Europe. This is not intended. I use the term below in a generally descriptive sense. I mean, quite simply, ideas of erotic love as they evolved in the largely courtly and urbane milieu which has been the topic of this study. Yet if the interpretations suggest comparison with any other traditions, this is welcome, for it seems to me that the dangers of comparison are far less than those of isolating the Indian materials from important concerns in the name of civilisational uniqueness.

Courtly love and its sources

Several sorts of sources tell us about the sexual lives of people at court. The most famous of these is undoubtedly the Gupta-period treatise by

Volkes (Berlin: Verlag von H. Barsdorf, 1911); also useful are De, *Ancient Indian Erotics* and N. N. Bhattacharya, *History of Indian Erotic Literature* (Delhi: Munshiram Manoharlal, 1975). For recent thematic approaches, generally placing 'sexuality' and 'renunciation' as civilisational tendencies in tension with one another, see Lee Siegel, *Fires of Love, Waters of Peace: Passion and Renunciation in Indian Culture* (Honolulu: University of Hawaii Press, 1983), and Shulman, *The King and the Clown*. For a psychoanalytic approach, see Sudhir Kakar and John Munder Ross, *Tales of Love, Sex and Danger* (Oxford: Blackwell, 1986).

[4] See Roy, 'The King's Household', pp. 18–38; and her 'Unravelling the *Kamasutra*', in Mary E. John and Janaki Nair, eds., *A Question of Silence: The Sexual Economies of Modern India* (Delhi: Kali for Women, 1998). See also the useful introduction to Doniger and Kakar's translation of the *Kāmasūtra*.

Vātsyāyana Mallanāga, the *Kāmasūtra*, discussed briefly above, which purports to advise men of twice-born affiliation on the proper pursuit of sexual pleasure. The *Kāmasūtra* forms the first and most capacious of a genre of literature which was widely produced and read in courtly environments until as late as the eighteenth century. It advised on a number of topics: the general lifestyle and attributes of the ideal courtly paramour; the sexual compatibilities of lovers; the specific phases and activities of the sex act itself; the ways and means of winning and acquiring a virgin; the conduct and management of sexual relations with one or many wives; liaisons with the wives of other men; dealings with courtesans; and esoteric formulas for achieving one's sexual goals.

Besides the prescriptive literature like the *Kāmasūtra*, there is also a vast body of poetic writings in various genres on courtship, love and sex. There are, for example, numerous plays (*nāṭaka*s) which depict the courtship and integration of princess-maidens into the royal household, particularly those of the famous legendary King Udayana of Kauśambi. There are also story cycles of famous lovers like Kādambarī and Candrāpīḍā and Nala and Damayantī depicted in prose, verse and drama. Beyond these, there are literary texts which deal with the love affairs of courtesans, notably the famous *prakaraṇa* plays about the brahmin merchant Cārudatta's infatuation with the courtesan Vasantasenā, and the *bhāṇa* monologue plays, narrated by that comic and wry voluptuary, the *viṭa*, as he moves through the courtesan's quarter of the royal city and discourses at *goṣṭhī*s. To these latter plays, which have an element of the picaresque, may be added sections in longer prose and poetic narratives (*ākhyāyika*, *kathā*, *carita*) as well as court epics (*mahākāvya*) which include extended erotic descriptions of courtly women and courtesans. Finally, and importantly, are large numbers of anthologised and free-floating independent verses commenting on, or sketching scenarios between, lovers. These verses, stretching from the sublime to the vulgar, are typically populated by anonymous and generic 'lovers'.

Completing the picture is an extensive technical literature on poetics, beginning with the *Nāṭyaśāstra*, and continuing throughout medieval India, which instructs poets and readers on the conventions for writing and appreciating love poetry. It sets out the qualities, scenarios and behaviours appropriate to the male and female character/lover, known respectively as *nāyaka* and *nāyikā*, as well as a cast of supporting characters who appeared in connection with their affairs. This literature is in many respects crucial, for in setting out the conventions of literary representation, it makes reference to and shares terminology with the prescriptive literature on erotics proper. The different types of lovers in the *Kāmasūtra*, for example, are also designated generically as *nāyakas* and *nāyikā*s, and many of the specific practices mentioned in the *Kāmasūtra* (scratching, biting, symptoms of 'lovesickness', etc. . . .) form frequent themes in love poetry.[5]

It would seem, then, that the different sorts of literature on erotic love reveal a coherent 'world', at once courtly and urbane. There are, of course, important differences of perspective and subject matter between various poetic genres and, further, between those texts which advised lovers how to behave and those which advised poets how to write about love. Some poems, for example, present rustic, village or even 'pastoral' scenes – though it must be said that such depictions were markedly courtly in their vision.[6] In general, poetic discourses are far less explicit with regard to the sexual act itself than erotological, being more concerned with various aspects of the wider process of courtship – from wooing, seduction and the symptoms of desire, to sexual longing and lovers' quarrels. Poetic discourses divided the experience of erotic love into the categories of 'union' and 'separation', and became increasingly preoccupied with the experience of love-in-separation – the affective world of the lover longing for the beloved. This preoccupation was not only a clever poetic technique, it also allowed and contributed to a general proclivity to invest erotic love with wider social concerns.

Nevertheless, the general convergence of the different types of sources is significant in at least two senses. First, it suggests that it is not enough to regard the poetic treatment of erotic love in isolation from the actual practices they represent, as a purely 'literary' experience, savoured in the name of greater aesthetic rapture or spiritual realisation. While the aesthetics of erotic love may indeed at times have been put to such uses (which themselves are hardly excused from sociological scrutiny in any case), it hardly justifies the rampant formalism that has usually accompanied the study of Indian poetry.

Second, and far more importantly for this study, the close connection of poetic discourses and the erotic manuals suggests that representational and aesthetic concerns of poetry were also those of lovers in the courtly context. Sanskrit plays give us ample evidence of the use of poetry in the courtship of lovers. Accomplished paramours frequently broke into verse to capture the emotional ambience of the moment or to convey their inner feelings to one another. Indeed, the capacity to do so is almost

[5] The close connection between the normative treatises on erotics and poetic representations has been noted by De, *Ancient Indian Erotics*, p. 20.

[6] I take the 'rustic' motifs and village scenes found in collections like the Prakrit *Gāthāśaptaśatī* and Tamil *akam* anthologies, usually attributed to the first centuries of the Common Era, to be essentially courtly in nature. Not only do they explicitly claim association with royal courts, but are also highly 'mannered' in literary style.

always regarded positively from the prescriptive side, and it is thus not surprising that so many of the supplementary skills of the accomplished *nāgaraka* according to the *Kāmasūtra* concern the interpretation and composition of poetry (table 2.1). Vātsyāyana would thus have his ideal lover cultivate both the techniques of sensual love as well as the finer points of its representation. The sympathetic *rasika* sensibility we encountered in the previous chapter was a badge of distinction for the courtly lover.

The close link of sexual relations to the larger aesthetic culture of the court also helps to explain some aspects of the *Kāmasūtra*'s peculiar treatment of sex which, I think, has not been sufficiently appreciated. The division of the sexual act itself into discrete phases and activities – embracing, kissing, scratching, biting, coitus, slapping, moaning and oral sex – each with their own varieties, positions and suitability for different sorts of lovers, suggests, when placed alongside the careful attention to gesture, facial expression and comportment we have encountered above, that sex for the people of the court was a highly mannered and tutored experience, an 'art', which like other aspects of the courtier's life, was to be refined and perfected.[7] Vātsyāyana treats scratching and biting, for example, as activities which were not only pleasurable in themselves as outbursts of fiercely felt passion, but also notes that they formed a sort of non-verbal 'language' between lovers both during sex and, even more importantly, afterwards, when the often surreptitious sight and display of scars or marks became reintegrated into the excitative economy of courtship. This added layer of semioticity to action is precisely characteristic of the general attention to demeanour and gesture in other courtly sources. Vātsyāyana calibrates these scratches and bites into different varieties depending on the shape of the mark left on the body. He justifies the seemingly arbitrary variety of his classification with a telling argument – an apology for 'variety' itself. For variety, according to Vātsyāyana, increased desire and was generally approved in other accomplishments, like archery.[8] The word for 'variety' here, *vicitra*, had significant aesthetic overtones, as it was a term used to denote the brightly and variously coloured clothes, jewellery and diverse artifice of courtly decoration, and could often stand in for the idea of 'ornamented' itself. The point is that the trend towards elaboration and classification in the *Kāmasūtra* was motivated in part by the same aesthetic concerns we have seen earlier with regard to the material life of men and women at court.

[7] I believe that this courtly/aesthetic concern better explains the seemingly hair-splitting and pedantic obsession of the *Kāmasūtra* with positions and other minutiae of sexual behaviour than existing explanations of it as an example of brahmanical number crunching.

[8] *KS* 2.4.25.

In literary representations, the trend towards aetheticisation is clearly apparent if we compare a brief passage from the story cycle of Nala and Damayantī found in the *Mahābhārata* (an early 'epic' text whose concerns were certainly political but 'proto-courtly' at best), with a later courtly *kāvya*, the *Naiṣadacarita* of Śrīharṣa, composed during the reign of the Gāhaḍvāla king Jayacandra of Kanauj (1170–93 CE). In the *Mahābhārata*'s account of the initial lovesickness of Nala, we find the following description: 'unable to bear the desire in his heart, Nala at once left secretly and sat in a grove besides the women's quarters'.[9] In Śrīharṣa's rendition, this event is preceded by a rather long conceit about the god Kāmadeva's attempt to subdue Nala through the form of Damayantī – a conceit I shall comment on below – in which Damayantī's excellence is said to be 'made by the king the guest of his ears'. Śrīharṣa says that:

> powerful Nala, though consumed by desire, did not ask the king of Vidarbha for the hand of his daughter, for the proud would rather renounce both life and happiness than forsake the single vow never to beg. Feigning to be depressed on account of something, he concealed his many sighs caused by his separation from her, and denied his paleness by attributing it to an excess of camphor in the sandal paste applied to his body. Luckily, even amidst company, he was able to conceal during the vīṇā recital both his deluded words to his beloved, as well as the fact that he fainted. The king who had a reputation of being the foremost of those whose senses were conquered, was ashamed when the irresistible power of Kāmadeva became slowly manifest in him. Neither his power of discrimination nor other virtues could restrain Nala's disquiet; for where there is desire, Kāmadeva produces an unrest that is never restrained – such are the ways of the world! When, in spite of his efforts, he became unable to sit in the royal assembly even for a moment without betraying signs of being in love, he longed to retreat to a secluded place under the pretext of recreation in his pleasure garden.[10]

Śrīharṣa's expansion here is significant. The great relish taken in describing the gradual manifestation of desire in Nala's body and his acute suffering as a lovestruck hero, largely absent in the *Mahābhārata*'s account, represent a new set of concerns around erotic love. In the several hundred years which separated these accounts, Nala had been transformed from an epic hero to a courtly lover, or *nāyaka*. Relations between lovers had come to be structured by courtly protocols, 'adorned' by courtly concepts of personal bearing, beauty and ethical self-regard, and structured by the court's formulaic and mannered set of affective and gestural correspondences.

[9] *MhB* 3.50.17–18.

[10] *Naiṣadhacaritam* 1.49–55. In the garden, Nala's problems only worsen as a host of flowers afflict his mind and make him pine even more.

Protagonists and audiences

What do we know about the 'hero' (*nāyaka*) and 'heroine' (*nāyikā*) of courtly literature? The prescriptive traditions have much to say about different types of *nāyaka*s and *nāyikā*s, dividing them into numerous categories and sub-categories according to a wide variety of criteria, which need not concern us centrally for the moment. I would like, instead, to focus on the basic definitions of the *Kāmasūtra*, since they tend to be more generic and sociologically revealing than those of the *Nāṭyaśāstra* (which are typically more modal and dispositional). The *Kāmasūtra* provides at least two schemes of different sorts of *nāyaka*s and *nāyikā*s which we will come to momentarily, but it also contains general lists of attributes ideally possessed by each group (male and female) as a whole.

The male lover or *nāyaka*, who is conflated and identified with the larger category of the urbane man, or *nāgaraka*, was, according to Vātsyāyana, to possess a prodigious set of qualities: noble birth (*mahākulīna*), learning, knowledge of all spiritual paths, skill in poetry and storytelling, eloquence, confidence, knowledge in the arts, regard for the learned, ambition, great energy, firm devotion, absence of spite, generosity, fondness of friends, familiarity with playing games, with joining associations, and spectating among assemblies, good health, manliness, friendliness, being a guide and protector of women while not being subjected to them, independence of means, gentleness, lack of envy and lack of attachment.[11]

The ideal female lover, or *nāyikā*, was bestowed with an equally elaborate set of qualifications. She was to possess beauty, youth, favourable bodily marks, sweet speech, attraction to virtue (but not to wealth), inclination towards affection and sexual union, firmness of thought, similarity of birth (to the *nāyaka*), a desire to achieve distinction, perpetual avoidance of miserliness in conduct, and a fondness of skills performed at *goṣṭhī*s.[12] Vātsyāyana adds a further list of more 'general' (*sādhāraṇa*) characteristics that she was to possess, including having well-considered and good conduct, knowing the proper place and time for things, honesty, gratitude, foresightedness, politeness, proficiency in the science of *kāma*

[11] *KS* 6.1.12. To these must be added the largely similar attributes of the *nāgaraka*: twice-born affiliation and residence among good people (*sajjana*) and, crucially absent from the above list, the possession of wealth, *KS* 1.4.1–2. Compare with those listed in the fourteenth-century *Pañcasāyaka* 1.4: having good conduct, filled with compassion, having resolve, generous, having a clean heart, desirable, an abode of the arts of *kāma*, well-spoken, beautiful in the thoughts of women, wealthy, skilful in policy, patient, curious, brave, of good family, youthful and proficient in music.

[12] *KS* 6.1.13.

and its allied knowledges and possessing the qualities of the *nāgaraka*. Moreover, she was to avoid contradicting herself, avoid begging, excessive laughter, backbiting, blaming others, anger, greed, arrogance and fickleness.[13]

At one level, there is an obvious parity between these categories which mark them as belonging to the courtly classes – people who possessed the advantages of birth, wealth, winning appearances and a host of virtues. Importantly, these men and women were to share a general inclination towards erotic love which presumably distinguished them from others of equal birth and advantage who did not, or were not able to, cultivate themselves in this capacity. This is an important point, for it suggests that not every person of birth at court necessarily conducted their sexual affairs in the manner set down by the erotic and aesthetic manuals. That is, the role of being a courtly lover was less a regulatory norm than, as mentioned earlier, a badge of distinction or prized avocation.

Apart from such similarities, the lists show some significant differences. The qualities of the ideal man, for example, tend to be expressed positively, while many of the woman's are stated negatively, a distinction which plausibly suggests what Vātsyāyana and other authors thought were the typical attributes of women: tendencies towards backbiting, anger, greed and fascination with money, arrogance, blameful of others, fickleness and frivolity. This is confirmed by the numerous free-floating and anthologised single-stanza verses on the 'qualities of women' which circulated at court in prodigious numbers.[14] These verses exalted the beauty of women but at the same time denigrated their inherent weaknesses. Such images of women, which as we shall see later are crucial for understanding courtly masculinity, reveal a basic disparity in perspective about gender ideals.[15]

Matters become further muddied if we turn to the distinctions within the categories of *nāyaka* and *nāyikā*. Vātsyāyana treats this problem in two ways, one physiological and the other sociological. The former sought to determine the suitability of different temperamental and physiological types in sex. It divided men into hares (*śaśa*), bulls (*vṛṣa*) and horses (*aśva*) and women into deer (*mṛgī*), mares (*vaḍavā*) and she-elephants (*hastinī*).[16] The latter scheme sought to divide lovers with reference to their social identities, a problem which is posed in the first instance as a question of propriety – a man should have relations with a woman of

[13] *KS* 6.1.14.
[14] See, for example, entries indexed under women in *MSS*, vols. 1–7.
[15] No such free-standing verses, for example, exist on men as such, but on particular types of men, good and bad.
[16] *KS* 2.1.1–2, *passim.*

similar rank for happy conjugal life with progeny, and should never, under any circumstances have sexual relations with a woman of higher station or who was married, but could, if he so desired, have relations without consequence, 'for the sake of pleasure' (*sukhārthatvāt*) with women of lower rank.[17] He thus concludes that *nāyikās* were of three basic varieties – unmarried virgins (*kanyā*), women once-married who sought the company of a man out of wedlock (*punarbhū*) and courtesans (*veśyā*). Vātsyāyana goes on to engage various contemporary authorities over the question of other categories of *nāyikā*s, implicitly conceding two more varieties – a married woman enjoyed for some purpose other than pleasure (*pakṣikī*), and those of the 'third nature' (*tritīyaprakṛti*), classified as neither man nor woman.[18]

Whatever the implications of these categories themselves, the discourse assumes a stable male subject-perspective, and it is indeed significant that Vātsyāyana never develops a parallel typology of male social types. In fact, he says later that for the various types of *nāyikā*s, or female lovers, there was really only one type of *nāyaka*.[19] As far as the discourse of the *Kāmasūtra* was concerned, male lovers might be divided by their physiognomies and temperaments, but they were united in their social location to the extent that the topic never requires discussion.[20] Instead, the emphasis in later texts, even physiologically, came to revolve around *nāyikābheda*, or the 'classification of women'.[21]

This comparatively 'unmarked' status of the male lover in the *Kāmasūtra* highlights a general perspectival bias in the sources which reveals the assumed 'subject' of the discourse on love to be men of courtly standing. In this connection, it is probably worth stating the obvious: that the authors of the courtly manuals on erotics and the voluminous literature which took love as its subject were, without exception, male. The

17 *KS* 1.5.1–3.

18 *KS* 1.5.5, 27. Varieties of *tritīyaprākṛti* are discussed in more detail at *KS* 2.9.1–8, in connection with the practice of oral sex (*auparișṭaka*).

19 *KS* 1.5.28–9. Vātsyāyana qualifies his remark with a 'second type of *nāyaka*', which turns out to be modal rather than sociological in definition, as one who achieved his goal covertly.

20 The *Nāṭyaśāstra* shows similar perspectival imbalance in its rather generalised sociological definitions of *nāyaka*s and *nāyikā*s. While the text notes that any high or middling rank of character is suitable for the role of *nāyaka*, it is much more specific in regard to *nāyikās*, which it divides into goddesses (*divyā*), queens (*nṛpapatnī*), women of high families (*kulastrī*) and courtesans (*gaṇikā*). See *NS* 34.17–18; 25–7.

21 See for example Kokkoka's twelfth-century *Ratirahasya*, a greatly attenuated *kāmaśāstra* which retains Vātsyāyana's physical division of *nāyaka*s and *nāyikā*s (ch. 3), but adds to it various classifications which are discussed only in relation to women – astrological considerations based on the lunar calender (chs. 1–2), by age, disposition, and region (chs. 4–5).

audiences of courtly literature, the participants in the cultivated conversation on love at the *goṣṭhī*, and the students of the science of pleasure, were also largely composed of men.

Yet it is also true that women were expected to cultivate themselves to be suitable for the practice of courtly love, and thus were encouraged, in some capacity, to acquire some of the knowledges associated with *kāma*. Indeed, Vātsyāyana himself makes a case at the outset of his treatise for the instruction of the *Kāmasūtra* to women, who were otherwise forbidden *śāstric* knowledge. He remarks that the highest classes of courtesans (*gaṇikā*s), princesses (*rājaputrī*s) and the daughters of men of ministerial rank (*mahāmātra*s) could have their intelligence 'sharpened' (*prahata*) by instruction in the *śāstra*.[22] They were also urged to acquire competency in the sixty-four arts or *kalā*s deemed by Vātsyāyana as 'auxiliary knowledges' (*aṅgavidyā*) to the *Kāmasūtra* itself. Women of noble households, however, were to learn this knowledge 'privately' (*rahasi*) from trusted female companions or special instructors brought into the household discretely. The *Kāmasūtra* lists various women who could instruct the noble-born virgin – including a foster-sister who grew up with her, a girlfriend, one of her mother's sisters who is her age, an old servant-woman, a nun with whom she is close or her own sister.[23] The assumption here is that the young woman, unlike her male counterpart or the courtesan who moved more freely in the circles of noble men, was educated in this knowledge primarily within a limited domestic context. Unfortunately, our understanding of exactly how the women of the nobility came to possess this knowledge is vague, considering our almost total ignorance of how, and to what degree, they acquired skills of literacy as well as obvious constraints to their mobility. What is clear, however, is that through whatever path such women entered the open world of the court and its sexual relationships, they generally did so with far fewer 'cultural resources' than their male counterparts. The entire edifice of courtly love from the prescriptive treatises on sexual positions to the emotional dynamics reflected in *kāvya*, is decidedly oriented towards the male point of view.

The contexts of courtship

Understanding the contexts of courtship presents a vexed set of problems for a number of reasons, not least of which is that the literary sources tend to present a range of scenarios, some of which are plausible but many of which are almost certainly either partially or entirely 'fictive', given our knowledge of the lives of courtly people. Ironically, or perhaps not, the

[22] *KS* 1.3.12. [23] *KS* 1.3.13–15.

more frank and 'realistic' literary depictions of the sexual world of the court tend to be from the less exalted genres of courtly literature, often partly or entirely comic, which included relatively low characters like profligate kings, ministers' sons and that denizen of pleasure who formed the cynosure of courtly moralists, the courtesan. The comic genre of the *bhāṇa* is perhaps the most telling example of this literature. It is narrated by a *viṭa* as he moves through the courtesans' quarter of the royal city, where he encounters court officials, sons of ministers and assemblies (*goṣṭhīs*) of urbane men. But as we ascend the courtly genres and approach the righteous king and the goings-on in his household, usually in the form of palace dramas and romances, the depictions become markedly fantastic and unlikely – a fact which deserves some explanation. A preliminary condition for explaining this problem, I believe, is to place the *Kāmasūtra*'s presentation of *nāyikās*, adumbrated above, in the context of what we know about the gender organisation and sexual codes of noble and élite households.

As noted above, polygamy was the norm among the courtly and urban élite, particularly among men of royal status. In the households of more powerful men, large numbers of women were also retained as servants and sometimes as concubines (*bhoginīs*). In all households of men of rank that we have any information on, there would seem to be some basic principles of spatial organisation with regard to gender. Vātsyāyana divides the *nāgaraka*'s household (figure 1.4), into two sections, distinguishing between the women who appeared in its 'inner' (*antara*) and 'outer' (*bahirs*) portions.[24] The inner portions of the residence, minimally described, were reserved for wives, while in the outer parts of the house the *nāgaraka* met his friends and various women through arrangement.[25] Vātsyāyana's description of the outer rooms – with a lute on the wall, an attached garden with parrot cages and a swing – makes it clear that this was the place of seduction, but a seduction which was not an invitation to the inner regions of the house.[26] Sexual relations were consummated on a couch in the middle of the outer room.

The royal household, though certainly more complex, had a broadly similar spatial logic (see figures 1.2, 1.3).[27] At the centre of the palace was the residence of the king. Close by were the residences of various

[24] The following account is based on *KS* 1.4.4–15.

[25] The inner quarters of the *nāgaraka*'s house, according to Yaśodhara, were reserved for the sleeping quarters of the wives, *KS* 1.4.5, comm: *ābhyantaraṃ vāsagṛham antardārāṇam śayanārtham*.

[26] Yaśodhara notes that the outer rooms of the house were for the purpose of sex, *KS* 1.4.4, comm.

[27] The plan following Bāṇa's *Harṣacarita* does not include details of the larger area of the king's quarters, where both his own residence as well as the *antaḥpura* were located.

queens, whose houses formed part of the *antaḥpura*, a place where women alone resided and perhaps additionally a specific place therein where the king met these women collectively.[28] The women of the *antaḥpura*, or 'interior' (*ābhyantara*), were quite diverse. According to the *Nāṭyaśāstra*, they included not only the chief queen (*mahādevī*), and her 'sister' queens (*devī*s), as well as other high-born and ordinary wives (*svāminī*s, *śāyinī*s), but concubines (*bhoginī*s), craftswomen (*śilpakāriṇī*s), actresses (*nāṭakīyā*s), dancers (*nartakī*s), numerous types of female servants (*anucārikā*s, *paricārikā*s, *sañcārikā*s, *preṣaṇacārikā*s), matrons (*mahattarī*s), doorkeepers (*pratihārī*s), maidens (*kumārī*s), older women (*sthavirā*s) and female overseers (*ayuktikā*s).[29] Though Vātsyāyana's account is less expansive, including within the *antaḥpura*, besides the king's wives, only concubines (*punarbhū*s), actresses (*nāṭakīyā*s) and courtesans (*veśyā*s), it is equally revealing, for in discussing these women, Vātsyāyana suggests that each had an 'appropriate' place or room (*kakṣa*), which his commentator explains to mean that queens occupied the central place near the centre of the palace and concubines, courtesans and actresses successively 'outer' (*bahirs*) rooms.[30] The 'outer rooms' of the *nāgaraka*'s house had their counterparts in the many pavilions and 'playhouses' within the palace, and the royal gardens, often called 'pleasure gardens' (*krīḍāvana*) in sources from Gupta times. And it is within this region, particularly the garden, as we shall see that the king, like the *nāgaraka*, engaged in the activities of courtship.

Given this domestic context, what were the typical scenarios in which sexual relationships developed? Most obviously, there were the relations that men had with wives and wives-to-be, or virgins (*kanyā*) as they are designated by Vātsyāyana. Yet a man's marriage did not, in and of itself, prohibit extramarital sexual liaisons, as is clear from Vātsyāyana's enumeration of *nāyikā*s beyond the maiden. Sexual pleasure with such women was effectively valourised by the *Kāmasūtra*, which presents only 'exogenous' obstacles to his sexual conquests – the standard prohibitions of relations with women of higher social standing, married women and those attached to other households. Yet Vātsyāyana assures his listeners that if a man regarded even such forbidden women as having 'freedom of will' (*svairinīya*) he could treat them as a *nāyikā*s in the category of *punarbhū*.[31] Vātsyāyana suggests that the real problem was entering into

[28] On the origin of this term in the *Arthaśāstra*, see the discussion in chapter 1. Discussion of the *antaḥpura* in the *Kāmasūtra* in connection with the king's daily meeting of its women implies that he meets them collectively, at some designated place.

[29] *NS* 34.31–4.

[30] *KS* 4.2.77–9 and comm. Vātsyāyana describes these latter categories of women as 'inner' (*ābhyantarikā*), which Yaśodhara understands as 'of the *antaḥpura*'.

[31] *KS* 1.5.6–7. Yaśodhara glosses *svairinīya* as *svatantra*, or 'independence'.

other men's houses, on both moral and practical grounds.[32] Vātsyāyana, thus, is concerned with how women could be lured into the king's own household, for the seduction of a woman, once within the confines of the palace, was a much simpler and safer affair, since she was surrounded by the king's people. Vātsyāyana's advice here reflects an important reality at court, that almost any woman of equal or lower rank, and even those 'unavailable' or of higher rank, were deemed *potentially* accessible to the *nāyaka*.

The large numbers of women retained in the *antaḥpura*s of powerful aristocratic households also meant that there was considerable potential for illicit sexual liaisons between these women and other palace personnel or even men of rank from outside the palace. If we follow Vātsyāyana, this was a major and constant concern for the king, perhaps not least because Vātsyāyana himself provides the courtier-lover several strategies about how to enter the *antaḥpura* to unite with its women.[33]

The princes of aristocratic households probably also engaged in sexual liaisons with women from the larger retinue of women retained by the palace. The attraction of palace women to the young prince formed a common theme in courtly literature, and in the case of Bāṇa's *Kādambarī*, the prince Candrāpīḍā is appointed a female companion by his father after his formal education was completed.[34] These women, in part, were seen to complete this education, for though the prince remained celibate during his instruction as a child (*bālya*, until age sixteen), he was now permitted, even expected, to pursue *kāma* legimately as one of the three goals of worldly life. Indeed, youth was deemed the most appropriate life-stage for *kāma* according to Vātsyāyana.[35] Through these liaisons the prince developed proficiency in the skills of courtship which, as we have seen from inscriptions, was a universally applauded skill among men of the court. Moreover, as we shall see, the successful negotiation of these liaisons was probably a matter of some importance for his overall reputation and 'training' for his life at court.

All of these relations could, to varying degrees, take on the 'courtly' inflections I have referred to above. In one sense this is indicated by their

[32] *KS* 5.1.1–2; 5.5.1–2, 29–30. In the latter verses, Vātsyāyana makes clear that the practical reasons for not entering other men's houses involved the safety of the *nāyaka*.

[33] See *KS* 5.6.1 ff. The concerns for the king were not only guarding the sexual continence of his wives, but because these women were potentially close to him, they could also be seduced by men, not for sex as such but for a variety of ulterior motives. See Vātsyāyana's discussion of Gonikaputra's idea of the *pākṣikī* (a woman enjoyed for some purpose other than pleasure or offspring) as a type of *nāyikā*, *KS* 1.5.5 ff.

[34] For descriptions of palace women longing for the young prince, see *BC* 4.1 ff., *Kd*, p. 135–40. For the appointment of Patralekhā, a captured princess from the queen's retinue, as the betel-bearer to prince Candrāpīḍa, see *Kd*, p. 165–6.

[35] *KS* 1.2.3.

very inclusion in the *nāyaka*/*nāyikā* dyad. In Vātsyāyana's treatment, they all consequently shared some practical features – the use of intermediaries, acts of wooing and refusal, the sharing of gifts and courtesies, and the use of games and arts as part of the rituals of seduction. Having said this, not all of these relationships were deemed suitable for thematisation in courtly literature. So while less socially desirable liaisons were treated *inter alia* in some narrative *kāvya*, they typically do not form the centrepiece of courtly literature. It is only the courtesan who gains a certain prominence in the courtly literature as an instance of non-conjugal erotic love. In most courtly dramas the preferred scenario was a romance between a maiden of noble rank and a king which culminated with her accession to the royal household.

Many prescriptive texts discuss sexual relationships against the overall framework of marriage. As an institution of 'good society', marriage was ideally to be secured by arrangement between the two families in question. According to Vātsyāyana, when a girl reached marriageable age her family was to make known her 'availability' among men of suitable rank and receive potential suitors for a predetermined duration of time, before giving her away (*kanyādāna*, or the 'gift of a virgin') to the man of their choice.[36] Vātsyāyana represents this arrangement as typically occurring through one or more meetings known as a 'selection', or *varaṇa*, where the bride-to-be's family displayed their daughter for inspection and reviewed potential suitors. Some have considered this process of mutual selection and negotiation to be a sort of formal 'courtship'.[37] If this is so, it should be admitted as a rather peculiar one, as the courtship and wooing on the part of the *nāyaka* seems to have been directed not so much to the girl herself but to her family, particularly her mother. In this spirit Vātsyāyana recommends that the courtier and his companions use various methods to convince the girl's parents of his superiority over his competitors. A notable concern in these meetings was the examination of bodily marks and the search for other omens and portents as signs of future prosperity, success and (in the case of women) fertility.[38] At the conclusion of the review of suitors, the parents chose their favourite and 'gave' their virgin away to him in marriage.

A significant variant to this course of events was the *svayaṁvara*, or 'self-choice', where the bride herself chose the suitor in question from men of rank who came to her father's court at general invitation. The

[36] See *KS* 3.1.1–21. [37] As in Doniger and Kakar's translation of *KS* 3.1.1ff.

[38] Marriage selection among the nobility was no doubt one of the more important contexts in which Varāhamihira in the sixth century collected lists of auspicious and inauspicious bodily characteristics (*lakṣaṇas*) of different types of men and women in his 'Great Compendium' (*Bṛhatsaṁhitā*).

svayaṁvara is portrayed in both the *Rāmāyaṇa* and *Mahābhārata*. The most famous of these, that of Nala and Damanyantī, formed a popular theme of later courtly writers.[39] It did not, however, become a defining aspect of the ideology of courtship, and is rarely referred to in inscriptions or historical kāvyas which are not based on the epics. It is notably absent in Vātsyāyana's account in the *Kāmasūtra*.

The *svayaṁvara* notwithstanding, neither of these selection ceremonies had much scope for any substantial courtship (or even contact) between the bride and groom before marriage. This is confirmed by Vātsyāyana's devotion of a chapter entitled 'wooing' or 'creating confidence' in the virgin (*kanyāvisrambhaṇa*) which clearly takes as its context the first days *after* the marriage ceremony. The *Kāmasūtra* recommends three nights of sexual abstinence after the marriage ceremony which was to be followed by another seven during which time the couple were to bathe, dress up, eat together and visit and honour their relatives.[40] It is during this period that the man was to begin conversing with the bride (perhaps for the first time), wooing and approaching her, according to Vātsyāyana, with 'gentle courtesies' (*mṛdubhirupacāraiḥ*).[41] In the passages that follow, Vātsyāyana recommends various methods through which the *nāyaka* could gently coax his bride into physical intimacy, including formal requests, oaths, verbal conciliations and even prostration before her feet.[42] He also suggests that the girl should first refuse her husband's entreaties and then slowly return his courtesies (bringing him betel-nut, garlands and scented oils) before eventually submitting to his advances.[43] In short, what Vātsyāyana presents here is a sort of adumbrated courtship to be enacted by the husband and wife in the first days after marriage. This, according to Vātsyāyana, generated affection or attachment (*anurāga*), and prevented the wife from becoming alienated from her husband (which could potentially lead to her seeking liaisons with other men).[44] Vātsyāyana concludes that a man who knows how to win the confidence of women, increase

[39] Noted by Johann Meyer, *Sexual Life in Ancient India* (New York: Dorset Press, 1995), p. 78, n. 3 and Yadava, *Society and Culture in Northern India in the Twelfth Century*, p. 70. In addition to Śrīharṣa's *Naishadhacarita*, versions of this story include the *Nalodaya*, doubtfully attributed to Kalidāsa; the *Nalacampū* of Trivikramabhaṭṭa (ninth century); the *Naiṣadhānandanāṭaka* of Kṣemīśvara (tenth century); the *Sahodayānanda* of Kṛṣṇānanda (thirteenth century); and the *Nalobhyudaya* of Vāmanabhaṭṭabāṇa (fifteenth century).

[40] *KS* 3.2.1; see also the *Ratirahasya* 11.8. [41] *KS* 3.2.2.

[42] See Vātsyāyana's remarks on getting the bride to accept betel-nut directly from her husband's mouth, *KS* 3.2.11–12.

[43] See *KS* 3.2.18 ff. for the bride's behaviour.

[44] *KS* 3.2.4–6; 43–4; *Ratirahasya* 11.8, 21–2. Affection here is deemed a possible 'fruit of marriage' (*vivāhanam phalam*) rather than its precondition, see *KS* 3.5.30.

their attachment and cause their affection towards him, becomes beloved among them.[45]

In contrast to the ceremonies, with their forms of post-marital courtship, was what texts call the *gandharva* rite, a marriage which resulted from the mutual attraction and courtship between the *nāyaka* and *nāyikā* without the prior sanctioning or agreement between the families concerned. The *nāyaka*, in this case, was to win over the confidence of the girl from her childhood by numerous strategies of courtship. These included giving her gifts (toys, rare objects, cosmetics, clothing, jewellery, etc. . . .), playing games with her, telling her stories, showing her magic tricks and displaying his skill in the arts (like singing, etc. . . .). He was also to convince her foster sister to assist him in his designs. The courtship culminated in luring her away from her house, performing the wedding rites himself with the sacred fire and then informing the respective families of the marriage, specifically requesting her family to now formally offer her as a gift (*kanyādāna*).[46] Vātsyāyana begins by recommending this form of marriage only for those who could not attain a wife through the normal selection process because of some lack of qualification, but soon avers its advantages and conformity to dharma, and even suggests its superiority over marriage by selection, because of its basis in mutual affection (*anurāgātmakatvāt*).[47]

It is difficult to know what the reality of the *gandharva* or 'love-match' marriage might have been in courtly circles. It had been widely represented in the earlier epics like the *Mahābhārata*, where it formed a sort of *ex post facto* justification for non-marital liaisons which led to offspring. In subsequent times it may have acted as a similar justificatory strategy for a variety of unorthodox liaisons and methods of 'acquiring' (or abducting) women among the nobility.[48] Yet it was very unlikely that such 'love matches' were in any way common in courtly circles. This is for two basic reasons. First, because, as we saw above, marriage itself was not in any case a *necessary* end or precondition for the development of romantic attachment, and so, because men of rank could always enjoy erotic love outside the conjugal relation, there was little compulsion to make it either the basis or precondition of marriage. Second, and just as

[45] *KS* 3.2.41; repeated, with slight variance, in *Ratirahasya* 11.20.

[46] See *KS* 3.5.12–18. [47] *KS* 3.3.1, 4; 3.5.28–30.

[48] *PY* depicts an 'elopement' of the captured prince Vatsarāja and Mahāsena Pradyota's daughter Vāsavadattā from his palace at Ujjain. On learning of the elopement, Vāsavadattā's mother, Queen Aṅgarikā, tries to throw herself from the upper palace in shame before her husband stops her by saying that the marriage has been arranged through the *gandharva* way. Then, the royal couple (contrary to the directions of the *Kāmasūtra*, and tellingly) perform the marriage rite themselves with pictures of the two lovers.

important, was the fact that marriage was typically motivated not by individual love interest but by the socio-economic concerns of the families in question, for whom marriage represented the seal of some formal or informal alliance. This was always the primary concern in the marriages of men and women of rank. Among royal houses, as mentioned in chapter 1, marriage formed the 'seal' on various types of political alliance and was recommended by texts on polity as an instrument of political gain.[49] It was very typical for the fortunes of royal houses to be altered significantly by the effects of key marriage alliances. The Guptas, Vākāṭakas and Puṣyabhūtis, to name the most prominent of the dynasties we have been examining in this study, all rose to prominence in part through the inheritance of patrimonies from strategic marital alliances.

The more likely scenario for courtship in aristocratic households, given both the compulsions of dynastic marriage and the recommendations for 'courtship' after marriage, was probably in the king's negotiation of his relations with women of the *antaḥpura*. According to Vātsyāyana, women of the *antaḥpura* vied with one another for their interests (as diverse as they may have been) in relation to the king. If we follow Vātsyāyana, who recommends various courses of policy to this end for senior (*jyeṣṭā*) and junior (*kaniṣṭā*) wives as well as concubines (*punarbhū*), the *antaḥpura* had a potentially charged and antagonistic character – and a social texture largely homologous to that of the realm of 'open' politics, or the *sabhā*. This is manifestly evident in the way in which the king was to meet the women of the *antaḥpura*. According to Vātsyāyana, he met with them together each afternoon, assigned them places and conversed with each in a manner which suited their rank.[50] And each day, these women, like the *sāmanta*s who attended the assembly hall, deputed gifts to him (garlands, scented oils and clothes) which were returned to them as 'grace' or 'favour' (*nirmālya*). Later the king selected the woman he would sleep with that night by choosing from among the gifts presented to him with the seals of various queens and concubines.[51] The scope for antagonism here was considerable, and the king, as master of his household, had to negotiate his relations with the women of the *antaḥpura* carefully, assigning his attention to them in a matter befitting their various ranks, exercising *dākṣiṇya*, or kind courtesy, to all of his wives even as he

[49] See *AS* 7.22–9 and *NiS* 9.6. In *SV* King Udayana regains his kingdom from a usurper by marital alliance with the house of King Darśaka of Magadha. Such recommendations also applied to the lower-ranking court nobility. In the case of a prince in disfavour, for example, the *Arthaśāstra* recommends taking up residence at the court of a friendly neighbouring prince, accumulating troops, making compacts with forest chiefs, winning over seducible parties in one's father's kingdom, and entering into marriage alliances with arms-bearing men of rank, *AS* 1.18.7.

[50] *KS* 4.2.75–6.

[51] See *KS* 4.2.73–4; 80–1.

may have favoured one. Though this depiction of the *antaḥpura* is at one level highly idealised and simplistic, as Vātysāyana himself suggests when he treats the question of the sexual needs of the women residing within the *antaḥpura*, they are nevertheless clearly the operative dynamics presented to the audiences of most of the dramatic representations of courtship. Indeed, the dynamics of the women of the palace establishment forms the immediate backdrop for several key courtly dramas composed between the fourth and seventh centuries CE which I would like to examine more closely in the remainder of this chapter.

Fantasy and power in the palace drama

I want to explore briefly some of the salient features of a few Sanskrit plays which involve the courtship of a king and a maiden of noble rank. This theme was a popular one in early Sanskrit dramas, and no theme was more well-known than the love-exploits of the legendary king Udayana Vatsarāja of Kauśambī. We have at least four extant plays dealing with his career – the Trivandrum author's *Pratijñāyaugandharāyaṇa* and *Svapnavāsavadatta* and King Harṣa's *Ratnāvalī* and *Priyadarśikā*. To these may be added plays having similar themes, particularly Kālidāsa's *Mālavikāgnimitra*, and to a lesser extent, his *Vikramorvaśīya*.

All of these plays portray the erotic love between a king and an unmarried virgin of noble birth in the context of a largely polygamous royal household. I summarise the plots of the Vatsarāja plays and Kālidāsa's *Mālavikāgnimitra* for the purposes of my analysis. The 'first' of the Udayana plays,[52] *Pratijñāyaugandharāyaṇa*, treats King Udayana's capture and imprisonment at the hands of his rival Mahāsena Pradyota, king of Ujjain, through the ruse of a false elephant. While in captivity, Udayana wins the heart of Mahāsena's daughter Vāsavadattā, who is at the time being visited for selection by various suitors, and, through the designs of his minister, Yaugandharāyaṇa, escapes with her to Kauśambī where they are married by *gandharva* rite.

Harṣa's *Priyadarśikā* deals with King Udayana's love of the princess Priyadarśikā, daughter of the king Dṛḍhavarman of Aṅga. We are told at the beginning of this play that Priyadarśikā had earlier been promised to Udayana by her father, to the great annoyance of another suitor, the king of Kalinga, who, thinking Udayana to be still imprisoned by Mahāsena of Ujjain, attacks Aṅga with a view towards abducting her. Though he

[52] I have 'sequenced' these plays through a reconstruction of their dramatic action rather than by their chronological composition. They are roughly contemporaenous, with the Trivandrum plays probably dating to the eighth-century Pallava court and the Harṣa plays to the seventh century.

captures Dṛḍhavarman, Priyadarśikā is escorted safely to a neighbouring ally's realm by the king's loyal chamberlain who intends on making good his master's promise (*Svāminam anṛṇaṁ kariṣyāmi* literally 'relieve his debt') to Udayana. But before he can do so, Priyadarśikā is carried off by unknown assailants, who turn out to be King Udayana's avaricious generals. She thus arrives, unbeknownst to all, at Udayana's palace as war booty, and is placed in Vāsavadattā's retinue, where she is then courted by the king.

Svapnavāsavadattam begins with King Udayana's household and retainers living in a frontier encampment, having been ousted from Kauśambī by a usurper to the throne. Udayana's ministers can think of no other means of regaining the kingdom but an alliance with King Darśaka of Magadha, best achieved by marrying his beautiful daughter Padmāvatī. Darśaka, however, has flatly refused to give Padmāvatī as long as queen Vāsavadattā, Udayana's favourite, is still alive. So with the connivance of Vāsavadattā, the ministers inform Udayana that his wife has perished by a fire in the Lāvanaka forest. In actuality she is deposited, in disguise, at the court of Darśaka, where she acts as retainer and companion to Padmāvatī, who is soon given by her father to the still-grieving Udayana. Udayana's kingdom is restored and Vāsavadattā's identity eventually revealed during a visit of the newly wed couple to Mahāsena Pradyota's court.

King Harṣa's *Ratnāvalī* portrays a romance between King Udayana and Ratnāvalī, daughter of the Sinhala king Vikramabāhu. In this play we learn that Yaugandharāyaṇa, without Vatsarāja's knowledge, had earlier requested the princess Ratnāvalī from the Sinhala monarch because of a widely known prophecy that she would wed a universal sovereign. The Sinhala king, who like Darśaka is unwilling to be the instrument of Vāsavadattā's uneasiness, at first declines the suit, but afterwards, learning of Vāsavadattā's supposed demise, consents. But the princess is lost in a shipwreck en route to Vatsarāja's abode. Recognised by a merchant, Ratnāvalī is conveyed to the minister Yaugandharāyaṇa, who in turn deposits her in the queen's retinue, her identity concealed from all, where events take their course and a romance between her and the king begins.

The hero of Kālidāsa's *Mālavikāgnimitra* is not Udayana of Kauśambī but Agnimitra of Vidiśā, son of Puśyamitra, usurper of the Mauryan throne. We learn that King Agnimitra had been offered the sister of a Vidarbhan prince, one Mādhavasena, in order to seal a matrimonial alliance between the families. But while escorting the princess Mālavikā to her new home, the bride's party is ambushed by Mādhavasena's brother, Yajñasena. Mādhavasena is made captive, but Mālavikā escapes with the minister Sumati, who are in turn ambushed (and separated) by forest people on their way to Vidiśā. As a result of these events, Agnimitra deputes his general Vīrasena, bastard-brother of his queen, Dhariṇī, to punish Yajñasena. On his campaign Vīrasena comes across the princess Mālavika among the forest people and ignorant of her identity sends her to his sister where she enters the household of her destiny as a servant in Queen Dhariṇī's retinue. Noticed by the king, the courtship begins.

Several features unite these dramas. First, as the brief plot synopses make clear, each romance unfolds against the backdrop of high dynastic politics; and in each case there is significant political advantage for the king in marrying the maiden in question. In the case of Udayana, his successive marriages not only gain him alliances with the kings of Avanti (Mālwā), Aṅga, Magadha and Sinhala, but they also coincide with important political victories against his enemies and in one case even assist him in regaining his kingdom from a usurper. Likewise in the case of Agnimitra, Mālavikā's acquisition seals both an alliance with Mādhavasena and coincides with a pacification of his brother Yajñasena, who rule under him jointly as vassals at the conclusion of the play.

The plot narratives sketched above, however, actually occupy little more than the explanatory scaffolding for the more prominent dramatic action which unfolds in each play, namely the developing romance between the king and the maiden in question. It may be tempting, then, to see these intricately framed plots of political ambition as merely perfunctory requirements of the genre (which should see the hero lifted up into prosperity at the end of the play), without any other significance. But, for courtly audiences, these dimensions would have been necessary and thematically important elements of the dramas. Such scenarios would have had strong resonances with their own lives. Indeed, it has been convincingly argued that the events of Kālidāsa's *Mālavikāgnimitra* present a wholesale transposition of relations between the Gupta and Vākāṭaka courts onto Mauryan-Śuṅga times.[53] If this is true, then it would seem that Kālidāsa actually wished to tantalise his audience by veiled reference to events they would have been more than familiar with. It is not, at current, possible to present a similar analysis about the plays of the Trivandrum author or Harṣa. Having said this, it is also true that the court of at least one of these authors, that of King Harṣa, would have been well-familiar with the importance of marriage as an instrument of dynastic alliance.[54]

[53] Noted by Warder, *Indian Kāvya Literature*, vol. III, p. 129 ff. and developed more recently by Hans Bakker, 'Vidiśā in the Days of Gupta Hegemony: A Theatre of Broken Dreams', in *Festschrift für Hermann Kulke* (in press).

[54] Harṣa and the men of his court would have been witness to the effects of several important marital alliances in their lifetimes. Harṣa's grandfather Ādityavardhana (*c.* 555–80)

The significant point, however, may be that whatever evocations these plots may have had with contemporary political events, in all of these dramas the events are placed at the courts of legendary kings. This projection of present concerns onto a putative past may have indeed been preferred to the presentation of realities closer to home, where various members of the audience may have been implicated in any such representation. We may recall the anger of Vāsavadattā at seeing her own romance with King Udayana misrepresented on the stage in Act 3 of Harṣa's *Priyadarśikā*. While courtly praise literature openly celebrated the hero/patron by name, love literature, by contrast, tended to operate through either hypothetical, generic characters (*nāyaka* and *nāyikā*) or the settings of distant and legendary kings. This generic or once-removed depiction of love and politics in erotic poetry and palace romances, I would suggest, facilitated the creation of a relatively open and reiterable framework, particularly around the topic of erotic 'love', into which courtly agents could variously insert their own immediate relationships.

The main dramatic events in these plays take place almost entirely inside the palace, and more specifically, within the royal pleasure garden, or *krīḍāvana*, attached to the king's residence. The prominence of such arcadias in courtly literature, and their overwhelming association with erotic love, should prompt us to pause for a moment on this setting. Gardens have remained a largely neglected aspect of courtly life in early India, though their importance as a regularised feature of royal households long preceded the famous Mughal gardens which have been preserved and celebrated from colonial times.[55] The role of the garden is best understood, for the present purposes, if we keep in mind that daily life in the palace, with its minutely calibrated protocols, was open to the more or less constant scrutiny of its more powerful members, either directly or through the eyes of others. Nearly every space was 'marked' in some way. The garden, by contrast, provided a 'neutral' space for the king's

married Mahāsenāguptadevī, sister of the later Gupta king ruling at Magadha. The implications of the alliance that this marriage sealed meant that two later Gupta princes (after the family had moved to Malwa) were sent to the Puṣyabhūti household when Harṣa and his brother were children. Even more important was the marriage of Harṣa's sister, Rājyaśrī, to Prince Grahavarman of the powerful Maukhari family of Kanauj. It is their connection with this house which allowed the Puṣyabhūtis to rise to such prominence (and relocate to Kanauj) during the complex events which unfolded at the beginning of the seventh century. Later Harṣa himself secured the alliance of the Maitrakas of Vallabhi, crucial allies against the circle of *sāmanta*s under the influence of his enemy, the Cālukya king Pulakeśin II, by marrying his daughter to the Maitraka king Dhruvasena II in 632 CE.

55 Though ubiquitous in written sources from early historic times, few if any palace gardens have been preserved in city and palace excavations, barring the important site at the palace fortress at Sigiriya, probably dating to the fifth or sixth century CE.

liaisons – in contrast to those carried out in particular residences where the presence of the couple may have easily been detected. The garden thus provided a measure of secrecy and protection to the king's sexual life when it was needed. It functioned as a sort of 'outside' place at once beyond the scrutiny of the court yet within the safety of its confines. The garden, with its densely shaded bowers and pavilions, enabled lovers and their companions to constitute and violate intimacies very easily, a fact which made it the ideal convention in drama, where characters continually eavesdrop on one another to discern their true feelings. For members of the royal household, the garden was thus the place of seduction and intrigue *par excellence*.[56]

In the plays reviewed above, the garden intrigue is given its particular character by the impingement of the interests of the king's senior wife or wives onto the budding romance. The queen perceives the new entrant as a potential threat to her own position in the king's heart (and in the palace establishment). In Harṣa's and Kālidāsa's plays, the king is placed in the difficult position of assuring the queen that her pre-eminence remains unchallenged – a task requiring the skilful display of *dākṣiṇya*, or courteous consideration – while at the same time pursuing his love affair behind her back. In the face of the king's repeated intransigence in the matter, the queen, in three of the dramas (*Priyadarśikā*, *Ratnāvalī* and *Mālavikāgnimitra*) resorts to confining the heroine. It is only when the newcomer's identity is revealed as a princess of note, ostensibly already promised to or destined for the king, that she is accepted by the senior queen, who addresses her by the appropriate title of 'sister'.[57] In the case of Harṣa's plays, this is more than figurative, since the maidens in question turn out to be daughters of Vāsavadattā's maternal uncles. Queen Vāsavadattā signals her approval by herself offering the heroines in marriage to the king.

In *Svapnavāsavadatta* the dramatic conceit is inverted, and in order to acquire the needed dynastic alliance the queen must herself go into disguise and enter into the household of the prospective wife, silently witnessing the union of her husband with the new rival. Here it is not the king's incorrigible errancy but his unswerving devotion which is demonstrated to the queen. Though the roles are reversed, in all the plays the

[56] The garden also formed the setting for less salubrious sexual liaisons. See, for example, the narrative of Upahāravarman in *DK*, ch. 3, p. 113. The *Kāmasūtra* in its chapter on liaisons with other men's wives recommends that once such women were brought into the royal household, that they were coaxed into playing games and 'seeing the beautiful places in the palace'. These attractions were deemed 'delightful' (*rāmaṇīyaka*), and had the effect of predisposing the woman to the king's advances, *KS* 5.5.14–17.

[57] The senior wife was to treat the new entrant 'as if she had the quality of a sister' (*bhāginikāvat*), *KS* 4.2.5.

queen is vindicated and reaffirmed in her status, the new princess integrated into the household as a junior wife and happy 'sister' of the queen, with the desired political alliance being achieved, and news arrives of some military victory bringing the king political fortune. The external and internal politics facing the royal house are thus neatly resolved.

If we return for a moment to the sociology of the royal household, to note that though the intrigues of the garden, as is clear in the plays reviewed above, seem to mirror events happening in the wider world driven by the politics of the assembly, they also differed with respect to courtly audiences in one key respect. Though both were saturated with 'convention' and enmeshed in wider norms of court sociability, the politics of the *sabhā* remained relatively 'open' and 'visible' to the wider society of the court, the subterfuge and intrigue generated by its in-built antagonisms displayed through visible relations of deference and decorum. In the *antaḥpura*, while similar dynamics obtained – dynamics which invoked the wider political relations of the outside world in the case of dynastic marriages – they remained largely hidden from the court as a whole. Yet, ironically, it is the intrigues of the pleasure garden which formed the favourite theme of courtly representation, giving what may have been hidden in real life, the character of spectacle before the court as a whole. As the intrigues of the inner palace could be quite consequential for lives of the wider circles of courtiers and underlords who formed the audiences of courtly drama, it is possible to surmise that much of the pleasure gained by courtly audiences in the depiction of palace dramas was the palpable excitement of viewing a world, depicted through suggestion and disguise, which was normally hidden.[58]

The plays witness a further and crucial reversal. For, in marked contrast to the normative structuring of the royal household, the audience shared a particular sort of omniscience, privy not only to the inner desires of each character, but also to the wider political ramifications of the courtship itself. This knowledge, by contrast, is partially or wholly occluded to the various characters within the romance, most notably the king as main protagonist. The marriages are arranged either through the less-than-straightforward designs of the chief counsellor (the redoubtable Yaugandharāyaṇa in the Udayana plays, assisted in *Svapnavāsavadatta* by the queen) or through fate itself (in *Mālavikāgnimitra*). Yet in each play the king as main protagonist remains wrapped in a gauze of almost childlike innocence, concerned only with pursuing his love-infatuation.[59] To

[58] We are told in the prologues of the *Rv* and *Pd* that these plays were performed at the request of the assembly of *sāmanta*s 'dependent on the feet of Harṣa'.

[59] See the remarks of Goodwin, *Playworld*, pp. 163–76.

effect this ignorance in Harṣa and Kālidāsa, the heroine is introduced to the royal household under a concealed identity. Once placed in the queen's retinue, the lovers are almost instinctively drawn to one another, and fall in love at first sight. Their love, after being frustrated by the queen is vindicated in a moment of recognition when the heroine's identity is revealed.[60]

The device of the princess's concealed identity allows the effective separation of their romantic and political narratives and provides the fundamental and necessary narrative tension which drives the plots to their conclusions. The effect of this separation was to create a kind of hermetically sealed affective world where love took its course. Yet, interestingly, this device is not meant to exalt love beyond or set it against the exigencies of political life, to redeem it or make it 'transcendent'. Indeed, the high and, to readers trained up in European courtly love, the disappointing degree of resolution at the conclusion of these plays would prevent any such interpretation – for the announcement of the maiden's identity seems to both allay the queen's jealousy as well as exhaust the king's infatuation, thus producing a happy ending, where both conjugal felicity and political success are seamlessly intertwined. Love in these dramas does not transcend political power, but rather is viewed as its necessary component.

The separation of the political and romantic narratives of these plays suggests instead, I think, two points, with which we can conclude this chapter. First, such narrative devices operationalised the explicit linkages between power and romance that were built into artistocratic society. The very topic of dynastic alliance and political conquest was highly aphrodisiacal; conversely the realm of love is deeply enmeshed with fantasies of power. While the perfect alignment of these realms was probably only rarely achieved by men at court, they nevertheless seemed to constantly dream of it.

But, more than this, and perhaps of greater significance, is that the separation of these realms creates for the courtly audience a sort of pleasure of 'deferred signification'. The plays split the worlds of romance and pleasure precisely so that the audience could repeatedly engage in linking and delinking them, as it moved from the occluded world of the pleasure

[60] Though from the vantage point of courtly sociology, it might be plausibly argued that such representations sought to plaster over the sometimes not so palatable methods through which women were 'acquired' (and in the case of *PY*, arguably, abducted) for the royal household, such an interpretation is vitiated by the fact that should such 'legitimacy' have been necessary, it would not have been facilitated by the projection of events into legendary pasts. It makes more sense, I think, to read these conventions in terms of courtly subjectivity.

garden with its sublimely unknowing hero, to the 'open' world of political fortune and strategic design as envisioned by the minister. The split subjectivity of the audience here, knowing what the king does not and yet sympathising with him as protagonist, gave the court intrigue its unique appeal to courtly audiences – allowing them a vantage point which they rarely gained in their own lives! It no doubt also helped to overdetermine love as a realm of self-regard, a topic which we shall examine in the final chapter of this book.

7 Anxiety and romance in court society

> How can a man who serves others savour the taste of pleasure?
>
> *MR* 3.4

It is now possible to take a closer look at the internal dynamics of sexual love and erotic pleasure in courtly texts. How were courtship and sexual love actually conceived and what were their 'psychological' dimensions? Such questions are prompted, in a sense, by the sources themselves, which, for all the prescriptive literature's emphasis on the different types of lovers (particularly in regard to *nāyikās*), tend to present scenarios of largely generic and unplaceable characters. Court poets produced thousands of shorter individual poems which describe particular scenes, emotions and contexts between unnamed or anonymous lovers. To this sort of representation may be added the highly sexualised yet generic descriptions of 'courtly' women which formed standard sections of narrative genres. We noted this earlier in the *Mānasollāsa*'s recommendation that the king be surrounded by onlooking women dressed in their finery as he held court.

This chapter will place under critical scrutiny courtly conceptions of erotic love. The tendency towards universalisation is both remarkable and significant, not because courtly literature represents a meditation on the universal experience of love (as typically conceived by modern humanistic scholarship), but quite the opposite, because in its tendency towards abstraction, courtly literature perhaps assumes its greatest specificity. The generic and abstract character of *nāyaka* and *nāyikā* in courtly poetry made these personae eminently open and 'habitable' categories which members at court were implicitly encouraged to 'enter'. This is perhaps obvious enough. But it also made them susceptible to investment with wider concerns of self and society. It is this investment, which this chapter hopes to tease out, which explains the hypertrophied role of erotic love in the mental world of the court.

I will argue below that through a close attention to the courtly commentary on erotic pleasure as well as to the language used to denote wider courtly affiliations, it is possible to show why erotic love remained the preferred topic of courtly poetry. This is not because of any innate cultural tendency towards sensuality or openness of sexual morality, but because people at court preferred to 'think' about wider social relationships through the world of erotic love.

First, a note about terminology. Understanding the discursive provenance of the terms which come to refer to romantic love in medieval India is particularly difficult because their interrelation shifts between aesthetic and religious traditions, and over time. Nevertheless, reading the early texts, one can distinguish between two different types of words: those that refer to the physical desire for and pleasure arising from sexual union, which generally include terms like *kāma* and *rati*; and those terms which refer to the more general dispositions of adoration, attachment, affection and participation that lovers were to share to varying degrees with one another, typically designated by terms like *rāga*, *anurāga*, *śṛṅgāra* and *bhakti*. In drawing this distinction, I am not suggesting that these terms functioned to distinguish between physical sex and a higher form of love. In the case of the relations between lovers, as described in the *Kāmasūtra*, *Nāṭyaśāstra* and other texts of *kāvya* tradition, these two types of terms are seen to be related and complementary, rather than opposed. These latter terms could encompass or include *kāma* within themselves. This does not mean, however, that these two sets of terms were identical. The latter set of terms, particularly those of *bhakti* and *anurāga*, were used more generally to characterise various relations between men in medieval Indian society. Significantly, the rise of these terms in political parlance occurs precisely at the time when *kāvya* emerges as a discursive form and love as a courtly theme. And it is through some attention to the wider usages of these terms that we may learn something of the preponderance of erotic themes among the ruling discourses of medieval India.

The jewel of games

We might begin with an early representation of frustrated erotic love from Aśvaghoṣa's *Buddhacarita*, a verse poem which casts the Buddha's princely life into a courtly mould. Attributed to the Kuṣāṇa court in the first century CE, this text forms one of our first examples of what would later become a stock scenario for courtly poets: the young prince's procession through the royal city. In Aśvaghoṣa's account, the young prince Gautama comes forth from his residence, as directed by his father's loyal chief minister Udayin, to enter the Padmaṣaṇḍa pleasure garden, with its beautiful lotus ponds, flower pavilions and lovelorn women. Incited by Udayin, the women approach the prince and an elaborately described encounter ensues in which the women literally assault the prince in order to seduce him. They 'arm themselves' (*prāvṛtya*) and 'attack' the prince through various means: binding him with garlands and striking him with words, according to Aśvaghoṣa, as if they were elephant goads.[1] One woman tells the prince to look around him at the various trees, flowers and birds, for each signified desire in some way.

Perhaps expectedly, the prince remains impervious to their blandishments, a point which underscores his growing dissolution with worldly life. I want to put aside for the moment this apparent renunciatory theme to highlight the chief metaphor used to describe his encounter with the women – that of 'battle'. Aśvaghoṣa here anticipates what would become perhaps the chief courtly conceit used to describe relationships between lovers. Courtship and sex were conceived of as an elaborate contest or 'game' between the parties concerned – indeed, it was known as the 'jewel among games' (*krīḍāratna*).[2] Nearly all elements of courtship and sex were understood from the vantage point of a 'combat' between lovers. Lovers quarrelled and fought for a variety of reasons, most typically the male lover's wayward tendencies. Such fights required strategies of conciliation and even acts of propitiation. In the *bhāṇa* plays we learn that lovers used agents or 'ministers' (recall that *viṭa*s, *pīṭhamarda*s or *vidūṣaka*s were the 'ministers' (*mantrin*s) of the *nāyaka* and *nāyikā*) to negotiate 'treaties' as if they were conducting high politics. Love-quarrels were just the beginning, for all the moments of courtship can be understood as tactical moments (glancing, playing garden games and sexual union itself) in the larger warfare which was love. Biting, scratching and striking were common accoutrements to the sexual act itself for lovers of intense passion, as they were thought to train the body to be attentive to the senses.[3] The sources present a certain delectation and pleasure in this contrariness as a mark of the sophisticated appreciation of courtly love. When a royal scribe in the *Pādataḍitilaka* complains bitterly before the *goṣṭhī* that his paramour, the courtesan Madanasenikā, has meted out to him the greatest of humiliations by kicking him in the head, and seeks redress, he becomes the laughing stock of the assembly. This is because, it is announced, he is too foolish to understand that 'being received' by

[1] *BC* 4.26 ff.

[2] See the discussion of love as a game, but primarily in the context of *kṛṣṇabhakti*, in Lee Siegel, *Sacred and Profane Dimensions of Love in Indian Traditions as Exemplified in the 'Gitagovinda' of Jayadeva* (Delhi: Oxford University Press, 1990).

[3] These activities are treated at length in the *Kāmasūtra*, though Vātsyāyana cautions that they be practised with restraint as they could potentially lead to the injury or even death of a female partner. See *KS* 2.7.27–9. For the justification of their use as heightening sensual awareness, see *DhVS* 42.

the feet of one's lover, like that of a king, was not a humiliation but an honour, an expression of the lover's favour![4]

As in courtly traditions which grew up in Europe, erotic love itself was deemed a form of suffering, a suffering that in one sense grew from the inevitable separation which was part of the conventions of courtship. But even more generally, sexual attraction was deemed a form of suffering. Recall how the hero Nala suffers unbearably once 'smitten' by the arrows of Kāma, in the form of Damayantī. He retreats from the assembly to the pleasure garden, with distress and 'shame' (*sāpatrapatā*) at the manifestation of his condition. Part of the suffering and shame which Nala experiences at this point has little to do with Damayantī except in the most general of senses, for he has, we should remember, not even laid eyes upon her yet. To understand this deeper sense of affliction which erotic love represented, I want to turn to what the didactic texts have to say about the matter.

The conquest of the self

In this section I will place the courtly understanding of erotic pleasure, in the context of discourses of self-mastery. I will limit myself strictly to the treatises on polity which purport to instruct the prince and, to a lesser degree, the *Kāmasūtra* itself. The sorts of concerns which I will be addressing have usually been seen as an impingement of 'brahmanical' or religious ideology into a world of untrammelled pleasure or Machiavellian politics.[5] Yet while the theories I am dealing with here relied to some extent on ideas developed in religious and philosophical circles, their concerns were entirely worldly. Courtly life presented its own set of exigencies and problems which demanded particular strategies and solutions. These problems were 'ethical' to the extent that they sought to formulate the general relations that a man was to have both with himself and with those around him. As we shall see, these concerns were almost entirely male, and when the discourses of polity speak of inner workings of pleasure, they always have in mind a man of noble birth.

We saw in chapter 2 that Vātsyāyana defined pleasure with specific reference to a notion of the self comprised of the senses, the mind and the

[4] See Viṣṇunāga's lament, *Pādatāḍitaka* 9, 13, and the *goṣṭhī*'s response, playing on the idea that honour and grace were bestowed by being 'accepted by the feet' (*pādaparigṛhīta*) of one's lord. His punishment is that he should watch (as a jealous lover) Madanasenikā 'grace' the leader's own head with her lac-dyed and ornamented foot! On the other hand, the kicking of a lover on his head was the limit of violence a *nāyikā* could inflict on a man, according to Yaśodhara's commentary on *KS* 2.10.45.

[5] See Lee Siegel, *Fires of Love*.

soul. This concept of self, drawing on firmly implanted theories across the philosophical spectrum in early India, is also represented, almost identically, in the manuals on political conduct. It may be represented visually, following Kāmandaka's *Nītisāra*, in the following manner:[6]

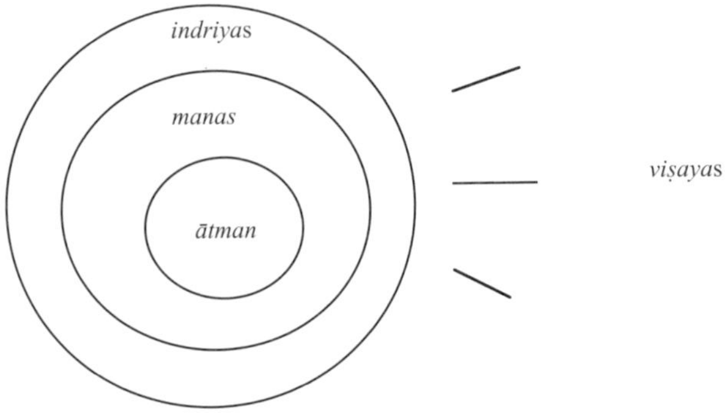

The central constituent here, which could stand in for the whole, was the *ātman*. In both the *Kāmasūtra* and *Nītisāra* the next entity mentioned was the mind, or *manas*.[7] The outermost constituents of the self were the five sensory organs or *indriyas* – ear, skin, eyes, tongue and nose – along with five other 'external' organs – the sexual organ, the anus, hands, feet and mouth – which together formed the ten faculties of action and cognition.

The self's most important and defining element, the soul (*ātman*), stood at the centre of the structure as its permanent core. It was comparatively inactive, preferring instead to act through the agency of less permanent sheaths which surrounded it in successive layers. Consequently, the outer layers of the self surrounding the *ātman* were considered to be *karaṇas* – 'instruments' or 'means' of knowledge and action, ultimately in the service of the *ātman*. The *karaṇas* were further divided into internal and external 'instruments' or 'organs' (*antaḥkaraṇa, bāhirkaraṇa*). The major internal organ which Kāmandaka and Vātsyāyana are concerned with is the *manas*, or mind.[8] The external organs consisted of the *indriyas*,

[6] *NiS* 1.33–6.

[7] In other formulations different evolutes or layers like *buddhi*, *cit* and *ahaṃkāra* interposed themselves between the *ātman* and the *manas*. Kāmandaka is aware of these entities but regards them as identical to the mind: 'perfect knowledge (*vijñāna*), the heart (*hṛdaya*), consciousness (*citta*), the mind (*manas*) and the intellect (*buddhi*) are synonymous and are caused by the *ātman* to discriminate between what should be done and what should not be done', *NiS* 1.30.

[8] Other formulations include *buddhi*, *cit*, etc. as *antaḥkaraṇas*. Kāmandaka considers not only *manas*, but also *ātman* as an *antaḥkaraṇa*, *NiS* 1.35. This would seem atypical. He implies in 1.30 (see fn. 7) that the *ātman* has a more determinative role. For different formulations of the *antaḥkaraṇas*, see John Grimes, *A Concise Dictionary of Indian Philosophy* (Albany: SUNY Press, 1996), s.v.

limbs, speech and the excretory organs. Each of these organs, both internal and external, had an activity (*kriyā*) appropriate to it, according to Kāmandaka. The sensory organs (*indriyas*), for example, were to engage with their appropriate fields (*viṣaya*). The activity of the sense organs formed the basis for more complex internal processes. So the mind (*manas*) organised incoming but indeterminate sensory data into determinate perceptual forms in a process called *saṁkalpa*. As a result of this, various affective or volitional states (*bhāvas*) arose in the mind like doubt, imagination and, relevant to the topic at hand, pleasure and desire. The mind was crucially situated; it formed the link between the outer sense organs and the more internal parts of the self and was the first element of sentience in perception.

Relations between elements of the self were not simply based on function, but also implied hierarchy and mastery. Conceptions of the self had long deployed political imagery in conceiving of the inner relations of the self. The famous formulation in the Upaṇiṣads, for example, compared the *ātman* to a king in his chariot, with his driver (the intellect) using his reigns (the mind), to control the five horses (the senses) as it ranged across the paths of his realm.[9] By the period with which we are concerned, the image had changed considerably. In an eighth-century inscription of the Rāṣṭrakūṭa king Amoghavarṣa, the soul is compared to the king, the mind to his minister, the group of senses to his circle of feudatories and speech and the other organs to various royal servants.[10] Such metaphors not only reveal the evolution of political structures as ways of imagining the insides of people but, just as importantly, reveal something about the relationships that men at court were enjoined to have with themselves. So the normal and properly 'functioning' self not only implied relations of internal hierarchy, but also involved active mastery and even coercion. The mind's activity of resolving indeterminate sensory matter received from the *indriyas* was not simply a generic psychic process, but a marshalling and discipline of the senses as instruments in the same manner a minister bearing the burden of rule effected the will of his master with regard to his feudatories. The mind ruled the external organs, which in turn engaged with the objects of the senses, regarded as 'domains' or 'fields' (*viṣaya*) of mastery.

The texts on polity are emphatic that the training of the prince should begin with a turning inward to master the various elements of his own self, particularly his senses. This was known as 'conquering the senses' (*indriyajaya*) and according to Kāmandaka, it made a young prince fit for the knowledge of the *śāstra*.[11] Kauṭilya calls it the whole of his teaching.[12]

[9] See *Kathopaniṣad*, 1.3.3–4. [10] *EI* 18 (1925–6), no. 26, p. 255.
[11] *NiS* 1.22. [12] *AS* 1.6.3.

Since in the hierarchic logic of the self's structure, the command of the mind included mastery over all that it should command, the conquest of the senses presupposed an ordered mind. And an ordered mind was a prerequisite for success in policy. Kāmandaka puts it like this: 'How can one who cannot subdue the mind (*manasaḥ sannirbahane*), conquer the earth bounded by the oceans?'[13] Conquest of the senses was to be effected through that paramount quality which we have encountered above, *vinaya*, discipline or humility.[14] It is perhaps worth noting that the term *vinaya* was conceptually (and etymologically) related to concepts of 'policy' (*nīti*) and 'directed conduct' (*naya*) which formed the goal of the prince's and the courtier's training. While *naya* and *nīti* generally referred to conduct in relation to others, *vinaya* denoted conduct towards oneself. The position of the manuals is thus that an individual's conduct and policy at court was presupposed and sprung from 'self-policy' or self-discipline. As Kāmandaka put it, 'self-discipline (*vinaya*) is the root (*mūla*) of policy (*naya*)'.[15] This is because, according to Kāmandaka, perfect knowledge of the *śāstra* could only be obtained through discipline.[16] The prince was to begin with the practice of self-discipline as the means to effect mastery over the senses and gain proper instruction in policy. The important point behind these assertions is that in the manuals that trained ministers, princes and other men of the court, the ideal foundation of one's external policy at court was a sustained labour and care (or to use the language of the sources, a conquest) with regard to one's own mind and body.

Self-discipline and mastery over the senses were recommended to men at court in all of their pursuits, including sexual relationships. The *Nāṭyaśāstra*, for example, includes *dhīra*, or self-control (the capacity to direct one's own actions), as an integral characteristic in all of its categorisations of *nāyaka*s, even the sporting and playful hero (*dhīralalita*).[17] The *Kāmasūtra* too recommends that 'he who knows the principles of this *śāstra* is one who has conquered his senses (*jitendriya*) and will be able to conduct himself in the world and firmly guard *dharma*, *artha* and *kāma*'.[18] This point is also made by Kauṭilya, who warns that the king should not deprive himself of pleasures but pursue *kāma* without contravening the other goals of human life.[19] It is perhaps peculiar to conceive of the enjoyment of pleasures as entailing self-discipline. Yet we may recall that it is implied in Vātsyāyana's very definition of pleasure as the activity of the sense organs when favourably engaged in their fields of operation,

[13] *NiS* 1.36. [14] Kāmandaka equates victory of the senses with *vinaya*, *NiS* 1.22.
[15] *NiS* 1.21. [16] *Ibid.* Cf. *AS* 1.6.1. [17] *NS* 34.18–19.
[18] *KS* 7.2.58. [19] *AS* 1.7.3.

as directed by the mind along with the soul.[20] The relation of the mind to the senses, here is expressed by the word *adhiṣṭhita*, literally to 'stand over' or 'superintend'. The idea was that sexual pleasure arose not in the senses themselves, but in the mind as it directed and organised incoming sensory data.[21] The mind, once again, was crucial; for as the immediate superintendent of the senses it predisposed them towards their sense-objects. In the event of sensual excess, the mind was ultimately to blame.[22] The point here is that the discipline in regard to the senses, which texts like the *Arthaśāstra* and *Kāmasūtra* recommend, need not be seen as part of some other-worldly yearning for ascetical transcendence. The control of the mind and victory over the senses recommended in courtly manuals, then, had less to do with any critique of worldly life as such, but instead were forms of ethical self-regard that men of the world were to develop within themselves driven largely, I shall show, by exigencies at court. In these manuals the discipline of the senses was not opposed to sensual and worldly enjoyment, it was its precondition.

The dangers of the senses

Why then were sensual pleasures problematic for men of the court? Control over the senses, according to the *Arthaśāstra*, assured an 'avoidance of errors' (*avipratipatti*), errors which most often arose from the excessive pursuance of a particular sense domain.[23] Goaded on, according to Kāmandaka, by an undisciplined mind, 'running wildly like an elephant in the forest of the sense-objects',[24] the senses fixated on the outside world to the detriment of the self. Each of the five senses, according to the *Nītisāra*, was sufficient to bring about the ruin (*vināśa*) of a man.[25] Kāmandaka proceeds to give an example, for each sense, of an animal killed by its pursuance – a deer lured by the melodious sound of the hunter's flute, an elephant ensnared by his desire for the touch of a she-elephant, and so on. In these cases, to which other authors add numerous human examples, the danger was that the pursuit of pleasure had the potential of leaving one vulnerable to attack by one's enemies through neglecting the other demands on the life of a man at court.[26]

The most general idea used to refer to the deployment of the senses in this manner was 'attachment' – denoted in Sanskrit by a number of

[20] *KS* 1.2.11.

[21] Giving rise to pleasure's epithets 'mind-born' (*manasija*, *manoja*) and 'resolution-born' (*saṃkalpaja*).

[22] Kāmandaka says that the mind excites (*prerayate*) the senses with greed for sense-objects as if they were meat preparations, *NiS* 1.29.

[23] *AS* 6.1.2.

[24] *NiS* 1.27.

[25] *NiS* 1.52. ff.

[26] Examples are numerous, but see *AS* 1.6.5; also *KS* 1.2.44.

terms with differing connotations. There were derivatives from the verb root √*sañj* (*sakta*), which had a potentially negative sense of sticking or adhering to something. There were also derivatives of the root (*anu*) + √*rañj*, 'to redden', or 'become impassioned', or 'attracted to' (*rāga*, *rakta*, etc.) which had a far greater range of connotations, a great many of them positively associated with human attraction. Yet both terms, and others, were connected to a general principle in early Indian soteriological thinking which sought to distinguish between involvement in worldly activities and detachment from them. Attachment referred to a specific relation of *involvement*, through the mind and the senses, with the outside world. Renunciative philosophies attributed it to different cognitive and mental errors.[27] Release and liberation from the fetters of worldly life for various religious ideologies thus began with a 'detachment', variously conceived, from the objects of the senses.

'Attachment', however, was an equally important concern at court. Overattachment resulting from desires was a concern for courtly discourses at a number of levels. I want to begin with the generalised anxiety over attachment to pleasures as such, specifically its effects on the body as detailed in the manuals concerned with the king's health. Caraka's medical treatise gives a detailed account of the origin, etiology and treatment of an affliction known as *rājayakṣman*, 'the royal disease' or 'king of diseases'.[28] According to Caraka, Dakṣa or Prajāpati gave his twenty-eight daughters to the moon (*soma*) in marriage. But the moon became overly attached (*atisakta*) to one of these daughters, Rohiṇī, and neglected to take care of his body, which suffered a diminishment of unctuousness (*snehakṣaya*) due to the loss of vital fluids.[29] Because the moon married all of the daughters of Prajāpati but did not deal with them equally, being excessively attached to one, the god became angry and exhaled his anger from his mouth. And 'despised by the great, treating his wives unequally, filled with *rajas* and weakness, the moon was attacked by *yakṣmā*'.[30] After seeking the refuge of the gods, Prajāpati was pleased and allowed the moon to be treated by the physicians of the gods, the Aśvins, who cured him. *Yakṣmā* was then dispatched to the human world by the Aśvins, where it entered into human beings through various etiologies.

Two points are worthy of note. First, the cause of the moon's affliction in this account was not sexual union as such, but an *over*-attachment to

[27] See the discussion of the term *rāga* in relation to orthodox schools of philosophy in Surendranath Dasgupta, *A History of Indian Philosophy*, vol. I (Cambridge University Press, 1922).

[28] The double-meaning of *rājayakṣman* is noted and discussed by Zimmerman, *Jungle and the Aroma of Meats*, p. 177.

[29] *CkS* 6.8.4 ff. [30] *CkS* 6.8.7.

one of his wives and the consequent neglect of the others.[31] Caraka says that among the causes of the disease in the human world were both pining for an absent lover as well as overindulgence in sexual intercourse.[32] The emphasis, thus, is not so much on the sex act itself as wasting the body, but on an excessive predisposition or inclination *of the mind* towards sexual desire which was potentially dangerous. Second, the chief physical symptom of *rājayakṣman* was 'excessive thinning' (*atikarśana*) which, according to Caraka, was due to a loss of fluid or unctuousness (*snehakṣaya*).[33] Again, this symptom was the result of a mental disposition rather than the sex act itself. Thinning as a result of pining for one's lover is widely known in both literature and the prescriptive texts on love. If sexual attractiveness and beauty was expressed physiologically, as we saw above, through a plumpening of the body in the manner of the new growth of a budding plant, then the excessive inclination to pleasure could give rise to the reverse process of wasting and desiccation.

The final book of the *Raghuvaṁśa* ends with the blight of *rājayakṣman*, the story of King Agnivarṇa. Installed on the throne by his father, the king conducts his affairs for some years in person, and then consigns them to his ministers, devoting himself entirely to the pleasures of the *antaḥpura*. Kālidāsa describes at length the king's dalliances with the various women of the palace – his wives, courtesans, dancers and attendants. But all is not right:

> unable to bear even the interval of a single moment without the enjoyment of the objects of the senses (*indriyārtha*), spending day and night in the interior (of the palace) he had no regard for his longing subjects. If upon the counsel of his ministers he deigned to give appearance (*darśana*) to his expectant subjects, he did so by hanging a foot from the opening of a window.[34]

The king's neglect of his courtiers and supplicants forebodes the worst. Though due to his power the king remains safe from his enemies, he begins to thin (*akṣiṇot*) from a disease 'born of attachment to sexual pleasures' (*ratirāgasaṁbhava*).[35] Agnivarṇa ignores the counsel of his physicians as symptoms become apparent. His face pales, his voice weakens, he is unable to adorn himself, and can walk only when supported by his servants. Raghu's family, according to Kālidāsa, was now like the sky with the moon on its last digit. The comparison is significant. The moon, or Soma, who was progenitor of the rains, and the waters, was the first

[31] Literally the 'non-enjoyment' (*asaṁbhoga*) of his other wives, *CkS* 6.8.5.
[32] *CkS* 6.8.24.
[33] *Ibid.* Zimmerman notes that the commentator specifies a loss of semen and vital fluid in the case of the moon, *Jungle and the Aroma of Meats*, p. 177.
[34] *RghV* 19.6–7. [35] *RghV* 19.48.

victim of *rājayakṣman*.[36] Agnivarṇa is not as fortunate as Soma; he eventually dies in his palace garden, attended by his ministers and the royal physician.

But the case of *rājayakṣman* in a sense was only a pathological manifestation of a deeper notion of erotic love as affliction which was common among people of the court. According to the texts which were concerned with the subject, the whole dynamic of sexual attraction had the potential to evolve into forms of attachment which could be mentally and physically debilitating. Take, for example, Vātsyāyana's enumeration of the 'ten stages of desire' (*kāmasthāna*).[37] Desire began with pleasure taken by the eyes (*cakṣusprīti*), followed by a fixation of the mind (*manasaṅga*), and then the birth of resolution or discrimination (*saṁkalpa utpatti*).[38] This progression so far conforms to the description above of the definition of *kāma* itself as an attraction of the senses and mind. Afterwards, particularly when separated from one's beloved, a series of physical symptoms arose which afflicted the body: loss of sleep (*nidrāccheda*), physical emaciation (*tanutā*), turning away from (other) objects of the senses (*viṣayebhyo vyāvṛtti*), loss of shame (*lajjāpraṇāśa*), madness (*unmāda*), fainting (*mūrcchā*) and, finally, death (*maraṇa*).

The idea here is that one was smitten with erotic love for another person, usually at first sight, which afterwards led to suffering if the lovers could not be united. For Vātsyāyana this formed the basis for pursuing rather than avoiding sexual liaisons, as only sexual union could avert the inexorable course of suffering in separation.[39] In most courtly texts love-suffering was, in fact, seen positively. It was a mark of refined sensibility and formed a standard element in the structure of courtship itself. Examples of such afflictions are numerous. Love in nearly all the palace dramas begins with the king and the heroine seeing one another (usually in the garden) and falling in love immediately, after which they begin to suffer in

[36] The metaphor should be extended in the case of the king, who was also the bringer of rain and prosperity to his kingdom. His wasting led to the inevitable ill health of his realm.

[37] *KS* 5.1.4.4–5.

[38] The mind literally became 'stuck' (*saṅga*, from the root √*sañj*) to the external object. *Saṁkalpa*, as noted before, refers to the mind's organisation of the diffuse sensations coming from the senses into desire, will or volition.

[39] Self-preservation in the face of wasting from overattachment becomes the pretext for Vātsyāyana to prescribe not merely sexual relations, but the violation of patriarchal privilege by sleeping with another man's wife. 'When he sees desire progressing from one stage to the next, then, with the goal of preserving his own body from harm, he may approach another's wife', *KS* 5.1.3. Compare this to the remark in Dāmodaragupta's eighth-century *Kuṭṭanīmata* 812, that while sexual intercourse with one's wife was necessary for progeny, having sex with servants (*ceṭika*) may be necessary for the abatement of sickness (from excessive desire), cited in *GkS* 3.

love until they are united at the play's conclusion.[40] In Bāṇa's *Harṣacarita*, too, Sarasvatī and the young prince Dadhīca fall in love at their first meeting. When later, Prince Dadhīca's messenger Vikukṣi brings tidings of the prince to Sarasvatī, she is delighted to learn, upon enquiring after his health, that he is not entirely well, his body thinning and mind rather distracted.[41] This was a clear sign that her desire for him was reciprocated.

To summarise the observations made thus far, sexual love in the courtly sources was conceived not merely as an engagement of the senses and attachment of the mind but a disposition to the outside world which, by its definition, had the potential to compromise and even destabilise the internal hierarchy and proper order of the self. On the one hand, this was viewed positively, for attachment was 'love' itself, and thus the suffering that the lover felt in separation was a mark of devotion. On the other hand, attachment either in separation or union also had the very real potential, in the eyes of the men of the court, of disarticulating the carefully balanced internal order which was deemed to constitute an individual's capacity to act in the world. This was apparent not only as a structuring concern in the discourse on love itself but in anxieties over bodily health and the ubiquitous warnings in all the courtly sources in guarding against one's senses. I will return shortly to the language of courtship but first it will be useful to turn to another aspect of courtly life, which, I believe, will illuminate the courtly conception of erotic love even further.

Attachment and autonomy

The discourse on self-mastery as detailed in the texts on polity, necessarily and explicitly drew parallels to the wider political arena of the court. They were concerned, after all, with training the political élite. For them mastery of self was the first and necessary step for a successful career at court. The king's mastery over the subordinate agencies which composed his realm – conceived as a body of which he was the central 'organ' – both began with and was homologous to 'ruling' the elements of his own self. For the texts on polity, the king's proper self-mastery, in other words, ideally entailed, *ipso facto* the proper mastery of his kingdom. Yet as the comparison with the self suggests, the king's mastery was complex, for it relied upon and subsumed within it the agencies of those other elements ('organs', or *karaṇas*) of the body politic, each of whom exercised relative

[40] In *MkA* the king sees his beloved Mālavikā in a picture drawn of the queen with her attendants. Likewise Nala and Damayantī fall in love with one another and begin pining on the basis of words alone.

[41] See *HC*, ch. 1, p. 28.

mastery over its own sphere(s) of competence. Self-discipline on the part of ministers, who were conceived variously as the 'eyes' or the 'mind' of the king, entailed not only mastery of their own competencies, but also submission to the king as a superordinate and ruling element of the polity conceived as self. The conception here, as Ronald Inden has noted, was one in which subordinate agencies were 'encompassed' or subsumed by more powerful agencies.[42]

This, at any rate, is the theory assumed in the political thought from the Gupta period. It is perhaps not so hard to see how the supposedly 'ascetical' values of 'restraint', 'discipline' and 'humility' (captured by the word *vinaya*) functioned in this régime – on the one hand to enable a variety of individual capacities at court, while on the other to safeguard its hierarchical order. A disciplined and restrained man at court exercised mastery over himself and his proper spheres of influence, even as he recognised through this very discipline (as humility) the mastery of his superiors. But this image is not enough, for it conveys neither the dynamism nor the anxiety so obvious in courtly sources. To understand these aspects of courtly 'selfhood', it is necessary to enquire into the language used to talk about affiliation at court.

It is perhaps germane to mention again the larger political context already outlined at the beginning of this book. For the theories we are dealing with here emerged during the overall expansion of the royal household as an institution and the widespread growth of political hierarchies founded on land. A key feature of this dispensation was the 'divided' and overlapping nature of economic and political power. From Gupta times, numerous categories of 'intermediaries' swelled the ranks of political hierarchy, both within the royal household and beyond. Men throughout these hierarchies, whether petty kings and lords within a circle of kings or upper service personnel within royal households, sought to rearticulate their positions within existing political hierarchies whenever opportunities presented themselves. There was, in other words, considerable space for movement and mobility within the political hierarchies of the court.

Within this network of relationships, the lives of men could be viewed along a continuum at the ends of which were two opposed ideas: 'dependence on oneself' (*svatantra*), and 'dependence on another' (*paratantra*). The latter was usually denoted by conditions like entering the service of (*sevā*), taking refuge with (*āśrayin*) or subsisting on (*anujīvin*, *upajīvin*) another person, while independence was generally denoted by terms suggesting living by 'one's own arm' (*svabāhu*) or being of 'independent means' (*svatantravṛtti*). The discourses of the court, as we shall see, have

[42] See Inden, 'Lordship and Caste in Hindu Discourse', pp. 159–79.

quite complex relations with these concepts, but I want to begin by noting that much courtly literature denigrates dependence on others and elevates independence. There is a vast gnomic literature inaugurated largely in Gupta times which laments the condition of the courtier servant.[43] Indeed, according to the *Mudrārākṣasa*, the courtier as one 'dependent on another' (*paratantra*) 'sold his body (*śarīram vikrīya*) to the wealthy and lost all ability to discriminate'.[44] Among kings, submission to another was deemed humiliating, and numerous inscriptions appear from Gupta times boasting of the deeds of kings performed by the strength of their 'own arms'. A ninth-century inscription which records the Pratīhāra king Nāgabhaṭṭa's defeat of Cakrāyudha of Kanauj, who was in the service of the Pāla king Dharmapāla, says that Cakrāyudha had a 'lowly demeanour clearly obvious from his dependence on another'.[45]

Such attitudes, however, must be placed within a political context where few were independent in any absolute or unqualified sense. Even the emperor, or king among kings, who sat atop the putative hierarchy of kings and 'ruled the earth', could be represented as dependent upon his powerful servants and ministers.[46] Yet it is in (and perhaps because of) this context that we find a constant celebration of forms of relative independence, often enjoyed by virtue of service or subordination to higher powers. Interestingly, when such relative 'independence' is imagined in the discourses of the court, it often appears as the capacity not to act as a 'free agent' but to dispense favour and support others as one's own dependants. In an exchange between the jackal courtiers of the *Pañcatantra*, Damanaka lectures his companion that no one served at court merely to fill his stomach: 'Surely no one enters royal service except to gain distinction . . . to help friends and harm foes . . . for he truly lives on whose life the lives of many depend'.[47] This conception of power also informed the courtly discourse about wealth and poverty. The goal for people of the court was not merely the accumulation or possession of wealth as an end in itself, but instead its enjoyment and, particularly, its

[43] Among the prominent early examples of such literature are verses contained in the *Pañcatantra* (see particularly the story of Caṇḍarava, in M. R. Kale's edition 1.10.266 ff.), in the palace dramas of Kālidāsa, Harṣa and others, as well as in Bhartṛhari's *STr*.
[44] *MR* 5.4.
[45] *EI* 18 (1925–6), no. 13, p. 108. See also the fifteenth-century *Puruṣaparīkṣā*, in which the ambitious prince Malladeva proclaims: 'cowards, children and women live by taking refuge in others', *Puruṣaparīkṣā* 1.3.2. He subsequently challenges a more powerful king before entering his service.
[46] See *MR* 1.15+; 16.
[47] *PT* 1.7–8. See the sixth-century inscription of the Naigama ministers, who, though servants of the Aulikāra kings, boast of having their own brilliant ministers (*nijasucisaciva*), *CII* 3 (1888), no. 35, p. 155.

distribution to worthy recipients.[48] The prominence of generosity among the courtly virtues is in part explained by the fact that giving implied the capacity of granting favour and, by extension, of being a 'refuge' for large numbers of men as one's servants. Courtly aphorisms tirelessly reiterate that being generous (*dātara*) attracted others to oneself regardless of one's birth and other virtues.[49] Put more cynically, in the shrewd words of Īśvaradatta's *viṭa*, 'making gifts was a means of bringing others under one's control'.[50]

So it is that kings and courtiers sought to acquire relative autonomy – in terms of power and wealth – within the context of service at court and within its chain of dependencies. While their capacities to do so differed radically according to their rank and the avenues through which they entered the court, the discourses which circulated among them shared a common preoccupation with autonomy and dependence. It is these men who formed the audience for the prescriptive and aesthetic literatures of the court and, I should add, whose worldview is encoded in them.

If we turn to the official representations of relationships between superiors and inferiors – between relatively autonomous and relatively dependent agencies – we find that they were expressed in terms quite relevant for the discussion thus far. Inscriptions from Gupta times frequently describe the relations of lords and their subordinates through the very language of 'attachment' (*anurāga*, to a lesser extent, *sakta*) which we have encountered above. As we noted in chapter 3, *anurāga* along with *bhakti* denoted the ideal disposition that any dependant or servant was to have towards his superior and, as such, they formed common virtues of courtiers celebrated in inscriptions.[51] Having men 'devoted' or 'attached' to oneself thus also formed a common boast in inscriptional eulogies. An eighth-century inscription of a Maitraka king in western India refers to the hereditary servants of his family as being 'attached to the king through

[48] A *viṭa* in *DhVS* 59, says that 'there are three ends of money: making gifts, enjoyment and hoarding. Of these gifts and enjoyments are superior, and hoarding has been censored. Why? In hoarding money there is no benefit, and being without benefit, it creates no satisfaction. Hence hoarding is improper.' This feudal sentiment towards wealth is widespread. See *STr* 1.34 and the many anthologised verses on the subject collected in *MSS*. It should be noted that this courtly/aristocratic conception of wealth probably also characterised 'city' life. It is, for example, clearly apparent in Śūdraka's depiction of the merchant Cārudatta's lament on poverty in *MK*, a point which prevents, in my mind, this play from being considered a 'bourgeois' drama.

[49] *NiS* 5.60. [50] *DhVS* 29+.

[51] The fifth-century Junagadh rock inscription, celebrates the courtier Parṇadatta, appointed to rule Saurāṣṭra, as 'devoted' (*bhakti*) and 'attached' (*anurakta*) to his lord Skandagupta, *CII* 3 (1981), no. 28, p. 300.

affection' (*anurāgānurakta*), and *sāmanta*s paying obeisance to the king through the 'attachment (*anurāga*) produced by his splendour'.[52]

Sovereignty itself, in the form of the feminised personification of Fortune, or Śrī, was thought to be 'attached' to kings. In Viśākhadatta's *Mudrārākṣasa*, the minister Rākṣasa asks Śrī why she has abandoned his master the Nanda king and become 'attached' (*sakta*) to Candragupta.[53]

Once we see 'attachment' in this interpersonal manner, as a relation between individuals rather than with the external world as such, then we may also understand the recommendations of the political treatises on discipline and policy somewhat differently. The *Arthaśāstra* and *Nītisāra*, for example, set out lists of qualities which were to 'attract' others to oneself called *abhigāmikaguṇa*s.[54] These included not only wealth, fortune and generosity, but a host of other moral qualities as well. The point is that for men at court, one of the explicitly stated ends of self-cultivation was to make oneself attractive, by developing qualities which drew others towards oneself. Numerous inscriptions praise men as exhibiting these 'qualities of attraction'.[55] In an eighth-century Gurjara inscription, even the goddess of fortune is said to be attracted to the 'inviting qualities' (*abhigāmikaguṇa*s) of the king Ahirola.[56]

In the inscription cited above, the poet tells us that it is the mind (*manas*) of Lakṣmī that was fervently attached to the king.[57] The mind, as the seat of the emotions, formed a sort of 'zone of engagement' for the dynamics of affiliation at court, and the *Arthaśāstra* makes clear that one of its goals of policy was the 'winning over' of the minds of others at the *sabhā*. Interestingly, this is underscored in the final sections on 'secret' (*aupaniṣadika*) practices in both the *Arthaśāstra* and *Kāmasūtra*. These sections purported to advise men in special and covert methods to obtain what they otherwise could not by the straightforward policy recommendations which formed the positive teaching of these treatises. They were, in other words, last resorts for men in desperate circumstances and are significant because they present in sometimes rather crude fashion the goal of much more complicated advice found elsewhere in these manuals.

[52] *CII* 3 (1888), no. 39, pp. 173, 178. The only pre-Gupta examples of this terminology I have found are the well-known inscriptions of Kharavela and Rudradāman which speak of these kings as having their subjects (*prakṛti*) 'attached' to them, *EI* 20 (1929–30), no. 7, p. 79 and *EI* 8 (1905–6), no. 6, p. 44.

[53] *MR* 2.6. [54] *AS* 6.1.3; *NiS* 4.6–8.

[55] Typical is the seventh-century inscription of the Kāmarupa king Bhāskaravarman, where the king is described as 'having people attached to his inviting qualities' (*ābhigāmikaguṇānurāga*), *EI* 19 (1927–8), no. 19, p. 118.

[56] *CII* 4 (1955), no. 24, p. 105. [57] *Ibid.* See also *CII* 4 (1955), no. 12, p. 41.

In both cases, the courtier/king is recommended to resort to the secret rites of the *Atharvaveda*, a knowledge which had a long and intimate relationship with the development of courtly practices from late Vedic times, and which continued throughout the period under study to have 'esoteric' uses at court. The knowledge of the *Atharvaveda* is far too complex to treat properly here, but the tenor of certain hymns is revealing enough. Several hymns speak of 'drawing the minds' of others to 'take delight' (*ramatāṁ*) in the aspirant, of 'bending' (*namayāmasi*), 'grasping' or 'seizing' (*gṛhnāmi*) the minds of others with one's own mind.[58] Although they do not use the term *anurakta*, they anticipate its logic by referring to the drawing of the opponent's mind to oneself where it would 'take delight'. The imagery of 'seizing' another's mind or 'causing it to bend' is also highly significant, for it treats the mind with the same gestural vocabulary which informed courtly etiquette. The comportment of the body mentioned in previous chapters was ostensibly linked to the disposition of the mind, and becoming attached to someone entailed bodily gestures which reflected the condition of the mind. Attachment was thus envisioned as a 'leaning towards', or 'inclination' of the mind in the direction of another. It is thus not surprising that the feudatory prostrates before his lord from attachment to his splendour (*pratāpānurāgapraṇata*).[59]

Yet such inclinations could be far more subtle. In any case, any inclination of one man to another was at one level a matter of 'control' or 'influence', typically referred to in courtly sources by the term *vaśa*. This concept returns us to the idea of self-mastery with which we began this discussion, for *vaśa* was a capacity one could exercise (or lose) not only with respect to others, but also in regard to oneself.[60] More commonly it arose in regard to effecting one's own will or influence onto that of another person. The goal of royal policy, according to the *Arthaśāstra*, was for the king to use the benefits of livelihood, along with his wealth and the army, to 'bring under his control' (*vaśīkaroti*) both his own party (*svapakṣa*) and other parties (*parapakṣa*) through various strategies.[61] It was also the policy of lower court officials. A thirteenth-century inscription of the later Rāṣṭrakūṭas refers to a counsellor who exercised 'fascinating influence (*vaśikāra*) over his friends'.[62]

58 *Atharvaveda* 7.12; 6.94. The recitation of these hymns was to be accompanied by various rituals. For details, see the remarks in the translation of Maurice Bloomfield, pp. 543, 360–1.

59 *CII* 3 (1888), no. 39, p. 178.

60 See the description of Parṇadatta as exercising self control (*ātmavaśa*), *CII* 3 (1981), no. 28, p. 300; cf. the courtier Varāhadāsa, *CII* 3 (1888), no. 35, p. 155. For loss of control, see the description of a woman moving unsteadily during the spring festival 'under the influence of intoxication' (*madanavaśa*), *Rv* 1.12+.

61 *AS* 1.4.2.

62 *EI* 13 (1915–16), no. 3a, p. 20.

To us, the discourse of attachment, influence and control between individuals may seem to be a greatly impoverished and even banal conception of political life. But to grasp their importance for the men of the court, it is necessary to remember that the goal of the prince's policy was not commitment to a 'social ideology' or the 'improvement of society' (insofar as it was not connected to quelling disturbance), but simply acquiring and retaining his kingdom – attracting virtuous and powerful servants, retaining their support and winning over 'seducible parties'. In this context, the struggle for the minds of men was of utmost importance as a political instrument and the problem of attachment and autonomy formed the very ballast of the courtly political mentality.

As should be obvious by now, ideas of attachment, inclination and influence all had a potentially agonistic dimension. Attachment was essentially a submission of one's mind to another which compromised the self's autonomy. Under such circumstances, the internal order of the self, which I represented schematically above, was disrupted as the mind and the external instruments it controlled became inclined towards another person. Of course, such human dispositions were endemic to the very fabric of society at court, giving a fillip to the ascetical orders' critique of worldly life. Moreover, they were even valorised both at court and in theistic religious orders which placed a high premium on 'devotion' and 'attachment' as the highest of dispositions. But the fact remains that just below the surface of such normative affiliations (and often protrudingly visible) was a vast world of agonistic social relationships. When an eighth-century inscription from western India describes *sāmanta*s prostrating before the Maitraka king Kharagraha because they had been 'violently subdued (*sarabhasavaśīkṛta*) by excessive attachment (*atiprakṛṣṭānurāga*) for him,' more than a hint of coercion is certainly implied.[63] The end of the policy of war was the submission of the defeated king to the victor which was expressed as an attachment of the defeated king's self/mind as ruler of its own organs/instruments with their external domains, to a new lord.

The same antagonism could potentially characterise the courtier's attachment to his lord. As one verse from Hāla's anthology eloquently puts it 'though being self-controlled (*ātmavaśa*), a good man of noble birth may submit to another, even if hated, with the complexion (or attachment – *rāga*) of his face unchanged, and follow his wishes'.[64] There is probably no better example of such 'policy' than that of the jackal courtier Damanaka in the first book of the *Pañcatantra*. When he sees his master Piṅgalaka's weakness, he confides to his companion that 'this very

[63] *CII* 3 (1888), no. 39, p. 177. [64] *Gāthāsaptaśatī* 3.65.

day I will catch him while he is overcome with fear and by the power of my intelligence bring him under my control (*prajñāprabhāvenātmīyaṁ kariṣyāmi*)'.[65] Using the policy of sowing dissension between friends, Damanaka brilliantly achieves his goal of promotion by effectively bringing his master under the sway of his political design.

The tensions which underlay all relationships at court are best revealed, I would submit, by the persistent ambivalence to attachment and dependency in the aphoristic literature which I have pointed out above. Servitude, devotion and attachment were, on the one hand, elevated to the most perfect of virtues and, on the other, denigrated as the basest of conditions. Moralists of the court decry the pathos of servitude and denigrate lords for their pride and cruelty to the honest servant, while at the same time blaming servants for their greed. The apparently simple posture of devotion that a servant was to have towards his lord, along with the reciprocal disposition of favour the lord was to display towards his dependant – relations which formed the basis of relationships at court – were undergirded by complex antagonisms which the language devotion and attachment was only partly capable of sustaining.

The warfare of love

This excursus on the 'psychology' of courtly affiliations is in the first part justified, I believe, by the fact that a number of the key terms encountered in the discussion above – *anurāga*, *vaśa*, *mano* $\sqrt{}$*grah* – were the very ones used widely to conceptualise courtship and erotic love. This congruence of language deserves serious consideration, for the agonism of attachment is even more apparent in the discourses on courtly love. The remainder of this chapter will explore the dimensions of this congruence and its wider significance for courtly life as a whole. This section will draw on both prescriptive texts as well as poetic representations of erotic love. Prominent among the latter will be the corpus of some 680 'graffiti' inscriptions in Sinhala dated between the eighth and tenth centuries which have been recovered from the environs of the Sigiriya Palace complex in Sri Lanka probably built sometime in the fifth century CE. These inscriptions take the form of short stanzas addressed to the famous 'palace women' depicted in paintings on the citadel's rockface (see figure 7.1).[66] They are typical if delightful specimens of a certain type of love poetry common in the immediate post-Gupta period.

[65] *PT* 1.18+ .

[66] There is some debate as to the identity of these women. Some of the inscriptions clearly address them as the forlorn members of the dead king's palace retinue.

Figure 7.1 Painting of palace maiden, stucco, from Sigiriya, Sri Lanka, fifth century CE.

Let us begin with the prescriptive literature on erotic love. It is perhaps obvious that the elements of 'courtship' detailed in the previous chapter – creating confidence (*visrambhana*, *viśvāsa*) and soliciting (*prārthana*) – were all embraced within the larger strategy of 'winning over' a lover to oneself, or what the texts call *anurañjayati*, literally 'causing one to be attached'.[67] The methods which the *nāgaraka* was to ideally employ in achieving this goal were considerable, for wooing was to be a gradual and even elaborate process, which required various skills depending on the circumstances. Therefore the ideal lover was to have a vast array of accomplishments at his command, which ranged from the possession of winning personal qualities which, like those of the king, were deemed 'inviting' (*abhigamya*), to skills in interpreting the inner feelings of a woman by knowledge of her facial expressions and gestures, and a host of others, most prominent of which were the sixty-four arts (see table 2.1).[68]

The essential dynamic of the courtship interaction, as noted above, was that of a 'game'. It is worth pausing over this association, for the 'play' aspect of courtship is of immense importance in understanding both its internal dynamic and its larger significance in the lives of people at court. Games and contests of a bewildering variety were themselves very prominent activities for men and women at court. They were, of course, first experienced during childhood, frequently as the miniature imitations of the adult activities using diminutive carts, dolls, cooking utensils, houses and weapons.[69] Such games obviously introduced particular skills and masteries to children. As they became more elaborate and complex, the performance of games was directly continuous with the contests and examinations necessary for advancement within the circles of the court.[70] The game known as *caturāṅga*, for example, named after the four parts of the army, introduced the prince to the principles military strategy. The crucial point, however, is that the playing of games continued well into adulthood. As men grew up, childhood games were supplemented (rather than displaced) by more sophisticated contests and games which often relied on verbal and poetic skills. To give a flavour of

[67] *KS* 3.3.2.

[68] *KS* 6.1.11; 3.3.22; 3.3.24; 3.4.34; 5.3.1 ff. Vātsyāyana recommends displaying one's facility in the sixty-four arts as a way of impressing the potential *nāyikā*, *KS* 3.3.21.

[69] For carriages and dolls, see *KS* 1.3.16, *kalās* nos. 48, 61, see table 2.1. Cf. *MK* 6.1 ff.; also Auboyer, *Daily Life in Ancient India*, pp. 165–6.

[70] Games, as Norbert Elias has noted in the context of the warrior societies of medieval Europe, educated children for adult life in a much more direct way than in modern societies, for children, as a result of political exigency, often had to assume political responsibility at a very early age. See Norbert Elias, 'The Civilizing of Parents', in Johan Goudsblom and Stephen Mennell, eds., *The Norbert Elias Reader* (Oxford: Blackwell, 1998), pp. 202–3.

this we need only consider the representation of King Tārāpīḍa's court in Bāṇa's *Kādambarī*:

seated inside the audience hall as befitted their rank, some kings were dicing; some were playing *caturaṅga*; others playing the lute; others were drawing images of the king on painting boards; others were holding conversations about poetry; others were telling funny stories; others were making out which letters correspond to which dots in the Bubble Verse game; some were pondering verse-riddles; others were considering well-turned verses composed by the king; others were reciting poems in the *dvipadī* metre; others were praising various poets; others were making leaf-and-streak decorations on their bodies; others were conversing with courtesans; and others listening to the songs of bards.[71]

Bāṇa presents this image of the court at play to emphasise the power and majesty of King Tārāpīḍa's house as a place of untold enjoyments. Yet the tendency towards 'play' was more than simply ideological in this sense. The games men played as adults were a continuation of those played as children, and served not merely to provide pleasure, but to isolate and refine the verbal and strategic skills necessary for their formal 'policy-relationships' with one another.

Courtship too entailed the playing of games, according to Vātsyāyana, and skill at contests of various sorts featured prominently among the sixty-four arts which were to support the activities of courtship. The generic 'court-women' who long for the prince in *kāvya* are typically depicted as playing various games suitable to their age. In many cases this was because such women were, in fact, very young and Vātsyāyana recommends that the *nāyaka* use games appropriate to the age of the women he sought to seduce as a means of endearing himself to them.[72] The transition of childhood games to youthful pleasures is seamlessly demonstrated by the progression of his gifts to the girl, which begin with balls and string and give way to rarer objects of enjoyment like mechanical toys, doll houses, talking birds and eventually to the standard accoutrements of the courtier's life like cosmetics, betel-nut and musical instruments. Vātsyāyana also lists numerous games to be played as adults.[73] Games and toys formed a sort of communicative idiom in courtship through which intentions and affections could be suggested indirectly to one's prospective lover amidst friends and companions. Vātsyāyana, for example, recommends that the *nāyaka* make gifts of miniature couples of animals and humans to the girl to suggest his affections for her.[74]

Such diversions formed tactical moments in the larger game which was courtship itself. And like many (but not all) other games at court, courtship was posed as a 'contest', one in which lovers sought to discern

[71] *Kd*, p. 88. [72] See *KS* 3.3.5. [73] *KS* 1.4.42–3. [74] *KS* 3.3.14.

each other's feelings, while concealing their own. Vātsyāyana says that the woman, though she might feel attraction to a man, will not act on her feelings, and because of this men also had to conceal their intentions, approaching the woman neither too directly nor too slowly, but in a proper cadence.[75] This concealment was part of a larger ritualised incompliance. For a woman was never to submit too readily to a man's advances, because a woman gained easily was eventually detested by men, according to Vātsyāyana.[76] Nor was a man to accede immediately to the requests of his beloved. Vātsyāyana says that the *nāyaka* was to have neither too compliant nor contrary a method for gaining women, but instead to strike a middle path.[77] These incompliances were translated into courtship in a number of ways. They created a sort of meta-language of gesture and expression which operated through hint and suggestion rather than open statement. So since a fixation of the eyes indicated the state of being 'smitten', the sidelong or darting glance, which only hinted at attraction, was preferred. The idea was that the glance 'caught' and 'fixed' the eyes of the beholder, initiating the evolution of desire. Most generally, incompliance was translated into the progression of courtship through a pattern of variously subtle and bold advances on the part of the man and hinted invitations and feigned refusals on the part of the woman. Yet each insinuation and deferral formed an excitatory stimulus in the game of seduction.

'Victory' in this ritualised contest was conceived in the same ways as the contests for minds at court we saw above. Lovers sought to 'capture' or 'seize' one another's minds. The covert methods recommended by the final book of the *Kāmasūtra* include recipes which enabled a man to exert 'influence' or 'control' (*vaśīkaraṇa*) over a woman.[78] Once again, the importance of these formulae lies less in their secrecy than in the fact that they make quite plain the goal of overt strategy recommended by Vātsyāyana. Such ends were clearly recognised and discussed in the conversations at the *goṣṭhī*. In Īśvaradatta's play the *viṭa* Devilaka is asked how one can bring under one's 'influence' (*vaśyā*) a woman who shows no signs of desire, refuses one's advances, remains distant, or avoids one

[75] On women's reluctance to indicate their feelings and reasons for this, see *KS* 3.3.23; 5.1.7–43. For Vātsyāyana's recommendation to the *nāyaka* to conceal his intentions, see *KS* 3.4.32; also *DhVS* 47. For the proper cadence of approach, see *KS* 3.2.42–3.

[76] For the maiden, see *KS* 3.4.43; for the wife of another, *KS* 5.1.16; for the courtesan, *KS* 6.1.21.

[77] *KS* 3.2.40; *Ratirahasya* 11.19.

[78] *KS* 7.1.25–8; 31–5. These formulae remained important in later erotic manuals as well. Cf. *Ratirahasya* 1.23+; 14.1 ff.; *Pañcasāyaka* 4.14–18. See also the entry in Ram Kumar Rai, *Encyclopedia of Indian Erotics* (Varanasi: Prachya Prakashan, 1983) which draws heavily on Kalyānamalla's late-fifteenth-century *Anaṅgaraṅga*.

at the opportune time. The *viṭa* relishes the question, saying that one must first know the nature of the woman before adopting a suitable strategy.[79] Women, too, are recommended to take control of men, though not so much during courtship itself, where they are generally attributed the 'passive' role of 'receiving' the advances of the man, but rather in the struggle for her husband's affection in the context of the polygamous household. So Vātsyāyana says that a king's or minister's daughter who knows the sixty-four arts will make her husband conform to her influence (*svavaśe kurute patim*) even if there are a thousand other women in the *antaḥpura*.[80] Exercising control over one's husband also entailed mastering the other women of the household, and Vātsyāyana advises the young wife to conquer her own anger and cultivate herself in accord with the *Kāmasūtra* in order to stand above (*adhitiṣṭhati*) and control (*karoti vaśyam*) both her co-wives and her husband.[81]

The preoccupation with winning, capturing and controlling the affections of one's lover tended to push courtship towards metaphors of battle and struggle which we have noted above. Vātsyāyana himself is explicit about this, saying that erotic love takes the form of a combat (*kalaharūpa*) because it is essentially a contest (*vivādātmakatvād*) and because of its innate contrariety (*vāmaśīlatvāt*), which his commentator Yaśodhara explains as arising 'because man and woman each tries to accomplish their own goal (*svārthasiddhaye*) by overcoming the other (*parasparābhibhavena*)'.[82] This battle, however, was not fought by equal partners or through equal strategies. Vātsyāyana always puts the man in the aggressive stance and the female in the defensive one. A forward virgin or even a prostitute were never to make open advances to a man – they were at best to indicate their receptiveness to his potential advances.[83]

When we turn to literary representations, we find even more markedly eristic conceptualisations. The most common images connect the bodies and gestures of women to weaponry in general, as when Bhartṛhari says that women's sidelong looks, darting glances with raised eyebrows, soft speech, shy laughter and playfully indolent movement all constitute at once their ornaments (*bhūṣaṇa*) and their weapons (*ayudha*).[84] More particular is the iconography of Kāmadeva, the bowman of love, who pierces the hearts of lovers with his flower arrows. The most developed

[79] *DhVS* 46+. Devilaka recommends forcible seizure in the case of proud women.

[80] *KS* 1.3.22. See also *NS* 24.224 for the woman whose husband is under her control (*svādhīnanabhartṛkā*).

[81] *KS* 4.2.90.

[82] *Kāmasūtra* 2.7.1 and comm. The description of lovers evokes the political treatises' definition of an enemy, as one who, according to Kāmandaka, pursued the same goal as oneself (*ekārthābhiniveśa*), *NiS* 8.14.

[83] *KS* 3.4.41; 6.1.21.

[84] *STr* 2.3.

imagery is resolved around the eye, with the eyebrow compared to the bow, the eyelash to the bowstring and the glance to the arrow. In a typical example from Vidyākara's anthology, a woman's glance (*vīkṣita*) is likened to a poison arrow, bringing paralysis, dizziness of mind, fever and, in the last event, loss of consciousness.[85]

The graffiti poems at Sigiriya present themselves as a vast collection of battle epigrams commemorating the melees between their authors and some 500 women depicted in murals which once adorned the side of the mountain. The authors fancy that the glances of the women, which are shot like arrows, 'allure' (*polobā*) and 'entice' (*harava layi*) them, as their own eyes become 'captured'.[86] The fixation of the eyes led, of course, to the agitation of the mind, which forms a general theme in the graffiti.[87] The mind is 'attracted' (*adanu, haja*) and eventually 'captured' (*gata, banda*) or 'bound' (*daga*) by the women.[88] We encounter the metaphor of the inclining, or bending (*nama*), of the mind towards the object of attraction. One Leṇ Siv, of the house of Lord Kasäba, remarks that his mind is 'bent' (*mananāma*) and then captured by the women.[89] Other poems speak of the poet's mind being 'controlled' or 'subdued' (Sinhalese *visī* = Sanskrit *vaśa*): 'having looked at you, my mind is as if subdued (*visī*); by mere sight of you I am enslaved', or 'you have bent and controlled (*visī*) my mind'.[90]

The minds of the women are in turn described as 'hardened' (a favourite conceit at Sigiriya, given their appearance on the rockface of the citadel) in contrast to the soft and tender hearts which befitted women.[91] In most cases the authors of the graffiti claim to meet 'defeat' before the women, but occasionally claim victory for themselves.[92] What is remarkable here is not so much that the women of Sigiriya tend to emerge victorious in these struggles, for in many similar accounts (cf. those of Aśvaghoṣa and Bāṇa) the poisonous glances of women are merely their initial engagements, first attempts to stave off their own impending

[85] *Subhāṣitaratnakośa* 496. Following the progression of Vātsyāyana's *kāmasthānas*.
[86] *SG*, see variously nos. 5, 66, 114, 126, 176, 194, 249, 284, 291, 364, 438, 442, 457, 486, 521, 639, 661.
[87] *SG*, nos. 232, 263, 268, 327, 359, 374, 405, 416, 432, 484, 601.
[88] Poems using this or similar vocabulary are numerous: *SG*, nos. 5, 6, 8, 13, 53, 72, 85, 96, 106, 119, 123, 125, 154, 167, 168, 231, 233, 234, 237, 239, 248, 313, 316, 324, 345, 350, 357, 358, 361, 371, 377, 401, 402, 408, 422, 442, 449, 450, 463, 473, 498, 504, 529, 544, 560, 587, 598, 618, 628, 639, 642, 656, 657, 663, 666, 674, 677.
[89] *SG*, no. 350, see also nos. 48, 51, 119, 166, 357, 374, 393, 470, 513.
[90] *SG* nos. 273, 166. Other inscriptions at Sigiriya using the term *visī* include nos. 211, 494, 547.
[91] *SG*, nos. 59, 87, 92, 158, 213, 319, 352, 353, 414, 415, 434, 487, 521, 523, 573, 673.
[92] In some cases, the eyes of the women are attracted or given to the viewers or their minds become inclined towards them, *SG*, nos. 21, 200, 393.

lovesickness. Indeed, in the battle of love it is typically the male who emerges victorious despite the heroine's initial victories. That is, the heroine desires more intensely for her male counterpart, for she is 'weaker'. Women, both in the prescriptive literature as well as in poetic representations, succumbed more easily to desire and attachment – a curious disability considering their passive role in courtship as depicted in the prescriptive treatises.[93] We shall return momentarily to this point. What I want instead to note as remarkable – inasmuch as it is typical – is the degree to which the entire language of sexual attraction was open to martial imagery and agonistic conceptions. Indeed, erotic attachment (*rändi*, *laga*) at Sigiriya, effectively indistinct from 'capture' and 'enslavement', is conceived in the most agonistic of ways.[94]

What are we to make of these descriptions? I began by noting the similarities between the discourses on sexual love and those which obtained between men at court. At one level, this is perhaps only natural for relations between courtly lovers were often fraught with the same complex tensions. Indeed, this is because at one level marriage, concubinage and prostitution – the institutions that governed such relations – were, in fact, hierarchical relationships intimately associated with authority and property to begin with, which overlapped and were largely continuous with those which obtained between men. The contexts of courtship, in other words, were the contexts of the court, and as such were governed by the same principles and strategies. It is thus only natural that these tensions formed the internal dynamics of courtship.

Yet this explanation can be only partly adequate, for it is these very tensions which the men of the court seemed to collectively cherish as the very basis of their concern with erotic love. The antagonisms of love were viewed as its highest pleasures, and the moments of incompliance and indirection – whether it be the furtive indirection of lovers' eyes, the furious rebukes of the jealous woman, or pining in separation – formed the preferred themes of courtly poetry. It is no wonder that the sophisticates of the *goṣṭhī* laugh at the stupidity of Viṣṇunāga in feeling insulted by the touch of the courtesan Madanasenikā's foot.

Moreover, the hypertrophied signification around erotic love in general at court and its overwhelming pre-eminence as a theme in courtly poetry suggests that it was invested with wider concerns. Erotic poetry, as we have seen, was hardly a straightforward depiction of sexual relations between men and women at court. This is manifestly evident from the court's view of women as temptresses whose charms ensnared the minds

[93] See Vātsyāyana's remarks on this point at *KS* 5.1.9–13.
[94] *SG*, for example, nos. 525, 654,

of men, and yet passive agents in the *telos* of actual courtship. Women, deemed more susceptible to desire than men, were, on the one hand, viewed as sort of naturally 'sexualised' – beautiful, tender-hearted and charming. On the other hand, they were derided as inherently weak in capacities of self-restraint, overly sensual and naturally unsteady. Given such contradictions, we might accuse these discourses of a massive displacement, and indeed a displacement which reveals more about courtly masculinity than the nature of women. The women of *kāvya* are perhaps not so different from the 'painted ladies' at Sigiriya – for however alluring and captivating they might have been, in the end they were not much more than pretty pictures.

I believe we are on firmer ground if we return to the predominantly male context which I set out in the middle of this chapter – the context of the *sabhā*, the assemblies of men who were the predominant authors and audiences of the discourse on erotic love. Courtship, I would submit, both as a sophisticated accomplishment and a representational realm, had a sort of double life, as at once an introduction to the sexual politics of the élite household, but also as a sort of 'enactment' of the affiliative dynamics which obtained between men at court. Courtship during youth allowed the men of the court to learn the strategies of conduct and forms of self-discipline necessary for participation in the life of the *sabhā*. The detection of concealed feelings, the use of deception and indirection required in courtship and other skills prepared men for courtly existence as a whole. In a world where discerning the strategies of others and concealing one's own was an accepted necessity, the game of courtship could provide no better training. And judging from the sources, continued success at courtship was an indication of one's self-perfection as an accomplished man at court. The king as the most powerful man at court had to constantly represent himself as the most perfectly skilled player in the contest of love.

Yet as a discourse, I believe that the language of love also reveals important ambivalences and anxieties. I have noted that the crucial axis of convergence between the language of pleasure and political affiliation was the idea of attachment. On the one hand, attachment was considered a necessary relation and even ideal virtue in the basic affiliations between the upper echelons of title-holding men at court. On the other hand, as the conceptual opposite of self-mastery and autonomy, it formed an obviously limiting and compromising condition, all the more so because attachment implied submission to another individual. The significant 'problem' for men at court – an 'ethical' problem, I would submit, since it concerned the central features of one's relationships with others – was how to think about and resolve this dual aspect of attachment, a problem all the more salient because each man of rank at court was more or less precariously situated within a web of such social and political 'affections' or 'attachments' which at once afforded him agency and power and at the same time limited it. And erotic love formed the 'palette' upon which the essential ambiguity of these relationships were continually projected and thought about. I believe that this, more than anything, explains both the nature and prominence of the depiction of love in courtly literature.

Postscript: conclusion and further directions

This book began by asserting that in order to fully understand the nature of political action and the texture of political life in early medieval India it is necessary to take some account of the activities and lifestyles of people who lived at royal courts as something other than superstructural froth to be summarily dispatched in the name of real history. The chapters that followed tried to make an initial, if largely partial, attempt at approaching the sources with this framework in mind. By way of conclusion, I want to review some of the key arguments made in this study and chart out possible further directions of inquiry suggested by the research for this book.

Most centrally, this book has tried to examine closely the internal dynamics of courtly life. I have been specifically concerned to show how the structure of courtly life, the relations between its members as embodied in the royal household, variously conditioned the bodily proclivities, verbal affinities and mental inclinations of its members in ways which scholars of early India have not sufficiently appreciated. This conditioning served to interpolate individuals into the society of the court as an institution and facilitated the development of specific *capacities* within them to act in the spheres of 'good society'. An important dimension of courtly accomplishment, in other words, was its ability in facilitating the skilful negotiation of relations with others through formalised verbal registers, gestural protocols, and the display and interpretation of a set of highly mannered affective codes (which entailed familiarity with the previous two).

The texts on policy are clear that the first and most important relationship which a man of rank was to guard and cultivate for a successful life in the circles of the court was with himself – a point which gave courtly discourse a strong reflexive dimension. The persistent and remarkable exhortations in courtly sources towards discipline, humility and self-mastery, routinely ignored by secondary literature or attributed to 'brahmanical' religious influences, I have argued, show instead an important ethical orientation to the texture of courtly life. This ethics was not so much concerned with moral judgements about what was right and wrong, or adherence to 'dharma' as a cosmo-moral order, but rather with the careful and considered cultivation and disposition of virtues in one's life and the 'public' society of the court. It is against this ethical background that I have placed courtly aesthetic preoccupations of the court, for virtue among the people was always clearly envisioned as a form of very palpable beauty in one's appearance, behaviour and surroundings. The enjoyment of material and literary pleasures, the beautification of the world and oneself – one's speech, body and soul – were all viewed as forms of 'self-fashioning', at once aesthetic and moral. Aesthetic sophistication and ethical self-regard presupposed one another in a mutually reinforcing relationship.

Yet my analysis of the realm of erotic pleasure suggests that this relationship was not entirely seamless. In the final chapters of this book, I turned to the courtly preoccupation with romance in both its practice and ideology to reveal not only how it was integrated into the wider norms of court sociability, but, more importantly, how its highly exaggerated profile in the sources rested on its ability to act as a 'palette' for the projection of court society's peculiar ethical anxieties. The chief of these, I suggested, was the problem of 'attachment' and 'dependence', conditions which, as integral as they were to the very fabric of courtly life, always evinced ambivalent responses from the court as a whole, from the most powerful of emperors to the lowliest of servants, from mid-ranking vassals to ministers, poets and intellectuals of various types. The discourse on love as it developed in courtly circles was pre-eminently suited for this investiture, a point which is clearly highlighted by its profile in later religious literature as a way of experiencing divinity.

Courtly sources, even while celebrating the battlefield valour and martial prowess of kings and vassals (a topic largely untreated in this study), also emphasised what I called at the beginning of this book an 'irenic' form of lordship. Proper rule entailed the celebration of happiness, fructification and compassion. These irenic values were upheld in nearly all aspects of lordship; ethical self-perfection, political fortune, righteous rule and aesthetic delectation were deemed, together, the existential felicities of a life properly lived in the world by men of rank. This is everywhere apparent in courtly representation, from the gently reposeful postures of courtly bodies in their brilliant surroundings to the tender emotions of lovers sporting in the garden – all of which continue to evoke an enduring 'message' for modern aesthetes.

Yet this felicity, and all it entailed, was an image of power which both united and divided the court in different ways. The court attributed, as we have seen, fundamentally different external and internal characteristics to the noble and the low-born. The people of the village were deemed ignorant of proper ways of expression – untutored in the grammatical rigours of courtly speech and its unique expressive codes which operated through indirection and suggestion. Men of the forests and hills were thought to be characterised by unmitigated cruelty, harshness and violence. At the same time, bearing and speech were graded within the society of the court. Menials and low-ranking servants, our sources continually emphasise, were not thought to possess the benefits of proper speech and bearing. Women, though always present in the representation of power and felicity as embodiments of fortune, tenderness and delicacy, were denied access, or so our sources suggest, to the verbal refinements of the court and were viewed as petty, frivolous, inconstant, mentally weak and inherently concupiscent. The courtly preoccupation with erotic love was not only premised on a substantial displacement of male desire onto a hypersexualised image of the feminine, but also offered very restricted forms of agency for women in the activities and representations of courtship. Whatever its pretensions to incorporate irenic values, the institution of the court was founded on clear and incessant rules of hierarchy and exclusion.

But this exclusionary aspect of court life must be set against two processes, one historical and the other institutional. First, at the 'macro'-historical level, the period under question saw the continual absorption of local lineages and élites into the penumbra of 'good society'. The number of new ruling houses which appear on the historical record throughout the subcontinent between the fourth and eighth centuries (and beyond) is considerable. While the fate of such ruling families varied greatly, their almost universal adoption of the practices and discourses outlined in this book suggests that the culture of the court was more inclusive than it claimed and that the boundaries of the ruling classes were more porous than is often assumed. In this sense, the culture of the court may be seen as an acculturative mechanism, whereby men and women were integrated into a mutually intelligible pan-regional culture with its own distinctive protocols of sociability, gestural and mental proclivities, modes of communication and ethical preoccupations.

Second, sources suggest that within the society of the court, there was considerable scope for social mobility. The rank of families could often rise and fall within generations. The emphasis on high and low which organised the spatial imagination of courtly élites, their bodily composure and oneiric fantasies, also mapped, in a very real sense, their careers and fortunes. Numerous inscriptions speak of the rise (and sometimes decline) of courtier-families from one generation to the next at court, as they themselves offered favour to others and raised their own friends and dependants. The court in a way formed a place of opportunity where men, often of relatively diverse birth, could make their fortunes and careers. The hundreds of verses decrying the dangers and humiliations of service and servitude in Sanskrit gnomic literature may be read as a testament to the powerful draw that courts exercised over educated and ambitious men in medieval India.

One question which has not been taken up by this study, partly because the evidence remains problematic, is the interaction of courtly norms and values with the cultures of the local élites who were gradually integrated into the power structures of political society. This evidence is elusive, as Sheldon Pollock has argued, because the culture of the courts, which such men adopted, tended to elevate the universal and non-locative over the particular and the local. These interactions, however, become more traceable in the courtly dynamics in the second millennium of the Common Era, when, as Pollock has again argued, royal courts formed the chief vehicles in the process of what he has called the 'literization' of vernacular languages – their simultaneous displacement and appropriation of key features of earlier cosmopolitanism in explicitly marked and 'regional' cultural spheres.[1] The interpretive and literary-historiographical difficulties in understanding this process, as Pollock has noted, have been considerable, and no comprehensively informed account has been possible to date.[2] The research for this book has suggested that this problem may also be approached at the level of practices rather than simply linguistic history and literary registers. Questions which need to be asked are how forms of sociability, ethical practice and aesthetic self-fashioning changed in response to new political, literary and economic realities in the ongoing centuries of the second millennium?

Yet like literature, the history of courtly life in the second millennium presents an extraordinarily complex set of problems, the most pressing of which is the need to develop some account of the relationship between what Pollock has called (rather unhappily) 'vernacular' polities and the new 'cosmopolitan' culture of Persianate Islam as articulated under the successive Turkish warrior lineages of the Delhi Sultanate from the twelfth century. In the first place, there needs to be a sustained account taken of the courtly practices of the ruling élite in Delhi and other centres like Jaunpur, Gujarat, Bengal and the Deccan. Barring K. A. Nizami's valuable but largely descriptive study of royalty and a few important studies

[1] And not, as is often imagined, 'popluar' or religious movements, see Pollock, 'The Cosmopolitan Vernacular', pp. 28–31.

[2] For a preliminary exploration of these problems, see the various contributions in Sheldon Pollock, ed., *Literary Cultures in History: Reconstructions from South Asia* (Berkeley: University of California Press, 2003).

of political history, there have been very few sustained scholarly examinations of the lifestyles and culture of the ruling élite in this period.[3] Understanding these aspects of the life of élites would require a re-examination and reading along new lines of the copious Persian literature which circulated in the wider political contexts of the Delhi Sultanate, including genres of 'advice' literature, historical chronicles, inscriptions and various types of poetry in Persian produced and/or read in India.[4]

This is no easy task, for the proportions of this cultural formation were as vast as that which it supplanted and, from the South Asian perspective, much of its ballast came from regions beyond 'al Hind'. Indeed, the origins of one strain of sultanate courtly culture may be traced to the Persianised courts of Central Asia and Iran – the Samainids, Saljuks and Ghaznavids – as they evolved between the tenth and twelfth centuries. This court culture itself claimed to be a reworking of earlier Central Asian and Iranian notions of lordship and protocol (which also had connections with India) as embodied in Firdawsī's eleventh-century poem, the *Shāhnāma*. Although the courts of India would come to have an important contribution to make to this larger world (like the ornate literary register of *sabk-i-hind* which gained currency in Central Asia), many leading Indian court intellectuals writing in Persian were variously but crucially aware of the wider spheres where Persian *belles lettres* had currency, and this cultural world, therefore, stretching throughout Central Asia, cannot be ignored.[5]

The evolution of courtly culture in north India in the context of the ongoing integration of both Central Asian and indigenous élites into the structures of the newly formed Sultanate forms an important historical problem. While important studies have been done on the composition and evolution of the ruling class of the early Sultanate, notably the *iqtā'* system and the institution of military slavery, work on norms of behaviour, codes of social interaction and literary cultures among these classes has been less forthcoming.[6] Further, is the question of how

[3] See K. A. Nizami, *Royalty in Medieval India* (Delhi: Munshiram Manoharlal, 1977).

[4] The distinction is important. Nizami cites Zia-ud-Din Barani reporting that Iltutmish obtained books on princely conduct from Baghdad for the education of his sons. See Nizami, *Royalty in Medieval India*, p. 101.

[5] These ideas have been in part formed through discussions with Nilanjan Sarkar.

[6] See Irfan Habib, 'Formation of the Sultanate Ruling Class of the Thirteenth Century', in Irfan Habib, ed., *Medieval India 1: Researches in the History of India, 1200–1750* (Delhi: Oxford University Press, 1992), pp. 1–21; and Iqtidar Husain Siddiqui, 'Social Mobility in the Delhi Sultanate,' in *Medieval India 1*, pp. 23–49. Also, more recently, Sunil Kumar, 'When Slaves were Nobles: The Shamsi Bandagan in the Early Delhi Sultanate', *Studies in History*, vol. 10, no. 1, n.s. (1994), pp. 23–52, does treat a number of issues of crucial importance for the understanding of service culture in the Sultanate.

indigenous Indian and newly introduced Persianised or Central Asian vocabularies of authority, norms of sociability and images of heroism interacted with one another. Evolving norms of comportment, sumptuary codes, material cultures, aesthetic traditions and ethical styles are also in need of close scrutiny. Once again, this history is complex and operated at a number of levels, for while it is clear that despite vast differences between Hindu concepts of universal lordship and Perso-Islamic ideas of righteous rule, on the ground élites faced many similar problems, which tended to create a seemingly commensurable world of communicative practice.[7] The Sanskrit sources indicate that intellectuals were indeed prepared to translate across cultural and linguistic divides. There are, for example, numerous celebrations in conventional Sanskrit of various Turkish and Persian élites in inscriptions from the tenth century which raise questions of 'cultural translation'.[8] One of the problems which lies before historians, as Peter Hardy has put it, is the role of the 'homonyms and homophones' in the evolution of what clearly became a viable and shared political culture.[9] The vast number of Sanskrit works written after the twelfth century, largely untouched or ignored by secondary scholarship, needs to be examined in the light of these processes of cultural translation and historical change.

Unfortunately, much of the older historiography on this period has been overdetermined by communal and/or nationalist approaches which have provided a largely debilitating set of frameworks for understanding these changes. These important interactions can only partly be grasped through the prism of religious identity as conceived in the modern world, and then quite inadequately so. Importantly, this was explicitly recognised by the intellectuals of the Sultanate itself, who acknowledged that much of the political theory and ethical style they sought to imitate was itself built on appropriations from earlier pre-Islamic Persian practices. So it is that the Indian-born scholar and court-official (*nadim*) of Muhammad bin Tughluq, Zia-ud-din Barani, represented both Balban and Mahmud of Ghazni as recommending that kings follow the court ceremonials of

[7] See Peter Hardy, 'Growth of Authority over a Conquered Political Elite: Early Delhi Sultanate as a Possible Case Study', in J. F. Richards, ed., *Kingship and Authority in South Asia* (Delhi: Oxford University Press, 1998), pp. 216–41.

[8] See Pushpa Prasad, *Sanskrit Inscriptions of the Delhi Sultanate, 1191–1526* (Delhi: Oxford University Press, 1990). For an analysis of the treatment of Muslims in Sanskrit sources, see Brajadulal Chattopadhyaya, *Representing the Other: Sanskrit Sources and the Muslims* (Delhi: Manohar, 1998), esp. pp. 28–60.

[9] Peter Hardy, 'Growth of Authority over a Conquered Political Elite: Early Delhi Sultanate as a Possible Case Study', in J. F. Richards, ed., *Kingship and Authority in South Asia* (Delhi: Oxford University Press, 1988), p. 226.

the ancient kings of Iran, despite his own distrust of things not sanctioned by the *shari'a*.[10] One particular practice which has recently been taken up in detail, is the ceremony of 'robing' (*khil'at*), or the gift and acceptance of robes as a sign of political submission and acceptance. Robing came to supplement (and partially displace) indigenous practices of demonstrating favour and fealty between 1200 and 1700 CE. As Stewart Gordon and others have shown, robing was not an exclusively 'Islamic' practice and found no specific sanction in Muslim religious discourses. Nevertheless, it was widely practised throughout Islamic Asia, and formed an important public ritual from Byzantium to China.[11] Numerous aspects of this cosmopolitan ecumene (banqueting, dress styles, manners and concepts of love) have yet to be explored, but an adequate understanding of them cannot be grasped simply through dichotomous religious categories like 'Hindu' and 'Muslim'. Indeed, it would seem that the claims and practices of *both* 'Hindu' *and* 'Muslim' courts of this period related themselves in some way to this ecumene and the wider cosmopolitan world which it represented.[12]

The complex history of the linguistic and literary cultures of these states is yet to be fully worked out, but it is clear that imperial courts had to negotiate a far wider range of linguistic registers than was previously known. Most imperial kingdoms had a number of different language cultures within their realms which, due to the processes which Pollock has set out, had to be accommodated in some way. It is perhaps possible here to see new hierarchies emerging between 'new nobilities' and 'old nobilities', which were more palpable than ever before, and between 'imperial' and 'provincial' courts, a process which had certainly crystallised by Mughal

[10] Irfan Habib, 'Ziya Barani's Vision of the State', *Medieval History Journal*, vol. 2, no. 2 (1999), pp. 28–9; for a discussion of Barani's political thought in relation to *shari'a* and his disdain for pre-Islamic Iranian notions of kingship (against the larger trend of medieval Islamic political thought), see Muzaffar Alam, '*Shari'a* and Governance in the Indo-Islamic Context,' in David Gilmartin and Bruce Lawrence, eds., *Beyond Turk and Hindu: Rethinking Religious Identities in Islamicate South Asia* (Talahassee: University Press of Florida, 2000), pp. 220–7.

[11] See the important essays in the recent groundbreaking works on the subject of *khil'at*: Stewart Gordon, ed., *Robes and Honor: The Medieval World of Investiture* (New York: Palgrave, 2001) and particularly, Stewart Gordon, ed., *Robes of Honour: Khil'at in Pre-Colonial and Colonial India* (Delhi: Oxford University Press, 2003).

[12] See the suggestive and important study of Philip Wagoner on courtly titles and sartorial codes at the Vijayanagara court, (unnecessarily handicapped by the framework of 'Islamicization'), Phillip Wagoner, '"A Sultan among Hindu Kings": Dress, Titles, and the Islamicization of Hindu Culture at Vijayanagara', *JAS*, vol. 55, no. 4 (1996), pp. 851–80; see also the discussion of Richard M. Eaton, *Essays on Islam and Indian History* (Delhi: Oxford University Press, 2000), who follows Marshall Hodgson's idea of an 'Islamicate' culture. See M. Hodgson, *The Venture of Islam*, vol. 2, The Expansion of Islam in the Middle Periods (University of Chicago Press, 1977), pp. 3–11.

times. These cleavages are consequential not simply at the level of language, but courtly practice, manners and literary-cultural styles as well. In the Deccan, for example, the rise of the Kākaṭīya, Hoysaḷa and Vijayanagara kingdoms led to a new sort of political culture, in which the older noble families of the lowland agrarian empires were gradually displaced by warrior lineages who preferred mixed wet/dry zone agriculture, and who ruled the river deltas, at least at first, from without. Exactly how were these changes reflected in political culture, aesthetic traditions and everyday practice?

By mid-millennium, the sources begin to become very complex indeed, and it is possible to speak of the relationships between courts and the sub-cultures of quasi- or non-courtly locales within both provincial and imperial contexts. The scribal classes, for example, though present throughout the period of this study, began to develop their own literate subcultures from the fourteenth century in the context of the gradual but widespread transition from lithic and copperplate inscriptions to paper record-keeping. Their importance is not only indicated by the appearance of the scribe (*kāyastha*, *divira*) as a villified character in courtly literature, but the compilation of handbooks on letter-writing for their benefit which circulated widely from the fourteenth century.[13] By the time we reach the sixteenth century, there seem to have been pockets of vibrant scribal subcultures with their own political ideas and worldviews in various regions throughout the subcontinent.[14] What is the relationship of these cultures to norms and manners of the court? Similarly, Mughal period documents show the emergence of quasi-aristocratic and military cultures emerging among military groups, lower imperial servants and landed gentry which while interacting partly or entirely with imperial courtly structures, articulated lifestyles in opposition to the conspicuous material displays of the higher echelons of Mughal service.[15] A key insight of this recent scholarship on later medieval or 'early modern' India has been to distinguish and differentiate cultural styles among various classes of service-personnel at court and among lower and higher nobilities, at particular historical

[13] See Kṣemendra's eleventh-century *Narmamāla* for a satire on scribes. For an early published example of a manual on letter-writing for scribes, see the Sanskrit (mixed with Old Gujarati) *Lekhapaddhati*. For a brief review of other literature on the subject, see K. V. Sharma, 'Introduction', *The Praśastikāśīka of Bālakṛṣṇa Tripāṭhin* (Hoshiarpur: Vishveshvaranand Institute, 1967), pp. xi–xiii.

[14] See the apposite remarks and important study of Velcheru Narayana Rao, David Shulman and Sanjay Subrahmanyam, *Textures of Time: Writing History in South India, 1600–1800* (Delhi: Permanent Black, 2001), pp. 19–21; 93–139.

[15] See Rosalind O'Hanlon, 'Manliness and Imperial Service in Mughal North India', *JESHO*, vol. 42, pt. 1 (1999), pp. 47–93; also, her 'Issues of Masculinity in North Indian History: The Bangash Nawabs of Farrukhabad', *Indian Journal of Gender Studies*, vol 4, no. 1 (1997), pp. 1–18.

junctures. While the records of the period treated in this book appear less amenable to such differentiation, these studies provide important issues to think about, which, given modification, may be fruitful research in early medieval India.

The more immediate implications of the study of early modern courts, however, point in the other direction. Scholars have only recently begun to pose the question of the relationship of this complex palette of practices to the rise of colonialism. In general, the debate has been polemical, revolving around the characterisation of the nature of modernity in India. Reacting to the assumptions of those critical of 'orientalism', recent interventions in this debate have stressed 'dialogue' and continuity rather than rupture, with some arguing strongly for the roots of modernity in India within the regional linguistic and political cultures of the sixteenth to eighteenth centuries.[16] In one sense this is a positive development. Yet the polemical underpinnings of much of this historiography has led to somewhat simplistic accounts of this historical change based on overly uncritical acceptance of the claims of modernity itself. Colonialism continues to present a seemingly intractable problem, for though it is obviously possible to see continuity in Indian social practice across the 'colonial' divide, the ideological pillars and institutional frameworks of the Indian state hardly proceed from entirely indigenous paradigms. To wit, the Hindu right's claim to a Hindu *rāṣṭra* notwithstanding, Indians today live within an 'official modernity' not dissimilar to that of the west. Of course such a position hardly captures the reality of life lived anywhere in India (or the west, for that matter), and this is where the important insights of recent scholars into the gradual transformation of early modern and colonial periods have the potential to present a far more nuanced account of social transformation than we currently possess.

Thus understanding the evolution of manners and courtly culture, and their wider social resonances from polemical frameworks may be less helpful than a methodogically structuralist attention to the reorganisation of practices both in medieval India and then later under colonial rule. In the latter case, with the emergence of the ideology of the rule of law, the structure (however tenuous and gradual at times) of the colonial state, the reframing/removal of existing political structures, both provincial and imperial, the consolidation of new professional identities and the appearance of that famous figure, the Indian clerk, we must ask exactly

[16] On history, see Narayana Rao, *et al. Textures of Time*; on linguistic identity, see Cynthia Talbot, *Precolonial India in Practice: Society, Religion and Identity in Medieval Andhra* (New York: Oxford University Press, 2001).

how the complex array of existing systems of practice were transformed. How were forms of sociability re-articulated with the introduction of new institutions operating with 'bureaucratic' or universalist principles, which sought less to standardise all social practice than to provide a standard for different social practices? While it is clear that manners, aesthetics and forms of sociability which once had courtly (or quasi-courtly) moorings and inflections continue to persist, they do so in clearly changed environments – environments which effect their relation with other practices and, thus, however imperceptibly, their own internal composition and functioning. It is only through a careful appraisal of the differential evolution of social practices, considering also their relationships with their own pasts, that we can grasp the significance of the transformation of everyday forms of lived experience that have led to India's modernity. This study has tried to make a very modest contribution to an early chapter in such a history.

Bibliography

PRIMARY SOURCES: TEXTS AND TRANSLATIONS

Abhidānaratnamālā:
Halāyudha's Abhidānaratnamālā. Ed. T. Aufrect, with Sanskrit–English glossary. Delhi: Indian India, 1975.

Abhijñānaśākuntala:
Abhijñānaśākuntalam of Kālidāsa with the Commentary (Arthadyotanikā) of Rāghavabhaṭṭa. Ed. N. B. Godabole. Bombay: Nirnayasagar Press, 1913.
Amarakośa: see Nāmaliṅgānuśāsana.

Āpastambadharmasūtra:
Āpastamba Dharmasūtra. Ed. A. Chinnaswami Sastri and Ramanatha Sastri. Benares: Jai Krishnadas Haridas Gupta, 1932.
The Sacred Laws of the Aryas as Taught in the Schools of Āpastamba, Gautama, Vasiṣṭha and Baudhāyana. Vols. 2 and 14, 2 parts of *Sacred Books of the East*. Trans. G. Bühler. Delhi: Motilal Banarsidass, 1978.

Atharva Veda:
Atharvavedasaṁhitā. Ed. R. Roth and W. D. Whitney. Berlin: Dümmlers Vergalgsbuchhandlung, 1924.
Hymns of the Atharva-Veda. Trans. M. Bloomfield. Oxford: Clarendon Press, 1897.

Arthaśāstra:
The Kauṭilīya Arthaśāstra. Sanskrit text ed. and trans. R. P. Kangle. 3 vols. Delhi: Motilal Banarsidass, 1988.

Baudhāyanadharmasūtra:
Baudhāyanadharmasūtram with the Commentary of Govindaswamin. Ed. Chinnaswami Sastri. Benares: Chowkhamba Sanskrit Series Office, 1934.
The Sacred Laws of the Aryas as Taught in the Schools of Āpastamba, Gautama, Vasiṣṭha and Baudhāyana. Vols. 2 and 14, 2 parts of *Sacred Books of the East*. Trans. G. Bühler. Delhi: Motilal Banarsidass, 1978.

Bhāsanāṭakacakra:
Bhāsanāṭakacakram: Plays Ascribed to Bhāsa. Ed. C. R. Devadhar. Poona: Oriental Book Agency, 1951.
Thirteen Plays of Bhāsa. Trans. A. C. Woolner and Lakshman Sarup. Delhi: Motilal Banarsidass, 1985.

Bṛhatsaṁhitā:
Varāhamihira's Bṛhat Saṁhitā. Sanskrit text ed. and trans. M. Ramakrishna Bhat. 2 pts. Delhi: Motilal Banarsidass, 1981.

Buddhacarita:
The Buddhacarita or the Acts of the Buddha. 2 vols. Sanskrit text ed. and trans. E. H. Johnston. Delhi: Motilal Banarsidass, 1972.

Caṇḍakauśika:
The Caṇḍa-Kauśika of Ārya Kṣemīśvara. Ed. Sibani Das Gupta. Calcutta: Asiatic Society, 1962.

Cāṇakyarājanīti:
Cāṇakya-Rāja-Nīti: Maxims on Rāja-Nīti Compiled from Various Collections of Maxims Attributed to Cāṇakya. Ed. Ludwik Sternbach. Madras: Adyar Library, 1963.

Carakasaṁhitā:
Agniveśa's Caraka Saṃhitā. Sanskrit text ed. and trans. R. K. Sharma and V. B. Dash based on Cakrapāṇidatta's Āyurveda Dīpika. 3 vols. Varanasi: Chowkhamba Publications, 1976–88.

Caturbhāṇī:
Glimpses of Sexual Life in Nanda-Maurya India: Translation of the Caturbhāṇī Together with a Critical Edition of the Text. Ed. and trans. Manomohan Ghosh. Calcutta: Manisha Granthalaya Ltd., 1975.
Pādatāḍitaka of Śyāmalika. Sanskrit text ed. and trans. G. H. Schokker and P. J. Worsley, 2 vols. Dordercht: D. Reidel, 1966.

Darpadalana: see Kṣemendralaghukāvyasaṅgraha

Daśakumāracarita:
The Daśakumāracarita of Daṇḍin. Ed. and trans. M. R. Kale. Delhi: Motilal Banarsidass, 1966.

Daśarūpaka:
Daśarūpam with Dhanika's Commentary. Ed. F. E. Hall. Calcutta: Asiatic Society, 1865.

Dhūrtaviṭasaṁvāda: see Caturbhāṇī

Dhvanyāloka:

Dhvanyāloka of Ānandavardhana, with the commentary of Abhinavagupta. Ed. Pattabhirama Shastri. Varanasi: Chowkambha Sanskrit Series Office, 1940.

The Dhvanyāloka of Ānandavardhana with the Locana of Abhinavagupta. Trans. Daniel Ingalls, J. M. Masson and M. V. Patwardhan. Cambridge, MA: Harvard University Press, 1990.

Dīgha Nikāya:

The Dīgha Nikāya. Ed. T. W. Rhys Davids and J. E. Carpenter. Oxford: Pali Text Society, 1995.

'Mahaparinibbana Sutta' in *Buddhist Suttas.* Vol. 11 of *Sacred Books of the East.* Trans. T. W. Rhys Davids and Hermann Oldenberg. Delhi: Motilal Banarsidass, 1965.

Gaṇikāvṛttasaṁgraha:

Gaṇikāvṛttasaṁgraha or Texts on Courtezans in Classical Sanskrit. Ed. Ludwik Sternbach. Hoshiarpur: Vishveshvaranand Institute Publications, 1953.

Garuḍapurāṇa:

The Garuḍapurāṇam. Ed. Ramshankar Bhattacharya. Varanasi: Chowkhamba Sanskrit Series Office, 1964.

Gāthāsaptaśatī:

The Gāthāsaptaśatī Compiled by Sātavāhana King Hāla. Ed. and trans. Radhagovinda Basak. Calcutta: Asiatic Society, 1971.

Gautamadharmasūtra:

Śrīgautamadharmaśāstram [The Institutes of Gautama]. Ed. A. F. Stenzler. London: Trübner and Co., 1876.

The Sacred Laws of the Aryas as Taught in the Schools of Āpastamba, Gautama, Vasiṣṭha and Baudhāyana. Vols. 2 and 14, 2 parts of *Sacred Books of the East.* Trans. G. Bühler. Delhi: Motilal Banarsidass, 1978.

Gṛhyasūtra:

The Grihya-Sûtras: Rules of Vedic Domestic Ceremonies. Trans. Hermann Oldenburg. Vols. 2 and 14, *Sacred Books of the East.* Trans. G. Bühler. Delhi: Motilal Banarsidass, 1978.

Harṣacarita:

Harshacharita of Bāṇa with the Commentary (Saṅketa) of Śaṅkara. Sanskrit text ed. Kāśināth Pāṇḍurang Parab and rev. Wāsudev Laxman Shastri Paṇśikar (5th edn). Bombay: Nirnaya-Sagar press, 1925.

Harṣacarita of Bāṇabhaṭṭa (Text of Ucchvāsas 1–VIII). Ed., with notes, P. V. Kane. Delhi: Motilal Banarsidass, 1986.

The Harsa-Carita of Bana. Trans. E. B. Cowell and F. W. Thomas. Delhi: Motilal Banarsidass, 1968.

Hiraṇyakeśi Gṛhyasūtra: see Gṛhyasūtras

Kādambarī:
Bāṇa's Kādambarī (Pūrvabhāga Complete). Ed. M. R. Kale. Delhi: Motilal Banarsidass, 1968.
Bāṇa's Kādambarī (Pūrvabhāga Complete). Trans. M. R. Kale. Bombay: Wāman Yashvant and Co., 1924.

Kāmasūtra:
Kāmasūtram. Sanskrit text ed. Goswami Damodar Shastri. Benares: Jai Krishnadas and Haridas Gupta, 1929.
The Kāma Sūtra (or Science of Love) of Sri Vatsyayana. Trans. K. Rangaswami Iyengar. Lahore: Punjab Sanskrit Book Depot, 1921.
Kamasutra. Trans. Wendy Doniger and Sudhir Kakar. Oxford: Clarendon, 2002.
Kama Sutra of Vatsyayana. Trans. S. C. Upadhyaya. Bombay: Taraporevala, 1961.
The Kama Sutra of Vatsyayana. Trans. Sir Richard Burton and F. F. Arbuthnot. Ed. W. G. Archer. London: Unwin, 1981.

Kathopaniṣad: see Upaniṣads

Kāvyālaṁkāra of Bhāmaha:
Kāvyālaṁkāra of Bhāmaha. Ed. with an Introduction, Batuk Nāth Śarmā and Baldeva Upādhyāya. Varanasi: Chaukhambha Sanskrit Sansthan, 1981.

Kāvyālaṁkāra Sūtra of Vāmana:
Vāmana's Kāvyālaṁkāra-Sutra-Vritti. Trans. Ganganatha Jha. Poona: Oriental Book Agency, 1928.

Kāvyādarśa:
Kāvyādarśa of Daṇḍin. Ed. and trans. S. K. Belvalkar. Poona: Oriental Book Supplying Agency, 1924.

Kāvyamīmāṁsā:
Kāvyamīmāṁsā of Rājaśekhara. Ed. C. D. Dalal and R. A. Sastri. Baroda: Central Library, 1924.

Kṣemendralaghukāvyasaṁgraha:
Kṣemendralaghukāvyasaṁgraha (Minor Works of Kṣemendra). Ed. V. V. Rāghavāchārya and D. G. Padhye. Hyderabad: Sanskrit Academy, 1961.

Lakkhana Sutta: see Dīgha Nikāya

Lekhapaddhati:
Lekhapaddhati. Ed. Chimanlal D. Dalal. Baroda: Central Library, 1925.

Mahābhārata:
Mahābhāratam. Ed. V. S. Sukthankar and S. K. Belvalkar. Poona: Bhandarkar Oriental Research Institute, 1961–.

Mahāparinibbāna Sutta: see Dīgha Nikāya

Mahāsubhāṣitasaṁgraha:
Mahāsubhāṣitasaṁgraha: An Extensive Collection of Wise Sayings and Entertaining Versers in Sanskrit. 7 vols. Comp. Ludwik Sternbach, ed. Bhaskaran Nair, *et al.* Horshiarpur: Vishveshvaranand Vedic Research Institute, 1974–99.

Mālavikāgnimitra:
Mālavikāgnimitram of Kālidāsa. Ed., with English notes, and trans. C. R. Devadhar (3rd edn). Delhi: Motilal Banarsidass, 1980.

Mānasāra:
Architecture of Manasara. Sanskrit text ed. and trans. P. K. Acharya. Vols. III and IV. Delhi: Oriental Reprint, 1980.

Mānasollāsa:
Mānasollāsa of King Someśvara. Sanskrit text ed. G. K. Shrigondekar. 3 vols. Gaekwad's Oriental Series, nos. 28, 84, 138. Baroda: Oriental Institute, 1925, 1939, 1961.

Mānavadharmaśāstra:
Mānava Dharma-śāstra. Ed. J. Jolly. London: Trübner, 1887.
The Laws of Manu. Trans. Wendy Doniger with Brian Smith. New York: Penguin, 1991.

Mayamata:
Mayamata: An Indian Treatise on Housing Architecture and Iconography. Trans. Bruno Dagens. Delhi: Sitaram Bhartia Institute of Scientific Research, 1985.
Mayamata: Traite Sanskrit d'Architecture. 2 vols. Ed. and trans. Bruno Dagens. Pondichery: Institut Francais Indologie, 1970.

Mṛcchakaṭika:
Mṛcchakaṭika of Śūdraka. Sanskrit text ed. and trans. R. D. Karmakar. Poona: Aryabhushan Press, 1937.

Mudrārākṣasa:
Mudrārākṣasa of Viśākhadatta. Sanskrit text ed. and trans., with the commentary of Ḍuṇḍirāja, M. R. Kale. Delhi: Motilal Banarsidass, 1976.

Mūvarulā:
Mūvarulā. Ed. U. Ve. Cāminātaiyar. 1946. Reprint, Madras: U. Ve. Cāminātaiyar Nul Nilaiyam, 1992.

Naiṣadhacarita:
Naiṣadhacaritam. Ed. Narayana Rama Acarya. Bombay: Nirnaya Sagara Press, 1952.

Nāgarasarvasva:
Nāgarasarvasva of Padmaśrī. Hindi trans. Srirājadhara Jhā. Calcutta: Venkatesvara Book Agency, 1929.

Nāmaliṅgānuśāsana:
Nāmaliṅgānuśāsanam, with the commentary Amarakośodhāṭana of Bhaṭṭa Kṣīrasvāmin. Ed., with English equivalents, H. D. Sharma and N. G. Sardesai. Poona Oriental Series, no. 43. Poona: Oriental Book Agency, 1941.

Narmamāla: see Kṣemendralaghukāvyasaṁgraha

Nāṭyaśāstra:
The Nāṭyaśāstra Ascribed to Bharatamuni. 2 vols. Sanskrit text ed. Manomohan Ghosh. Vol. I, Delhi: Manisha Granthalaya, 1967; vol. II, Calcutta: Asiatic Society, 1956.
The Nāṭyaśāstra Ascribed to Bharatamuni. Trans. Manomohan Ghosh. Bibliotheca Indica, no. 272. 2 vols. Vol. I, Calcutta: Royal Asiatic Society of Bengal, 1950; vol. II, Calcutta: Asiatic Society, 1961.

Nītivākyāmṛta:
Somadev Suri's Nitivakyamritam [10th-Century Sanskrit Treatise on Statecraft]. Sanskrit text ed. and trans. Sudhir Kumar Gupta. Calcutta and Jaipur: Prakrita Bharati Academy and Modi Foundation, 1987.

Nītiśataka: see Śubhāṣitatriśatī

Nītisāra:
The Nītisāra by Kāmandakī. Sanskrit text ed. and trans. Raja Rajendralal Mitra. Calcutta: Asiatic Society, 1861.

Pādatāḍatika: see Caturbhāṇī

Padmaprābhṛtaka: see Caturbhāṇī

Pañcatantra:
The Panchatantra Reconstructed. 2 vols. Sanskrit text ed. and trans. Franklin Edgerton. New Haven, CT: American Oriental Society, 1924.
Pancatantra of Viṣṇuśarman. Sanskrit text ed. and trans. M. R. Kale. Delhi: Motilal Banarsidass, 1986.

Pañcasāyaka:
Pañcasāyaka of Śri Kaviśekhara Jyotiśvara. Ed. Dhundhirāja Śāstri. Benares: Jaya Krishna Das and Haridas Gupta, 1939.

Pratijñāyaugandharāyaṇa: see Bhāsanāṭakacakram

Priyadarśikā:
Priyadarśikā: A Sanskrit Drama by Harsha, King of Northern India in the Seventh Century AD. Sanskrit text ed. and trans. G. K. Nariman, Williams Jackson and Charles Ogden. New York: AMS Press, 1965.

Puruṣaparīkṣā:
Puruṣaparīkṣā of Vidyāpati Ṭhākkura. Ed. Ganganatha Jha. Allahabad: Belvedere Steam Press, 1911.
Puruṣaparīkṣā. Ed. G. K. Śāstri. Bombay: Nirṇaya Sāgara Press, 1881.

Raghuvaṁśa:
The Raghuvaṁśa of Kālidāsa with the Commentary of Mallinātha. Sanskrit text ed. and trans. G. R. Nandargikar. Delhi: Motilal Banarsidass, 1982.

Rasakalikā:
Rasakalikā of Rudrabhaṭṭa. Sanskrit text ed. and trans. Kalpakam Sankaranarayanan. Madras: Adyar Library and Research Centre, 1988.

Ratirahasya:
Ratirahaysam of Kokkoka with the Dīpika Commentary of Kāncīnātha. Ed. Ramananda Sharma. Varanasi: Krishnadas Academy, 1994.
The Koka Shastra. Trans. Alex Comfort. London: Tandem, 1964.

Ratnaparīkṣā:
Les Lapidaires Indiens. Sanskrit text ed. and French trans. Louis Finot. Paris: Librarie Bouillon, 1896.

Ratnāvalī:
Ratnāvalī of Harṣa. Sanskrit text ed. and trans. C. R. Devadhar and N. G. Suru. Poona: Ganesh Printing Works, 1925.

Ṛtusaṁhāra:
Ritu-Samhāra of Kālidāsa. Ed., with Sanskrit commentary, S. D. Gajendragadkar, and notes by A. B. Gajendradkar. Poona: A. P. Bapat, 1916.
The Seasons: Kālidāsa's Ṛtusaṃhāra. Sanskrit text and trans. John Roberts. Centre of Asian Studies: Arizona State University, 1990.

Saddharmapuṇḍarīka Sūtra:
Saddharmapuṇḍarīkasūtram. Ed. P. L. Vaidya. Darbhanga: Mithila Institute, 1960.
The Saddahrma-Puṇḍarīka or Lotus of the True Law. Trans. H. Kern. Vol. 21 of *Sacred Books of the East*. Delhi: Motilal Banarsidass, 1994.

Sāhityadarpaṇa:
Sāhityadarpaṇa. Ed., with Hindi commentary, Shalgram Shastri. Delhi: Motilal Banarsidass, 1977.

The Mirror of Composition. Trans. J. R. Ballantyne and Pramadadasa Mitra. Delhi: Motilal Banarsidass, repr. 1956.

Śatapatha Brāhmaṇa:
Śatapatha Brāhmaṇa. Ed. Albrecht Weber. Varanasi: Chowkhamba Sanskrit Series Office, repr. 1964.
Śatapatha Brāhmaṇa. Trans. Julius Eggeling. In *Sacred Books of the East*, 5 parts, vols. 12, 26, 41, 43 and 44. Delhi: Motilal Banarsidass, repr. 1963.

Sevyasevakopadeśa: see Kṣemendralaghukāvyasaṁgraha

Si-Yu-Ki:
Si-Yu-Ki: Buddhist Records of the Western World. Trans. Samuel Beal. 2 vols. Delhi: Low Price Publications, repr. 1995.

Subhāṣitaratnakośa:
The Subhāṣitaratnakośa Compiled by Vidyākara. Sanskrit text ed. D. D. Kosambi and V. V. Gokhale. Cambridge, MA: Harvard University Press, 1957.
An Anthology of Sanskrit Court Poetry: Vidākara's "Subhāṣitaratnakośa". Trans. Daniel H. Ingalls. Cambridge, MA: Harvard University Press, 1965.

Subhāṣitatriśatī:
Subhāṣitatriśatī of Śrībhartṛhari with the Sahṛdayānandini Commentary of Śrī Rāmachandra-bhudendra. Ed. and rev. Narayana Rama Acarya and D. D. Kosambi. Varanasi: Chaukhamba Sanskrit Sansthan, 1987.
The Nīti and Vairāgya Śatakas of Bhartṛhari. Ed. and trans. M. R. Kale. Delhi: Motilal Banarsidass, 1971.

Sukhāvyativyūha Sūtra:
In *Mahāyānasūtrasaṅgraham*. Ed. P. L. Vaidya. Darbhanga: Mithila Institute, 1961.
In *Buddhist Mahāyāna Texts*. Trans. Max Müller. Vol. 49 of *Sacred Books of the East*. Delhi: Motilal Banarsidass, 1972.

Svapnavāsadattam: see Bhāsanāṭakacakram.

Ubhayābhisārikā: see Caturbhāṇī

Upaniṣad*s*:
The Principal Upaniṣads. Sanskrit text ed., with Introduction, trans. and notes S. Radhakrishnan. Atlantic Highlands, NJ: Humanities Press, 1992.

Vasiṣṭhadharmasūtra:
Aphorisms on the Sacred Laws of the Aryas as Taught in the School of Vasiṣṭha. Ed. A. Führer. Bombay: Grout Central Book Depot, 1882.

The Sacred Laws of the Aryas as Taught in the Schools of Āpastamba, Gautama, Vasiṣṭha and Baudhāyana. Vols. 2 and 14, 2 parts of *Sacred Books of the East.* Trans. G. Bühler. Delhi: Motilal Banarsidass, 1978.

Vikkirimacoḻaṉulā: see Mūvarulā

Vikramorvaśīya:
The Vikramorvaśīyam of Kālidāsa. Ed. and trans. M. R. Kale. Delhi: Motilal Banarsidass, 1991.

Viṣṇu Purāṇa:
Viṣṇu Purāṇa. [1840] Sanskrit text, ed. and trans. H. H. Wilson. Delhi: Nag Publishers, 1980.

Vyavahāramayūkha:
The Vyavahāramayūkha of Nīlakaṇṭha. Trans. P. V. Kane and S. G. Patwardhan. Bombay, 1933.

PRIMARY SOURCES: EPIGRAPHIC AND NUMISMATIC MATERIAL

Allan, John. *Catalogue of the Coins of the Gupta Dynasties and of Śaśāṅka, King of Gauḍa.* London: British Museum, 1914.

Bhandarkar, D. R. *Inscriptions of the Early Gupta Kings.* Rev. edn of vol. III of *Corpus Inscriptionum Indicarum*, ed. B. Chhabra and G. S. Gai. Delhi: Govt. Epigraphist for India, 1981.

Epigraphia Indica. Vols. 1–42 (1892–1978). Delhi: Archaeological Survey of India.

Fleet, J. F. *Inscriptions of the Early Gupta Kings and their Successors.* Vol. III of *Corpus Inscriptionum Indicarum.* Calcutta: Government Press, 1888.

Göbl, Robert. *System und Chronologie der Münzprägung der Kusanreiches.* Wien: Verlag der österreichischen Akademie der Wissenschaften, 1984.

Indian Antiquary. Vols. 1–62 (1872–1933).

Journal of the Epigraphic Society of India. Vols. 1–19 (1975–92). Mysore: Epigraphical Society of India.

Mirashi, V. V. *Inscriptions of the Kalachuri-Chedi Era.* Vol. IV of *Corpus Inscriptionum Indicarum.* Ootacamund: Govt. Epigraphist for India, 1955.

Inscriptions of the Śilāhāras Vol. 6 of *Corpus Inscriptionum Indicarum.* Delhi: Govt. Epigraphist for India, 1977.

Inscriptions of the Vākāṭakas. Vol. 5 of *Corpus Inscriptionum Indicarum.* Ootacamund: Govt. Epigraphist for India, 1963.

Nagaswamy, R. 'Archaeological Finds in South India: Esālam Bronzes and Copper-plates'. *Bulletin de l'École Française D'Extrême Orient* 76 (1987): 1–51.

Paranavitana, S. *Sigiri Graffiti: Being Sinhalese verses of the Eighth, Ninth, and Tenth Centuries.* 2 vols. London: Oxford University Press, 1956.

Prasad, Pushpa. *Sanskrit Inscriptions of the Delhi Sultanate, 1191–1526*. Delhi: Oxford University Press, 1990.

Rastogi, N. R. *Inscriptions of Aśoka*. Varanasi: Chowkhamba Sanskrit Academy, 1990.

Shastri, A. M. *Inscriptions of the Śarabhapurīyas, Pāṇḍuvaṁśins and Somavaṁśins*. 2 vols. Delhi: Indian Council of Historical Research, 1995.

Sircar. D. C. *Select Inscriptions Bearing on Indian History and Civilization*. Vol. I. University of Calcutta, 1965.

South Indian Inscriptions. Vols. 1–24 (1890–1982). Madras: Arachaeological Survey of India.

Thaplyal, K. K. *Inscriptions of the Maukharis, Later Guptas, Puṣpabhutis and Yaśovarman of Kanauj*. Delhi: Indian Council of Historical Research, 1985.

Tewari, S. P. and K. V. Ramesh. A *Copper Plate Hoard of the Gupta Period from Bagh, Madhya Pradesh*. Delhi: Archaeological Survey of India, 1990.

SECONDARY WORKS:

Agesthialingom, S. and S. V. Shanmugam. *The Language of Tamil Inscriptions 1250–1350 AD*. Annamalainagar: Annamalai University Press, 1970.

Agrawal, Ashvini, 'A New Copper Plate Grant of Harshavardhana from the Punjab, Year 8'. *Bulletin of the School of Oriental and African Studies*, vol. 66, no. 2 (2003), pp. 220–8.

Agrawala, V. S. *The Deeds of Harsha: Being a Cultural Study of Bāṇa's Harshacarita*. Varanasi: Prithvi Prakashan, 1969.

Terracotta Figurines of Ahichchatrā. Varanasi: Prithvi Prakashan, 1985.

Aklujkar, Ashok. 'The Early History of Sanskrit as a Supreme Language'. In Jan E. M. Houben, ed., *Ideology and Status of Sanskrit: Contributions to the History of the Sanskrit Language*. New York: E. J. Brill, 1996, pp. 59–85.

Alam, Muzaffar. '*Shari'a* and Governance in the Indo-Islamic Context'. In David Gilmartin and Bruce Lawrence, eds., *Beyond Turk and Hindu: Rethinking Religious Identities in Islamicate South Asia*. Talahassee: University Press of Florida, 2000.

Ali, Daud. 'Technologies of the Self: Courtly Artifice and Monastic Discipline in Early India'. *Journal of the Economic and Social History of the Orient* 41.2 (May 1998): 159–184.

Arditi, Jorge. *A Geneaology of Manners: Transformations of Social Relations in France and England from the Fourteenth to the Eighteenth Century*. University of Chicago Press, 1998.

Artola, George. 'The Title: Pañcatantra'. *Wiener Zeitschrift für die Kunde des Morgenlandes* 52 (1955): 380–5.

Auboyer, Jeannine. *Daily Life in Ancient India, from 200 BC to 700 AD*. Trans. Simon Taylor. New York: Macmillan, 1965.

Babb, Lawrence. 'Glancing: Visual Interaction in Hinduism'. *Journal of Anthropological Research* 37 (1981): 387–401.

Bakker, Hans. *The Vākāṭakas: An Essay in Hindu Iconology*. Groningen: Egbert Forsten, 1997.

'Vidiśā in the Days of Gupta Hegemony: A Theatre of Broken Dreams'. In Festschrift für Hermann Kulke (in press).

Basham, A. L. 'The Mandasore Inscription of the Silk-Weavers'. In Bardwell Smith, ed., *Essays in Gupta Culture*. Delhi: Motilal Banarsidass, 1983, pp. 93–105.

Berger, Harry. *The Absence of Grace: Sprezzaturra and Suspicion in Two Renaissance Courtesy Books*. Stanford University Press, 2000.

Bhattacharya, Narendra Nath. *History of Indian Erotic Literature*. Delhi: Munshiram Manoharlal, 1975.

Bourdieu, Pierre. 'Rethinking the State: Genesis and Structure of the Bureaucratic Field', *Sociological Theory*, 12.1 (1994): 1–18.

Bosch, F. D. K. *The Golden Germ: An Introduction to Indian Symbolism*. Mouton: Hague, 1960.

Bremmer, Jan, and Herman Roodenburg. *A Cultural History of Gesture: From Antiquity to the Present Day*. Cambridge: Polity/Blackwell, 1991.

Bryson, Anna. *From Courtesy to Civility: Changing Codes of Conduct in Early Modern England*. New York: Oxford 1998.

Bühler, G. 'The Indian Inscriptions and the Antiquity of Indian Artificial Poetry'. *Indian Antiquary* (1913), p. 29 ff.

Bühnemann, Gudrun. *Pūjā: A Study in Smārta Ritual*. Vienna: De Nobili Research Library, 1988.

Bumke, Joachim. *Courtly Culture: Literature and Society in the High Middle Ages*. Trans. Thomas Dunlap. New York: Overlook Press, 2000.

Burnley, David. *Courtliness and Literature in Medieval England*. London: Longman, 1998.

Castiglione, Baldesar. *The Book of the Courtier*. Trans. George Bull. Harmondsworth: Penguin, 1964.

Chakladar, H. C. *Social Life in Ancient India: A Study of Vatsyayana's Kamasutra* [1929]. Reprint, Calcutta: Susil Gupta, 1954.

Chandra, Moti. 'Indian Costumes from the Earliest Times to the First Century BC'. *Bharatiya Vidya* 1.1 (1939): 28–56.

Chartier, Roger. *Cultural History: Between Practice and Representation*, trans. Lydia Cochrane. Ithaca, NY: Cornell University Press, 1988.

Chattopadhyaya, Brajadulal. *The Making of Early Medieval India*. Delhi: Oxford University Press, 1994.

Representing the Other?: Sanskrit Sources and the Muslims. Delhi: Manohar, 1998.

'The City in Early India: Perspectives from Texts', *Studies in History* 13.2 (1997): 181–208.

Claessen, H. J. M. and P. Skalnik, eds. *The Early State*. The Hague: Mouton, 1978.

and P. Van Velde, eds. *Early State Dynamics*. Leiden, E. J. Brill: 1987.

Coomaraswamy, A. K. 'Ornament'. In *Coomaraswamy: Selected Papers*. Princeton University Press, 1977.

Curtain, Michael. 'A Question of Manners: Status and Gender in Eitquette and Courtesy'. *Journal of Modern History* 57 (1985): 395–423.

Dasgupta, Surendranath. *A History of Indian Philosophy*. 5 vols. Cambridge University Press, 1922–.

Dawoo, V. B. *A Guide to the Purush-Pareeksha Matric Sanskrit Course for 1915 and Onwards Containing Full Notes in Translation*. Nagpoor: Desh Sewak Press 1914.

De, Sushil Kumar. *Ancient Indian Erotics and Erotic Literature*. Calcutta: Firma K. L. Mukhopadhyaya, 1969.

Studies in the History of Sanskrit Poetics. 2 vols. London: Luzac and Co., 1925.

Derrett, J. Duncan M. '*Bhūbharaṇa, Bhūpālana, Bhūbhojana*: An Indian Connundrum,' *BSOAS* 22.1 (1959): 108–23.

Desai, Devangana. 'Art under Feudalism in India (*c*. 500–1300).' *Indian Historical Review* 1.1 (1979): 10–17.

Deshpande, Madhav. 'Changing Conceptions of the Veda: From Speech Acts to Magical Sounds', *Adyar Library Bulletin* (1990): 1–41.

Devahuti, D. *Harsha: A Political Study* (3rd edn). Delhi: Oxford University Press, 1998.

Dirks, Nicholas. *The Hollow Crown: Ethnohistory of an Indian Kingdom*. Cambridge University Press, 1987.

Disalkar, D. B. 'Indian Epigraphical Literature'. *Journal of Indian History* 37.3 (1959): 319–39.

Doniger, Wendy. See O'Flaherty.

Duby, Georges, and Philip Aries, eds., *A History of Private Life: vol. 2, Revelations of the Medieval World*. London: Harvard University Press, 1988.

The Chivalrous Society. Berkeley: University of California Press, 1977.

William Marshall: The Flower of Chivalry. Trans. Richard Howard. New York: Pantheon, 1985.

Dwivedi, R. C. 'Concept of Obscenity (aślīlatā) in Sanskrit'. In Pushpendra Kumar, ed., *Aesthetics and Sanskrit Literature*. Delhi: Nag Publishers, 1980.

Eck, Diana. *Darśan: Seeing the Divine Image in India*. Chambersburg: Anima Books, 1985.

Eagleton, Terry. *The Ideology of the Aesthetic*. Oxford: Blackwell, 1990.

Eaton, Richard M. *Essays on Islam and Indian History*. Delhi: Oxford University Press, 2000.

Elias, Norbert. *The Civilising Process: The History of Manners and State Formation and Civilisation*. Trans. Norman Jephcott. Oxford: Blackwell, 1994.

The Court Society. Oxford: Blackwell, 1983.

'The Civilizing of Parents'. In Johan Goudsblom and Stephen Mennell, eds., *The Nobert Elias Reader*. Oxford: Blackwell, 1998, pp. 189–211.

Foucault, Michel. *The History of Sexuality: An Introduction*. Vol. I of *The History of Sexuality*. New York: Vintage, 1980.

The Use of Pleasure. Vol. II of *The History of Sexuality*. New York: Vintage, 1985.

'Governmentality', in Graham Burchell, Colin Gordon and Peter Miller, eds., *The Foucault Effect: Studies in Governmentality*. University of Chicago, 1991, pp. 87–104.

'Technologies of the Self'. In Luther Martin, *et al.* (eds.), *Technologies of the Self: A Seminar with Michel Foucault*. Amherst: University of Massachusetts Press, 1988.

Ganguly, A. B. *Sixty-Four Arts in Ancient India*. Delhi: English Bookstore, 1962.

Geertz, Clifford. *Negara: The Theatre State in Nineteenth Century Bali*. Princeton University Press, 1980.

Gerow, Edwin. *Indian Poetics*. Vol. v, fasc. 3 of Jan Gonda, ed., *A History of Indian Literature*. Wiesbaden: Otto Harrassowitz, 1977.

Gode, P. K. *Studies in Indian Cultural History*. 3 vols. Hoshiarpur: Vishveshvaranand Indological Institute, 1960–.

Gombrich, E. H. *The Sense of Order: A Study in the Psychology of Decorative Art*. Ithaca, NY: Cornell University Press, 1984.

Gonda, Jan. 'The Meaning of the Word *Alaṁkāra*'. In J. Gonda, *Selected Studies*, vol. ii, Sanskrit Word Studies. Leiden: E. J. Brill, 1975.

'*Ābharaṇa*'. In J. Gonda, *Selected Studies*, vol. ii, Sanskrit Word Studies. Leiden: E. J. Brill, 1975.

Goodwin, Robert. *The Playworld of Sanskrit Drama*. Delhi: Motilal Banarsidass, 1998.

Gopal, Krishna Kanti. 'The Assembly of Samantas in Early Medieval India', *Journal of Indian History* 42.1–3 (1964): 241–50.

Gordon, Stewart, ed. *Robes and Honor: The Medieval World of Investiture*. New York: Palgrave, 2001.

ed. *Robes of Honour: Khil'at in Pre-Colonial and Colonial India*. Delhi: Oxford University Press, 2003.

Granoff, Phyllis. 'Maitreya's Jewelled World: Some Remarks on Gems and Visions in Buddhist Texts', *Journal of Indian Philosophy* 26 (1998): 347–71.

Greenblatt, Stephen. *Renaissance Self-Fashioning from More to Shakespeare*. University of Chicago Press, 1980.

Grimes, John. *A Concise Dictionary of Indian Philosophy*. Albany, NY: SUNY Press, 1996.

Gupta, D. K. *A Critical Study of Daṇḍin and his Works*. Delhi: Meharchand Lachhmandas, 1970.

Habermas, Jurgen. *The Structural Transformation of the Public Sphere*. London: Polity Press, 1999.

Habib, Irfan. 'Ziyā Barani's Vision of the State'. *Medieval History Journal* 2.2 (1999): 19–36.

'Formation of the Sultanate Ruling Class of the Thirteenth Century.' In Irfan Habib, ed., *Medieval India 1: Researches in the History of India, 1200–1750*. Delhi: Oxford University Press, 1992.

and Faiz Habib. 'India in the Seventh Century – A Survey of Political Geography'. *PIHC*, 60th Session, pp. 89–128.

Hardy, Peter. 'Growth of Authority over a Conquered Political Elite: Early Delhi Sultanate as a Possible Case Study'. In J. F. Richards, ed., *Kingship and Authority in South Asia*. Delhi: Oxford University Press, 1998.

Heesterman, J. C. *The Inner Conflict of Tradition: Essays in Indian Ritual, Kingship, and Society*. University of Chicago Press, 1985.

Heitzman, James. *Gifts of Power: Lordship in an Early Indian State*. Delhi: Oxford University Press, 1997.

Henige, David. 'Some Phantom Dynasties of Early and Medieval India: Epigraphic Evidence and the Abhorrence of a Vacuum'. *Bulletin of the School of Oriental and African Studies* 38.3 (1975) 525–49.

Hirschman, Albert, O. *The Passions and the Interests: Political Arguments for Capitalism before its Triumph*. Princeton University Press, 1977.

Hocart, A. M. *Caste: A Comparative Study*. London: Methuen, 1950.

Hodgson, Marshall G. *The Venture of Islam*, vol. II: The Expansion of Islam in the Middle Periods. University of Chicago Press, 1977.

Huizinga, Johan. *Homo Ludens: A Study of the Play Element in Culture*. Boston: Beacon Press, 1955.

Huntington, Susan. *The Art of Ancient India: Buddhist, Hindu, Jain*. New York: Weather Hill, 1985.

Inden, Ronald. *Imagining India*. Oxford: Blackwell, 1990.

'Changes in the Vedic Priesthood'. In A. W. Van den Hoek, D. H. A. Kolff and M. S. Oort, eds., *Ritual, State and History in South Asia: Essays in Honor of J. C. Heesterman*. Leiden: E. J. Brill, 1992.

'Hierarchies of Kings in Early Medieval India'. *Contributions to Indian Sociology*, n. s., 15.1–2 (1981): 99–125.

'Lordship and Caste in Hindu Discourse'. In Audrey Cantile and Richard Burghart, eds., *Indian Religion*. London: Curzon Press, 1985.

Ingalls, Daniel. 'Introduction'. In Ingalls, *et al.*, trans. *The Dhvanyāloka of Ānandavardhana with the Locana of Abhinavagupta*. Cambridge, MA: Harvard University Press, 1990.

'Words for Beauty in Classical Sanskrit Poetry'. In Ernst Bender, ed., *Indological Studies in Honor of W. Norman Brown*. New Haven CT: American Oriental Society, 1962.

Jaeger, Stephen. *The Origins of Courtliness: Civilizing Trends and the Formation of Courtly Ideals, 923–1120*. Philadelphia: University of Pennsylvania Press, 1985.

Jain-Neubauer, Jutta. *Feet and Footwear in Indian Culture*. Ahmedabad: Mapin, 2000.

Jha, D. N., ed. *Feudal Social Formation in Early India*. Delhi: Chanakya Publications, 1987.

Jolly, J. and R. Schmidt. 'Introduction'. In Jolly and Schmidt, eds. and trans. *Arthaśāstra of Kauṭilya*, vol. I. Lahore: Motilal Banarsidass, 1923.

Kaeuper, Richard. *Chivalry and Violence in Medieval Europe*. Oxford University Press, 1999.

Kakar, Sudhir and John Munder Ross. *Tales of Love, Sex and Danger*. Oxford: Blackwell, 1986.

Kale, Pramod. *The Theatric Universe: A Study of the Nāṭyaśāstra*. Bombay: Popular Prakashan, 1974.

Kane, P. V. *History of Dharmaśāstra*. 5 vols., 2nd edn. Poona: Bhandarkar Research Institute, 1968–75.

A History of Sanskrit Poetics. Delhi: Motilal Banarsidass, 1971.

Kant, Immanuel. *Lectures on Ethics*. Trans. L. Infield. New York: Harper Torchbooks, 1963.

Keen, Maurice. *Chivalry*. New Haven, CT: Yale University Press, 1984.

Kulke, Hermann, ed. *The State in India 1000–1700*. Delhi: Oxford University Press, 1995.

Kumar, Sunil. 'When Slaves were Nobles: The Shamsi Bandagan in the Early Delhi Sultanate'. *Studies in History*, n. s. 10.1 (1994): 23–52.

Laidlaw, James. *Riches and Renunciation: Religion, Economy and Society among the Jains*. Oxford: Clarendon Press, 1995.

Larson, Gerald. *The Meaning of Classical Saṁkhya*. Delhi: Motilal Banarsidass, 1979.

Lienhard, Siegfried. *A History of Classical Poetry: Sanskrit-Pali-Prakrit*. Vol. III, fasc. 1 of *A History of Indian Literature*, ed. Jan Gonda. Wiesbaden: Otto Harrassowitz, 1984.

Liu, Xinru. *Ancient India and Ancient China: Trade and Religious Exchanges AD1–600*. Delhi: Oxford University Press, 1988.

Silk and Religion: An Exploration of Material Life and the Thought of People, AD 600–1200. Delhi: Oxford University Press, 1996.

Loth, Anne-Marie. *Les Bijoux*. Fascicule IX (Première Partie). *La Vie Publique et Priveé dans L'Inde Ancienne (IIe Siècle av. J. C. -VIIIe Siècle Environ)*. Paris: Presses Universitaires de France, 1972.

Les Costumes. Fascicule VII (Première Partie). *La Vie Publique et Priveé dans L'Inde Ancienne (IIe Siècle av. J. C. -VIIIe Siècle Environ)*. Paris: Presses Universitaires de France, 1979.

Lynch, Owen. 'The Social Construction of Emotion in India'. In Owen Lynch, ed., *Divine Passions: The Social Construction of Emotion in India*. Berkeley: University of California Press, 1990.

Marriot, McKim. 'Hindu Transactions: Diversity without Dualism'. In Bruce Kapferer, ed., *Transaction and Meaning: Directions in the Anthropology of Exchange and Symbolic Behaviour*. Philadelphia, PA: Institute for the Study of Human Issues, 1976.

Meisami, Julie Scott. *Medieval Persian Court Poetry*. Princeton University Press, 1987.

Meyer, Johann. *Sexual Life in Ancient India*. New York: Dorset Press, repr. 1995.

Miller, Barbara Stoller, ed. *The Powers of Art: Patronage in Indian Culture*. Delhi: Oxford University Press, 1992.

Minson, Jeffrey. *Questions of Conduct: Sexual Harassment, Citizenship, Government*. London: Macmillan, 1993.

Mitter, Partha. *Much Maligned Monsters: A History of European Reactions to Indian Art*. University of Chicago Press, 1977.

Morris, Ivan. *The World of the Shining Prince: Court Life in Ancient Japan* (repr.). New York: Kodansha, 1994.

Nandi, R. N. *State Formation, Agrarian Growth and Social Change in Feudal South India, c. 600–1200 AD*. Delhi: Manohar, 2000.

Narayana Rao, Velcheru, David Shulman and Sanjay Subrahmanyam. *Textures of Time: Writing History in South India, 1600–1800*. Delhi: Permanent Black, 2001.

Nizami, K. A. *Royalty in Medieval India*. Delhi: Munshiram Manoharlal, 1977.

O'Flaherty, Wendy Doniger. *Śiva: the Erotic Ascetic*. New York: Oxford University Press, 1973.

O'Hanlon, Rosalind. 'Issues of Masculinity in North Indian History: The Bangash Nawabs of Farrukhabad'. *Indian Journal of Gender Studies* 4.1 (1997): 1–18.

'Manliness and Imperial Service in Mughal North India'. *Journal of the Economic and Social History of the Orient* 42.1 (1999): 47–93.

Olivelle, Patrick. 'Introduction'. In Patrick Olivelle, trans., *The Pañcatantra: The Book of India's Folk Wisdom*. New York: Oxford University Press, 1997.

Pandey, Anupa. *The Nāṭyaśāstra Tradition and Ancient Indian Society*. Jodhpur: Kusumanjali, 1993.
Parasher, Aloka. *Mlecchas in Early India: A Study in Attitudes towards Outsiders up to AD 600*. Delhi: Munshiram Manoharlal, 1991.
Pathak, V. S. 'Vedic Ritual in the Early Medieval Period: An Epigraphical Study'. *Annals of the Bhandarkar Oriental Research Institute* 40 (1960): 218–30.
Pollock, Sheldon, ed. *Literary Cultures in History: Reconstructions from South Asia*. Berkeley: University of California Press, 2003.
'Bhoja's Śṛṅgāraprakāśa and the Problem of Rasa: A Historical Introduction and Annotated Translation'. *Asiatische Studien* 52.1 (1998): 117–92.
'The Cosmopolitan Vernacular'. *Journal of Asian Studies* 57.1 (1998): 6–37.
'India in the Vernacular Millennium: Literary Culture and Polity, 1000–1500', *Daedalus* 127.3 (1998): 41–74.
'The Sanskrit Cosmopolis, 300–1300 CE: Transculturation, Vernacularization, and the Question of Ideology'. In Jan E. M. Houben, ed., *Ideology and Status of Sanskrit: Contributions to the History of the Sanskrit Language*. New York: E. J. Brill, 1996, pp. 197–249.
'The Theory of Practice and the Practice of Theory in Indian Intellectual History'. *Journal of the American Oriental Society* 105.3 (1985): 499–519.
Raghavan, V. *Bhoja's Śṛṅgāraprakāśa*. Madras: Purnavasu, 1978.
Studies on Some Concepts of the Alaṃkāra Śāstra. Madras: Adyar Library, 1973.
Rai, Ram Kumar. *Encyclopedia of Indian Erotics*. Varanasi: Prachya Prakashan, 1983.
Rawson, Philip. 'An Exalted Theory of Ornament'. In H. Osborne, ed., *Aesthetics in the Modern World*. London: Thames and Hudson, 1968.
Ray, Amita. *Villages, Towns and Secular Buildings in Ancient India c. 150 B.C.–350 A.D.* Calcutta: Firma K. L. Mukhopadhyay, 1964.
Ray, Niharranjan. 'The Medieval Factor in Indian History'. *Proceedings of the Indian National History Congress*, 29th session, Patiala (1967): 1–29.
Renou, Louis and Jean Filliozat. *L'Inde Classique: Manuel des Études Indiennes*, 2 vols. Paris: École française d'Êxtreme Orient, 2001.
Richards, John. 'Norms of Comportment among Imperial Mughal Officers'. In Barbara Metcalf, ed., *Moral Conduct and Authority: The Place of Adab in South Asian Islam*. Berkeley: University of California Press, 1984.
Rose, Jenny. 'Sasanian Splendour'. In Stewart Gordon, ed., *Robes and Honor: The Medieval World of Investiture*. New York: Palgrave, 2001.
Roy, Kumkum. 'The King's Household: Structure/Space in the Sastric Tradition'. In Uma Chakravarti and Kumkum Sangari, eds, *From Myths to Markets: Essays on Gender*. Delhi: Manohar, IIAS, 1999, pp. 18–38.
'Unravelling the *Kamasutra*'. In Mary E. John and Janaki Nair, eds., *A Question of Silence: The Sexual Economies of Modern India*. Delhi: Kali for Women, 1998.
Salomon, Richard. *Indian Epigraphy: A Guide to the Study of Inscriptions in Sanskrit, Prakrit, and the Other Indo-Aryan Languages*. New York: Oxford University Press, 1998.
'New Inscriptional Evidence for the History of the Aulikaras of Mandasor'. *Indo-Iranian Journal* 32 (1989): 1–36.

Sastry, Shama R. 'A Note on the Supposed Identity of Vātsyāyana and Kauṭilya'. *Quarterly Journal of the Mythic Society* 7 (1917): 210–16.

Scharfe, Hartmut. *Investigations in the Kauṭalya's Manual of Political Science*. Wiesbaden: Harrassowitz, 1993.

The State in Indian Tradition. Leiden: E. J. Brill, 1989.

Schmidt, Richard. *Beiträge zur Indischen Erotik. Das Liebesleben des Sanskrit Volkes*. Berlin: Verlag von H. Barsdorf, 1911.

Sharma, Baijnath. *Harṣa and his Times*. Varanasi: Susma Prakashan, 1970.

Sharma, K. V. 'Introduction'. In K. V. Sharma, ed., *The Praśastikāśīka of Bālakṛṣṇa Tripāṭhin*. Horshiarpur: Vishveshvaranand Institute, 1967.

Sharma, Ram Sharan. *Early Medieval Indian Society: A Study in Feudalisation*. London: Sangam, 2001.

Indian Feudalism: C. 300–1300 (2nd edn). Delhi: Macmillan, 1980.

Material Culture and Social Formations in Ancient India. Delhi: Macmillan, 1983.

Urban Decay in India (c.300–c.1000). Delhi: Munshiram Manoharlal, 1987.

Shulman, David. *The King and the Clown in South Indian Myth and Poetry*. Princeton University Press, 1985.

and Velcheru Narayana Rao. *A Poem at the Right Moment: Remembered Verses from Premodern South India*. Berkeley: University of California Press, 1998.

Siddiqui, Iqtidar Husain. 'Social Mobility in the Delhi Sultanate'. In Irfan Habib, ed., *Medieval India 1: Researches in the History of India, 1200–1750*. Delhi: Oxford University Press, 1992.

Siegel, Lee. *Fires of Love, Waters of Peace: Passion and Renunciation in Indian Culture*. Honolulu: University of Hawaii Press, 1983.

Sacred and Profane Dimensions of Love in Indian Traditions as Exemplified in the 'Gitagovinda' of Jayadeva. Delhi: Oxford University Press, 1990.

Singh, B. K. *The Early Chālukyas of Vātāpi (Circa A.D. 500–757)*. Delhi: Eastern Book Linkers, 1991.

Sircar, D. C. *Indian Epigraphy*. Delhi: Motilal Banarsidass, 1965.

Indian Epigraphical Glossary. Delhi: Motilal Banarsidass, 1966.

The Successors of the Sātavāhanas in the Lower Deccan. University of Calcutta Press, 1939.

Studies in the Yuga Purāṇa and Other Texts. Delhi: Oriental Publishers, 1974.

Smith, Brian K. *Classifying the Universe: The Ancient Indian Varṇa System and the Origins of Caste*. New York: Oxford University Press, 1994.

'Eaters, Food, and Social Hierarchy in Ancient India'. *Journal of the American Academy of Religion* 58.2 (1990): 177–202.

Smith, David. *Ratnākara's Haravijaya: An Introduction to the Sanskrit Court Epic*. Delhi: Oxford University Press, 1985.

Srimannarayana Murti, M. 'On the Nomenclature Saṃskṛta'. *Adyar Library Bulletin* (1993): 58–71.

Srinivasan, S. A. *On the Composition of the Nāṭyaśāstra*. Reinbek: Verlag für Orientalistische Fachpublikationen, 1980.

Srivastava, B. N. *Harsha and His Times: A Glimpse of Political History during the Seventh Century A.D.* Varanasi: Chowkhamba Sanskrit Series, 1976.

Sternbach, Ludwik. *Subhāṣita, Gnomic and Didactic Literature*. Vol. IV of Jan Gonda, ed., *A History of Indian Literature*. Wiesbaden: Otto Harrassowitz, 1974.

Talbot, Cynthia. *Precolonial India in Practice: Society, Religion and Identity in Medieval Andhra*. New York: Oxford University Press, 2001.

Tarlekar, G. H. *Studies in the Nāṭyaśāstra*. Delhi: Motilal Banarsidass, 1975.

Thapar, Romila. *The Mauryas Revisited*. Calcutta: K. P. Bagchi, 1987.

Thapylal, K. K. 'Kumārāmātya – A Reappraisal'. In B. C. Chhabra, *et al.*, eds., *Reappraising Gupta History (for S. R. Goyal)*. New Delhi: Aditya Prakashan, 1992, pp. 224–3.

Tieken, Herman. 'The So-Called Trivandrum Plays Attributed to Bhāsa'. *Wiener Zeitschrift für die Künde Südasiens* 37 (1993): 5–44.

Trautmann, Thomas. *Dravidian Kinship*. Cambridge University Press, 1981.

Kauṭilya and the Arthaśāstra: A Statistical Investigation of the Authorship and Evolution of the Text. Leiden: E. J. Brill, 1971.

Tripathi, R. S. *History of Kanauj to the Moslem Conquest*. Delhi: Motilal Banarsidass, 1989.

Upadhyaya, S. C. 'Introduction'. In S. C. Upadhyaya, trans., *Kama Sutra of Vatsyayana*. Bombay: Taraporevala, 1961.

Venkatasubbiah, A. and E. Müller. 'The Kalas'. *Journal of the Royal Asiatic Society* (1914): 355–67.

Vogel, Claus. *Indian Lexicography*. Vol. v, fasc. 4 of J. Gonda, ed., *A History of Indian Literature*. Weisbaden: Otto Harrassowitz, 1979.

Waghorne, Joanne P. 'Dressing the Body of God: South Indian Bronze Sculpture in its Temple Setting'. *Asian Art* 5.3, (1992): 9–33.

Wagoner, Philip. '"A Sultan among Hindu Kings": Dress, Titles, and the Islamicization of Hindu Culture at Vijayanagara'. *Journal of Asian Studies* 55.4 (1996): 851–80.

Warder, A. K. *Indian Kāvya Literature*. 5 vols. Delhi: Motilal Banarsidass, 1972–.

Whigham, Frank. *Ambition and Privilege: The Social Tropes of Elizabethan Courtesy Theory*. Berkeley: University of California Press, 1984.

White, David Gordon. *The Alchemical Body: Siddha Traditions in Medieval India*. University of Chicago Press, 1996.

Wilhelm, Friedrich. 'The Quotations in the Kāmasūtra of Vātsyāyana'. *Indological Taurinensia* 7 (1979): 401–12.

Winternitz, Maurice. *A History of Indian Literature*. Vol. III. Delhi: Motilal Banarsidass, repr. 1963.

Yadava, B. N. S. *Society and Culture in Northern India in the Twelfth Century*. Allahabad: Central Book Depot, 1973.

Zimmer, Heinrich. *The Art of Indian Asia*. 2 vols. Princeton University Press, 1960.

Zimmerman, Francis. *The Jungle and the Aroma of Meats: An Ecological Theme in Hindu Medicine*. Berkeley: University of California Press, 1987.

Index

Cambridge Studies in Indian History and Society

Other titles in the series

1 C. A. Bayly, *Empire and Information: Intelligence Gathering and Social Communication in India, 1780–1880*
2 Ian Copland, *The Princes of India in the Endgame of Empire, 1917–1947*
3 Samita Sen, *Women and Labour in Late Colonial India: The Bengal Jute Industry*
4 Sumit Guha, *Environment and Ethnicity in India from the Thirteenth to the Twentieth Century*
5 Tirthankar Roy, *Traditional Industry in the Economy of Colonial India*
6 Claude Markovits, *The Global World of Indian Merchants, 1750–1947: Traders of Sind from Bukhara to Panama*
7 Prasannan Parthasarathi, *The Transition to a Colonial Economy: Weavers, Merchants and Kings in South India, 1720–1800*
8 Nandini Gooptu, *The Politics of the Urban Poor in Early Twentieth-Century India*
9 Norbert Peabody, *Hindu Kingship and Polity in Pre-Colonial India*